Jeo Olander

tic Ocean

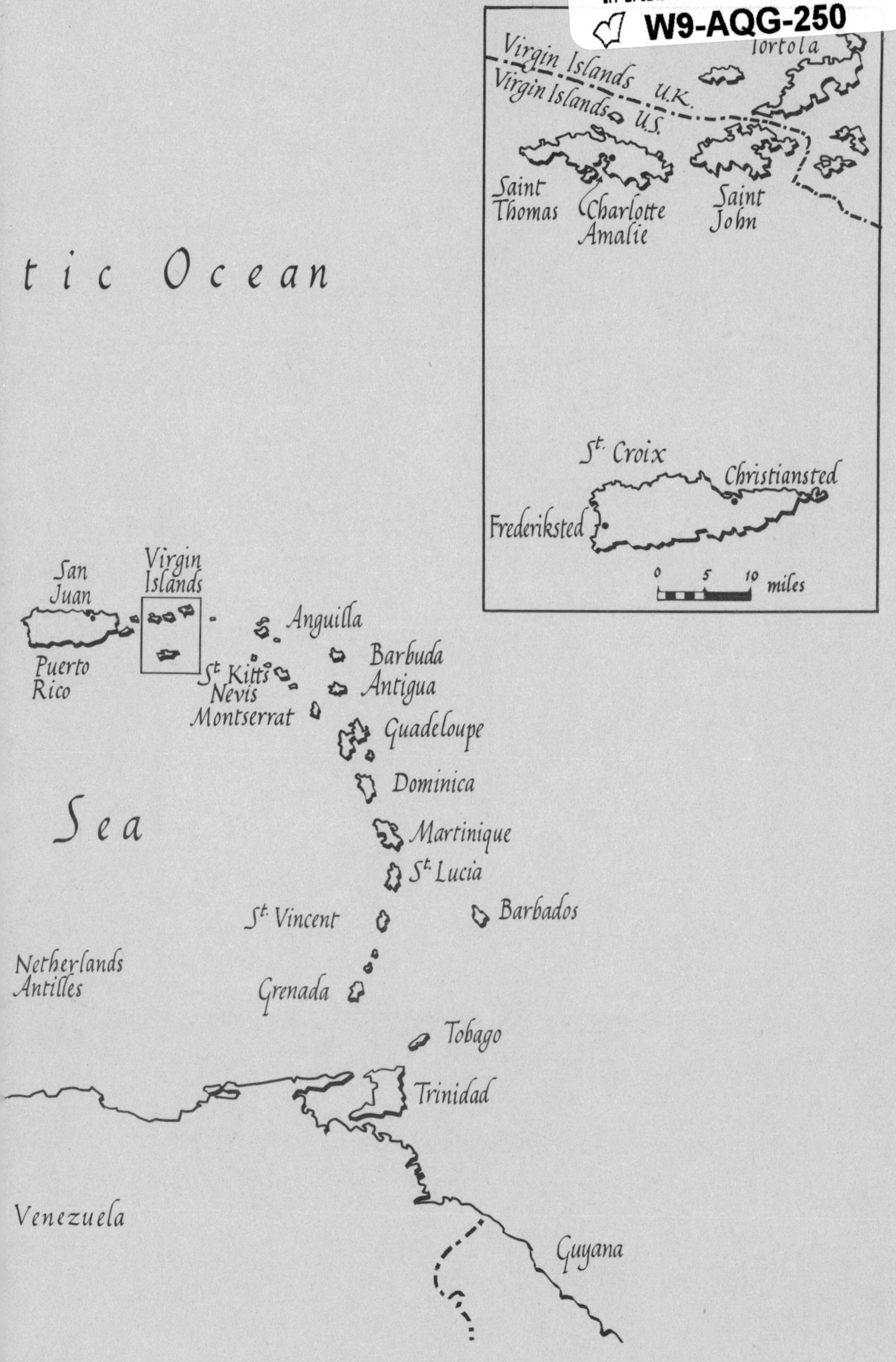

Virgin Islands U.K.
Virgin Islands U.S.

Tortola

Saint
Thomas

Charlotte
Amalie

Saint
John

S. Croix

Christiansted

Frederiksted

0   5   10   miles

San
Juan

Virgin
Islands

Anguilla

Puerto
Rico

Barbuda

St. Kitts
Nevis

Antigua

Montserrat

Guadeloupe

Dominica

Sea

Martinique

St. Lucia

St. Vincent

Barbados

Netherlands
Antilles

Grenada

Tobago

Trinidad

Venezuela

Guyana

GIFT OF

DR. JOSEPH OLANDER

THE VIRGIN ISLANDS

THE
VIRGIN
ISLANDS

*A Caribbean
Lilliput*

GORDON K. LEWIS

NORTHWESTERN UNIVERSITY PRESS

Evanston   1972

A version of the Introduction in this volume appeared in
Caribbean Studies, Vol. VIII, no. 2 (July, 1968).

Gordon K. Lewis is professor of political science
at the University of Puerto Rico.

*in love
and
affection
for*

JACQUELINE
and
DAVID

CONTENTS

PREFACE

The tiniest and most truly Lilliputian societies of the Caribbean region—those that rank below, for instance, Cuba or Martinique or Jamaica in being well known or enjoying traditional fame—have been curiously neglected by both West Indian and metropolitan scholarship. What local work exists has usually been done by teachers or priests struggling valiantly against tremendous odds and carries, inescapably, the mark of the amateur historian or anthropologist; correspondingly, existing scholarly work by the outsider has tended to concentrate on a single aspect of the society under investigation, thus reproducing the microscopic specialization typical of most academic research. Although they are now moving slowly out of their Caribbean oblivion, most of these islet groups—the Bahamas, the Caymans, the Virgin Islands, the Netherlands Antilles—still await the sort of study that would bring their past and present together within the holistic framework of a comprehensive analysis. Until scholarship, and preferably Caribbean scholarship, fills that gap they will continue to attract the merely spurious and evanescent attention that accompanies their inclusion, as with the Bahamas, in the James Bond type of novel or their role, as with Anguilla, as hapless victims in the imbroglio of post-independence Caribbean politics and diplomacy. Until the product of that scholarship, in turn, helps confer upon their folk-peoples a sense of their own independent worth as members of the Caribbean family, they will continue to suffer from the disdain, even contempt, of the larger Caribbean territories for the "small islander," reflecting as it does the form of secondary colonialism, as it were, to which they have been exposed.

This book on the American Virgin Islands is an effort to redress

(ix)

the imbalance of scholarship here noted. For whereas neighboring Puerto Rico has for years constituted a veritable laboratory for a formidable avalanche of able and often outstanding American social scientists of practically every discipline, the Virgins have been scarcely noted. The establishment of the College of the Virgin Islands has only begun to attract the visiting scholar, as against his ubiquitous presence at the University of Puerto Rico over the years. The fact that there exist jokes about the Virgins group even in faraway British politics, usually concerning their exact geographical location or some sort of feeble play, in the tradition of what passes for English humor, on their name, testifies to their relative obscurity and the low status they have occupied in the outside world's image of the Caribbean area. Their recent emergence as a tourist center has served in some ways only to intensify that low esteem, since by their very nature tourist playgrounds in an acquisitive society become notorious for their least pleasing aspects. Las Vegas and Miami Beach are hardly the highest forms of American civilization; and their Caribbean counterparts come to share a similar image. All of this, in sum, constitutes a severe handicap when Virgin Islanders put forward their claim, along with all other colonial and ex-colonial societies, to be taken seriously at the bar of world history. This book seeks, both in its evidence and in its argument, to support that claim.

The book is based on periodic visits to the islands over a period going back to 1955. I am grateful to the Institute of Caribbean Studies at the University of Puerto Rico for help in the form of various modest sums covering traveling and living expenses. I am equally grateful to all of those people, ranging from acquaintances to friends, who over that period of time have helped me in different ways to understand the Virgins scene. I can still remember, early on, sitting out a hurricane with Professor Robert Manners and his visiting student group from Brandeis University on the Cruz Bay promontory on St. John, the sort of experience graphically described in René Puisseseau's *Quelqu'un mourra ce soir aux Caraibes*; and I take this opportunity to acknowledge the memory of Professor Manners' friendship during my first Puerto Rican period, when Rio Piedras was a sleepy college township, and later, during my Brandeis stay. Nor must I forget to acknowledge my debt to another old friend, Professor John Augelli, whose early *Geographical Review* article (1956) helped to stimulate my interest in the Virgin Islands problems. The acknowledgment brings back memories, too, of early days in Puerto Rico when we energetically discussed the nature of Caribbean society, while surrounded by the splendid Rabelaisian vulgarity of the old Santurce dens of low pleasure, which have now regrettably disappeared under the avalanche of the new moral respectability that has accompanied Puerto Rican "progress."

Many Virgin Islanders, of course, of all groups have been enormously helpful. The Public Libraries and Museums service has been at my disposal throughout, for which I must thank especially its able director, Miss Enid Baa; and, after her, Miss June Lindquist and the willing staff of the microfilm-photocopy department. I am also indebted, among others, to Geraldo Guirty, Valdemar Hill, Felix Bello, Tram Combs, Sydney Burset, Mavis Brady, Eldra Shulterbrandt, Gustav Danielson, Darwin Creque, Dr. Randall James, Jean Larsen, and, of course, the late Allen Grammer, whose senseless murder robbed me of a friendly but mercilessly acerbic critic.

Henry O'Neal has helped me to understand the British Virgins group. I have benefited much, too, from conversations with Dr. Alonzo Moron, whose recent death has ended one of the finest careers of a native Virgin Islander in American public service. Nor must I neglect to offer my thanks to the anonymous reader of the Northwestern University Press, whose trenchant and knowledgeable comments on the manuscript of the book helped me to fill in lacunae and rectify inconclusive argumentation; and to Mrs. Joy Neuman, Assistant Director of the same Press, whose skillful editing and advice in their own turn helped to improve the manuscript. I am grateful to my friends Irene Delano and Peter Hawes for their preparation of the map.

In the Caribbean area, work is never far removed from pleasure. So, I have enjoyed throughout the warm hospitality of Mrs. Lydia Blanca Sandin in her old Danish villa-hotel in Charlotte Amalie and of Mr. and Mrs. Stanley Coulter in their fine Danish West Indian residence in Frederiksted, and it gives me real pleasure to record how so many visits have been made even more enjoyable by the prospect of staying with them. Then, too, there is the legendary Erva Boulon, whose Trunk Bay hostelry in St. John was for so many years a favorite haunt of connoisseurs of Caribbean travel. She may not perhaps remember me, but I always recall her culinary skill and knowledge of the folk-people of St. John with poignant nostalgia. As for the British Virgins group, it is especially pleasing to recall my various stays at Mrs. Creque's little island boarding house in Roadtown, with all its various idiosyncratic encounters which it would take the genius of a Dickens to describe fully.

Finally, and not least of all, I must thank all of those anonymous working-class Virgins Islanders, of all ethnic groups, who have welcomed my intrusions into their lives with tolerance and good humor, a welcome all the more appreciated because for many of them life is a daily struggle against the pressures of a society frequently unfeeling in its social attitudes. Polite manners, unhurried personal relationships, and dignity of person are all on the decline in the "advanced" industrial societies of our time. They still survive, however, in the common folk of the Caribbean area. No really worthwhile book on any Caribbean society can be written that is not a testimony, consciously rendered or not, to that fact.

THE VIRGIN ISLANDS

Introduction

Their geographical position alone—situated forty miles east of Puerto Rico on the northernmost point of the Lesser Antilles and constituting the easternmost point of all United States territory—has given to the Virgin Islands group of St. Thomas, St. Croix, and St. John a unique significance. Right in the middle of the great curving archipelago of Caribbean islands that stretches from Cuba to Trinidad, they have rarely, except for certain limited periods, been isolated communities living out a precarious existence but have played, historically, a vital role in the movement of West Indian life and commerce. In its heyday, indeed, St. Thomas enjoyed a status and reputation rivaling those of Jamaica in the outside world's conception of the West Indies. The purchase of the island territories by the United States in 1917, dramatized in the 1967 commemorative exercises celebrating the first fifty years of American suzerainty, rescued them in the long run from the sort of almost complete oblivion and neglect that characterized the neighboring Leeward and Windward Islands under British colonial rule, and incidentally helped to shape the attitude of disdain and indifference that Virgin Islanders display toward their Caribbean cousins. Only the modernization of maritime technology has lessened the usefulness of the island complex as a midway station for the great trade routes of Europe and the Americas.

The ancestral origins of the islands are shrouded in mystery. As far as is known they were originally populated by the Taino branch of the Arawak Indian culture group. That first population was probably decimated by the Caribs, as that warrior tribe made its way up the archipelago en route to Puerto Rico and Hispaniola. From the time of their discovery later on by Columbus on his historic second voyage in 1493 the islands were shaped, of course, by the same concatenation of massive forces that shaped the Caribbean area as a whole—conquest and colonization, European commercial and military activity, sugar capitalism, slavery, and the abolitionist movement that slavery provoked. From the second quarter of the seventeenth century, the period of the original European settlement of the Virgins group, to the middle of the nineteenth century those forces were the controlling factors in the growth of the island society. They were, in essence, the *differentiae specificae* of the New World society in the West Indies and the Spanish Main as a whole. But their imprint upon each particular island or island group was different to the degree that local conditions created idiosyncratic variations on the general theme. Despite the fact, then, that the Virgins were part and parcel of the universal history of the *homo caribiensis* as he emerged, slowly, out of the Caribbean melting pot, Virgin Islanders, as much as Barbadians or Haitians, came to nurture the stubborn belief that they were a uniquely different folk-people, set apart from others and endowed with a peculiar historic destiny denied to others.

It is worth emphasizing the peculiarities of Virgin Islands historical experience that explain, and partly excuse, that spirit of cultural particularism. In the first place, the islands came to belong to the Protestant segment of the European colonization process, being subject, after a few French and Spanish skirmishes, to the Protestant state of Denmark-Norway, first under the private rule of the Danish West India Company, and later, after 1755, under the system of royal government. All three islands—St. Thomas after 1671, St. John after 1717, and St. Croix after its purchase from the French Crown in 1733—to the degree that as New World frontier trading settlements they received any cultural impress at all received that of northern European Protestant commercial capitalism. Though they have been popularly associated with buccaneers and pirates, as the Kidd and Bluebeard legends attest, they were in fact dominated by the figures of the trading company official and the merchant adventurer, who, of course, were mainly Danish. But the general cultural atmosphere was European. In fact, the prevailing tongue among the St. Thomas and St. John planters in the seventeenth and eighteenth centuries was Dutch (the Dutch had preceded the Danes in the islands), while the main language of the Creole folk-people at the time of the historic transfer in 1917 was English.

The Spanish presence was close enough in Puerto Rico, and during the greater part of the history of the Danish West India Company there was a lively diplomatic relationship between St. Thomas and San Juan, mainly concerned with the vexing question of the return of fugitive slaves to the Spanish territory. But the Hispanic-Catholic influence went little further than that and, paradoxically, the Puerto Rican influx into the islands took place after, not before, 1917. That explains why Christopher Columbus is a figure much honored in Puerto Rico but little regarded in the Virgin Islands. Indeed, if a country's feelings about its past can be gauged from its commemorative statuary it is suggestive that the two major statues in Charlotte Amalie and Christiansted commemorate King Christian IX and Governor Peter von Scholten, the leading figures in the 1848 drama of slavery abolition. There is certainly nothing to match the astonishing production of books put out by Puerto Rican controversialists on Columbus, or the amiable habit of those nationalist groups in the small island of Tobago who for years reenacted the (historically dubious) landing of the Ocean Admiral on their shores under the colorful patronage of the local political leader "Fargo" James.

All this meant, as a second salient feature of the islands' life and society, their rapid emergence, early on, as outposts of European commercial capitalism. The story of the foundation of the Danish West India Company after 1671, stimulated by the successes of the West Indian exploits of private Danish adventurers in the 1660s, makes it plain beyond a doubt that Danish tropical colonization was seen by the court officials and the burgher-shareholders who sponsored it as a purely capitalist venture, to be run for profit only and based upon the emergent triangular system of the Guinea slave trade, the West Indian plantation economy, and the controlling Copenhagen import-export emporium.[1] There were present none of the motives of military conquest and religious proselytization that characterized Spanish operations in the Hispanic seaborne empire. The Dutch, who had been in the area at least fifty years before the Danish arrival, were permitted to set up shop in the island ports, especially Charlotte Amalie, as long as Copenhagen reaped the lucrative customs income; and that fact explains why Dutch rather than Danish became early on the leading

1. Waldemar Westergaard, *The Danish West Indies under Company Rule, 1671–1754* (New York: Macmillan, 1917), chap. 1. See also, for the Danish period generally, *Vore Gamle Tropekolonier*, Vol. I: J. O. Bro-Jorgensen, *Dansk Vestindien indtil 1755: Kolonisation og Kompagnistyre* (Fremad, Denmark, 1966); Manuel Gutierrez de Arce, *La Colonizacion Danesa en las Islas Virgenes: Estudio Historico-Juridico* (Seville: Escuela de Estudios Hispano-Americanos, Universidad de Sevilla, 1945); Mabel Thurston Murray, "The Virgin Islands: Their History, Strategic and Political Value to the United States" (Master's thesis, Clark University, 1918); Herman Justus Thorstenberg, "Chapters in the History of the Danish West Indian Islands" (Master's thesis, Yale University, 1906).

language of the islands. Danish settlement was made even more prob-lematical by the failure of the initial policy of using the dregs of the white population of Copenhagen as outgoing cargoes, for, as elsewhere in the Caribbean where white settlement was attempted, white can-didates for a colonial frontier found the climate difficult and the con-ditions of service, frequently little different from those of outright slavery, too onerous. Danish white settlement in St. Thomas, then, like English white peasant settlement in Barbados, turned out to be a mistake.

As the hardheaded Company directors saw it, the slave trade was to provide a ready flow of usable labor in Company ships under a system of mercantilist protectionism; the plantation economy would pro-vide the return cargoes of sugar for Danish ships; and that trade, in its turn, would feed the Company's monopoly in the lucrative business of refining and distributing sugar in the Danish-Norwegian market. The leading beneficiary of that mercantilist system was, naturally, the metropolitan bourgeois class in alliance with the Danish-Norwegian re-gime of enlightened absolutism. As Adam Smith noted, it bore all the marks of the state-chartered company monopoly. For European mer-cantilism, as its foremost modern historian has shown, was a system of national power that had as one of its economic functions the prevention of the development of the potentialities of the overseas colonies so that they would not be able to stand on their own feet and become po-litically independent.[2] It ought also to be added that the mercantilist policy sought to strengthen the national defense system of the metro-politan country by means, for example, of using the merchant marine engaged in the triangular trade as a nursery of seamanship. The argu-ment that the trade would thus help train the ordinary seaman became, later on, an important argument used by the slave interests against the abolitionists, both in the Danish and the English case. The national defense theory even had the support of those economic thinkers, like Smith himself, who on other grounds wholly condemned the mercan-tilist theory.

For two centuries the system returned profits to the Copenhagen mercantile houses. At the same time it is vital to note that the spirit of capitalism, being in essence universalistic, tended at all points to burst those nationalistic boundaries; more particularly, it generated in the colonies themselves new classes of Creole merchants and traders with local interests and local prejudices, potentially hostile toward the "home" country and the *métropolitains*. Westergaard's history,

2. Eli F. Heckscher, *Mercantilism*, trans. Mendel Shapiro, 2d ed. (London: Allen and Unwin, 1955), II, 41.

Introduction

The Danish West Indies under Company Rule, 1671–1754, has fully documented the rise of such a class in the case of early St. Thomas. Theoretically, the Company's officials concentrated all administrative, legislative, and judicial powers in their own hands. In practice, a process of delegation of those powers into Creole hands was under way from the beginning. In the selection of governors, for example, able men like Lorentz, Hansen, and Moth were more or less the choice of the planters; and the fact, indeed, that of the eight governors who held office between 1702 and the vital year 1733 only two had not had their preliminary training in St. Thomas indicated how much the local colony had become a training ground in the art of administrative statecraft in the service of the Danish state. Danish mercantilist policies likewise became diluted under West Indian pressure. The planned monopoly of Danish shipping rapidly broke down under the competition of Dutch and English interlopers; the growing trade with New York and New England skippers edged out the Company trade; and a gradual relaxation of onerous duties and taxes between 1724 and 1764 finally converted St. Thomas into a free port, thus firmly establishing the basis of its prosperity. By the time that Company rule ended, in 1754, far from being "the Company's Negroes," the new class of Creole planter-capitalists had become a solid phalanx of West India gentry, self-confident in their new wealth, and learning, like their Jamaican counterparts, the art of being a powerful pressure group in metropolitan politics.

The third point to make about all this is that the St. Thomas and St. Croix economies, and to a lesser degree that of St. John, became open societies, in contrast to the closed society of Puerto Rico. The nascent Puerto Rican shopkeeping class was prevented by Spanish exclusivism from becoming a powerful capitalist group; its St. Thomas counterpart, on the other hand, soon became the foundation of the old commercial houses, many of whose lineal successors still flourish there; and the difference in the effects of Spanish and Danish economic policies was noted by the St. Thomas historians.[3] Just one illustration of that difference was in the religious field, for whereas Spanish Puerto Rico was a clerico-Iberian state overseas, St. Thomas from the beginning was a tropical Protestant city-state in which Calvinist and Lutheran were permitted free *exercitium religionis* and Catholic and Jew were given the right to hold private services. The Sephardic Jewish trader came from St. Eustatius after Rodney's devastation in 1781, just as

3. John P. Knox, *A Historical Account of St. Thomas, W.I.* (New York: Scribner, 1852; reissued and edited, St. Thomas: Adolph Sixto, 1922, and St. Thomas: College of the Virgin Islands, 1966), pp. 104–6. (Page references are to the 1922 edition.)

the French Huguenot came after the Edict of Nantes of 1685. Denmark, indeed, became, by the historic royal ordinance of 1814, the first modern European nation to pass laws for the protection of its Jewish citizens, and the fact that as early as 1684 Gabriel Milan was appointed the first Jewish governor of St. Thomas, and that in 1950 Morris de Castro was appointed governor of the Virgin Islands under the American regime, testifies to the historic continuity of the Jewish presence in Virgin Islands life. The historic relationship between religion and the rise of capitalism in the Europe of the sixteenth and seventeenth centuries was thus repeated in the Caribbean area. Religious strife hindered profit-making, while the Protestant religion, with its emphasis on the virtues of economic individualism, favored the growth of the business type. Religious toleration thus went hand in hand with business enterprise.

Similarly, despite the fact that the Lutheran Church was the national religion, various European religious sects—Dutch Reformed, Moravian, Catholic—made their own mark after an initial period of planter hostility, and Oldendorp's volumes of 1777 constitute the classic account of early Moravian missionary efforts in the islands. The Dutch influence, of course, was understandable, for the Dutch constituted the majority element of the population almost from the very beginning; in 1765, when Martfeldt visited the islands, that was certainly the case, with the Danes coming next in point of numbers, and followed by the less numerous French, German, English, and Irish. Père Labat's description of the infant colony in 1701, with its portraiture of the small brick Dutch-style houses, with their tiled pavements and whitewashed interiors, certainly indicates that very early there existed in the town of St. Thomas that sense of the tropical *ambiente holandés* which has drawn from visitors ever since a literature of praise extravagant even by Caribbean standards. All in all, St. Thomas was a classic illustration of the close relationship between capitalism and religion in the history of the New World, and the lesson was not lost on those liberal elements in Spanish Puerto Rico that wanted to emulate Danish policy. An enlightened policy, in the words of a nineteenth-century Puerto Rican deputy to the Spanish Cortes (or Parliament), could have made of Puerto Rico, with its strategic position between the Pacific and Atlantic oceans, a great mercantile emporium, especially since Columbus' dream of an isthmian canal looked like becoming a reality within the century. As it was, the opportunity was seized by the more enlightened Danish government, so that neighboring St. Thomas, with its free port, rather than San Juan, became the flourishing center of the Caribbean commerical system.

All of these three generic factors—European Protestant colonization, a more or less undiluted spirit of capitalist enterprise, and economic and social openness, as contrasted to other, hermetic West Indian societies— helped to shape Virgin Islands life and society over the centuries. The shaping, of course, did not take place overnight. As for all of the New World societies, it was a brutal struggle against massive odds: devastation by hurricane, official and unofficial piracy, raids by hostile colonists from other islands, and, later, uprisings by the slave class, as, most famously, in St. John in 1733 and St. Croix in 1848. Colonial mercenary warfare exacerbated by the export of European politico-religious passions to the colonies—like the rivalry between bourgeois Huguenot and aristocratic Catholic in the early history of St. Croix—always made life marginal and precarious; in 1650 alone, for example, St. Croix was occupied by three different European war parties. Governor Iversen's edict of 1672 graphically portrayed a young colonial community struggling desperately to stay alive, huddled around the twin bastions of the church and the fort, battling incipient social anarchy with enforced Lutheran piety, each householder ready at a moment's notice to repel the ever possible raiding party from outside with sword and gun.[4] Social bonds were always fragile, and neither missionary nor town burgher could hope to control in any full measure the combative lawlessness of tropical frontier communities. The heavy expenses of a "maroon hunt," following a slave rebellion, could cripple such vulnerable economies; indeed, St. John reverted to bush for a generation after the ordeal of 1733. What saved St. Thomas from such disasters was the fact that it very early became a trading community rather than a plantation economy, turning away from the land to the sea, which made survival easier.

Why the Virgin economies did in fact survive, as compared with failures during this early period in St. Bart's, St. Kitts, and New Providence, to mention only a few, must be related to the seminal formative factors already noted. While the Danish West India Company had conceived of its enterprise as a closed port for Danish trade and shipping, the local merchants and planters, on the contrary, saw their manifest destiny in the role of an open port serving the needs of a flourishing international commerce and navigation in the Caribbean area. The story of the Virgins, in one way, is the story of that destiny fulfilled. St. Thomas, in effect, became a free-trade magnet in a region of economic protectionism. It attracted, then, the enterprising adventurer: the Dutch trader willing to sell his wares on credit, the English slaver eager to undercut the Company boats that plied the Middle Passage, and the North American skipper bringing in plantation provisions to planter magnates

4. In J. Antonio Jarvis, *Brief History of the Virgin Islands* (St. Thomas: Art Shop, 1938), pp. 33–35.

anxious to circumvent Danish commercial regulations. All that was reinforced, in turn, by catering to the urgent needs of the smuggler and the privateer. Under its more unscrupulous governors, in fact, St. Thomas on occasion became a "nest of pirates," and a Virgin Islands historian's recent account of the burning of the pirate ship *La Trompeuse* in the local harbor in 1683 sufficiently demonstrates that there were always servants of the Danish Crown, like the disreputable Esmit brothers, who were willing to connive with planter factions to welcome roving pirates if a profit was to be gained.[5]

But English and French vigilance, as well as official Danish reluctance to countenance piracy as a permanent source of colonial strength, always made such schemes hazardous. This, it should be noted, was not a moral scruple; the slave trade, after all, was only a legitimized form of piracy. But piracy, by its very nature, struck at the roots of that safety of shipping transportation so absolutely necessary to the growth of large-scale capitalist sugar production; in the long run, a corporate enterprise offering such massive profits to the European shareholders made it impossible for piracy, always an individualistic undertaking, to compete. It was by serving more permanent needs that St. Thomas made itself indispensable —the needs, in particular, of a region in which the movement of trade was complicated by the pressures of war. War and trade, indeed, constituted the twin polar stars of West Indian life and society in the seventeenth and eighteenth centuries, and their intense and continuing interaction required the emergence of institutions to give the interaction some form and logic.

The St. Thomas entrepôt was one such institution. It provided fiscal, mercantile, and governmental agencies for the resolution of all the problems generated by the perennial warfare of the European colonizing powers in the Caribbean cockpit. It provided a money mart for the sale of captured ships and cargoes, and the courts necessary for the disposition of prizes brought in by the privateers of different national flags. Every major European war—of the Spanish Succession, the Seven Years' War, the prolonged Napoleonic Wars—became a tremendous source of prosperity that laid the foundations for the wealth of the "old families" of St. Thomas society. It was a form of capital accumulation only made possible, of course, by the Danish foreign policy of neutrality within the structure of the European balance of power system; that is, it was made possible by the fact that policies at the Copenhagen court were made by business-statesmen whose guiding principle was that of national economic gain,

5. Isidor Paiewonsky, *Account of the Burning of a Pirate Ship La Trompeuse in the Harbor of St. Thomas, July 21, 1683* (St. Thomas: Isidor Paiewonsky, 1961).

more or less undiluted by considerations of dynastic or military ambition. A man like State Councillor von Plessen, for example, who undertook the reorganization of the Danish West India Company in 1733–34, was clearly made in the Colbert mold; and if Colbert laid the economic foundations of the age of Louis XIV, Danish state planners like von Plessen created a national prosperity out of the general European anarchy. St. Thomas was quick to adapt those policies to its own use, so that its merchants, in Père Labat's phrase, profited by the misfortunes of the vanquished and shared the spoils of victory with the conquerors. It is suggestive that the colonial system collapsed only when the metropolitan policy faltered, as can be seen from the fact that the two successive English occupations of the West Indian islands, in 1801 and 1807, came as a result of the diplomatic situation in which Denmark-Norway had been practically forced to become an ally of the French state. It was, perhaps, a touch of poetic justice that the destruction of the Danish fleet off Copenhagen in 1801 should have been accomplished by Nelson, who had learned his naval strategy in the waters of the West India stations.

The history of the Virgin Islands, in sum, is the history of the strenuous application of business enterprise, as well as the Calvinist economic virtues that historically accompanied such enterprise in the world of northern European Protestantism, to the needs of the Caribbean area. It is tempting to write about this in romantic terms, as many have in fact done; Luther Zabriskie's *The Virgin Islands of the United States of America* (1918) is only one example of the rash of popular books that appeared after the transfer of 1917 which were written glowingly in the manner of the "romance of business" school of publicists. Yet the enthusiasm is perhaps pardonable, for St. Thomians, as much as Barbadians, were a superb example of how a tropical community with tiny resources could lift itself into prosperity by keeping an eye on "the main chance" and by living imaginatively, by its wits, so that the traditional commercial supremacy of Barbados in the southern Caribbean was matched by that of St. Thomas in the north. The character of demand, of course, changed with changing times; thus, after 1815, the old war trade of the eighteenth century gave way to the new commerce of the Industrial Revolution, and St. Thomas became a rich transshipment point for the expanding triangular commerce between Europe, Latin America, and the United States, as well as a coaling station for the new cargo ships of the period. It would be difficult to underestimate, for example, the contribution made to the economy by the decision of the great Hamburg-American line in 1873 to make St. Thomas its chief depot in the Antilles. In the long run, however, the advent of steam transportation killed St. Thomas as a staple port for both intercolonial and intercontinental commerce, and the twentieth century produced new problems of adjustment. It was ironic, in fact, that the accession of the islands to the United States in 1917 coincided with economic decline, and the great expectations unleashed by that event died in the prolonged depression of the interwar years. The postwar period following 1945, after a brief flirtation with the experiment of being a "divorce mill" for Americans, has culminated, for the present, with the explosion of the tourist boom as the Virgins begin to exploit their natural beauty in response to the revolution of travel habits that has taken place in the North American affluent society.

This, altogether, constitutes the historical background of life and society in the Virgin Islands of the present day. The character of Virgin Islanders has been shaped by the social relations arising out of that general economic process. The character of the society has grown out of the vast migratory movements of the Caribbean populations, and if Trinidad can be seen as the magnetic hub of the internal-migration area of the southern Antilles, St. Thomas can be seen as the axis of a similar area in the northern Antilles. That, in turn, has helped to produce its mixed, polyglot character, and the present-day mosaic of black Creole, upper-class Jew, resident "continental," Puerto Rican Crucian, and West Indian alien is only a difference of degree, not of kind, from the mixed pattern of earlier periods. The figure of the tourist, who frequently decides to come back and stay, also adds a new ingredient; and the debate as to whether he is a necessary evil or the latest desirable addition to the Virgin Islands mix can be seen in one way as not unlike the discussions that must have taken place in seventeenth-century governors' houses and Danish West India Company board meetings as to what sort of welcome to give the visiting pirate. The need of a mercantile community to watch the market, to calculate the risks of each enterprise, to respond with economic cunning to the vagaries of war and commerce, while at the same time lacking (except in St. Croix) the stabilizing force of a solid agricultural tradition, helps to explain the peculiar plasticity of the Virgin Islands character. This has led to much romantic exaggeration. Thus the leading local historian has extravagantly claimed:

> It may be truthfully said of the Virgin Islanders that they are very imitative, adaptable and self-possessed, in contrast with people from the larger Leeward and Windward Islands. A St. Thomian or Crucian has the ability to lose himself in a London crowd, or on the San Francisco waterfront, and become for the moment one of the people of that section. He will speak like a Cockney, or like

a Connecticut Yankee upon occasion. Perhaps his background has made it easy for him to learn languages and he avails himself of every opportunity to acquire some alien tongue, much to the wonderment of foreigners who are often astonished at meeting natives conversant with German, French, Spanish, Russian, Dutch and Danish.[6]

Charlotte Amalie and Christiansted, certainly, are far from realizing that fancy of being, as it were, trading seaports of the ancient Mediterranean throbbing with a dozen languages. At the same time, they do possess an enriching mixture of American and Caribbean qualities. The mixture has undoubtedly contributed to the astonishing transformation of the society that has taken place within the last decade. The local business acumen has skillfully used every asset of geography, climate, scenic beauty, political stability, and the rest to build up a surging tourist boom that already looks as if it might even begin to threaten Florida's status as the major American East Coast winter playground. A secondary boom in the services and catering industries, in turn, begins to change quite fundamentally the old-style economic structure. The recent advent of the twin industrial enterprises of Harvey Alumina and Hess Oil Refinery marks the beginning of that industrial base which many islanders hope will become the economic foundation of statehood. Half a dozen growth statistics—in per capita income, revenue collections, air traffic flow, real estate turnover, the construction industry—testify to the emergence of yet a new era in the history of this tropical business civilization.

The tremendous rise in population figures especially illustrates all this. The total population, although exact figures are not available, certainly escalated in the first seven years of the 1960s by a phenomenal 70 per cent; and it is generally agreed that as of today (1972) there must be, even at a conservative estimate, at least some 65,000 permanent residents in the three islands. It is worth noting that the federal Census Bureau estimated in 1971 a total of just over 62,000 persons, and that Virgin Islands officials immediately attacked the figure as being hopelessly wrong, themselves estimating the total to be at least 80,000. It is at least generally conceded that, whatever the real total figure, at least 50 per cent of the total now live on St. Croix. Only a brief visit to the islands will bring dramatically to notice the astonishing cosmopolitan variety of islanders: the Tortolan maidservant, the Puerto Rican shopkeeper, the continental mainlander, the Swiss hotelier, the Canadian technologist, the St. Lucian hotelworker, the Trinidadian East Indian store clerk, the Anguillan laborer, the semi-resident international nomads

6. Jarvis, *Brief History*, p. 188.

of the "jet set," even the "fabulous phonies" to whom Mrs. Harman felt obliged to contribute a special chapter in her book of 1961.[7] Much of the population growth, of course, is the economic consequence of the American political connection, on which many Virgin Islanders, like Puerto Ricans, enthusiastically congratulate themselves in the mood of the American Celebration. Former Governor Paiewonsky told his people several years ago:

> On Transfer Day in 1917 we had no cruise ships, no expanding tourist trade, few of the busy and prosperous shops now operating within our islands, no modern airports, no salt water conversion plants, no heavy industry, no public housing, no matching funds, no Federal assistance programs, no universal suffrage. I was a young boy when the islands changed hands, and I have grown up here with the opportunity of seeing progress on the march. It is to the everlasting credit of the Congress of the United States and the Executive Branch that over the course of the years increasing measures of self-government have been afforded to the people of the Virgin Islands.[8]

The international status of the Virgins has been profoundly changed. An obscure and only dimly known Caribbean backwater just a few brief years ago, the islands now begin to match southern California and Florida in the American imagination. In part, it has been a matter of easy communications: getting to the islands in 1917 meant, at best, a slow trip of five to six days on one of the steamship lines out of New York; today it merely involves an expeditious jet flight of only some three or four hours. In part, it is the fact that being United States possessions, the Virgins, like Puerto Rico, offer both the unique charm of a different "culture" (although the difference is easily exaggerated and frequently misunderstood) and the safety of life and property under the American flag, an advantage gratuitously nurtured by the quaint belief of many Americans that the rest of the Caribbean is a wild anarchy of personal dictatorship, social strife, and political instability, a sort of Hemingway-Bond syndrome. Despite the purple tourist literature, the Virgins are no longer an exciting yet safe frontier fun area so much as a settled, possibly oversettled, community just beginning to come to grips with the socio-cultural consequences of a rapidly enforced "development." So, the escapist

7. Jeanne Perkins Harman, *The Virgins: Magic Islands* (New York: Appleton-Century-Crofts, 1961), chap. 12. For later estimates of the Virgin Islands population count, see report by Social, Educational Research and Development, Inc., under Title I of Higher Education Act of 1965, 1968.

8. Governor Ralph Paiewonsky, *State of the Territory Message to the Seventh Legislature of the Virgin Islands,* Regular Session, 1967, reprinted in *Daily News* (St. Thomas), Jan. 18, 1967. For more material on Virgin Islands attitudes to the United States on the occasion of the semicentennial celebrations, see also *Daily News,* Virgin Islands Golden Jubilee issue, Apr. 3, 1967.

who came, just yesterday, fleeing the dullness of American social life after having read books like Holdridge's *Escape to the Tropics,* is now being pushed out by the resident continental, the real estate speculator, and the mass-produced tourist, pretty much like the pathfinder being replaced by the colonizer in the great American movement westward. For him, the islands are "spoiled"; he goes elsewhere. His tragedy demonstrates that the island group is no longer, for good or ill, isolated or forgotten. Its inhabitants are no longer forced to tolerate the bad jokes made about them by Americans who did not know where the islands were. Once again they are in the limelight. The earlier image of all of these Caribbean tourist playgrounds has been based mainly on notorious events, the 1943 Christie murder case in the Bahamas, for example. The Virgin Islands, at least, seem to be successfully developing a new respectability. Herman Wouk becomes an author in residence. The big names of the national Democratic and Republican parties meet regularly at the Rockefeller Caneel Bay resort in St. John. The new College of the Virgin Islands puts on speakers as prominent as the Vice-President and the First Lady. In cultural terms, of course, all this can be seen as part of the Americanizing process in the society, slowly destroying the *dolce vita* myth. Most Virgin Islanders feel, however, with typical small-island pride, that recognition has come at last to a tiny human community which has bred such eminent people as the designer of the capitol building in Washington, the founder of the Medical Society of London, the artist Camille Pissarro, and, of course, Alexander Hamilton. Bonaparte could not feel prouder of Corsica, nor Rousseau of Geneva.

The study of the Virgin Islands, then, is the study of a community in transition, moving from comparative isolation to incorporation, more and more intense, into the body of American society. The problems generated by that process are, in essence, social, economic, and political. The social problem, to begin with, is that of building up a healthy and effective community out of a congeries of different groups who, among them, have developed a system of class-color stratification of a quite astonishing complexity. The official thesis, of course, is that while the rest of the United States has still to complete the unfinished business of the Civil War the Virgin Islands offer the unique spectacle of people of diverse races, creeds, and national origins living together in harmonious accord. That the entirely different trajectory of cultural evolution in the Virgins, as throughout the Caribbean district as a whole, has produced a structure of race patterns *sui generis* is not debatable. The frequently noted difference between the psychology of the U.S. Negro and that of the Virgin Islands Negro goes back, historically, to the growth, in the "free colored" class, of a social composure and a quiet self-confidence springing from the fact that its members were rarely a physically oppressed minority with a minority psychology; and every new white resident is rapidly made to feel that it is the white minority that lives on sufferance, as it were, in a society in which an aristocracy of mixed blood, of high social status, and of considerable wealth calls the tune.

But this, at the same time, does not create the racial democracy of the official propaganda. As the Americans brought their own style of racial classification to the new territory, it came into conflict with that older style; the conflict is as yet unresolved, and in fact will probably become more acute as the proportion of whites increases. Alien groups like the "Cha-Chas," the "poor white" descendants of earlier French settlers, still survive, suffering the scorn that only a Negro can feel for the white man who has fallen socially to his level. There is little social mixing between the old aristocracy of upper-class Negro birth and the new aristocracy of American wealth; both the upper-class and the lower-class Negro worlds, in fact, constitute hermetic cultures sealed off, with the occasional exception, from even the most friendly of Americans. Nor is it as yet certain that the portrait of the resident continentals as a group of refugees successfully escaping from the "rat race" of the brutally competitive American way of life corresponds to reality; there is evidence to suggest that as they confront their old problems in a new form—the reappearance in island life of traffic problems, high living costs, housing pressure, combined with the local problems of expensive power, costly water, bad roads, and exorbitant telephone rates—they revert to American competitive attitudes. All this, it is true, may not constitute a completely disintegrated variant of the colonial pluralist society in which, in Furnivall's phrase, the different groups mix but do not combine. The absence of common norms, however, or at least the difficulty in determining what is the common norm, suggests a degree of social atomization that has grave, if not frightening, implications.[9]

The economic problem is no less intractable. The marginal character of the traditional sugar economy, along with high cost factors, has made sugar a declining industry in poor competitive condition with other sugar producing areas. The famous Crucian rum, hard hit in the beginning by Prohibition, has likewise declined as an export commodity, save when artificial conditions, such as the wartime scarcity of liquor after 1941, have helped its sales in the continental market. Since the 1950s, then, the economy has increasingly turned first to organized tourism and second to incentive-based industrialization after the Puerto

9. For a socio-psychiatric analysis of the various ethnic conglomerates of Virgin Islands society as a whole, see Edwin A. Weinstein, *Cultural Aspects of Delusion: A Psychiatric Study of the Virgin Islands* (Glencoe, Ill.: Free Press, 1962).

Rican style. Both of those enterprises, however, are notoriously hazardous as foundations for a permanent prosperity to replace the old agricultural and trading economy.

Industrialization, to begin with, means entering into a fiercely competitive drive to attract the outside investor, a drive in which the Virgins economy is handicapped by problems of low income, relative smallness of size, inadequate water supplies and power facilities, deficiency of skilled labor, and lack of natural resources. There is the further structural weakness of a high import and excessive living-costs economy, which has the additional consequence, among much else, of driving the more ambitious worker to the continental market, to be replaced by alien labor from the British and French West Indian islands. This, in turn, generates the dangerous situation of an economy based on exploited alien workers. Even the success of such a program, paradoxically, may prove harmful, for, based as it is on expatriate capital, it tends to repeat all of the traditional features of the West Indian sugar structure: a structure of local demand shaped by expatriate needs; the destruction of local industry, as can be seen in the disappearance of the St. Thomas handicraft industry; and the growth of absentee landlordism under a new guise, in which the outside shareholder replaces the colonial planter. All of those features are already far advanced in the Puerto Rican situation; it is ironic that the Virgin Islands seek to emulate "Operation Bootstrap" at the moment when the Puerto Rican planners themselves have begun to be aware of the massive alienation of the local economic patrimony that it has entailed.

The fragility of the tourist program, on the other hand, is openly recognized in Charlotte Amalie. The tourist is notoriously fickle; his demands are often socially undesirable; and he is easily frightened away by political upheaval, which at times can come pretty close to the islands, such as the secessionist revolt of the neighboring islet of Anguilla against the St. Kitts government in 1969. Yet such a program, once launched, can rapidly get out of hand, and signs are not wanting that as tourism has become the major dollar earner the politicians and the entrepreneurs of the Virgins economy have become so many sorcerer's apprentices pursuing a force they can no longer fully control. As the tourist establishment and the tourist hotel proliferate, a struggle for the land takes place, the most well-known instance being the clash over the last few years between the Rockefeller interests and the small native property owners in St. John. New social tensions arise as the continental hotelier brings his gospel of efficiency to bear upon a native labor force whose work attitudes have been shaped by different historical forces; and the result, only too often, is the sort of comic drama portrayed in Herman

(17)

Wouk's novel *Don't Stop the Carnival.* A Negro population electing to earn its living by catering to the holiday fancies of affluent whites on vacation scarcely makes an edifying picture in any case, even when the more offensive Bahamian-like elements are missing; and the growth in Virgin Islands society of, more and more, a blasé expatriate middle class and a docile indigenous native majority must be seen as one of its consequences.[10]

All of this, finally, is tied up with the politico-constitutional problem. For the islands, since 1917, have been constituted as U.S. territorial possessions, with administrative responsibility centered in Washington: first, after 1917, under the jurisdiction of the Navy Department, and later, after 1931, under the rule of the Department of the Interior. The inhabitants are wards of the federal Congress and its committees, who until recently have been governed by a presidentially nominated chief executive (since 1970 by a popularly elected governor), are subject to congressional legislation in which, like Puerto Ricans, they have no participating share and over which, consequently, they have little, if any, control. Their status, generally, is that of second-class citizens ruled not by the declarative commands of the Constitution but by the whims of "congressional government" (they were not even granted full American citizenship until 1927). Their economy rests on the vagaries of congressional trade policy: sugar on the federal quota system (now terminated), tourism on the "free port" status inherited from the Danish regime, the industrialization program on the vital provision of the Revised Organic Act of 1954 permitting the duty-free entry into the U.S. market of certain defined categories of articles assembled in Virgin Islands factories. The fact that any of those provisions may be unilaterally redrawn by Congress generates the air of traumatic uncertainty and fearful expectation so characteristic of Virgin Islands attitudes toward Washington; for, in effect, the islanders are subject to the arbitrary rule of the powerful chairmen of the strategic congressional committees. The local politics in one respect revolves around the dual response to the American suzerainty that results from all this: on the one hand, Virgin Islanders, like Puerto Ricans, are grateful for American economic benevolence, in the form, for example, of the massive federal matching funds that help finance the embryonic welfare state in both communities; on the other hand, they lampoon American political arrogance as it treats their demands for rapid constitutional reform with indifference or

10. There exists no comprehensive study of the Virgin Islands economy. For an overall but uncritical study, see Earl Fernando Brady, "The Economy of the U.S. Virgin Islands," mimeographed (Rio Piedras: School of Public Administration, University of Puerto Rico, May, 1963).

at best a glacial pace of change. Their economic benefactor becomes, paradoxically, their major political irritant. Equally paradoxically, the economic largesse helps to blunt the temper of political agitation, giving rise to a spirit of happy indifference to public affairs that so many critics find disconcerting in Virgin Islanders.

The politico-constitutional development of the islands, clearly, is a generation behind that of the rest of the Caribbean, where national independence is the order of the day. Congressional conservatism, combined with specious rationalizations about Virgin Islanders' "immaturity," has retained a system of colonial dependency increasingly anachronistic in a democratic age. It took Congress nearly twenty years to amend the Organic Act of 1936, and even then some of the new provisions considerably reduced, rather than enlarged, the scope of self-government; the wholesale revision of the 1954 instrument demanded by the 1965 Constitutional Convention still remains a dream only, while it speaks volumes for the general assumptions underlying both congressional and local attitudes that the main feature of the agitation in the years since 1960 was that of the elective governorship, something enjoyed by Puerto Rico since as far back as 1947. The peculiar savagery of Virgin Islands politics, noted by every observer, probably owes something to this struggle between colonial status and imperial power, immeasurably exacerbated by the fact that it is also a struggle between Negro subject-citizen and white federal bureaucrat. The very future of the society rests upon the outcome, difficult to imagine, of that struggle.[11]

All this must be seen, finally, within the context of the cultural framework of Virgin Islands life. Although politically American, Virgin Islanders are in large part culturally West Indian. This is not always appreciated even by Virgin Islanders themselves. Jarvis thus notes that the three salient traits in the personality of his people, as he sees it, are, first, their conviction that the sun actually shines just a little brighter

11. There is no comprehensive study of Virgin Islands government and politics. For brief discussions of some of the main issues, see Carl J. Friedrich, "Report to the Organic Act Commission of the Virgin Islands Legislature on Five Proposals for the Amendment of the Organic Act, with Reasons," mimeographed (Cambridge, Mass.: Harvard University, March 1, 1957); and Roger Baldwin, "A Report to the Virgin Islands Constitutional Convention," mimeographed (St. Thomas, March, 1965). For two recent narrative surveys of local government and politics since 1917 by native authors, see Valdemar A. Hill, Sr., *A Golden Jubilee: Virgin Islanders on the Go under the American Flag* (New York: Carlton Press, 1967); *idem, Rise to Recognition: An Account of U.S. Virgin Islanders from Slavery to Self-Government* (St. Thomas: Valdemar A. Hill, 1971); and Darwin D. Creque, *The U.S. Virgins and the Eastern Caribbean* (Philadelphia: Whitmore, 1968).

in the Virgins than any other place in the world; second, while other less fortunate mortals must go to school to learn to be a mechanic or an architect, or whatever, the Virgin Islander is born knowing how to do all those things; and, third, the Congress of the United States has very little else to do but concern itself with the problems of the island inhabitants.[12] Yet those traits are, all of them, uniquely West Indian. They are all expressions, in different ways, of small-island pride, of the helio-centric image that all of the islanders hold of themselves. Their con-viction of their own uniqueness, for example, is so pronounced in Barbadians that it has generated a special brand of West Indian humor directed at the "Bajan" personality, while the most famous of all books written by the Puerto Rican Creole intelligentsia, Pedreira's *Insularismo*, is an essay on the sociocultural exclusivism of the Puerto Rican *jíbaro* people. The insular chauvinism, then, that is so marked a character trait in Virgin Islanders does not prove their singularity so much as indicate how much they belong to the general West Indian culture patterns.

There are signs that thoughtful Virgin Islanders are becoming con-scious of this truth, evidenced, for example, in the recent debate over the question of a cultural center after the fashion of the Institute of Puerto Rican Culture. A spirit of cultural nationalism, that is, emerges as the counterpoise to the legacy of cultural imperialism. For since the history of the area has been, almost exclusively, the history of the im-position of European civilization upon the detribalized and deculturated masses, first in the slave society and later in the post-Emancipation Creole society, the advent of political independence almost automatically un-leashes a search for a new cultural identity. The process of compulsory Europeanization was, of course, different in each colony; in Jamaica it took place through the prism of the English influence, in Martinique through that of France, and in the Virgin Islands through that of Denmark and, more latterly, that of the United States. This tension between the old colonialism and the new nationalism, the one being as it were the logical response to the other, is at the heart of the modern Caribbean revolution.

The tragedy of the Virgin Islands, in a sense, is that their awareness of Caribbean identity and their willingness even to recognize that there is such an issue at stake have been blunted. This was caused, first, by the temptation to seek psychological compensation for the Americanizing pressure, at times so unbearable, in a romantic nostalgia for the Danish past (as evident in books like Pastor Larsen's *Virgin Islands Story* [1942] and Knud-Hansen's *From Denmark to the United States* [1947]), and,

12. Quoted in Harman, *The Virgins*, p. 144.

second, by a readiness to enjoy, without asking too many awkward questions, the economic benefits that flow from the American relationship. A book like Valdemar Hill's *A Golden Jubilee* (1967) is a characteristic expression of that latter attitude, constituting a hymn of praise to most things American, so that reading it makes it easy to understand how, in the Caribbean, American largesse makes it difficult for small-islanders to adopt a stance of critical independence. A book, in turn, like Darwin Creque's *The U.S. Virgins and the Eastern Caribbean* (1968), although more critical in tone, is on the whole equally euphoric in its general argument. Even the heroic efforts of the great names in the history of the Virgin Islands political struggle after 1917—Rothschild Francis, Hamilton Jackson, Lionel Roberts, Caspar Holstein, Ashley Totten, and the rest—can be seen not so much as a struggle against American rule as such, but rather as an effort to gain for Virgin Islanders as many of the rights and privileges that pertained to that rule as possible. Not even Jarvis, the remarkable historian of the Creole patrimony, could ever bring himself to undertake a thoroughgoing critique of the American colonial system, despite the fact that he saw clearly enough at times the damage it was doing to Virgin Islands life and society. It is worth noting that as the basic character of the continentals in the insular life changes, moving away from being a marginal sea of escapists and beachcombers (on which theme many mediocre novels have been written) to becoming a functionally operating group of resident business and professional people, their role as culture carrier of American values becomes more and more pronounced. The implications of that process cannot forever be avoided by native Virgin Islanders despite their characteristic retreat into ghettos of private life and of the public sector of the economy which they still control by means of their elaborate machine of patronage politics.

Both of these attitudes—the temptation to resurrect the myth of the Danish past and the temptation to turn uncritically to the American protecting power—are evasive devices. For if the first dreams of solving the problems of the present by invoking the ghosts of the past, the second dreams of solving the problems by the pretense that they do not in fact exist. Both commit the cardinal error of assuming that conduct and society in the Virgin Islands experience can only be understood in Danish or American terms, whereas they can only be fully understood in Creole terms. What little scholarly work there is on the islands has tended to encourage that distorting metropolitan bias; thus Westergaard could preface his book, seminal study as it was, with the sweeping and denigrating assertion that "Treated of itself, colonial history is well-nigh meaningless. Only when considered as part of European history

—indeed, when related somehow to universal history—does it become vital." [13] It is hardly surprising that most Virgin Islanders today, like the majority of Puerto Ricans, prefer as it were a second-class status in the privileged great house of the American planter-master class to a position of equality in the Antillean slave barracks. Whether they can break away from the cruel pressures of that position remains to be seen.

13. Westergaard, *Danish West Indies*, p. vi.

Part One

THE PAST

1

The Danish Background

The leading features of Danish colonization have already been noted. The Danish impress upon the islands, however, prolonged over a period of centuries—like that of England upon Jamaica—left behind it a legacy worth examining in greater detail. There is, of course, the visible legacy of architectural style: the thick masonry walls and heavy iron doors of the old St. Thomas warehouses now converted into elegant shopping centers, the old patrician houses, the superb public buildings like Government House, the austere beauty of the religious centers like the Sephardic Synagogue and the Dutch Reformed Church, much of it recognized by the Historic American Buildings Survey. St. Thomas, as the National Park Service claims, probably possesses more hundred-year-old buildings still in use than any other community of its size in America. The Danish engineer and craftsman left their mark as emphatically as did their Spanish counterparts in San Juan and Havana. They instinctively made the most of the natural setting, the vast amphitheater of the St. Thomas harbor surrounded by the rising heights of the three great ridge spurs upon which the town is built. They received a final recognition with the decision of the Royal Danish Academy of Fine Arts in 1960 to undertake a complete inventory of their work in the form of drawings and sketches by its leading experts.

The less visible forms of the metropolitan legacy, those that concern the culture-historian, are not of course as easy to identify and interpret. These were consolidated in the last century of Danish rule between the return of the islands from the British in 1815 and their sale to the Americans in 1917. The early schemes of home settlement by white emigrants failed, as elsewhere in the area, and were rapidly pushed aside

(25)

by the demands of sugar capitalist enterprise; the indentured white servant and the deported criminal were thus replaced early on by the large-scale planter, the merchant-capitalist, and, of course, the slave. The eighteenth-century society was described, variously, by the Danish residents or visitors of the period—Höst, Haagensen, Oxholm, Martfeldt, and others—and the nineteenth-century society by the peripatetic writer of the Victorian age of travel who was almost certain to pass through St. Thomas if he were on a West Indies tour. What these observers reported, altogether, was a highly stratified society based on caste and color, following in part the patterns of the Danish absolute monarchy at home. The usual West Indian scheme of the small white European class at the top, the mulatto "free colored" in the middle, and the Negro freedmen and slaves at the bottom repeated itself, with the usual numerical imbalance. Governor Bredal's complaint to the Danish West India Company directors in 1719 that the foreign ships lying in St. Thomas harbor sometimes had four times as many men on board as the entire fort and island together was typical of the fears that the preponderance of the Negro element engendered in the mind of the ruling group. Politically, the Danish paternalistic tradition took the form of more or less authoritarian rule by a governor, usually a military man, appointed exclusively by the Crown and unhampered by anything comparable to the old representative system of the British West Indian colonies. It was not until 1865 that the twin Colonial Councils of St. Thomas and St. Croix were granted a limited franchise allowed to a handful of property owners, the same year in which the Jamaican planter-class elected to surrender their far more democratic representative regime of internal self-government to the Crown Colony system.

It was, first and foremost, a tremendously mixed society, a fact noted unanimously by all observers. In part, of course, this was owing to the racial admixture arising out of the mutual confrontation of the massive forces of sex and slavery in the West Indian white capital–black labor framework. In part, however, it was the occupational heterogeneity that developed out of the peculiar structure of St. Thomas as a port-colony. From the beginning, the Danes were rarely the determined settlers that the Dutch were, by comparison, in the Guianas. They were, at best, a handful of administrators, soldiers, and professional men, comprising at the time of the transfer of 1917 not more than 30 per cent of a white population of less than 2,000. They were surrounded by a cosmopolitan sea of other nationalities. An 1837 census listed 450 Creoles, 400 Jews, 250 Danes and Germans, 250 British and Americans, and 132 others; while at much the same time, of the 41 large importing houses, 13 were English, 11 French, 6 German, 4 Italian and Spanish, 4 American, and only 3 Danish or Danish West Indian. This led Westergaard to comment that the population was nearly as cosmopolitan at that time as in the mining camps then opening up in California. It was, as Trollope described it in 1860 with characteristic asperity, a "Hispanic-Dano-Niggery-Yankee-doodle population"; and he further noted how Danish officialdom looked on with disdain at this riffraff that, according to them, had overrun the island.[1] Yet the Danes themselves seem not to have cut a much better figure, and another visitor a few years later noted that the only visible evidence of the Danish presence were "somewhat seedy-looking soldiers in shabby blue uniforms, with red facings."[2] It was suggestive that with almost the single exception of von Scholten none of the Danish governors matched the quality of the great van Gravesande tradition in Surinam or the Olivier tradition in Jamaica. The achievement of the Danes was essentially negative rather than positive, in that their liberalism permitted the political exile and the economic adventurer to build up a bustling and vigorous colonial capitalist society they were concerned only to administer rather than to operate themselves. That, of course, was particularly so in the later period of Danish rule, when the government of the Danish West India Company, essentially economic in character and motive, was replaced by that of the Crown, essentially more administrative in its bias.

All this, it should be noted, was St. Thomas. For the complexity of Virgin Islands life was made even more complex by the geographical bifurcation of the islands. St. John has always felt like a little family on its own. There persists up to the present time a real sense of separatism, even mutual disdain, between St. Thomas and St. Croix, and most natives consider themselves Crucians or St. Thomians rather than Virgin Islanders. The feeling goes back to the difference in the historical evolution of the two island communities in the Danish period. St. Croix was a plantation economy, based on sugar, while St. Thomas was a commercial township. Profound differences of social attitude were born out of that difference of economic structure. The Negro in St. Thomas was urbanized, while his Crucian counterpart was a slave tied to the land; thus, in 1848, at the time of Emancipation, half of the St. Thomian Negroes were already free while the Crucian Negroes were still chained to estate serfdom. The Negro in commercial-maritime St. Thomas was, generally, a craftsman, a warehouse or waterfront worker, a house servant, even entering the lower echelons of shopkeeping and office manage-

1. Anthony Trollope, *The West Indies and the Spanish Main* (London: Chapman and Hall, 1860), p. 236.
2. Greville John Chester, *Transatlantic Sketches in the West Indies, South America, Canada, and the United States* (London: Smith, Elder, 1869), p. 4.

(27)

ment; he had alternatives to working on the despised land. The result was an enlarged self-respect, a vigorous individualism, a self-confidence, all of them well-known components of urbanized life-styles. By contrast, the Crucian land worker was ruled by a planter class with more seignioral attitudes. The history of Danish West Indian slave rebellions, consequently, is the history of St. Croix and St. John. The bitter struggle of master and slave was followed, after 1848, by the equally bitter struggle between employer and servant, and only the very recent surcease of the sugar dominion in St. Croix gives promise of the growth of more liberal social relations. As late as 1917 an American anthropologist visitor noted the striking difference between the twin communities: on the St. Thomas waterfront there was a welcome by a grinning boatman and a willing, if ineffective, porter; in Christiansted there was, by contrast, an atmosphere of surliness, although the discourtesy had to be understood by the visitor less as evil intentions toward himself and more as a general resentment against social conditions.[3] An earlier account, of 1852, describing the St. Thomas laborer as, variously, a carpenter, mason, tailor, shoemaker, cigar maker, or shipwright enjoying comparatively high wages and always able to command employment along with his female counterparts, the cook, house servant, seamstress, and market vendor, illustrates to what extent the island was, as it were, a house slave economy while St. Croix was a field slave economy.[4]

Much has been made of the liberal quality of Danish rule. To some extent, that was so. But it is open to doubt as to whether the claim, in any real sense, is anything more than romantic nostalgia. It is true that Denmark was the first European nation to abolish the slave trade, and the struggle of the domestic liberal forces in the last quarter of the eighteenth century toward that end has been documented in Holm's *Danmark-Norges Historie under Kristen VII, 1766–1808*. But that did not prevent St. Thomas remaining a center for the continuing illicit trade, with local official connivance, well into the following century. It is equally true that Governor von Scholten is known as the great architect of the 1848 Emancipation. Yet Danish historians still debate as to whether he connived at the insurrectionary movement that precipitated the events of that year in St. Croix, or whether his hand was forced by them; and the truth is, in any case, that the act of freedom, dramatically announced at the drumhead from the ramparts of the Frederiksted fort, was

3. Theodore de Booy and John T. Faris, *The Virgin Islands, Our New Possessions and the British Islands* (Philadelphia: Lippincott, 1918), pp. 212–13.

4. John P. Knox, *A Historical Account of St. Thomas, W.I.* (New York: Scribner, 1852; reissued and edited, St. Thomas: Adolph Sixto, 1922, and St. Thomas: College of the Virgin Islands, 1966), pp. 125–26. (Page references are to the 1922 edition.)

primarily the result of slave militancy. It is true, finally, that Danish official policy actively fostered the social elevation of the free colored elements, even going so far, in the remarkable royal edict of 1831, as to
permit the legal registration of colored persons as white citizens, on the
basis of good conduct and social standing. From this legislation there
no doubt rises the dominating influence of the concept of social color in
the communal psychology of Virgin Islanders today. Yet even those
measures, revolutionary as they were, can be interpreted less as evidence of
racial egalitarian ideas in the ruling group than as proof of a "divide and
conquer" policy designed to prevent a united front between lower-class
Negro and upper-class mulatto. That the policy succeeded admirably is
evident from the history of the Danish colonial statute book, which is
crowded with measures seeking to punish certain behavior patterns—the
wearing of precious stones and silk stockings, the holding of masked
balls, the use of ceremonial gunfire at funerals—that point to the existence, quite early on, of a rich colored community guilty not so much
of harboring dangerous Haitian-like ideas about racial justice as entertaining bold social aspirations. Social snobbery thus supplanted racial
brotherhood, and the Virgin Islands free coloreds, like their counterparts
elsewhere in the Caribbean, became known as a group given more to
lavish social display than to radical mental activity.

Yet the real test of metropolitan attitudes was, of course, slavery. On
that score the Danish record was no more liberal than that of the
Dutch or the English. The original Danish occupation of the islands,
after all, had been for the express purpose of facilitating the slave trade,
a fact not always emphasized by historians. The trade in its turn became
the basis of a slave economy as monstrous, for what it meant in the
daily life of the bond Negro, as any in the New World. The St. Thomas
planters, early on, certainly treated their slaves far more harshly than the
Spanish in Puerto Rico, and Governor Gardelin's slave mandate of 1733
reflected in its awful severity the paranoiac fear of conspiracy that was the
natural result of such treatment. Danish benevolent paternalism sought,
admittedly, to ameliorate the system. But legal provisions for ameliora-
tion, as Gurney noted when he visited the St. Croix plantations in 1840,
were generally of little use, for metropolitan measures, as the British
experience had shown, were constantly frustrated by local influence. It is
worth noting that, quite apart from corrupting the moral sense of the
Creole plantocrats, the system evoked an apologetic literature from the
Danish historians. Thus, Pastor Knox's unreliable history of 1852 sought
to justify repressive measures on the ground that the society faced the
danger of insurrection from slaves "still ignorant, vicious, and even
savage," while as late as 1917 Westergaard could not make up his mind to

wholly condemn slavery, evading the question with the assertion that the Danish treatment of the slave was probably no worse than in the English, French, and Dutch islands. It is ironic that in 1966 the new College of the Virgin Islands should have decided to reprint the Knox history, without comment and with an apparent unawareness that it was giving a new lease of life to a book which, apart from its numerous inaccuracies, contained a libelous slander on the character of the island masses under the slave regime. The extent of the slander is evident from the fact that after having excitedly described the "mad destruction" of the revolting Crucian Negroes in 1848 the author was obliged to confess that the damage to property was in fact limited and not a single white person had been harmed, a contradiction he sought weakly to resolve with the assertion that both planter and slave had become imbued with the moral principles of missionary Christianity.

The social legacy of slavery remained, after Emancipation, to frustrate the growth of a liberal free enterprise economy. The Labor Act of 1848 revealed how deeply the planter still thought of the laborer in chattel terms, for despite its intent of codifying the mutual obligations of estate proprietor and laborer much of it perpetuated the old outlook, seeking to hold down the worker, by contractual obligation, to work on one estate only, and legalizing the power of management to fine workers for trifles and to determine their private lives. The very essence of slavery had been compulsory work at the behest of others; freedom, for the ex-slave, meant above all else complete escape from such a condition, under whatever guise. Even Knox saw that, and in an oddly perceptive passage he noted how slavery left behind, with much justification, a series of social prejudices that still remain firmly entrenched in the Virgin Islander. There was the aversion to work, always identified with slavery; the feeling that to be able to command attendance from a social inferior or a juvenile apprentice or a house servant was the height of gentility; the love of extravagance, since slavery failed to generate any sense of the real value of things; and the unblushing readiness to solicit charity, even on the part of those well able to do without it. All of these prejudices led, generally, to a spirit of social and personal irresponsibility, mitigated only by the fact that despite the availability of cheap rum a drunk man in the street, unless he were an American or English sailor, was a rare sight. It is not surprising, then, that although Denmark brought to the islands the whole baggage of Protestant economic virtues, their assimilation by the islanders was sharply limited, since the slave heritage endowed them with completely different meaning. The American influence since 1917 has done something to change this, but not too much. It is still the overt prestige value of a job, not work performance, that

(30)

is important. The economical use of leisure is still not much appreciated, and leads to much ridicule of the hard-playing continentals. There is, certainly, a "get-rich-quick" mentality. But the average St. Thomian is more likely to satisfy it through dreams about finding hidden pirate treasure—on which topic there is a whole wealth of local folklore—than through the cultivation of thrift and industry.

The most illuminating aspect of the Danish legacy, however, was the interaction of slavery and religion. The steady erosion of European marriage forms under the relentless pressure of black-white sex is a well-known story, and Danish Lutheran pietism gave way in the Virgins as readily as elsewhere. The story of Anna Heegaard, the colored mistress of Governor von Scholten, culminating in the idyll of their life together in the enchanting hillside mansion of Bulows Minde, illustrates how color and illegitimacy could become, in the hands of clever and attractive women, royal avenues to wealth and respectability. The psychiatric price that Danish puritanism had to pay for the habit of *mésalliance* is not known, although it must frequently have been high. As far as the general institution of slavery was concerned, however, acceptance was easier, granted the general character of Lutheranism. For in its sociological theory the Lutheran ethic merely continued the neo-medieval world-view of the authoritarian social hierarchy divided into vocational "callings"; and from that point of view both serfdom and slavery were regarded as legitimate social categories whose members could enjoy inner liberty but had no right to seek external legal freedom. Luther himself even went so far as to enjoin patient acceptance of their lot upon the Christian prisoners of war of the time who had been enslaved by the Turks. That general social teaching was reinforced, in the Danish case, by the particular application of the Moravian sect ideal as it entered the Virgin Islands missionary field under the guidance of the quixotic figure of Count Zinzendorf. It is true that there were radical elements in the Moravian ideal. The emphasis on inward piety and Christ-mysticism, so firmly entrenched in the parent Hernhut community, was certainly in at least potential conflict with the Lutheran state-church position; the literature contains ample evidence of certain Anabaptist, that is, radical, millenarian, elements in the sectarian idea. Troeltsch has noted, even more, the affinity of Moravian social ideas with Calvinist business morality, for the sectarian concept of the mobile, voluntary religious community, free from state support and therefore dependent on the business enterprise of the community, gave an overwhelming industrial character to the Moravian ethic.[5]

5. Ernst Troeltsch, *The Social Teaching of the Christian Churches*, trans. Olive Wyon, 2 vols. (London: Allen and Unwin, 1931), II, notes, 460.

But the transfer of all this to the slave mission field had to meet the compromising power of slavery, and Moravian enterprise in the islands was characterized by the more conservative Lutheran-ecclesiastical bias rather than by the liberal-sectarian bias. The Moravian sect worked closely with the colonial state machinery, enjoying a monopoly of preaching rights as against visiting outside ministers. Its acceptance of slavery was dramatized by the fact, scandalous to many Christian visitors, that it owned its own slaves, Gurney noting that the Moravian religious influence, in his view, was seriously diminished by that fact, as well as by the practice of teaching the natives in the little understood Negro-Dutch tongue. Correspondingly, the industrial bias, so natural in the European setting, gave way to the older Lutheran agricultural bias in the colonial setting, and the main work of the missions, suggestively enough, was in the plantation economies of St. John and St. Croix. The pressure of slavery, in brief, inhibited the maturing development of the more libertarian elements within the Moravian ethic. The Moravian contribution to Virgin Islands life, as a result, has been dangerously exaggerated, and it is not surprising that nineteenth-century visitors, such as Hovey, commented on the obvious incapacity of the missions to overcome the widespread religious apathy of the populace, thus reinforcing the evidence of earlier residents like Nissen who noted the decline of Moravian congregations as compared, for example, with Roman Catholic congregations.[6]

The post-Emancipation society of 1848–1917 was thus shaped by all of these varied forces. Underneath the Danish patina it was a society economically American and linguistically English. The Zabriskie volume of 1918 printed some four pages of a directory of leading St. Thomas merchant houses engaged in the import-export trade with the principal distributing centers of the United States, thus emphasizing the close economic ties with the American economy, although the Crucian sugar economy remained to the last under the control of either the Danish

6. Sylvester Hovey, *Letters from the West Indies* (New York: Gould and Newman, 1838), pp. 30–31; Johan Peter Nissen, *Reminiscences of a 46 Years Residence in the Island of St. Thomas in the West Indies* (Nazareth, Pa.: Senseman, 1838; microfilm, St. Thomas Public Library), pp. 203–5. For the general character of Moravian missionary work, including Count Zinzendorf's support of slavery, see "Early Moravian Missions," *Daily News*, Golden Jubilee issue, Apr. 3, 1967. See also Herman Lawaetz, "Brodremeninghedens mission i Dansk-Vestindien 1769–1848" [The Moravian Mission in the Danish West Indies 1769–1848. Contribution to a description of the characteristics of the Moravian Church and its activities and of the attitude of the coloured race to Christianity] (Master's thesis, Kobenhavns University, 1902).

government or leading Danish companies.[7] English, being the traditional language of trade and piracy in the Caribbean as a whole, early became the popular street language, and later the elite prestige language, so much so that the later debates of the twin Colonial Councils were conducted in that language. Thurlow Weed remarked, noting that St. Croix in the 1840s was English in language and habits, that the Danes had "failed to nationalize" the island. A study of the local press during the whole period shows to what a large extent it was a businessman's journalism, concentrating on commercial news from Europe and the United States and taking little notice of Danish affairs at any time. Trollope remarked upon the fact that St. Thomas was a commercial empire operated by the rough money-making type of man. There was some English spleen in the remark. But the impression is reinforced by the diary of a resident merchant like Nissen, which almost reads like a ledger book as it describes, for a period of forty years or more, the laborious accumulation of business fortune by a hardheaded family entrepreneur.

The society was thus bifurcated between a Danish political power structure and a Creole socioeconomic power structure. In St. Thomas, as already noted, it was the rule of a commercial oligarchy, and in St. Croix that of a sugar oligarchy. That meant a more open-ended occupational mobility in St. Thomas than existed in St. Croix. Even so, it was a difference of degree, not of kind. The working classes of both economies were governed by a narrow-minded colonial master class still imbued with ideas of "moral slavery." The thirty years after the labor riots of 1878 in St. Croix were, in effect, a reign of intimidation of the worker by gendarme, judge, and prison official, all acting in concert. "The planters," observed the Crown member for the St. Croix Colonial Council in that body's debate on the 1878 explosion, "have for many years been driving their labor power at high steam pressure; the engine has now burst." But it was symptomatic of planter attitudes that the planter members in the same debate attempted to lay the blame on what they regarded as the local government's misguided retrenchment policy in military expenses—as if, in the governor's caustic reply to that evasion, one could "grow canes with rifles." [8] Yet examination of the punitive labor codes and various ordinances against begging, vagrancy, and trespassing suggests that even after 1878 the machinery of justice continued to be used as a means of class oppres-

7. Luther K. Zabriskie, *The Virgin Islands of the United States of America* (New York: Putnam, 1918), pp. 124–29.

8. *Proceedings of the Colonial Council of St. Croix* (microfilm, St. Thomas Public Library), sess. 1878–79, pp. 137–50.

sion, including arbitrary imprisonment simply on the basis of complaints from employers; and well into the twentieth century a barbarous penal code made it possible for laborers successively convicted of cane-stealing to be imprisoned for life. The mass of statutory legislation, in turn, that sought to control public behavior—from conspiracy and disobedience to masters to whistling and loud singing on the streets, not to mention the innumerable police regulations for the supervision of weddings, funerals, and concerts—suggests the continuing existence of a sort of social civil war between a resentful populace and a strait-laced alien bureaucracy.[9] The peasantry, naturally, sought relief from their quasi-serfdom under estate landlordry by escape to the towns, where some of them managed to save money, buy houses, and even become voters for the Colonial Councils; as the St. Croix Council chairman noted in the 1878 debate, it was a kind of ambition with them not to be considered as country laborers.[10] In mercantile St. Thomas the workers suffered, somewhat differently, the repressive rule of the merchant employer. Even as late as 1915, when liberal members of the Council sought to bring the world-wide shop-hours movement to St. Thomas, the representatives of the merchant community argued against the statutory limitation of a barbarous twelve- to fourteen-hour working day on the ground that it would give the clerks "more time to spree in." [11] The even more barbarous system of "coaling" the visiting steamers by local gangs of women workers, considered picturesque by most visitors, had to await the unionizing efforts of Hamilton Jackson during the same period before it yielded to some humane regulation.

None of these conditions was alleviated by any spirit of public-minded citizenship. Like all colonial societies, the Danish West Indies were, by their nature, anti-intellectual communities. The social tedium of middle-class life (artfully described in Taylor's charming book), only occasionally relieved by the *soirée* or the "fiddle dance," or by the visiting circus or dramatic company, was hardly calculated to encourage or sustain the arts.[12] There was, it is true, the occasional individual, like Taylor himself, whose restless mental energy at times enlivened the local scene. But it is clear that Taylor's influence was due as much

9. For examples of government ordinances respecting these various matters, including master and servant legislation, see *Proceedings of the Colonial Council of St. Thomas and St. John* (microfilm, St. Thomas Public Library), esp. sess. 1878–79, pp. 12–16, 22–26, and sess. 1881–82, pp. 10–16. For police regulations toward the end of the Danish regime, see *The Herald* (Christiansted), Nov. 30, Dec. 1, 10, 17, 1915.

10. *Proceedings of the Colonial Council of St. Croix*, sess. 1878–79, pp. 232–33.

11. *Proceedings of the Colonial Council of St. Thomas and St. John*, sess. 1915, pp. 5–26.

12. Charles Edwin Taylor, *Leaflets from the Danish West Indies* (London: Wm. Dawson and Sons, 1888), chap. 26.

as anything else to the accident of being a white stranger of varied accomplishments in a colored society; his ideas of social progress were basically limited to criticisms of a colonial system which made it almost impossible for the sons of respectable Creole burghers to obtain any of the higher offices under the Danish government. His attitude to the masses, as his chapter on the 1878 labor riots shows, was not much more advanced than that of his own adopted middle-class society. Taylor's influence, then, as editor, engraver, bookseller, and pseudo-doctor, died with him, leaving untouched the pervasive philistinism of the society. The average businessman, as a local newspaper sketch portrayed him, was a shopkeeper with little sense of humor but possessed of a certain dry sharpness of his own, not much interested in poetry, music, or literature, and infinitely preferring to converse about the latest speculations in sugar or to go home satisfied after a good day's transactions with his Santo Domingo purchasers. It is true that there was a certain permeation of liberal ideas through the English and American newspapers, and the presence of liberal elected Council members in the local politics, like Canegata and Stakemann in the last years of the Danish regime, as well as Taylor during the earlier period, testified to the real power of those ideas; it was not for nothing, after all, that, in Taylor's graphic phrase, the St. Thomian shook hands with the universe every day of his life. The story of public-spirited professional men, like Dr. Heyn, who devoted years of his life to the poor as communal physician, likewise demonstrated the existence of a real sense of social obligation, particularly significant considering that the medical profession was, by restrictive legislation, practically the closed preserve of a small clique of Danish expatriate practitioners.

The incapacity of the system to give birth to a significantly large class of Creole professional groups effectively insured that any sort of liberalism, in government or the professions, would be limited to a handful of individuals. The leading societal types were the planter and the merchant, full of a narrow colonial provincialism. Their concepts of public service rarely went beyond campaigns for financial conservatism in public expenditures. They could argue that since St. Thomas in earlier days, when it was a richer community, had never had a communal physician that post should now be abandoned and Poor Law medical work be done gratis by private doctors.[13] They wanted retrenchment on all items of public expense, from the upkeep of the local gendarmerie, which, they argued, should be taken over by the Danish state

13. *Proceedings of the Colonial Council of St. Thomas and St. John*, sess. 1882–83, pp. 22–28; also debate of Colonial Council reported in *St. Thomas Herald*, July 12, 15, 1882.

treasury, to the St. Thomas College, completely irrespective of the difference of purpose of the various items.[14] They insisted upon the use of the penal code to punish breach of contract, leaving it to the more liberal Crown members of the Councils to argue in defense of the more humane method of fines.[15] They could oppose the introduction of a municipal electricity service on the ground that since most people in St. Thomas went to bed between eight and nine o'clock the town did not require much lighting.[16] There was also the usual provincialist lampooning of any outsider with the temerity to criticize, as in the cases, successively, of the British consul who dared to write a satirical piece on St. Thomian life in the *Cornhill Magazine* and of the American consul who wrote a piece for the Demerara *Argosy* exposing the nefarious practices of the St. Thomas commission agents, especially the excessive storage charges they levied upon vessels in distress. In the case of the American consul, indeed, defenders of the local honor wrote angrily against a brand of American humor which, as they saw it, was a "compound of quaint absurdity and coruscating wit, invented and elaborated by Artemus Ward, Mark Twain, and Bret Harte," and even managed to drag in quotations from a speech by Lord Salisbury in the British House of Lords in order to answer their critic.[17]

The general climate of opinion, in short, was shaped by the commission agent mentality. It was the mentality of the middleman. Even technical progress usually came from outside, being instigated by the big transatlantic agencies, the Danish sugar companies, for example, or the great shipping lines like Hamburg-American. There was a similar backwardness in the technology of the professions, and it was at least suggestive that even the open-minded Taylor devoted much of his colonial lifetime to a reactionary struggle against the acceptance of the vaccination revolution in medicine. Taylor described, almost certainly with romantic exaggeration, how the planters of the previous century had been well-educated persons, knowledgeable in mathematics and history, and conversant with Virgil and Horace. The picture certainly did not apply to their nineteenth-century descendants. The most that could be said, perhaps, in defense of the Danish colonial civilization was that it was, as Taylor somewhat smugly congratulated himself, a politically peaceful community in which the Haitian type of violent

14. *Proceedings of the Colonial Council of St. Thomas and St. John*, sess. 1878–79, pp. 19–20, 22–26.

15. *Proceedings of the Colonial Council of St. Croix*, sess. 1878–79, pp. 246–68.

16. *Proceedings of the Colonial Council of St. Thomas and St. John*, sess. 1914, pp. 37–38.

17. *St. Thomas Herald*, Nov. 8, 18, 22, 29, Dec. 2, 1882.

revolution was impossible, in which, that is, the man of property could sleep peacefully at nights.

The Danish system of government itself reflected these values, being noted, above all else, for its qualities of economy and conservatism. As in the British Crown Colony system, with some peculiarly Danish modifications, the governor, under the effective direction of the king and the minister of finance in the metropolitan Diet, was the linchpin of local government, with the elective members of the Colonial Councils enjoying certain limited participatory powers through the medium of departmental commissions. Armed with a variety of weapons—repressive press laws, a set of appointed Crown members, and the ultimate power to dissolve the Councils—the governor ruled as a benevolent autocrat, surrounded by a court of Danish officeholders who gave the lie to the official credo that there existed no prejudicial differences between "native Danes" and "Danish natives." The official circle, then, with an overdose of legal personnel, was at once anti-local (the appointment of Customs Inspector Bjerg, a local man, was sufficiently rare to evoke special comment even as late as 1915) and anti-Negro (equally late in the day, it awaited the Socialist Brandes cabinet to appoint three colored natives as official Council members). Every new Danish official who arrived rapidly found himself in a situation where, finding every language spoken except his own and having no taste for local society, he was driven into the closed circle of his compatriots, thus reinforcing the line of demarcation between himself and the "outsiders." The local government employee, on the other hand, was always in a subordinate position, and his frustration was heightened by the fact that he could only qualify for a higher appointment by means of an expensive and lengthy education in Copenhagen, failing which he relapsed into colonial stagnation. The role of the governor, in all this, was to maintain the status quo and to make concessions merely sufficient to prevent another 1848 or 1878. The status he enjoyed in the more progressive elements of local opinion can be gauged from the fact that, almost on the eve of the transfer, Governor Helweg-Larsen could be popularly viewed as a "Negro hater" who had advised the planters not to pay a daily wage above the level of twenty-five cents.

Theoretically, appeal was always possible to the "home" authorities in Copenhagen. The effectiveness of this course of action was evident in the success of the union leader Jackson in persuading the Socialist Prime Minister Brandes during the First World War period to force the St. Thomas government to permit the holding of political meetings, as well as in receiving an affirmative response to a union appeal for an official grant to start a printing office in Christiansted. But the method had its limits, which were succinctly summarized by a local critic in 1882:

> As a matter of course we in our little community depend to quite a different degree on our officials than is the case at Home, where a mighty public opinion and a powerful public press are in a position to stimulate or to hold in check. Here, when once we have got the officials, we do not lightly make any complaints of them. For we have partly a conviction that at Home there is very little interest taken in our complaints, perhaps less interest just where we should look for the reverse; and besides, it is a difficult thing in Copenhagen to form an opinion as to personalities in the West Indies. When, on the presentation of a complaint, follows a "confidential" report from the official, which report the complaining party never sees, but in which is enumerated all the personal and malicious motives that have caused the dissatisfied rebel to get up in arms with his Superior Magistrate—it is but too natural that the Minister seeks his decision in this confidential report, and that the result must be naught, or even greater discomfiture for the self-constituted reformer.[18]

Not surprisingly, then, the Danish Antilles in 1917 hardly qualified as a model Caribbean colony. Economically, they had long since lapsed, like the neighboring British colonies, into the position of dependencies calling for state subsidies which "home" governments, would not or could not provide. Socially, they presented a massive problem of poverty, unemployment, begging, and malnutrition (the Danish expert Dr. Hindhede estimated that 64 per cent of all children between one and five years of age died in St. Croix in the period 1909–13).[19] Standards of public services were frequently medieval: up until the time of the transfer, sick persons in St. Croix were transported to town on open wooden carts, exposed mercilessly to the sun. The vaunted Danish record in education proved, as the new American teachers rapidly discovered, to be largely legendary, the educational system being in fact characterized by incompetent teaching by church "teachers" and untrained boy monitors, petty graft in administration, and a grand total of nineteen tumbledown "schools," a regime, in brief, as the first American governor reported, leaving about everything in the way of an adequate system to be desired. There existed, in fact, no proper records of schools, pupils, or parents. The Catholic schools taught practically nothing save a rudimentary religion, while the teachers in the "public" schools were possessed of an "English" which almost deserved to be ranked as an independent dialect. The *Herald*, a newspaper valiantly

18. *Ibid.*, Dec. 23, 1882.
19. Dr. Hindhede, Report on infant mortality, in *The Herald* (Christiansted), Dec. 30, 1915.

edited by Hamilton Jackson in the last years of the regime, fully catalogued the grievances of the Negro masses: police brutality, the
numerous petty abuses of the work contract system, the habitual mo-
lestation of citizens by arrogant gendarmes, absentee government in
both church and state (which could only be remedied by a policy of
local West Indian recruitment of candidates, as had been recommended
by the groups of leading colored citizens who had memorialized the
Danish Royal Commission of 1903), and much else, not to mention a
general culture so impoverished that about the only pleasure permitted
to the natives was the playing of their own brass bands.[20] About the only
affirmative thing the various American reports that followed the transfer
could say of the Danish system was that, unlike other European colo-
nizers of Caribbean islands, the Danes had not made any attempt to
enforce their language upon their subject peoples.

Thus it is possible, in assessing the record, properly to speak of the
myth of the Danish past. The final proof, of course, was the conspicuous
absence of any significant sentimental regrets when the prolonged
sale negotiations, going back to the Civil War period, finally terminated in 1916–17. The logical implication of an Americanized economy was, after all, an Americanized political system. There were few
voices to dispute the maxim. The editorial remarks of the *Bulletin*,
following the results of the Danish plebiscite of 1916, were typical, in
their mixture of relief and bitterness, of public attitudes:

> The merchandise is now off the counter, the undignified, unique business being
> at last closed. There will soon be no more Danish West Indies, and if the flag
> is lowered unhonoured and the name of Denmark by the great majority unsung,
> there is a reason, or reasons. To the credit of Danish administration however
> it should be said, at this time when misdeeds are grossly magnified and exag-
> gerated, that it has not been barren of good results. It has accomplished much,
> though it could have achieved much more. But the sale virus which tainted the
> national spirit could not be eradicated. That was the bane which with other
> contributory causes created a state of affairs in these islands without parallel
> anywhere, communities above all that were practically aliens to the mother
> tongue, without which there can be no true sympathy or love such as that
> welded by the strong link of language in the fraternal chain.[21]

Even the Reformed Dutch Church pastor who conducted the solitary religious service commemorating the transfer permitted himself the implied
rebuke of observing that economic reasons had proved stronger than
bonds of sentiment and there had certainly been no sale of an un-

20. See, for all this, *ibid.* through 1915.
21. *The Bulletin* (St. Thomas), Dec. 16, 1916, quoted in Zabriskie, *The Virgin
Islands*, p. 254.

willing people.[22] Those, of course, were the sentiments of the Creole respectability. The nascent forces of organized labor permitted themselves more radical observations. They anticipated a new deal for the majority under the American popular democracy. They saw the transfer as, in part, a logical step in their advance as a social element in the national life. They had started their organizational work in 1915 as a crusade to consummate the "sublime work" of emancipation started in 1848. They now saw themselves as a Negro race, constituting a "separate nationality, in relation to the Danish state." "Our long apprenticeship to the other race is ended. We no longer worship it as the incarnation of the deity; we have found it to be a race of 'mere men,' men in every relation of life like ourselves." [23]

The colonial rejection, understandably, was the consequence of metropolitan lack of interest. Neither Danish government nor people had ever shown much active interest in the Antillean dependencies. A more or less creolized *métropolitain* like Nissen could appreciate the Creole way of life, and he defended its quite remarkable society of elegant manners against European abuse. But that was hardly possible for the *métropole* itself. The history of the sale negotiations, starting perhaps with Secretary Seward's winter cruise of 1866 to the West Indies, revealed a not too reluctant seller willing to get' the most out of an anxious buyer and not above conducting the business by royal proclamations to colonial subjects who were not consulted. It is difficult to read the various self-righteous proclamations issued at different times by Christian IX and Christian X without agreeing with the American author who commented on manifestoes in which the royal person told his loyal subjects how grieved he was to part with them, assuring them, as fathers always do, that it was for their own good, but neglecting to mention that he needed the money.[24] Even more telling as an indictment of metropolitan attitudes was the fact that, as Professor Morse Stephens pointed out in his introduction to Westergaard's volume of 1917, no Danish scholar had ever bothered to attempt to write the history of the Danish West Indies, indicating that the feeling of historic pride had not gone very deep among the Danes. The result was that the first such history, written from primary sources, had to be

22. *Ibid.*, p. 280.
23. *The Herald* (Christiansted) , Dec. 31, 1915.
24. Harry A. Franck, *Roaming through the West Indies* (New York: Century, 1920), p. 315. For the various royal proclamations, see Zabriskie, *The Virgin Islands*, pp. 17–19, 22–24, 285–87. For the sale negotiations, see Charles Callan Tansill, *The Purchase of the Danish West Indies* (New York: Greenwood Press, 1932); and Marietta Pedersen, "The American Acquisition of the Danish West Indies" (Ph.D. diss., Georgetown University, 1962).

undertaken by the son of a Danish family who had emigrated to North Dakota and who himself had received his historical training at the University of California.[25] It was in a way fitting that the date of publication of the book should have coincided with the final Danish act, the sale of the islands to the American democracy.

25. Waldemar Westergaard, *The Danish West Indies under Company Rule, 1671–1754* (New York: Macmillan, 1917).

2

1917:
The American Beginnings

The acquisition of tropical possessions marked the advent of America as a modern world colonial power. Beginning in 1917, however, the Virgin Islands, like Puerto Rico and the Philippines, suffered from the fact that America, unlike France or Great Britain, lacked the administrative machinery appropriate to the government of colonial dependencies. Until the creation, in 1934, of an embryonic colonial civil service in the form of the Division of Territories and Island Possessions within the Department of the Interior, there existed no body of thought or administrative tradition to give continuous attention to colonial problems when public interest and congressional concern inevitably waned. Nothing was more dramatic than the immense contrast between the vast diplomatic energy that preceded the sale of 1917 and the almost casual manner in which the problems of the government of the new Caribbean possessions were treated after the sale. The treaty of sale itself bore the marks of the main American motive—fear that St. Thomas would fall into German hands—for only an inordinate haste could explain the curious fact that far from being a hardheaded "Yankee trade" it was, in fact, a curiously one-sided document which among other things obliged the U.S. government to maintain all the grants, concessions, and licenses left behind by the Danish administration. Once American fear of German motives had been allayed, national interest in the new possessions almost completely faded away, aided by the fact that preoccupation with the conduct of the war left nobody of importance in Washington with either the time or the inclination to remedy the neglect. Once the war was ended the history of U.S.–Virgin Islands relationships rapidly became a dismal story of unending conflict and recrimination between a federal administration unequal to its task and a local public opinion in which all shades of the Virgin Islands political spectrum, from radical to conservative, united in their agreement that the United States had acquired the islands for selfish purposes and then had proceeded to neglect, even forget, them.

The primary example of that conflict, and in itself a fecund source of even more conflict, was the issue of the constitutional status of the new territory. Virgin Islanders had confidently expected to be received as full members of the American family. No single factor, then, so shaped the character of postwar insular politics as the set of governmental institutions which was introduced by Congress as the new basic law of the territory and which bitterly belied those great expectations. Without any attempt to canvass the state of island opinion, Congress simply applied to the new possession the doctrine of the unincorporated territory previously laid down by the Supreme Court in the famous Insular Cases whereby, in essence, the leading principle of American constitutional development—the establishment of territories designed to graduate, after a period of apprenticeship, to statehood in the Union—was put aside in favor of a new and lower status of second-class membership. It was an anomalous status, for since, as the Court argued in *Downes* v. *Bidwell,* the Constitution was not intended to immediately embrace in its entirety the people of an annexed area, or to bestow upon them the full privileges of American citizenship, it followed that the traditional constitutional precepts restraining the power of president and Congress were no longer to apply to such areas.[1] The real power over the people of such areas, *Dorr* v. *United States* decided, was not the declarative command of the Constitution but rather the fiat of Congress as it flowed from the territorial clause.[2] Congress, under this argument, had been delegated to serve as the "constitution" for the unincorporated territories, and the sole limitations on its behavior in that role were "such constitutional restrictions upon the power of that body as are applicable to the situation." The ambit of congressional power clearly rested upon the definition offered at any given moment of "applicable" powers and provisions, an ambiguity not improved upon by the effort of Justice Brown to enunciate a distinction between the "fundamental" guarantees of the Constitution which must prevail everywhere and the "non-fundamental" guarantees which Congress might presumably abjure and need not extend to "unincorporated" territories unless it wished to do so.[3]

1. *Downes* v. *Bidwell,* 182 U.S. 244 (1901).
2. *Dorr* v. *United States,* 195 U.S. 138 (1904).
3. *Downes* v. *Bidwell,* 182 U.S. 244 (1901).

(43)

The extension of this novel doctrine—which had about it, in Justice Harlan's pungent phrase of dissent, some occult meaning difficult of apprehension [4]—to the Virgin Islands had momentous consequences. It meant that Virgin Islanders were governed not by the mandate of the Constitution but by an emergent congressional political science in which rights that were denied them by being deemed "non-fundamental" included, from time to time, the right to trial by jury, the right to indictment by grand jury, the traditional separation of powers between the judicial and executive and the civilian and military branches of government, as well as the advantages of a bill of rights. It meant, further, their acceptance as "nationals" but not "citizens," a dubious distinction that was only put an end to by the grant of full citizenship in 1927. But the practical result of that extraordinary status meant, for example, that between 1917 and 1927 a Virgin Islander who graduated from an American university in one of the professions could not practice his skills in any of the individual states, simply because he was not a citizen of the United States. An additional ignominy was that Virgin Islanders did not even have the satisfaction of being judged by the Supreme Court, since the decision about citizenship, for example, was made almost surreptitiously by means of a letter from the acting secretary of state in 1920 to the chairman of a congressional Joint Commission investigating the islands.[5] Yet the evidence suggests that the American negotiators of the 1917 treaty with Denmark were clear in their own minds from the beginning that citizenship would not be extended to the former Danish citizens of the islands.

Whether publicly intended or not, however, the *suma providentia* of the doctrine of nonincorporation—the exclusion of alien territories and peoples acquired by treaty or conquest from the full rights of American life—was extended to all of the new colonial possessions of the United States during these first phases of the American imperial career. The fact was not lost upon Virgin Islanders that the new doctrine of nonincorporation was used exclusively against communities in which significant elements of the population, as in Puerto Rico, or the overriding

4. *Ibid.* For a general discussion of the Insular Cases see, among much else, Pedro Capó Rodriguez, "The Relations between the United States and Porto Rico," *American Journal of International Law*, XIII, no. 3 (July, 1919), 483–525, and "Colonial Representation in the American Empire," *ibid.*, XV, no. 4 (October, 1921), 529–52; and Whitney T. Perkins, "American Policy in the Government of Its Dependent Areas: A Study of the Policy of the United States toward the Inhabitants of its Territories and Insular Possessions" (Ph.D. diss., Tufts University, 1949).

5. Luther H. Evans, *The Virgin Islands: From Naval Base to New Deal* (Ann Arbor, Mich.: J. W. Edwards, 1945), p. 62. See also letter of second assistant secretary, U.S. Department of State, to George Utendahl, November 15, 1922, in *St. Croix Tribune* (Christiansted), Dec. 29, 1922.

majority, as in the Virgin Islands, were of Negro origin. Altogether, Virgin Islanders rapidly came to feel, after 1917, that they had become the latest victims of American Manifest Destiny. For, as Bryan had argued earlier in a famous speech, the central idea of Manifest Destiny was, "This is the first time that we have been told that we must cross an ocean, conquer a people, drag them under our flag, and then tell them that they are never to be citizens, but are to be subjects, and to be treated with kindness by our people." [6]

The machinery of government set up by Congress reflected this humiliating second-class status. It bore all the marks of hasty wartime improvisation. In fact, the basic statute of March, 1917, by continuing in effect most of the provisions of the Danish Colonial Law of 1906, perpetuated a Danish constitutional system that went back to 1863 and conferred upon Virgin Islanders the further anomaly of being governed by an odd combination of American sovereignty and Danish institutions, with the minor modification, of course, of a changed nomenclature to conform to American usage. The lacunae inevitably created by this curious mode of legislating for the new territory had to be filled in by a mixture of administrative edict, congressional enactment (such as the extension of Prohibition to the Caribbean possession), and presidential executive order (such as President Hoover's order of February, 1931, transferring the islands to the Interior Department). The confusion attending the citizenship problem was the best-known example of the difficulties arising from all that. But there were other problems no less intractable: the vaguely defined jurisdiction of the local Colonial Councils retained from the pre-1917 days; the divided and at times conflicting obligations of the governor to, variously, the president, the Congress, the Department of the Navy, and the secretary of the interior; and the continuing bitter debate as to whether the system of government that lasted for the fourteen years up to 1931 was "naval government" or "civilian government." Collectively, these matters had the result of diverting Virgin Islands energy into a sterile debate about political status, just like the vexing status issue in Puerto Rican politics; exactly how sterile can be appreciated by even a cursory glance at the prolonged politico-constitutional agitation which over the weary years accompanied the reform movement for, first, the Organic Act of 1936 and, second, the Revised Organic Act of 1954.

6. U.S., Congress, Senate, *Congressional Record,* 56th Cong., 1st sess., 1906, 33, 6340. See, for a general discussion of all this, Raymond Lewis Cravens, "The Constitutional and Political Status of the Non-contiguous Areas of the United States" (Ph.D. diss., University of Kentucky, 1958).

It is worth looking at the particular details of that struggle in the period of Navy rule (1917–31), for they constitute a perfect example of how preoccupation with problems of constitutional legalism can lead to the neglect of the "condition of the people" question in colonial politics. The fact, to begin with, that the president nominated the Navy to take over the new local government in itself underlined the dangerously broad discretionary power conferred upon him by the congressional legislation, for he was not restricted to a choice of the armed services by that legislation. That a president as liberal as Wilson did so choose served to emphasize the fact that Washington viewed the new possessions almost exclusively from the narrow viewpoint of national security, an attitude further made evident by President Hoover's later disastrous remarks of 1931 viewing the islands as important only in terms of "remote naval contingencies." A mode of government—police action by the Marines— employed by the Americans in Haiti and Santo Domingo, both of them turbulent trouble spots for American interests, was thus extended to a peaceful community that had come into American hands by means of peaceful negotiations with a neutral European country. In theory, of course, the governor, as a representative of the federal government, was the president's man, accountable to him. But the general lack of interest in the Virgin Islands shown by most chief executives, combined with the fact that the new territory was in effect one vast naval defense base, meant that the Navy Department became not simply the channel of communication between president and governor but, much more, the controlling federal agency over the islands, exercising considerable power over both the financial relations between the insular and federal governments and the general administrative structure of the insular government. Presidential interest rarely went beyond the occasional writing of a letter to a private Virgin Islands citizen, and it is doubtful if any president read seriously the annual reports of the governor, those reports in any case not being regularly printed until 1926. The effective monopoly of the Navy was further strengthened by the fact that except for a few Navy officials no one in Washington really knew anything about the Virgins: Jarvis asserts that even at the State Department executives had classified the Caribbean group as part of the Philippines. The governorship, clearly, was a post of real power. An American official wrote:

In presiding over the destinies of 22,000 people who live on three islands of 132 square miles in area, in exercising the functions of a small town mayor combined with those of a county manager, the governor receives the perquisites of a governor-general, enjoys several weeks twice a year or oftener in Washington, has access to the Treasury of the United States, carries his problems directly to a Department head and even to the President, and is emancipated from dependence upon public opinion for anything except his insular legislative program.[7]

The local executive power, backed by all the glittering panoply of the
Navy, was made even more formidable by the general weakness of the
legislative institutions carried over from the autocratic Danish regime.
The twin Colonial Councils, certainly, were embryonic representative institutions. But their power to control the colonial administration, through
their participation in the budgetary and auditing processes, was severely
limited both by the governor's veto power over particular items and by his
extensive ordinance power. Further, the Councils' power to investigate
government departments was limited by the bifurcation of the administrative system into one central, federal administration and two municipal
administrations. This had the result of insulating an entire body of
Washington-appointed administrative officials from local control or local
accountability; and on at least one occasion the government secretary
flatly took the position that only the president was competent to investigate
a department of the insular government. It is true that the 1906 law
guaranteed the continuance of the peculiar feature of administrative
commissions in areas as varied as schools, taxes, poor relief, and sanitation. But in a moment of abject surrender to gubernatorial pressure,
later much regretted, the Councils first suspended and then completely
abolished the commissions. The governor exercised further legislative
power through the minority groups of his nominated members in the
Councils, and the crucial struggle with the St. Croix Council in 1925,
when the Council queried the appointment of two nominees on the ground
that they were aliens, decisively determined the legal incompetence of
the Councils to question his appointments in that field. What the nominated officials could not do, the gubernatorial power (in the last instance,
to dissolve a recalcitrant Council) could always do. It should also be
noted that the combined Councils, being based upon the narrow Danish
franchise, represented no more than 5.5 per cent of the island populations
at any time during this period, a fact that shattered their pose as democratic instruments of popular opinion.

A reading of the published debates of the two Councils during this
period makes it clear that the continuity in the machinery of government
from one regime to the other also meant a certain continuity in the

7. Evans, *The Virgin Islands*, p. 80. For the role of the governor in the American
colonial system, see Jack E. Eblen, "The Governor in the United States System of Territorial Government" (Ph.D. diss., University of Wisconsin, 1966). For a comparative
analysis of the American and British colonial systems in the area, see Hester Dorothy
Chisholm, "A Colonial Evaluation of the British Leeward Islands and the Virgin Islands
of the United States" (Master's thesis, Clark University, 1938).

personnel of the Councils. The old Danish conservative names carried on as before, plus new ones like Mylner. There were, of course, new liberal faces, such as Leroy Nolte, Lionel Roberts, and Rothschild Francis, as well as the occasional figure of a public-spirited professional man, like Dr. Knud-Hansen, who spanned both regimes. The typical councilman, however, was the reactionary white Crucian estate owner like Armstrong or the equally reactionary St. Thomas business oligarch like Moorehead. It is worth noting that this type frequently derived his electoral support from the anachronistic alien franchise comprising (1) the Danish residents who had elected not to opt for American citizenship but who retained their civil rights under the terms of the 1917 Convention signed by Washington and Copenhagen, and (2) the non-Danish European residents who had been given the right to vote, conditional on a five-year residency period, by the Danish Colonial Law of 1906, which right was carried over into the American regime. The result was an irregular situation in which the electoral roll in 1926 contained a mere 700 voters, of whom some 40 per cent were estimated to be aliens. The Armstrong-Moorehead type was generally supported by the conciliar nominated members (a system unique in the United States, since only the Virgin Islands had it), for most of the Navy governors used the appointing power to nominate upper-class aliens, members of the judiciary, federal office-holders, and candidates defeated at the polls (as with Governor Trench's appointment of Kuntz and Corneiro in 1926), instead of using it to fulfill its original purpose of securing representation for the disenfranchised.[8] As in the legislative councils of the Crown Colony system in the neighboring British islands, all this generated the characteristic disease of legislative individualism. Each legislator, legally, was responsible solely to his own conscience; and even if he was sponsored by an organized group outside, as with the early Progressive Party slate, such groups were powerless to control him once he entered the Council. In summing up the record of the Councils under the Navy regime, the leading progressive newspaper in 1930 editorialized as follows:

> Notwithstanding the fact that each member of the Colonial Council is the representative of everybody, but represents no party, he is there as an independent so long as personal interest, aggrandizement or political favors are his views. No party obligations, no pledge to the people to carry through a single measure for community benefit, nothing is required of a member other than the way he is able to practice his deceptions on an innocent public.[9]

The general record bore out the indictment. The majorities in the

8. *The Emancipator* (St. Thomas), Sept. 29, 1926.
9. Editorial, *ibid.*, Dec. 3, 1930.

Councils strongly favored the continuing presence of the Navy under the new governmental arrangements. Indeed, the debate of the St. Thomas and St. John Council in May, 1926, on the receipt of a petition by prominent local citizens asking the Council to request Congress not to pass any legislation that would cause the withdrawal of naval personnel from the local administration demonstrates the deep power of the colonialist mentality and its readiness to draw upon the most abject of reasons—that the Navy could give the natives better service than they could give themselves, for example—to justify the status quo, even when members could at the same time recognize that in doing so they were in effect "singing for their supper."[10] Councils could at times be more courageous, of course, as with the demands of the St. Croix Council from the beginning for expanded public works programs; but even then the demand for economic betterment was deemed so important that the Councils were willing to forego political and constitutional reforms as their part of the bargain.[11] The agitation for those reforms, as a result, came from other sources; the introduction and discussion of successive drafts for a new constitution during the period came either from liberal forces outside, such as the American Civil Liberties Union, or from federal governmental sources—for example, the 1926 draft presented by the Puerto Rican delegate to the House of Representatives on behalf of his Virgin Islands neighbors, or the various bills introduced by friendly congressional leaders like Representative Kiess and Senator Bingham. The Councils rarely went beyond recommendations in favor of resolving the confused citizenship issue, as in their joint resolution of February, 1924. It was symptomatic that when the St. Thomas Council went further and appointed a committee to study the constitution reform matter the resultant draft act prepared by one of the committee members, the St. Thomas police judge, George Mena, was apparently not even considered by the Council, and its author had to be satisfied with presenting it to the local Republican Club. The Councils, clearly enough, saw themselves as subordinate bodies in the system whose duty it was to cooperate with the executive, as the chairman of the St. Thomas Council put it, "through useful suggestions and reasonable objections, as may be needful." Psychologically, they saw themselves as the local allies of the governor in his struggle to Americanize the new possessions, a frame of mind aptly summed up in the speech of Robert L. Merwin to the St.

10. *Proceedings of the Colonial Council of St. Thomas and St. John,* May 28, 1926 (microfilm, St. Thomas Public Library), pp. 87–92.

11. *Proceedings of the Colonial Council of St. Croix,* June 2, 1927 (microfilm, St. Thomas Public Library). See also, for similar sentiments, petition of St. Thomas businessmen to Washington, in Evans, *The Virgin Islands,* p. 238.

Thomas Council in 1922, in which he described in lyrical terms his visit to the White House and how, after experiencing the influence of the "ethereal spirit" of former presidents in the anteroom, he bathed under the "kindly and magnetic smile" of President Harding.[12]

Council debates thus rarely concerned themselves with the seminal problems of the society and mostly with the odds and ends of public business, such as the methods of garbage collection, the system of road maintenance, or the question of pensions for individual government servants. There were, admittedly, moments of open confrontation, when Virgin Islands pride asserted itself. Lionel Roberts led an indignant St. Thomas Council in 1926 in a unanimous demand for the reinstitution of the municipal committees arbitrarily taken away by the administrative *coup d'état* of 1918, leaving the Councils with no means of controlling the spending habits of departments overburdened with useless employees enjoying fantastic salaries.[13] The same debate unleashed a storm of protest against the growth of reckless nepotism in the Department of Education, involving, among other things, the setting up of a new post to accommodate the American director's wife, to be financed by cutting down on the salaries of native teachers.[14] The iniquities of the new Civil Code—massive fines used as a means of prolonging imprisonment of offenders, the limitation of jury rights, including the right of pardon, the ridiculously high costs of appeal, all of them defects noted by both appeal courts and visiting congressional committees—were thoroughly exposed in the Council debate of February, 1927.

But two things must be noted about this aspect of legislative behavior. In the first place, the items that excited Council members into their occasional revolts usually concerned the interest groups of their tiny electorate; they displayed little interest in the glaring abuses under which the native masses labored, in particular a feudal system of land monopoly and a vicious tax system. Most of them would have agreed with the naval governor who told the Chamber of Commerce that it was not the province of the legislature to dictate to merchants when they should open and close their places of business. So antediluvian, indeed, were the social attitudes of the St. Croix Council that even a naval governor was moved to lecture its members severely on their obligations, advising them against sending a costly commission to Washington unless at the same time they took care that the commission spoke for all the people and not just for special interests. Second, legislative protest was

12. Quoted in *St. Croix Tribune*, Dec. 23, 1922.
13. *Proceedings of the Colonial Council of St. Thomas and St. John*, February 10, 1926, pp. 76–80. See also debate of April 9, 1931, quoted in *The Emancipator*, Apr. 29, May 2, 4, 6, 9, 1931.
14. *Proceedings*, February 10, 1926, pp. 80–81.

rarely effective, there being no means available of implementing legislative views at the administrative level. The series of naval governors did not even bother to attend Council meetings, despite invitations to do so, and the feelings of legislators were hardly assuaged by being informed by the government secretary in 1927 that the governor was in his office every morning and was always delighted to see the gentlemen of the Council.

The real struggle, the undeclared civil war between the Navy administration and the popular interests, took place outside the Council chambers. It could have been stated as an axiom deductively argued from the nature of things that the U.S. Navy was the wrong agency with which to entrust the government of a dependent civilian population. By training and disposition, the Annapolis mentality was not suited to the demands of popular government. The professional naval officer, imbued with the habit of authority, would find it difficult to work with civilians and humiliating to be accountable to them or, as a governor in a legislative council, to be subject to their criticisms. Administratively, the Navy possessed no training program to fit its candidates for what was, in effect, a colonial civil service. Appointment to the office of governor in the new dependent territories, then, was certain to be haphazard. In his outgoing speech of 1922 to the Virgin Islands people Governor Kittelle in fact revealed that his successor, Captain Hough, had been selected by a curious process. It seemed that the president, overwhelmed by domestic problems, had delegated the assistant secretary of the Navy to find him "the right man"; the secretary, in turn, had consulted with the director of naval operations and the chief of the Bureau of Navigation to select an officer whose claim to the appointment apparently was that he already had friends in the Virgin Islands local social aristocracy as the result of two visits to St. Thomas as an officer of visiting Navy cruisers some twenty years earlier.[15] Even worse, however, was the fact that for the period of its rule in the Virgin Islands the Navy was a completely segregated service, having adopted a policy of total racial exclusion in 1920 which was only partly relaxed in 1932; the supreme irony, then, was that an all-white service was granted the power to rule over an overwhelmingly Negro civil population. Perhaps the final humiliation was that Virgin Islanders were governed by a service which, whether as "nationals" or "citizens," they themselves could not join, the only exception to that rule being the recruitment of local colored musicians into the local Navy band for ceremonial occasions at the St. Thomas Naval Station. It is

15. Reported in *St. Croix Tribune,* Sept. 23, 1922.

worth adding, on that point, that although Virgin Islanders genuinely appreciated that gesture—which included a moving ceremony on board the U.S.S. *Vixen* in 1917, in which Captain White and his officers paid tribute to Lionel Roberts, the doyen of the Virgin Islands brass band tradition—they have not forgotten that the price they had to pay was the spectacle of Alton Adams, the appointed Navy bandleader, being sent by Admiral Kittelle on an official tour of American public schools as a publicity gimmick in defense of the Navy record in the islands.

The Navy system of government, in short, consisted of the private rule of naval governors generally ignorant of civic duties, lacking in experience, holding themselves aloof from local society, and generally delegating their authority to subordinates. All this was made even worse by the tendency of the Navy Department in Washington not to exercise any effective or close supervision over an area for which it was at least nominally responsible. The system almost immediately engaged the hostile attention of the radical Negro leaders, who were more skilled in political method than the naval bureaucrats, were infinitely better orators, and were supported by a class solidarity that went back in its roots to the local class struggles that predated the period of American rule. Guerrilla warfare in the legislative councils was increasingly replaced by guerrilla warfare in field and factory by way of strike action, and in the area of communications by way of a lively polemical press conducted by skilled Negro editors—Hamilton Jackson, Rothschild Francis, Ralph de Chabert, and others—deriving new ideological substance from their reading of the American Negro and white liberal press and supported in practice by their new relationships, rapidly forged after 1917, with the political bosses of Negro Harlem.

The professional naval mind, being no match for this sort of popular "muckraking" politics—the import of which into the Virgin Islands was one of the earliest and unanticipated consequences of the transfer—responded in the manner of petty autocrats. Government House used every method to destroy criticism. There was the repressive censorship of the press; and the imprisoned editor who found himself in jail on "contempt" charges had only the recourse of a costly appeal to the Supreme Court of the Virgin Islands, located, oddly, in Philadelphia. There was the use of deportation powers against "undesirable aliens," as the cases of assistant editors like Barrow and Morenga-Bonaparte notoriously illustrated.[16] There was the scandalous administrative interference with the

16. Editorial, *ibid.*, Sept. 21, 1922. These local press cases generated much interest at the time in the stateside liberal press. See, for example, Eric D. Walrond, "Autocracy in the Virgin Islands," *Current History* (October, 1923); Arthur Warner, "Bayonet Rule for Our Colonial Press," *The Nation*, March 7, 1923; Samuel S. Ripley, "Our Naval Autocracy in Samoa," *The Nation*, March 15, 1922. See also Donald D. Hoover, "The Virgin Islands under American Rule," *Foreign Affairs* (April, 1926).

local judicial processes; Judge Lucius Malmin's 1925 address to the American Bar Association demonstrated to what lengths the Navy would go to get rid of "uncooperative" judges, including measures to deprive them of the help of court officials and pressure in Washington to force their resignation.[17] There was even the method of highhanded physical abduction of critics, as in the case of the visiting woman botanist, a correspondent of the Smithsonian Institution, who found herself summarily placed on board a ship in St. Thomas and, on reaching her home state, declared insane on the testimony of a naval nurse and incarcerated in the state insane asylum. It is hardly surprising, then, that the files of the American Civil Liberties Union on civil liberties violations in the Virgin Islands rapidly became among the largest in its collection.

The mentality behind all this was that of the postwar "Red Scare," exported to the Virgin Islands not so much by visiting congressmen as by the resident naval bureaucracy. The early exchange of letters between Roger Baldwin and the acting government secretary in St. Thomas made it plain that, in reply to the libertarian thesis that American institutions ought to mean the same thing at home and abroad, the naval mind could doubt whether the concept of freedom of the press extended to a colonial possession and that "in a country where the people have not had the advantage of long residence under American institutions, the control of a radical press and the prevention of promulgation of doctrines inimical to American interests could . . . do no possible harm, and would, in all probability, do incalculable good." [18]

Most governors were engaged in a holy war between "red-blooded Americans" and "professional malcontents." They had no understanding of politics, which was typified by Governor Kittelle's naive outburst: "What we need is no politics and a lot of business. This place is too small for politics." [19] They would have agreed with Representative Ayres's view that to put the islands under another federal department would mean the growth of yet another expensive Washington bureaucracy, controlled by political office-seekers both in the federal capital and in St. Thomas, and organized along the lines of party politics—as if

17. Reprinted in *The Nation*, October 21, 1925, and in *The Emancipator*, Sept. 16, 1925. One of the crucial court cases in this struggle was *Francis v. People of the Virgin Islands*, IIF (2d) 860 at 863 (C.C.A. 3d, 1926).

18. Reprinted in *St. Croix Tribune*, July 11, 1922.

19. Quoted in *ibid.*, Sept. 23, 1922. One of the tactics of the naval bureaucracy and its stateside friends at this time was to disseminate the libel that American socialist groups were engaged in conspiracies to export socialism to the Virgin Islands. See *The Emancipator*, Oct. 14, 1922, quoting the *New York Call*. Another tactic was to smear the reputation of the local "agitators." See attack on Rothschild Francis in *St. Thomas Mail Notes*, Sept. 26, 1922, and 1922 Report of Governor of the Virgin Islands, quoted in Evans, *The Virgin Islands*, p. 221.

politics were some sort of "un-American" activity.[20] Most of them abstained from attendance at Council meetings because they found it intolerable to be placed in a situation where they could be cross-examined by Negro politicians by means of the right of legislative interpellation. That meant a studied neglect of popular interests. "It shows no respect or regard for the opinions and feelings of the people," expostulated a legislative critic with reference to the scandalous conditions in education, "when the Governor sits back all the time in the Executive Mansion and plays his fiddle while Rome burns in the Department of Education." [21]

Underlying all this, of course, was the American white racist contempt for the Negro population, provoking the open fights between local youths and Marines so prevalent during this period. This feeling of contempt was a pronounced feature of American travel literature on the area at that time, as was evidenced, for example, in Harry Franck's *Roaming through the West Indies* (1920). The Virgin Islands colony in New York summed it all up in its 1922 protest against

> the hitherto unheard of doctrine of political serfdom which puts the government of an American colony into the hands of the Navy Department. We can readily understand how a conquered territory, prior to the establishment of civil government, can be administered under martial law by the military forces which had effected its subjugation; but we fail to find any precedent in the history or laws of the United States, or any other English speaking country, for the present arrangement which turns over the civil rights of a free people whose territory was peaceably acquired by treaty and by purchase to the by no means tender mercies of that same Navy Department which has achieved such an unsavoury reputation in Haiti.[22]

It is true that the native propagandist literature, especially of the exiled New York groups, frequently exaggerated conditions; rapine and murder were hardly the order of the day. Nor was the real gravamen of

20. House, *Congressional Record*, 71st Cong., 2d sess., 1930, 72, pt. 8, 8801–3. But for more sympathetic congressional attitudes toward the islands see, for example, remarks of Senator Kenyon, Senate, *ibid.*, 67th Cong., 1st sess., 1921, 61, pt. 2, 1723–25; and House, *Citizenship of the Inhabitants of the Virgin Islands*, 69th Cong., 2d sess., 1927, H. Rept. 2093.

21. *Proceedings of the Colonial Council of St. Thomas and St. John*, February 10, 1926, pp. 80–81.

22. Resolutions on behalf of the Virgin Islands of the United States, by Virgin Islands residents in New York, quoted in *St. Croix Tribune*, July 7, 1922. For profiles of the island leaders during this period of struggle with the Navy regime see, as examples, Carlos Downing, remarks to Municipal Council of St. Thomas and St. John on life of Rothschild Francis, reprinted in *Daily News*, Apr. 27, 1946; Alton A. Adams, "The Man D. Hamilton Jackson," *ibid.*, June 8, 1946; Resolution of the Virgin Islands Legislature, in honor of Caspar Holstein, February 15, 1968, reprinted in *Home Journal*, Feb. 18, 1968.

the complaint against the Navy that it produced Captain Blighs in Government House. It was, rather, that psychologically the Navy was not equipped to understand the processes of civilian democracy in general or the peculiarities of Caribbean race relations in particular. Its officers thought, characteristically, in terms of the habit of authority. "There should be full recognition of the fact," wrote Major General McIntyre in an argument against civilian rule, "that in assigning small islands for supervision it is proper to keep in mind the specific object for which they were acquired. An island or a small group of islands acquired primarily for naval purposes does not differ greatly from a war vessel or fleet at anchor. It would be as improper to transfer the administration of such an island or island group from the Navy to another department as to turn over war vessels to any other than the Navy Department." [23] Looked at thus, Virgin Islanders were, so to speak, on active service as soldiers in a national emergency. The weakness of the argument was, quite simply, that with the end of World War I no such emergency existed. Nor were there problems of internal disorder to justify the continuation of military government.

The considerations that led Colonel Thompson, in his 1926 report on the Philippines, to advocate a civil regime in that Pacific possession—that there was no anti-Americanism to speak of, no problem of insurrection or sedition, and that the real problems were those of civil administration and economic development—applied even more forcibly to the Virgin Islands. Virgin Islanders, as a matter of fact, were (as they still are) a remarkably placid and law-abiding people, and even a Navy governor was constrained to note in an annual report, not without some malicious humor, that although unduly contentious most Virgin Islanders quite happily settled their differences diplomatically in the offices of the directors of police and that although sentimentally opposed to Prohibition they presented a "prohibition situation deemed satisfactory judged from continental American standards." [24] But the Navy as a whole was immune to such considerations and insisted to the last that it was engaged in a peace-keeping operation, with the resultant emphasis upon the priority of "law and order" concepts. Even when a governor like Evans managed to see beyond that narrow horizon into the social and economic problems of the islands, as his imaginative re-

23. "American Territorial Administration," *Foreign Affairs* (January, 1932). The article quotes from *A Proposal for Government Reorganization*, published by the National Budget Committee (Washington, D.C.: Government Printing Office, 1921).

24. *Annual Report of the Governor of the Virgin Islands to the Secretary of the Interior, 1926* (Washington, D.C.: Government Printing Office, 1926). See also comparable remarks on the social placidity of the island population in article by R. A. Sell, *Houston Chronicle*, Sept. 14, 1922.

ports show, he was still haunted by the reminder, as the American liberal press pointed out at the time of his appointment, that in his earlier career as a colonial administrator in American Samoa he had used his power to whitewash the notorious abuses of Navy rule, including the abrogation of the native forms of self-government.[25]

From all this there emerged a typical Navy regime, with typical virtues and typical defects. The director of education who dismissed the Council member from St. John with the insulting remark that "I did not come down here to mind your dirty business" personified the worst type of official. Yet most officials, granted their limitations, were imbued with a real sense of duty, and often devotion, to their jobs. There were Navy chaplains like Walter Steiner who believed deeply in the cooperative principle and who received the greatest compliment any native could have paid him when Rothschild Francis observed that being with him reminded one of Frederick Douglass' remark that Lincoln was the only man who did not make him feel that he was a Negro in his presence. The chief sanitation officer for St. Croix was capable of writing an indignant article in the local press attacking the filthy condition of most of the villages attached to the Crucian sugar estates as a reproach to managers and owners and a monumental discredit to the Department of Sanitation. Within the fiscal limits set by contributions from the U.S. Treasury, which were not phenomenally large—a typical figure was the amount of $270,150 for the year 1925—the Navy administration accomplished much in the field of public services. The educational system was revised and the first junior high school established. A badly needed water supply system was installed, comprising concrete catchment areas on the hillsides, concrete storage cisterns, and standpipes. The nucleus of a sewer system, to replace the primitive methods of open-soil disposal and pail collection, was set up. In the field of public health and medicine—the description of the general state of the Frederiksted hospital in 1917 by the new American doctor in charge still makes appalling reading—naval doctors and nurses undertook a frontal onslaught upon a multitude of diseases responsible for an excessive adult mortality rate and a fantastic infant mortality rate. There occurred, altogether, nothing less than a revolution in the general standards of hygiene and medical practice (including the establishment of the first professional nursing school), undertaken in general for scant reward (the head nurse in 1932 received a salary of $120 per month),

25. *The Nation,* February 9, 1927.

not to mention the popular obloquy occasioned by programs such as the physical inspection of school children, which a medically ignorant population could not properly understand.

Clearly, the Navy regime was strong in the purely administrative field and weak in the political and socioeconomic fields. Its outstanding achievements were essentially organizational; the 1930 annual report thus cited, as Captain Van Patten's greatest contribution when he was government secretary, the establishment of the local Chamber of Commerce and the creation of effective finance departments in the St. Thomas and St. Croix municipal governments.[26] Governors recognized the urgency of basic agricultural planning. But Governor Evans' acid remarks on the "fool scheme" of the Brown report of 1929–30, which advocated a federally sponsored homesteading plan, indicated that the naval mind thought instinctively in laissez faire terms. It was at least suggestive that when the Navy finally did set up a combined Department of Agriculture, Commerce, and Labor it was handed over, oddly enough, to the office of the naval chaplain. When the redoubtable Harry Taylor took over the work under the Pearson regime in 1931 he discovered that the files covering the activities of those three fields consisted of the contents of less than one-half of a standard file drawer, justifying his conclusion that, outside of health and vital statistics, the Navy's concern had been only with tennis, golf, fishing, social life, and the pleasantries of the then inexpensive island living.[27] The Navy official, as a type, was not interested in the fundamentals of the "condition of the people" question. Not unexpectedly, then, apart from the brief, standardized annual reports of the governor, the state documents which analyzed that question during this period came from other sources: the 1920 report of the congressional Joint Commission, and the massive 1929–30 report of the Bureau of Efficiency (the Brown report).

The great expectations unleashed at the time of the transfer, then, failed to bear fruit. Essentially, the expectations broke down into two categories: (1) that the federal government would undertake a vast spending program for the economic rehabilitation of the colonial economy; and (2) that the forces of American private capitalism would pour private investment capital into the islands. Optimistic reports after 1917 had spoken of the new opportunities for American firms in the islands, once they provided proper sales methods, and had anticipated that under the new American regime "thousands of dollars for investment, new and up-to-date ideas, progressive businessmen, and

26. *Annual Report of the Governor of the Virgin Islands to the Secretary of the Interior, 1930* (Washington, D.C.: Government Printing Office, 1931).
27. Letter in *Virgin Islands View* (St. Thomas), November, 1965, pp. 6–9.

shrewd speculators are sure to come this way in the near future." [28] The tragedy of the Navy experiment in colonial government was, in one way, that the Navy, through no fault of its own, possessed neither the machinery nor the connections to become what those expectations required of it: a political broker with Congress and a sales promoter with continental business. It could not be the latter because its young officers recruited from the gentlemanly class of the eastern seaboard societies had little contact with the business groups of the jazz age; this was not the Navy of the American "warfare state," where an alliance developed between government defense departments and big business as a result of the Second World War period. Its isolation from congressional politics likewise ill fitted it for the role of Virgin Islands lobbyist looking for the rewards of the federal "pork barrel." Navy governors did not know their way around the Washington bureaucratic labyrinth, and did not spend much time in the federal capital lobbying the strategic committees; the result was, all in all, that if there did exist anything approaching a definable congressional "policy" for the islands it was nothing much more than a compromise among the modest demands of governors, the even more modest requests of the Navy Department, and congressional ideas of economy.

An energetic secretary at the top, of course, could always make a difference. But the days of a Teddy Roosevelt pushing the Navy interests with a mixture of romantic militarism and expansionist braggadocio were over; on the contrary, a secretary like Josephus Daniels (1913–21) used up his Progressivist feelings in a running battle with the Navy conservative groups—the officer corps, the Navy league, and the clique that wanted to hand over the Navy's oil reserves in the west to the California oil men and their congressional allies. The liberal cause in the Virgins, alternatively, might have benefited from intervention by such a secretary. But a reading of the Daniels *Cabinet Diaries* makes it painfully clear, with their few bald references to the new Caribbean colony, that no secretary, however progressive, could hope to find time for the affairs of an obscure and tiny colonial possession thousands of miles away from the center of things. The promise of American life, if it came to the Virgins group at all, clearly would have to come through agencies other than those of the national armed services.

28. St. *Thomas and the Virgin Islands,* Souvenir Pamphlet, 1938, reprint of an earlier pamphlet published in 1917, compiled and published by the St. Thomas Bureau of Information, p. 12. For similar sentiments at the time of the transfer, see *The Virgin Islands: A Description of the Commercial Value of the Danish West Indies* (New York: National Bank of Commerce, April, 1917) ; and *The Danish West Indies: Their Resources and Commercial Importance* (Washington, D.C.: Government Printing Office, 1917).

1917: The American Beginnings

At the time of President Hoover's executive order of February, 1931, transferring the group to the jurisdiction of the Department of the Interior, the Virgins were substantially a depressed colonial society. Deeply rooted in an economy whose traditionally dominant occupations remained the same in 1931 as they had been in 1917, estate agriculture based on cheap Negro labor in St. Croix and harbor commerce based on hard-pressed clerks and stevedores in St. Thomas, the social structure remained rigidly conservative, grossly undemocratic, and profoundly inegalitarian. A perceptive American observer, writing in 1927, saw the island situation, generally, as the stubborn last stand of the old feudal system of work and industry against the practices of the modern economy. He stated:

> The feudal system, based on cheap and ignorant labor, autocratic and romantic-minded overlords and land monopoly, finds itself in startling contest with the systems of the twentieth century, based on scarce, high-paid and increasingly intelligent labor, efficient working executives risen from the ranks, and distributed land. Wherever this opposition occurs today the feudal system fails. Nowhere under the American flag is the system of feudalism so strongly entrenched as it is in the Virgin Islands. Nowhere is the price for maintaining it being exacted so inexorably.[29]

The facts of the case justified the indictment. Hereditary land monopoly—in St. Thomas over 60 per cent of total acreage was held by only fifteen owners, while in St. Croix twenty families and one alien industrial group owned 80 per cent of the island—produced its usual social consequences. The landowner made no pretense at proper capitalist use of his land, jealously holding it, especially after 1917, as a speculative property to be bought up at immoderate prices by wealthy American visitors who somehow never materialized. The laborer, in turn, was cut off from any responsible contact with the land. At best, he was permitted to become a squatter, paying exorbitant rent with no security of tenure, existing in atrocious living conditions, in ruined stone huts on the rundown estate villages. The monopolistic grip of sugar in St. Croix and of commerce in St. Thomas effectively prohibited the development of the fruit and vegetable industries so urgently needed to offset the irrational dependency upon imported foods, and the gross anomaly, for example, of an island people, surrounded by an ocean teeming with fish, existing on a deficient diet of imported dried codfish. Such an economic system, rewarding idleness and penalizing

29. Thomas H. Dickinson, "The Economic Crisis in the Virgin Islands," *Current History* (December, 1927), pp. 378–81.

thrift, pauperized first the worker and then the master. The above-mentioned American observer commented:

> The white owners of the island of St. Croix, constituting about two percent of the population, find themselves in possession of thousands of acres of fertile land which they are unable to cultivate on account of the lack of good labor. Meanwhile thousands of potential laborers live on starvation subsistence in huts and in the outbuildings of ruined sugar mills. The deadlock is complete. The owner will not or cannot give up his land; the field laborer will not or cannot do a good day's work for a good day's pay. The negro faces hunger every day; the planters are land poor.[30]

No single account of the period, perhaps, rendered so severe an indictment of all this as the remarkable report of the Hampton-Tuskegee Educational Survey of 1929. Ranging far beyond its strictly educational terms of reference, it painted a depressing picture of economic depression and social dislocation. The report stated clearly that it was not a simple question of blaming "Uncle Sam" or castigating "lazy" natives but rather one of progressive cultural deterioration predating 1917: "It may safely be assumed that conditions, as they are today, represent neither the ideal of the former Danish regime nor the ideal of the present American regime. They represent the necessary middle ground of transition between an order which for three-quarters of a century has been in a process of dissolution and a new order which has had a bare decade in which to operate." [31] The promise of the "new order" was, as yet, pretty meager. Fruit and vegetable cultures were frustrated by the habits engendered by the sugar and export trade monopolies. The older, once vigorous local craft industries, in turn, were being destroyed by the tendency, naturally encouraged by the merchant class, to buy from outside. The report stated:

> As the islands are at present constituted, there is little choice for the laborer. If he adapt himself to the dominant demand he must work on the docks or on the sugar flats. For the ambitious native the outlets are limited to clerical work for the Government and the activities of small trade. Under these conditions there is small wonder that for all classes the true path of opportunity should lead beyond the border, partly to the United States which has recently been opened to them. . . . The pressure of the industrial interests of the islands is always to reduce the standards of labor to the cheapest possible. Labor of the highest type is driven to the towns to compete for clerical jobs and places in

30. *Ibid.,* p. 379.

31. *Report of the Educational Survey of the Virgin Islands,* authorized by the secretary of the Navy and conducted under the auspices of Hampton and Tuskegee Institutes (Hampton, Va.: The Press of the Hampton Normal and Agricultural Institute, 1929) , pp. 54–55.

mercantile life and to the United States, leaving only the old and infirm and those of weaker calibre to work in the islands. The results are manifest in the labor conditions of the islands in a labor which tends to be lazy and shiftless. In the population itself there is taking place a gradual shifting of level downwards mentally, morally and physically. In the decade of American operation the Government has drawn a barrier up against this progressive deterioration, but the essential movement itself has not been stopped or stemmed. In the absence of a reconstruction of the dominant economic and industrial life of the islands, no procedure shows any promise of succeeding in stemming the tide of deterioration save education.[32]

Nor had any real leadership emerged to offer a way out of this social and economic bondage. Estate management was up to date in its technical processes, but did not show the same watchful care in handling the labor. Neither the St. Thomas industrialists nor the Crucian planters were keen supporters of education. Organized religion had also failed, concentrating too much on conducting religious services for the natives and too little on helping them develop a genuine religious life. Despite its obvious achievements, the real weakness of the new American educational system was that neither in structure nor in curriculum had it grown out of a specific inquiry into the needs of the local child. The most that could be said of industrial relations was that labor had moved out of the earlier stage of physical violence in the struggle for its rights into a period of economic adjustment through emigration and union negotiation. The local schools failed signally to prepare the bright boy or girl for entry into the professions, hence the grave lack of a native professional class, along with a weak spirit of social obligation. The report states:

The number of outstanding native teachers or preachers of whom the casual visitor hears is surprisingly small. Only in business are such men to be found as a rule, it seems, and success in this line appears to destroy their interest in the natives as such and to remove them from active leadership among the colored people. Graduates of the local schools as now constituted are likely to be lost in the mass of poorly trained people. The few who are able to continue their studies elsewhere rarely return for service in the islands.[33]

Nor, according to the report, had American policies under the Navy regime done much to solve the problem, stated in these terms. There had been a fatal imbalance of priorities, so that the preponderance of federal monies had been spent on items purely punitive or palliative— police and prison services, hospitals, insane asylums, poor relief payments, and so on. The local government, true enough, had worked

32. *Ibid.*, pp. 62–63.
33. *Ibid.*, pp. 50–51.

wonders in its engineering, road building, water supply, and sanitation projects; and to have reduced the death rate by one-third inside a decade was in itself a remarkable feat. But the statistics relating, for example, to poor relief or to pauper burials indicated that all this had not prevented in any way the continuing process of mass pauperization. The government spent four times as much on education as had the Danish regime; but it was still a fact that the total monies spent were lower than any other place under the American flag. Even the police systems of the islands had larger budgets than the schools. The government program, in brief, had been ameliorative only, treating symptoms of the social disease rather than the disease itself. The report asked:

> What is the use of providing excellent municipal hospital facilities for women to deliver babies in (two-thirds of them illegitimate) if some steps are not taken through education to build up the kind of family life, earning power, and knowledge of proper living that will tend to decrease the abnormally large number of births of children born into almost certain death before they are a year old, or, if they live, destined to repeat the career of poverty, disease, and anti-social behavior that appears to be indicated in the situation? [34]

It is clear that by 1931 thoughtful American observers and native progressives alike had concluded that Virgin Islands life had reached an impasse. What, then, had to be done? Despite the fact that the Hampton-Tuskegee report had been authorized by the secretary of the Navy, the Navy government in Charlotte Amalie, as Governor Evans' annual reports show, continued to believe in the program of increased spending on merely ameliorative social welfare schemes. The report of the commission appointed in 1924 by the secretary of labor advocated the establishment of a commissioner of conciliation on the islands to protect the native worker from harmful competition with alien labor by enforcement of the federal immigration laws.[35] Councilman Roberts, in his *Memorandum* of 1929 to a visiting congressional delegation, requested Washington to undertake a full survey of real productivity levels in the islands;[36] for in the seventeenth and eighteenth centuries St. Thomas alone had been able to produce and export tobacco, sugar, and rum, and although it could be contended that that was due to

34. *Ibid.*, pp. 24–25.
35. For this and other recommendations at the time, see generally Evans, *The Virgin Islands*, pp. 221–24. For the report of the 1924 federal commission, see *The Emancipator*, Oct. 23, 1929.
36. Quoted in *The Emancipator*, Mar. 25, 1929. For similar extensive reform proposals, see letter by Caspar Holstein to commissioner of conciliation, files of American Civil Liberties Union, New York Public Library, June 26, 1923.

the existence of a cheap slave-labor force, at the same time this might not have been the only reason, and it was possible that similar production levels could be reached again. *The Emancipator* suggested that a study, alternatively, of the pumpkin culture in Culebra and of the milk and corned-fish industries in Tortola might prove that what the Virgin economies needed was a new productive system based on the rental of small parcels of land with a concomitant right of ownership, education in truck farming and marketing processes, and a protective tariff for products in the U.S. market.[37] A local poet even managed to put all this in verse form.[38] The 1924 federal commission, after quite properly exploding the myth that the problem was political—for "civil rights give small comfort to women and children poorly housed and underfed"—proceeded to defend its own favorite myth that the thing above all else requisite for civil and industrial salvation was the termination of local Virgin Islands sex and marital customs and their replacement with the "moral code of our American standard."[39] There was something of that Puritan moralism in the Hampton-Tuskegee report, indicating, perhaps, the wide gulf that has always separated the value judgments of the American Negro from those of the Virgin Islands Negro. The main prescription of cure given by the report, however, was that of education, not morality, for it insisted categorically that "Many, if not most, of the problems of the Virgin Islands, can be solved only by the deliberative processes of education applied to the people of the islands themselves."[40]

This was, indeed, a veritable plethora of advice. Yet it is noteworthy that practically every analyst of the situation agreed on the thesis that change would have to come either from outside, that is, from the United States, or from liberal forces inside. The incapacity of the local Virgin Islands ruling groups to assume a position of positive leadership in favor of change was taken for granted. The occasional radical leader who was tempted to idealize the Danish regime as a reaction against the new American masters, like Caspar Holstein in 1922—he was reported as quoting approvingly the oldest planter on St. Croix, in a conversation on board ship leaving the island for New York, as having asserted that the Danish whites had always regarded all men as equals, and that it was the new American "land grabbers" who had brought in racialism—was rapidly reminded by his confreres of the crude mendacity of the claim.[41]

37. *The Emancipator*, Aug. 30, 1926.
38. J. P. Jimenez, "What I Would Do," *ibid.*, Sept. 28, 1925.
39. For the report of the 1924 federal commission, see *ibid.*, Oct. 23, 1929.
40. Hampton-Tuskegee report, p. 7.
41. *St. Croix Tribune*, July 14, 1922.

The local wealthy class was, on the whole, not only politically conservative but also entrepreneurially unadventuresome. In 1923 Adolph Sixto described how, twenty years earlier, he had unsuccessfully lobbied local businessmen to form a telephone company, with the result that the venture was finally undertaken by a Danish financial syndicate, with Governor Helweg-Larsen reputedly the principal shareholder.[42] And in 1929 Adolph Gereau described how, apropos the launching of a new company to start a local fishing industry, the company's stock book showed that most of the stockholders were mainland Americans, Danes, British subjects, and only a small percentage of Virgin Islands natives, since the latter group, as individuals, would always plead inability to buy shares in new ventures but would proceed at the same time to spend loosely on some temporary pleasure or idle luxury.[43] It is suggestive, furthermore, that during the Navy period the two leading demands that the local landowning oligarchy made upon the U.S. government were for (1) the reduction or abrogation of the export duty on sugar; and (2) permission to import cheap labor from the West Indian islands. Of the first demand, it must be remembered that, because of an archaic tax system, the sugar export duties constituted the only considerable source of local revenue in St. Croix, so that the planters were in reality asking for a measure which, if accepted, would have dealt a crippling blow to the local treasury; for at no time did the planter-dominated Colonial Council indicate its readiness to compensate such a loss by introducing alternative sources of revenue by means, for example, of direct land taxation. The second demand, if acceded to, would have produced the sort of exploited alien labor situation that had earlier been set in motion by the East Indian indenture system in Trinidad and British Guiana. At no time was there any evidence to suggest that the planter class would accept the sort of conditions which American experts from time to time set out as the price to be exacted for federal economic assistance: readiness to distribute the land at reasonable prices for productive settlement, acceptance of new taxation systems that no longer encouraged speculative holding as against the interests of production, and a crop rotation system to replace the dead monopoly of sugar.[44]

With a Creole oligarchy so Bourbonese in its outlook and with Republican America after 1920 anxious to forget anything in the nature of overseas obligations, the mantle of Virgin Islands leadership

42. Adolph Sixto, in *The Emancipator*, June 4, 1923.
43. Adolph Gereau, "The Virgin Islands' Newest Industry," *ibid.*, Feb. 23, 1929.
44. See, for example, Hoover, "The Virgin Islands under American Rule"; and House, 69th Cong., 2d sess., 1927, H. Rept. 2034.

fell by default on the shoulders of the local progressive groups. But their power to achieve anything was severely limited. They were never a united front so much as a series of disparate factions rent by personal jealousies and rival ambitions. Even before the transfer the trade union movement was divided, and after 1917 it was torn asunder by the internecine squabbling between the Francis and the Chabert forces, a rivalry that found further expression in the journalistic field as its star figures became editors of rival sheets. The record of their mutual recriminations in the *Herald* and *Emancipator* and *St. Croix Tribune* papers of the period demonstrates the deep power of personal abuse and vilification so characteristic of Virgin Islands politics; marital difficulties, skin color, private life, all were mercilessly paraded and lampooned in the general effort to besmirch the character of one's opponents. There was, indeed, more clashing between Negro cliques on the islands than there was between the Marines and the local citizens.

All this was made worse, however, by two additional sources of friction peculiar to the Virgin Islands. The first was the traditional rivalry between St. Thomas and St. Croix. Originally a rivalry of commercial and planter groups, it was taken over by the working-class groups, thus permitting island insularity to override questions of employee solidarity; nothing could have better illustrated the power of small-island pride in the Caribbean popular mentality. The differences of policy detail that divided the islands—St. Croix was always concerned with the drastic economic effects of Prohibition upon its rum and sugar industries, while St. Thomas was more concerned with, for example, preventing the application of U.S. coastwise shipping legislation to its mercantile interests—were thus permitted to become a major barrier to united action. The separate Councils could never agree on organizing joint delegations to Washington. Similarly, every time that the St. Thomian union interests advocated the gradual termination of sugar in St. Croix, to be replaced, for example, with organized cattle raising for the Puerto Rican trade, the Crucian interests denounced it as a nefarious scheme to convert their island into a "cattle ranch" in order to benefit St. Thomas. There was never, at any time, on the part of either employers or workers, a concerted effort to map out a system of priorities, based on impartial analysis of the real needs of each island, statistically verifiable, which could then have become the basis for joint lobbying action at the federal center. "We would rather write, criticise or advise the Congress of the United States or the Parliament of England," editorialized *The Emancipator* with fine disgust on November 13, 1929, "than to be so foolhardy as to clash with the nation of St. Croix."

(65)

The second aggravating factor was the rivalry that grew up after 1917, with truly tropical virility, between the progressive leadership resident in the islands and the leadership of the exile groups in New York. In one way, this was a Virgin Islands illustration of a general Caribbean phenomenon, the profound gulf separating the metropolitan psychology from the colonial psychology. Those who stay in the island home develop a temper of jealous possessiveness and suspect that those who have left are deserters; the exiles, they feel, have lost touch with local conditions and cannot speak authoritatively for the local interests. The exiles, in turn, build up attitudes of condescension toward the islanders, who, they feel, have become parochial, cannot see the larger perspective of things, and are isolated from events and people in the metropolis where the real decisions governing their destiny are made.

From the beginning this disease, so typical of colonial experience, bedeviled New York–St. Thomas relationships. The Harlem ghetto— estimated to contain some 20,000 Virgin Islanders by 1930—rapidly became a hive of political clubs frequently composed of people whose political apathy at home had soon changed to political consciousness under the heady influence of New York ghetto life. Their leaders were, at best, conscientious patriots, at worst skilled operators in the American "big fix" politics; in any case, they had to be listened to because they commanded sources of influence and money not available to their rivals in the islands. The result was a virulent hatred between the rival sides. The exchange of libelous correspondence between Caspar Holstein and Ashley Totten, Ralph de Chabert's shrill denunciation of the New York *Negro World* and its series of articles on conditions in St. Croix, and the ugly insinuations about the reasons for Jackson's original trip north to New York during the war period show the rich scandalous flavor of small-island politics, whose worst features were only exacerbated by coming into contact with the Tammany Hall quality of big-city politics.[45] If the New Yorkers pass resolutions demanding a new organic act for the islands, it is because they are people who imagine that they are Founding Fathers writing a Declaration of Independence for the Virgins.[46] If a governor is recalled from Charlotte Amalie, everybody claims that they engineered the coup, although some of them, their enemies assert, are so weak politically that they could not even com-

45. For examples of this, see articles by Ralph de Chabert, *St. Croix Tribune*, July 11, 22, 1922, which are in part a reply to an article by Caspar Holstein on conditions in St. Croix written in *The Negro World*. See letter of Ashley Totten concerning his opponents' exploitation of his marital difficulties, *St. Croix Tribune*, Dec. 20, 1922.

46. Editorial, *St. Croix Tribune*, July 7, 1922.

mand the attention of an elevator runner in the Navy Building in Washington.[47] Everything must be done to discredit the other side; so, a New York chieftain like Holstein must be disavowed because, it is claimed, his only means of livelihood is a professional gambling machine which he operates at the corner of 135th Street and Lenox Avenue.[48]

All of these lines of division, then, reinforcing one another, made quite impossible the sort of united action that the situation required, the grandiose scheme, for example, of a vast cooperative movement, to be endorsed by the local Colonial Councils and by all leading Virgin Islands newspapers, which would become "the recognised official agency for all matters political, industrial, and otherwise" and would help, among other things, the promotion of outside investment in the territory.[49] The failure made it all the easier for the forces of reaction, including governors, to spread the calumny that "unrest" was the work of racist "agitators," thus overlooking the particular fact, for example, that a man like Hamilton Jackson was more of a dreamy poet than the fiery apostle of polemics he was so often pictured as, and also overlooking the general fact that the "agitator" is usually the consequence, not the cause, of the conditions of his time. That the calumny was generally believed in Washington, however, is evident enough from the fact that there seems not to have been a single full-dress debate in either house of Congress during this period on the problems of the new dependency. Only a profound change in the climate of the national mood as a whole, forcing a revolution in congressional temper, could bring a promise of more sympathetic attitudes.

47. *Ibid.,* Aug. 29, 1922.
48. *Ibid.,* Oct. 14, 1922.
49. Article by Ashley L. Totten, *ibid.,* Dec. 14, 1922.

3

~~~

1931:
The New Deal Period

Nothing could have better illustrated the absence of any generative leading principles in American colonialism than the fact that the New Deal came to the Virgin Islands, quite by accident, some full two years before it took effect in the national capital. The immediate cause was the introduction of civil government, which was announced without any sort of prior consultation with the local legislatures, and was the outcome of the thoroughgoing report of 1929–30 undertaken by Herbert D. Brown of the Bureau of Efficiency. In the report that able official had argued for a vast new program of appropriations (the essential item of all later New Deal schemes) to foster, among much else, agrarian reform by means of an extended homesteading plan. The new program obviously required new men, a condition met by President Hoover's last-minute appointment, in his "lame duck" period, of the social-minded Pennsylvania Quaker Paul Pearson as the first civil governor. The withdrawal of the Navy in this way by the outgoing Republican president was indeed providential, for it is not idle to suppose that President Roosevelt, with his well-known affection for the Navy, might have been tempted to adhere to the status quo. In that case he might have indulged his penchant for nominating elderly retired admirals and generals to the St. Thomas post, after the fashion of his unfortunate appointment of General Blanton Winship to the Puerto Rican gubernatorial post. The change, of course, was welcomed by the local liberal forces. But they could not resist pointing out that the manner of its implementation seemed more like an act fraught with petty personalities than an act in which the gradual transfer of bodies functioning under one great institution of government passed by deliberative process from one department to another.[1]

1. *The Emancipator,* quoted in "Civil Government for the Virgin Islands," *Porto Rico Progress* (San Juan), Feb. 26, 1931.

The Brown report seemed finally to replace drift with direction. It indicated three possible policies: (1) discontinuation of federal appropriations with an eye to making the islands fully dependent upon locally raised revenues (the practice of the European colonial nations in the area), which would have the result of intensifying the exodus of the colored population to the United States and would·make it increasingly difficult to resist the demand of the white population for the removal of the barriers against imported foreign labor; (2) continuation of federal appropriations as usual, which would inevitably mean the same slow rate of progress; and (3) a vastly expanded appropriations program, "sufficient to do energetically at once the things that are necessary to bring about improved conditions and thus make it possible, by helping the Virgin Islanders to help themselves, to reduce gradually the federal aid with the ultimate result of making the islands entirely self-supporting." The report enthusiastically opted for that last alternative, which would have the merit, as its authors saw it, of replacing the old Navy spending program on unremunerative relief and welfare programs with the planned development of projects designed to be maintained by local revenues, naturally necessitating a fundamental overhaul of the local archaic tax structure. The central feature of the plan, in St. Thomas, would be the rehabilitation of the harbor, along with an imaginative planning of the tourist trade, and, in St. Croix, a homesteading development to break down the power of concentrated land ownership. These programs would be accompanied by a new educational policy (there is evidence that Governor Pearson had early on digested the Hampton-Tuskegee report). All this, its protagonists agreed, would take time. It would require the active assistance and good intentions of all concerned. The main problem, it had to be recognized, was economic, requiring outside assistance; in that task, as Secretary Ray Wilbur indicated, the Department of the Interior, with its administrative experience in Alaska and Hawaii and elsewhere, was peculiarly adapted to help. Good health, education, and economic independence, thus achieved, would pave the way for political autonomy, which should be granted as soon as possible.[2]

The story of the decade of the thirties is the story, frequently tumultuous, of the efforts of the Pearson regime (1931–35) and of the Cramer regime (1935–41) to implement that program. It is the story, in essence, of the application of the New Deal spirit to the colonial problem. It did not solve that problem, but it did much to alleviate its

---

2. For the Brown report, never printed, see résumé in *Annual Report of the Governor of the Virgin Islands to the Secretary of the Interior, 1930* (Washington, D.C.: Government Printing Office, 1931), pp. 6–7. See also letter of Secretary of the Interior Wilbur to Jos. Reynolds, member of Colonial Council, in *The Emancipator*, Feb. 16, 1931.

worst features. Its achievements, on the credit side, were not inconsiderable. For all of his limitations—essentially those of the Chautauqua-circuit lecturer—Governor Pearson, along with the young idealists he brought with him, was passionately concerned for the islands and their people. His own pet schemes were frequently naive, such as presenting Gilbert and Sullivan operettas (it would be difficult to think of a form of entertainment less capable of exciting the Virgin Islands masses) or setting up instructional classes in public speaking (which was hardly necessary since the islands have always suffered from a surfeit of born public speakers). But he knew how to appeal to local pride, and he was never guilty of the sort of crass insult to local sentiment illustrated by President Hoover's remarks at the very beginning of the Pearson regime, to the effect that the islands were an "effective poorhouse," which cost the governor so much in loyalty and cooperation in his difficult task. His program brought to the islands all the remarkable qualities of the New Deal—its willingness to try new ideas, its passion for innovation, its experimentalism, its infectious enthusiasm, its readiness to use the power of public government in areas where private enterprise had failed. In economic policy it took the form, most adventuresomely, of the entry of government, by means of the public corporation device, into the real estate field, and the Virgin Islands Company rapidly became the main weapon in the land redistribution program in St. Croix. Correspondingly, the bold application of the National Recovery Act, via the Works Progress Administration, to the islands made possible a vast spending policy never dreamed of by the fiscal conservatism of the Navy regime. Politically, the program enormously expanded internal self-government with the grant, in 1936, of universal suffrage by means of the Organic Act of that year. That went hand in hand with a new policy of appointing knowledgeable Virgin Islanders to administrative posts (as the new names testify—George Ivins as director of education, Leroy Nolte as prohibition director, Dr. Knud Knud-Hansen as commissioner of health, Alvaro de Lugo as St. Thomas postmaster, Alonzo Moron as commissioner of public welfare), thus implementing Governor Pearson's goal of helping ambitious young islanders, by means of an expanded scholarship program, to learn to look forward to careers of public service in the islands rather than on the mainland.[3]

The true measure, perhaps, of New Deal policies is to compare them with the colonial policy, or absence of policy, practiced at the time in the neighboring British Caribbean islands. It is symptomatic, at least, that

3. Governor Pearson, letter to acting chief municipal physician, in *Daily News*, Nov. 14, 1933. See also Governor Pearson, "Long Range Program for the Virgin Islands," *New York Times*, June 3, 1934.

the Virgin Islands situation did not deteriorate into the condition of explosive and widespread riots that swept over the British West Indies after 1935. This difference was surely traceable to the fact that the state of official attitudes in London during the period, as distinct from the national temper in Washington, was one of indifference to colonial affairs, a reluctance to entertain fresh ideas, and an unwillingness, due to the tyranny of the Treasury mentality, to spend money. The Organic Act, at the same time, brought to the American Caribbean profound constitutional changes, including universal suffrage, which did not come to the British Caribbean until after 1945. One result of the difference in attitude and legislation was that the quiet revolution whereby the old white Creole groups were replaced in politics by the new group of mulatto, popularly elected politicians took place a generation earlier in the Virgins than it did, say, in Jamaica and Barbados. It is suggestive that the British Moyne Commission of 1938–39, whose great report still stands as a massive indictment of British colonialism at the time, noted the U.S. Virgins only to refer approvingly to the right of the local municipal assemblies to be heard in Washington.

Thus the Virgin Islands became, during the thirties, a laboratory for New Deal planners, much like the Tugwell program in Puerto Rico a decade later. They received the attention of a veritable galaxy of New Deal eminences: Paul Banning, Ernest Gruening, Oscar Chapman, and, above all, Harold Ickes as the dynamic and unconventional secretary of the interior. The result was to put the Virgins on the map and to end, at least temporarily, the national neglect which had led Heywood Broun to expostulate angrily: "It is difficult to get any great number of Americans excited about the Virgin Islands. They are a long way off. They're tiny. They do not enter into the life of many of us. And yet our administration of this far flung group constitutes one of our greatest and one of our cruelest failures. . . . They did not ask to be taken into our empire. We were not out to better their condition and we did not." [4] The veritable absence of any mention of the Caribbean possessions in the Daniels diaries as compared with the prominent place they occupy in the later Ickes diaries is a measure of the distance that had been traveled since the islands were under the Navy's jurisdiction.

---

4. Quoted in editorial, *The Emancipator,* Aug. 31, 1931. For one of the very few pieces of academic research on the Virgin Islands experience during the 1930s, when most American progressive and radical opinion was preoccupied with the struggles of the American society proper, see John Frederick Grede, "The New Deal in the Virgin Islands, 1931–1941" (Master's thesis, University of Chicago, 1963).

Yet despite the initial enthusiasm a decade of the New Deal left basically unsolved the fundamental problems of Virgin Islands existence. The early "honeymoon period" was rapidly replaced with the organized opposition of both conservative white and radical Negro forces against the Pearson administration, ending in the Tydings Committee investigation of 1935 and the governor's final ouster, and characterized by a degree of bitterness, rancor, fear, and prejudice astonishing even by Virgin Islands standards. The local Colonial Councils petitioned for the return of the Navy. Local radical friends became converted, almost overnight, into archenemies, as in the case of both Rothschild Francis and Lionel Roberts. Erstwhile New York supporters like the wealthy Caspar Holstein became the financial mainstay of the massively abusive campaign against the governor after 1932. A new mood of romantic nostalgia for "dear old Denmark" made itself felt at this time, with all of its implied criticism of things American. Mass unemployment remained the order of the day, and it is suggestive that the statistics quoted by the local press in 1933—18 per cent of working group males and 28 per cent of working group females unemployed—were provided by the investigations of a private body, the St. Thomas Improvement Association. The various rehabilitation schemes failed throughout to generate full employment, and the decision to establish a Marine Corps air base in 1935 and a submarine base in 1939 indicated that the economy would have to fall back upon the medicine of locally established, federal direct-employment agencies. In the political field the Organic Act relieved tension somewhat but failed to treat the root cause of the colonial disease, the fatal division of authority between an alien-appointed executive and a popularly based legislature; and Governor Cramer's struggle of 1937–38 with the new joint Legislative Assembly indicated that the real problem was not, as the more rabid Pearson-baiters had insisted, a matter of personality, but the continuing imperial supervision from Washington. As late as 1939, to cite only one example of the problem, the St. Thomas–St. John Municipal Council was still debating, with reference to the question of obtaining refunds of Internal Revenue receipts to the local treasury, the gross inadequacy of its representational and lobbying devices in the federal capital, including the ineffective device of the visiting delegation.

Even for colonial politics, where the arrival of a new governor always became the occasion for a wild outburst of extravagant hopes, the Virgin Islands debacle was astonishingly extraordinary. What went wrong? In the first place, perhaps, there was the character of Governor Pearson and of the new administrative group he brought with him. The very method of his appointment indicated the grievous absence of a rational selective process in American colonial administration. For if Herbert Brown's testimony is to be believed, Pearson was initially chosen on the basis of Mrs. Brown's knowing some "fine people" in Swarthmore, Pennsylvania, who might be able to suggest someone, and a quick automobile trip to the Quaker center. Brown himself later confessed that his recommendation was the one blot in thirty years of his career as a government efficiency expert, and he hinted that President Hoover's failure to recall Pearson might have been influenced by the fact that Drew Pearson, the governor's son, was the powerful Washington columnist and that Governor Pearson's brother had contributed heavily to the Republican national campaign chest.[5] From the beginning, then, the new governor's Washington support, always vital to a colonial official, was compromised by Brown's defection; and from being popularly viewed as the kingmaker—Brown was obliged to write an open letter denying that he in effect controlled the new governor—the Bureau of Efficiency expert became a relentless critic of the new regime.

The views of such critics were naturally prejudiced, often violently so. Yet the opinion of visiting correspondents like Hanson Baldwin of the *New York Times* during the gathering storm of 1935 reinforced the feeling that Governor Pearson did not understand the local psychology, as his unfortunate remarks about a "moral crusade" against native "immorality" indicated; was disinclined to heed advice; was frequently tactless; was given to spectacular announcements of grandiose programs, many of which were at best small schemes of ordinary character; and was over-clever in his use of visiting correspondents to build up a favorable image of his work in the American liberal press. Many of his absurdities sprang from his conviction of the need for education, while he failed to appreciate that the last thing Virgin Islanders were prepared to admit was that they were ill-educated.[6] These delusional remedies, another American critic pointed out, became part of a court atmosphere in which the price of acceptance was one's readiness to eulogize the new occupant of the throne room: "If you would help to disillusion him, he is too busy. If you criticise, you are made to feel that the Virgin Islands is no place for you. If you have not sought him in order to worship, then the sooner you buy a ticket to the States, the better."[7]

The detail of the various New Deal programs bears out much of this indictment. The editor of *The Emancipator* noted that, at the time of the governor's arrival in 1931, he had advised the new incumbent of three

5. Brown, quoted in "How Paul M. Pearson Became Governor of the Virgin Islands," *The Emancipator,* Jan. 19, 1935.

6. Hanson Baldwin, in *New York Times,* reprinted in *The Emancipator,* Apr. 24, 1935.

7. Theodore Schroeder, in *Daily News,* Feb. 20, 1932, and *The Emancipator,* Mar. 7, 1932.

conditions of success: (1) the cooperation of the Councils must be sought in the fight to reestablish the municipal commissions; (2) there must be no color discrimination in public appointments; and (3) there must be a bold program of mass relief for the unemployed, not the old worn-out demand for "more taxation." It is not exaggerating to say that the new regime managed, ultimately, to fail all of those three tests. They related, successively, to the three leading problems of territorial life: the political problem, the question of color, and the problem of economic policy.

The question of the municipal commissions, to begin with, was inherited from the old dispute about the meaning of the relevant clauses in the Danish Organic Act of 1852 and in part constituted simply the defense of the constitutional privileges of a hopelessly unrepresentative legislative branch having little to do with the problems of the disfranchised laborer. At the same time the struggle became more acute with the sudden enlargement of the colonial executive-administrative branch and its new agencies, for the suppression of the commissions seriously handicapped any real legislative control. As Councilman Roberts pointed out, there was a solid historical precedent for the claim to have them resuscitated, for they had embodied the rights of the pre-1917 Councils, which in turn went back to the rights of the old Burgher Council of 1761. As for their present usage, Councilman Charles Smith noted that a continuing Poor Commission would have helped avoid the present abuses to which relief recipients were subjected by arbitrary officials, and that, to cite an example, had the old Cemetery Commission been still operative the vandalistic act of cutting down mahogany trees in the graveyards in order to work up furniture for the United States trade might have been prevented.[8] The Councils, in effect, were helpless in the face of a rapidly expanding executive machine, and their situation was made all the worse by their debarment from intervention in either the local or the federal appointive powers. The scandalous Gillette affair of 1932—in which the Colonial Council protested the appointment of a well-known racist of the Red Cross staff, the Missouri-born Miss Lucy Gillette, to the position of commissioner of public welfare—emphasized the anachronism of a situation in which the secretary of the interior could appoint persons to vitally strategic posts without any right of consultation on the part of the local councils. The 1932 exchange of correspondence between the secretary and the St. Thomas Council showed clearly that Washington would brook no interference in the matter of central ad-

8. For all this, see *Proceedings of the Colonial Council of St. Thomas and St. John,* April 9, December 10, 1931 (microfilm, St. Thomas Public Library), and reports of this in *The Emancipator,* Apr. 29, May 2, 4, 6, 9, 1931, Feb. 11, 1932.

ministration appointments financed by congressional appropriations, even though the power was frequently abused to create an entirely new bureaucracy of useless and highly paid offices not established under municipal laws.[9] Governor Pearson's response to all this was to invoke the doctrine of the separation of powers in the American form of government. This argument failed to take into account the difference between a bicameral situation of equality between White House and Congress and a colonialist situation in which the legislative assembly was a subordinate creature of the executive. The local constitutionalists in St. Thomas might indeed have pointed out, if they had cared to, that the power of the governor to sit in on the meetings of the Council (a power, incidentally, revived by Governor Pearson) was as much a violation of the "separation of powers" doctrine as any theory advanced by them.

A dogma that was liberal in Washington became, in colonial conditions, reactionary. Liberal officials in Washington occasionally half-recognized that. Ernest Gruening told a Senate committee hearing in 1937:

> It is fair when a community is not self-supporting that he who pays the piper has a right to call the tune. That might seem a reactionary policy if we had in view a continuation of this system in which the Federal Government always supports the islands. It may have to. But it is our problem, and it is the hope that just as rapidly as possible we will make the islands self-supporting. When they do arrive at that point, if they do, they may overrule our policy.[10]

The local reply to that casuistry was, of course, that so long as federal spending policies had the consequence, ironically, of making the island economies more and not less dependent on the metropolitan center, that hope was pretty illusory and the policy remained, by admission of its authors, reactionary. It was hardly surprising that, with their hands thus tied, the local assemblies failed to become aggressive champions of the popular cause, which passed, by default, into the hands of the radical orators of the Virgin Islands market places.

The political problem was mixed up with the question of color, especially as it made itself felt in the delicate area of appointments. Governor Pearson's liberalism on this point is well attested to, as his encouragement of young professional Virgin Islanders shows. But too many of his continental entourage, on a central administration payroll insulated from local control, did not share his views. Too many of them

9. Secretary of the interior to chairman of St. Thomas and St. John Colonial Council, January 18, 1932, reprinted in *The Emancipator*, Jan. 17, 1932; and St. Thomas and St. John Municipal Committee to secretary of the interior, January 26, 1932, reprinted in *ibid.*, Jan. 30, 1932.

10. Quoted in *ibid.*, Jan. 16, 1937.

were white "carpet baggers" masquerading as "moral uplift" specialists. Too many of them shared the prejudice of the continental nurse in St. Croix who was reported as saying that Dr. Canegata was a gentleman, but since he was a Negro she could take no orders from him; undoubtedly, such prejudice had much to do with the failure of the administration to reappoint the doctor to his position as municipal physician in St. Croix in 1935. Too many qualified natives were passed over for continental nominees, as in the Gillette affair. And at the upper reaches, certainly, the bureaucracy was all white. There was much to be said for the idea, advanced by Ashley Totten to the Joint Congressional Committee on Insular Affairs in 1933, that the appointment of continentals should be limited to the posts of governor and lieutenant governor;[11] but nothing ever came of it. As late as 1939 the St. Thomas Municipal Council could wonder why the board of directors of the newly formed Board of Business and Tourist Development should appoint yet another white American as secretary.[12] The Virgin Islands Company rapidly became another haven for white Americans, with its principal offices being filled with inexperienced continentals like Boyd Brown and Leslie Hunt, who replaced competent natives. And even when liberal America was assured by the Pearson propagandists that the administration was pro-native in its appointments policy, most·Americans failed to realize—as the *Afro-American* reporter Ralph Matthews pointed out— that most of the natives appointed were given half the salary and twice as much work as their white predecessors.[13] There was, finally, the minor scandal of the appointments to the powerful post of government secretary. The new governor might have suggested, in a fit of bright imagination, men like Dr. Canegata or Judge Jackson. Washington, however, chose to appoint men like the obscure American novelist Robert Herrick and, after him, the liberal Robert Morss Lovett, both of whom, whatever their liberalism, knew nothing about the Virgin Islands before being shipped there after a series of bizarre consultative procedures on the part of Secretary Ickes.[14]

In the light of all this it becomes difficult to accept the thesis of a stateside Pearson advocate that the history of the Virgin Islands during the New Deal period was "a fight between liberalism and the spoils

11. Quoted in letter of the executive secretary of St. Thomas Suffragette League, *Daily News*, Feb. 17, 1933.

12. Municipality of St. Thomas and St. John, *Municipal Council Record*, Vol. I, no. 8 (Charlotte Amalie, June 8, 1939).

13. *Afro-American*, May 25, 1935, reprinted in *The Emancipator*, June 5, 1935.

14. See Blake Nevius, *Robert Herrick: The Development of a Novelist* (Berkeley and Los Angeles: University of California Press, 1962), pp. 328–30; and Robert Morss Lovett, *All Our Years* (New York: Viking, 1948), pp. 272–75.

system." [15] It is true that there were real difficulties in a pro-native or pro-Negro policy. Most Virgin Islands doctors, for example, were white because, as local councillors looking into the matter in 1939 found out, young colored doctors were at a premium due to the discriminatory character of the American medical profession, a condition that not even the most belligerently liberal of governments in St. Thomas could alter. Nor was it a moralistically simple question of evil white forces discriminating against noble Negro aspirants, as the anti-Pearson campaign frequently pictured it. The situation was more complex. For the transfer to civil government had spawned, overnight, a new and powerful lobby of Negro politicians and their clients eager to get jobs out of the federal "pork barrel" in St. Thomas—to build up, that is, a Negro political empire in the potentially ripe pickings of a colored dependency. The National Negro Democratic Committee held meetings with Jim Farley; clubs like the Roosevelt-Garner Democratic Club in the islands came alive to join in the spoils; and the stateside Negro press mentioned Negro candidates for the office of governor, including names of Negro editors, educators, and army officers, even going so far as to print detailed lists, along with salaries, of the Virgin Islands government payroll. This would be a splendid opportunity, the idealists argued, to prove the ability of Negroes to conduct a colonial government. The politicians were franker: "Many a politician's slumber," one report put it, "is troubled with dreams of the grandeur of being Governor of the little principality down in the Caribbean." [16] Notwithstanding the fact that this dream faded, thus demonstrating the weakness of the Negro bloc in the national Democratic Party councils, the Pearson group could with some credibility portray themselves as the Galahads of New Deal liberalism defending the islands against "dirty politics."

It is, nevertheless, a thesis difficult to accept at face value. For the truth is that, in the absence of the extension of federal civil service regulations to the islands, the governor's selection of his enlarged official family had no limits placed on it, and his discretionary power was in fact increased further by the feeling on the part of his Washington superiors that since personal qualities of a somewhat intangible nature assumed a larger significance in a crowded little island town than they did in large impersonal departments at "home" the decisions of the "man on the spot" should not be readily interfered with. Almost inescapably, then, Pearson proceeded to build up his own spoils system. The temptation

15. Ralph Thompson, "The Promise of the Virgin Islands," *Current History* (March, 1935), pp. 681–86.
16. *Daily News*, May 18, 1933. For various reports on this matter drawn from the U.S. Negro press of the time, see *ibid.*, May 16, 17, 18, 24, 1933.

to do so was naturally made stronger by his realization that, as a "hold-over" Republican appointment, he was fair game for replacement by a Democratic secretary in Washington; and it was a testimony to his own not inconsiderable powers of political intrigue that he was able to survive until 1935. It could indeed be argued that, granted the nature of the American system, intrigue of a certain Machiavellian kind was a condition of mere survival. This, as much as anything, accounts for the steady deterioration in the state of colonial politics after 1932. There was the arbitrary dismissal of those New Deal appointees who in one way or another crossed the governor: Executive Assistant Paul Yates, Government Attorney Eli Baer, and others. There was the effort—if Yates's testimony in the 1935 hearings is to be believed—to buy off anti-administration editors with offers of appointments. There was the attempt, attested to by correspondence, to buy off local enemies like Ella Gifft, the St. Thomas suffragette leader, with the offer of a job from the director of education.[17]

Within a year of his appointment the governor had managed to build up an overstaffed bureaucratic machine of some sixty-four positions, many of them unclassified, that consumed in their total salaries one-half of the annual budget, with the added injustice of an unreasonable disparity of reward between the central administration appointments and the municipal administration appointments. It is true that much of the anti-Pearson material was maliciously put together by disappointed office-seekers such as the Chicago lawyer Lucius Malmin, whose crude attempts at blackmailing Secretary Ickes for the purpose of getting himself appointed to the Virgin Islands governorship finally ended in his own disbarment at the hands of the Illinois Supreme Court. But there was enough truth in the collected charges pressed by the island forces to perhaps justify the congressional investigation of 1935.

The story of that investigation shows that there was "politics" on both sides and that the Virgin Islands became the unwitting victim of a typical dispute between the administration and Congress, sparked by the acrimonious vendetta between Secretary Ickes and his archenemy Senator Tydings of Maryland. However, the construction implicitly put on that affair by one of the chapter titles of the Jarvis book of 1938—"Northern Party Politics and Departmental Struggles in Washington Interfere with Orderly Progress in the Virgin Islands"—is hardly tenable when it is remembered that by 1935 the internal situation in St. Thomas had so much degenerated that its ordinarily peaceful social life had become almost completely disrupted. The contem-

17. Ella Gifft to director of education, quoted in *The Emancipator*, May 20, 1935.

porary descriptions read like the political warfare of the medieval Italian city-states: jobs lost, men expelled from the Tennis Club for political views, personal assaults, a climate of fear that barred people from talking openly with strangers, and worst of all a widespread underground espionage system operated by both government and antigovernment factions. Editors vied with each other in the art of scurrilous personal abuse. And if Morris Davis was the Demosthenes of the crisis, Jarvis, as editor of the new *Daily News,* was the Platonic Socrates lamenting the raucous follies of his countrymen as he preached the virtues of more education as the solution to all. A collapse of general confidence between government and its opponents had clearly taken place. Even more, there was a collapse of meaningful communication; the fact, for example, that the local opposition groups could see the controversial District Court Judge Webber Wilson as a fine Southern gentleman with no trace of race feeling about him while the Northern liberal press saw him as a Southern racist indicated that the opposing sides were living in entirely different worlds of reference.

The Tydings investigation, properly assessed by Ickes as a veiled attempt to destroy him politically, naturally made the most of all this. It was symptomatic of what was wrong with the American conduct of colonial affairs that the first really important congressional investigation of the insular problem since 1917 was, in effect, a fierce intra-administration battle combined with a Senate-Interior conflict in which the real problem, by default, never was touched upon. "My theory is," wrote Secretary Ickes, "that since we are denied the right of cross-examination and since Tydings seems bent on smearing us all he can, we ought to fight back day by day through the newspapers, which is the only means available to us to meet the vague charges that are being produced before the investigating committee." [18] Nor was the secretary averse to using the questionable method of sending his private scouts into Baltimore in order to organize disaffection in the Negro centers of the senator's bailiwick, thus matching the use by the other side of private committee scouts scouring the islands for every piece of gossip and slander they could find. The whole tone and character of the hearings, concentrating as they did on hearsay and opinion evidence, were disgraceful, even by prevailing congressional standards. Senator Tydings, clearly, could not raise himself above the sort of sordid gossip which permitted him to attack governor-elect Cramer on the ground that the successor to Governor Pearson had had a book on nudism

18. Harold L. Ickes, *The Secret Diary of Harold L. Ickes,* Vol. I, *The First Thousand Days, 1933–1936* (New York: Simon and Schuster, 1953) , p. 393.

dedicated to him by the authors, who had been his house guests in St. Croix. On the basis of this kind of statesmanship Tydings' admirers in the islands were prepared to support his nomination for the presidency in 1936 and to declare his birthday a national holiday in the territory—a typical Virgin Islands touch. And it was symptomatic of Washington political ethics that when finally the circus was abruptly ended by the direct intervention of the president, the settlement of the quarrel imposed by him on both sides was worse than the quarrel itself. It involved transferring Governor Pearson to a post as assistant director of housing and Judge Wilson to a post as member of the Federal Parole Board, the latter vacancy being made possible by the arbitrary removal of the competent psychiatrist Dr. Amy Stannard from the board on entirely specious grounds. This violation of the merit system was so openly scandalous that even Secretary Ickes was moved to confess to his diary that "It does look rather raw." [19]

The end result of it all was to strengthen the feeling of the average American reader that, as *Time* magazine humorously portrayed the affair, it was all nothing more than a fight for colonial patronage between Republican incumbents and Democratic hopefuls, and Virgin Islands affairs were a comic opera "good for a laugh" but no more important than that. What, after all, could be expected from a tiny Negro community barely numerous enough in its population to fill two-thirds of the football stadium of the University of West Virginia? [20]

In its political aspect, then, the New Deal experiment in the islands became too deeply enmeshed in the Washington political jungle warfare to be able to concentrate its energy upon the local problems. In the absence of a trained colonial service too many colonial appointments, as in the case of Judge Wilson, were used as means of appeasing powerful opponents, in that particular case Senator Pat Harrison, the powerful chairman of the Senate Finance Committee. It meant, inevitably, government by the amateur. As one critic of the Virgin Islands situation put it, there existed in the Washington mentality the idea that any "fine fellow" was necessarily qualified, by temperament and wisdom, to solve complex problems of government and business. Accordingly, no man with administrative ability had ever been named as governor of any of the new colonial possessions. The defect was painfully evident in the annual reports of the Virgin Islands governors: "Here they usually write as an advertising agent, who is promoting a

19. *Ibid.*, p. 405.
20. *Time*, July 15, 22, 1935.

real estate or commercial boom; or, again, it is as if by a special plea and a lively imagination they were justifying their delusions of grandeur. Such official reports serve to fool the appointing power into the belief that something is being accomplished with the Federal appropriations." [21] The Pearson episode of 1935 must be seen as simply a symptomatic expression of that fundamental defect. Nor was it simply a matter of the absence of an efficient colonial administrative system. For, with patronage or without it, the basic fact was that, in an essentially colonial situation, there existed a fundamental and permanent principle of division between government and people which no gubernatorial personality, however compelling, could in the long run dispel. But American opinion, even liberal New Deal opinion, rarely appreciated that truth. In the case of the Virgin Islands, then, it was left to journals like the *Amsterdam News* to point out that in the long run the situation demanded that the territory be run by Virgin Islanders themselves, not by Democrats or Republicans from the north, black or white.[22]

The political situation influenced, understandably, the treatment of the colonial economic problem. In general terms, of course, the failure of the New Deal program, in St. Thomas as on the national level, was due to the fact that it was not a bold, coherent plan to reshape American economic society root and branch but rather a hasty and improvised response to sudden crisis; and it could be no more effective abroad in a dependent territory than it was at home. If it had any theoretical basis at all it was that of a revived economic Jeffersonianism in its campaign against the "economic royalists" and its predilection for the "small man" in business, a crusading liberalism that believed deeply that "something ought to be done" but that lacked any clear signposts to direct and channel the reforming energy. Mass unemployment finally was solved not by the haphazard schemes of the New Deal philosophy but by the war-preparedness program as it picked up steam after 1937, with the dependent economies like Puerto Rico and the Virgin Islands benefiting slowly from its overspill into the Caribbean.

It was inevitable, then, that the economic program in St. Thomas, for all of the criticisms of the previous Navy regime, really amounted to simply "more of the same," that is, an accelerated injection of public works and relief programs no more fundamentally reorganizational

21. Theodore Schroeder, "The Usual Psychologic Fallacy," *The Emancipator*, Apr. 9, 1932.
22. "The Rape of the Virgin Islands," *Amsterdam News*, quoted in *Daily News*, May 24, 1933. For stateside liberal comment on the 1935 episode, see *The Nation*, January 23, July 24, August 7, 1935.

than the varied schemes that the Navy governors had sponsored. Even
at that the new emphasis was upon relief, following the extension of the
federal Works Progress Administration program to the islands, with the
result that, paradoxically, some earlier programs, like sanitation and
water supply, began to fall from the standards set before 1931, while,
despite a decrease in the death rate (accomplished in any case almost
entirely by the earlier work of the naval physicians), malaria and ty-
phoid made their reappearance early in the Pearson regime. No problem was permanently solved by such devices, which were essentially
of a stopgap nature. The majority of unemployed laborers probably had
the period of partial starvation deferred, but the really permanent
benefits went into land values, without increased taxes to secure
those benefits. There was, it is true, a somewhat bolder touch in the
policy of limited land nationalization by purchase in St. Croix, designed
to return the land to the laborer by means of the homesteading program. But although that particular program was fought fiercely by the
Crucian landed oligarchy, its effects, in the long run, had no socialist
touch about them. There were two reasons for this. First, in the rehabilitation of the Crucian rum industry under the Virgin Islands Company, the future profits, following a ruling of the comptroller general,
were to be returned not to the islands but to the U.S. Treasury.
In addition, the company, being a quasi-governmental institution, was
not subject to local taxation, which meant a great loss of revenue to
the St. Croix municipality. Second, there was only a minor change in
the structure of land ownership, owing to the fact that the whole program was based on a fundamental misconception about the life
values of the Crucian laborer, who had little more than a sentimental
interest in landowning, and who rapidly failed as the well-known
limitations of peasant-proprietorship enterprise made themselves
felt over the years. Other programs, like the rug-weaving and basket-
making ardently supported by Governor Pearson's romantic advisers,
were doomed to failure since they lacked an organized sales effort in the
continental market and were based on a cheap domestic labor structure inevitably challenged by the growing local union movement. The
tourist program, likewise, could have little immediate effect since, by
definition, it depended upon cheap mass tourist travel from the American society, something hardly likely to develop within a mass depression economy. Nothing was done, alternatively, to develop the St. Thomas
harbor economy, for example, by means of a graving-repair dock, despite the fact that the island was fitted by its natural and historical
destiny to develop along such lines, as had been emphasized by its prosperity under the Danish occupation and recognized in fact by the United

States in its purchase. For the rest, both the Pearson and Cramer periods concentrated upon the relief program, and the agitated politics of the decade could be seen as little more than a sordid struggle between rival factions for the power to control that program.

The New Deal in the islands was beset by a series of serious internal contradictions of basic principle. There was the contradiction, already noted, of harsh criticism of the Navy program of "relief" in the name of a new program of "rehabilitation," which turned out to be a massive relief exercise under a new name. There was the second contradiction between the policy, announced by Governor Pearson in his initial statement of 1931, of cutting down the number of administrative offices for the sake of "economy," and the rehabilitation program itself, which of necessity led to the endless creation of new offices, the expansion of government inherent in the New Deal concept. There was the third contradiction of the endless moral exhortations to the islanders to learn the arts of "self-help" while at the same time official programs, by causing the economy to become more and more dependent on U.S. help, that is, more and more parasitical, made the adoption of the Puritan economic virtues increasingly difficult and, indeed, irrelevant. The slogan "Let the Navy do it" had early on become the expression of a settled attitude. This was to some extent justifiable for, as Representative Ayres had put it in 1930, something positive had to be done "before most of the people reach the conclusion that it is the duty of the U.S. Government to feed them, care for them in hospitals, and finally bear the expense of placing them in their final resting place. There are too many of that mind at this time and the sentiment is growing." [23] The contrast between preaching the virtues of economic individualism and practicing the habits of Keynesian government was not lost on perceptive natives. Jarvis noted ironically that when Governor Pearson spoke, in Booker T. Washington style, of "letting down your buckets where you are," the Virgin Islanders' response, not unnaturally, was that having been accustomed to Old Testament paternal government they felt that dipping water from any stream of idealism was too hard for their unaccustomed muscles and minds.[24]

Yet the matter was even more fundamental than that. Practically every American official, Navy bureaucrat or New Deal liberal, uncritically assumed that the colonial situation simply required the ex-

23. U.S., Congress, House, *Congressional Record*, 71st Cong., 2d sess., 1930, 72, pt. 8, 8802-3.

24. J. Antonio Jarvis, *Brief History of the Virgin Islands* (St. Thomas: Art Shop, 1938), p. 161.

tension to the islands, in gradual stages to be decided by him, of the American "way of life," regardless of whether local Caribbean conditions required that prescription of cure or not. Educational policy, constitutional structure, social life, economic plans—all provided examples of the resultant errors. Governor Pearson himself, arriving in St. Thomas fresh from his Chautauqua circuit, with nineteen trunks of theatrical properties to be used for the cultural uplift of the natives, was only the most maliciously noted example of many. Yet that, after all, was merely the amiable fault of a romantic liberal.

The consequences of the general fallacy here being noted were far more serious when it came to economic policies that affected the generality of the Virgin Islands "small man." When, for example, the Colonial Council passed a tick-eradication ordinance under pressure from the Puerto Rican cattle trade interests, it was the "small man" who grazed a handful of goats in the tiny off-islands or who used a donkey to ply his harbor livelihood in St. Thomas that suffered from the expenses involved in observing the law. Similarly, when the Council accepted a milk-pasteurization ordinance, its requirements penalized both the consumer and the ordinary housewife who lacked an icebox in which certified milk had to be kept, when the local custom of boiling milk assured cleanliness and safety equally well. The entire general direction of New Deal policies, only occasionally questioned by a stateside official, was to "Americanize" the native as rapidly as possible, encouraging him to embrace economic goals and expectations he had little capacity to satisfy. The result was a senseless exaggeration of the habit of consumption and the accompanying neglect of the problem of production. "The change in becoming Americans," noted one local journal at the time, "was more welcomed from the standpoint of sharing in the wealth of the nation than from adaptation to the nation's method of producing wealth." [25]

Social policy, in any society, is a function of social structure. No economic planner comes, like a Platonic utopia-maker, to construct a society all anew; and no public official finds, like Rousseau's Grand Legislator, a passive society all ready to receive the imprint of his schemes.

25. Editorial, *The Emancipator*, Sept. 20, 1937. For opinion of Robert Morss Lovett on the Pearson New Deal achievement, see *The New Republic*, March 3, 1937. For the opinion of native authors, see Jarvis, *Brief History*, chaps. 17, 18; and, later, Valdemar A. Hill, Sr., *A Golden Jubilee: Virgin Islanders on the Go under the American Flag* (New York: Carlton Press, 1967), chap. 8; and Darwin D. Creque, *The U.S. Virgins and the Eastern Caribbean* (Philadelphia: Whitmore, 1968). Both Hill and Creque rather uncritically follow Jarvis.

Least of all is that so in a colonial society where the leading prerequisite of planned change—mutual confidence between government and governed—is, almost by definition, absent. Most American colonial officials, even the most sophisticated, came to Manila or San Juan or Charlotte Amalie assuming that they were entering "simple" or even "primitive" societies because, unlike their British counterparts, they were unprepared by any inherited experience in the art of colonial administration. They rapidly became the victims of their anthropological naivete.

The history of the Americans in the Virgin Islands, extending to the present (1972), is in large part a series of illustrations of this general cultural ignorance. American officials had to learn to come to terms with an amazingly complicated set of class-color correlates rooted in constitutive principles and historical background quite different from those of their parent society. A system of color classification based on the subtle gradations of skin pigmentation contained grievous pitfalls for the American who mistakenly applied the North American simplistic black-white dichotomy; similarly, he could easily overlook the fact that the social and economic cleavage between the Negro masses and the tiny propertied mulatto group with whom any mainland administrator naturally dealt was almost as sharp as that generally found elsewhere between black and white. The knowledgeable field representative of the American Red Cross in the islands told a Senate committee in 1936:

> It is well to point out that the situation described is not racial, but economic. The dividing line in the islands between the propertied and the non-propertied is not at the same time a color line. Black, colored and white entrepreneurs and landlords make common cause together to protect the interests of their class against those of a laboring class which is also made up of black, colored and white, the latter represented by a colony of fishermen and basketmakers in St. Thomas of pure French descent.[26]

The North American stereotype of the illiterate and culturally ignorant "Step'n Fetchit" Negro, the general "lazy nigger" complex, also made no sense in this environment. The average Virgin Islands Negro, the same Senate committee witness pointed out, was highly literate (most of the minuscule 4 per cent classified as "illiterate" were adult immigrants from Puerto Rico and the British islands), a steady patron of the public libraries, an avid reader of a number of small newspapers

26. Testimony of Joanna C. Colcord, one-time field representative of the American Red Cross in the Virgin Islands, and departmental director of the Russell Sage Foundation, in U.S. Senate Hearings, May 31, 1936, reprinted in *The Emancipator*, Jan. 18, 20, 1937.

that were widely discussed in the three towns, a member of labor unions (one of whose remarkable features was the membership of men and women on an equal footing, including equal wages), an extremely law-abiding citizen, rarely given to alcoholism, a zealous churchgoer, and possessed of habits of natural courtesy and loyalty that made him and his like renowned as superior house servants throughout the West Indies—a general picture startlingly different from the image that the average white American entertained of the Negro in the world as he knew it.

In the sense that all this constituted a racial democracy (or at least a system of color relations far more democratic than anything to be found in racist America) the New Deal official who was genuinely liberal accepted it with delight. In the sense, however, that it was at the same time a social system carrying its own inner class struggle between the "haves" and "have nots," the sum total of New Deal policies left the colonial status quo essentially untouched. There was, one could say, a racial liberalism brought by the New Deal, but not much in the way of a political or an economic liberalism. So, an official like Government Secretary Robert Herrick did his bit, through his social entertainment, to open up Government House (hitherto kept "white" by the Navy) to guests of all shades. Yet most of those guests, almost by necessity, were representatives of the light-skinned local elite whose socioeconomic power held the masses in thralldom, and in the crucial test of challenging that power in the name of economic democracy the New Deal, on the whole, failed. Intimate social intercourse blunted, as it were, the edge of radical economic policy. That process, in turn, was encouraged by the fact that close relationships between government and business had always been an outstanding feature of Virgin Islands life, as it still is; nearly every leading businessman was under some form of obligation to the government, nearly every estate owner was indebted to the government for loans, while a peculiar contracts system meant that even the smallest piece of business—the right to publish legislative proceedings in newspapers or the right to supply sandwiches at Council luncheons—was fraught with great political significance. The New Deal administrators almost naturally fell into the atmosphere of mutual accommodation thereby engendered.

The long-term result of New Deal policy, then, was to consolidate the economic power of the elite group of wealthy merchants and landowners. With most of the government contracts in their pockets they reaped a large proportion of the profits from the rehabilitation program, in effect controlled the strategic position of the Virgin Islands

Company (the chartered corporation in charge of the homesteading program) in the St. Croix land program, and managed, through their representation in the archaic Councils, to shift the burden of taxation from their shoulders to those of the masses, with no very strenuous objections from the Government House bureaucracy. They thus became the staunch allies of the governor. The function of the Councils became, under such pressures, the protection of their privileges, and the concept of democracy that most Council members accordingly held was that of a narrow-minded legislative sovereignty unrelated to considerations of representation. Their legislative record, thus, was dismally uninspired. No measures were enacted to improve working-class conditions, such as compensation to injured workmen or legislation to compel landlord-employers to provide decent housing for their tenants. Welfare measures, suggestively, always came about through initiative from the executive branch. Suggestively, too, open warfare between the two branches only erupted on those occasions when the government sought to liberalize the income tax structure through its budgetary proposals.

The New Deal period thus ended with the economy structurally unchanged and characterized, as before, by (1) a disproportionate concentration of wealth in the hands of a mercantile oligarchy that usually went no further than individual or family savings; and (2) a chronically deficient buying power in an impoverished majority. Then, as federal expenditures began to decline after 1937 under the pressure of the economy drive from Washington—exemplified in the growing insistence upon the principle of only limited coverage of local colonial deficits by federal appropriations—a rejuvenated local production-investment power, which, according to New Deal theory, was supposed to emerge out of the rehabilitation program, failed to take the place of those federal funds.

Could all this have turned out otherwise? Would it have been possible, for example, for a really radical colonial administration leadership to challenge the hold of the local Negro aristocracy by seeking an alliance of interest and sentiment with the disfranchised common people? At least one American observer of the local scene at the time—Luther Evans in his book *The Virgin Islands: From Naval Base to New Deal*, substantially written in 1936 but not published until 1945—considered the possibility. Noting, correctly, that although natives of all classes were inordinately proud of the attainments of the more accomplished members of their race—always a persistent note in Virgin Islands literature—but that the common people at the same time were fearful of being exploited both by their upper-class brethren and by the "rabble-

(87)

rousers" whose power thrived on mass discontent, Evans recognized the potentiality of that class separatism for an imaginative official leadership.

> There is some evidence . . . that the ordinary laborer, whether coal carrier, cane cutter, or house boy, puts more reliance upon individual effort and entertains fewer mistaken notions about government and public policies than a majority of the local leaders. A local executive who could govern with their informed consent without the intervention of self-seeking local leaders, would be in a position to govern much better than an executive depending upon the consent of these leaders.[27]

Yet in terms of the concrete class situation this was a pipe dream based on romantic fantasy, not unlike the temptation of British colonial administrators in the neighboring British Caribbean possessions to make a facile distinction between the "reliable" folk-people and the "self-seeking" middle-class leaders, obviously a rationalization of their own chronic inability to come to terms with the new educated Negro intelligentsia coming to the fore in the colonial struggle of the period. The element of Tory Democracy was obvious, that is, the idea of an alliance of aristocrat and peasant against the new despotism of the capitalist businessman. But the social basis of Tory Democracy in England—the existence of a conservative labor aristocracy—was totally absent in the colonial situation, and without this the dream was bound to wither away. A further element of the same dream—the idea of a contented peasantry living peaceably on the land, as contrasted with the social evils of town life—was also evident in the St. Croix homesteading plan. But, here again, the dream ignored the harsh realities of the colonial economy, the fact that the Caribbean rural populations had been shaped not by a gentle pastoral tradition fostered by Tudor-like paternalistic governments but by a slave-labor system operated by a repressive plantocracy that left them, after the emancipation from slavery, with an ingrained antipathy toward the land and everything associated with it. Senator Hiram Bingham had early on seen this, in his perceptive observation that it would not be too easy to "turn hereditary stevedores into truck farmers," or even "hereditary plantation laborers into satisfactory raisers of diversified crops." [28] The distinctly political element of the dream, finally—the idea that somehow the political dimension could be bypassed in favor of an administrative leadership—quite overlooked the fact that, denied the right to vote, the man in the street naturally

27. Luther H. Evans, *The Virgin Islands: From Naval Base to New Deal* (Ann Arbor, Mich.: J. W. Edwards, 1945), pp. 93–94.
28. Quoted in *The Emancipator*, Aug. 18, 1926.

turned eagerly to extralegislative politics for his ideas, indeed for his social entertainment, a fact that continues up to the present day to be a distinguishing feature of West Indian politics.

In any case, the character of the American white administrators, if nothing else, insured the collapse of the ideal policy mapped out by critics like Evans. Everything about them—color, education, social convenience, the very pleasures of tropical life—made it only too easy for them to seek the social alliance of the local "upper-crust" elements. Most of them, as New Dealers, saw nothing wrong with a class social structure as such. This attitude was capable of producing comments like Governor Pearson's answer to his critics: "The merchants and representatives of the West India Company and their friends may possibly dominate the Colonial Council of St. Thomas and St. John, but these people are more fitted to assume responsibilities; they were the ruling class when we got here and in every country of the world, regardless of the system of government, there always will be a ruling class." [29] Nor should the slow corruption which the poison of power in a colonialist situation worked even in the most morally conscientious of officials be overlooked. The mainland administrator came from the vigorously democratic atmosphere of American life to the autocratic atmosphere of the colony where, merely by the fact of his skin color, he was welcomed as an aristocrat by a color-conscious aristocracy. He was given a taste of power unlike anything he had previously experienced. If he were governor, he became, in Jarvis' tart phrase, a little Pope in the Vatican of Government Hill. It was hardly surprising that even the humblest officials came to see themselves as a little larger than life. Herrick, for instance, with his growing disillusionment with American life, became an autocratic old man in his office of government secretary. "The truth is," he wrote his friend Robert Morss Lovett, "that the Virgin Islands don't need a secretary: what they need is a Boss who would reduce the salary roll by at least half, cut out the various grafts, divide up the lands, and tell them to go fishing and raising yams for a living." [30] A Virgins Islands Populist revolt, led by Government House, could hardly grow out of such attitudes.

All of the foregoing could be seen, generally, as the ineradicable contradiction between democracy and empire. Caught in the frustrations and disappointments spawned by that contradiction, the New Deal liberal, like the Navy officer before him, retreated into feelings of disgust and contempt. Nothing better illustrated that process than the Evans book.

29. Quoted in *ibid.,* Apr. 29, 1935.
30. Quoted in Nevius, *Robert Herrick*, p. 335.

For despite its plea for an enlarged suffrage and more doses of social democracy in future policy for the islands, it ended with a curious "Epilogue on Politics" which was nothing less than a full-blown apologetic for colonialism under the guise of presenting a scientific theory of statecraft. The ideal, the argument went, speaking both generally and particularly for the Virgin Islands, is a government-people relationship in which a "considerable degree" of representation must be permitted but in which complete self-government is not "essential." The race aspect of the problem can be met by treating the natives with "dignity," for "Negroes expect a separate status, but they do not expect that status to be accompanied by galling discrimination." The constitutional aspect of the problem—which arises from the fact that the colonial community "is by very definition in a position of inequality with respect to the mother country"—can be met by a type of administrator who, ideally, should not engage in heated public debate, should respect the local press but remember at the same time that a press which resorts to "alarmist tactics" must be "carefully watched" and "perhaps held in check," for "Government among Negroes must maintain its dignity; yet the more it secures respect without insisting upon it, the easier its tasks will be." The officials, furthermore, having earlier been warned that "The courageous forswearing of all seemingly devious or crafty methods of political action is most essential to successful administration," are then blandly advised to adopt various evasive tactics when faced with "unreasonable" demands: as a class, they can "make gestures in the direction of satisfying popular demands, or pretend to be pleading with the home government to answer the cries of justice. In extremely difficult cases they can advise the home government to refuse the demands which are being made, and then defend themselves before local opinion by pointing out that the home government has not yet yielded to their demands." If such a "removal-of-authority" strategy does not succeed, then the "appoint-an-investigating commission" technique is sometimes advisable. Nor should officials be restrained by an "unrealistic" democratic reluctance to "manage" opinion; recommended tactics in this area include the granting of discreet favors, "friendly cooperation" with the local churches, and a "complete indifference" to the opinions of expatriates about local conditions. All this, finally, according to the author, must go hand in hand with appreciation of the real character of Virgin Islanders as a people who are "petulant, irascible and unappreciative," traits probably traceable to tendencies of "degeneration." [31]

It is, altogether, an astonishing hodgepodge of ingenuousness, racism,

31. Evans, *The Virgin Islands*, pp. 321–26, also pp. 9–10.

(90)

and character assassination, not to mention the gratuitous assumption that the art of government in Negro communities somehow requires special laws not applicable elsewhere. The book makes it easier to understand the reasons for the failure of the New Deal in the colonial possessions. Its leading premise—like that of Governor Tugwell's autobiographical volume, *The Stricken Land,* in the case of Puerto Rico a decade later—was that the colonial problem was simply a morality play between "high-minded" American administrators and "irresponsible agitators." This view was aptly summarized in a quotation by Evans from another American official in the islands at much the same time with reference to "the perverse craving of this recently-enslaved population for a dictator—benevolent, urbane, just and terrible, to remove all responsibility from them and conduct their affairs; and their contempt for unassuming, plain-mannered Americans who lack the heavy dignity which the West Indies demands of its governing classes." [32] Apart from its tone of objectionable self-righteousness, it made the fundamental mistake of attributing certain supposed permanent traits of conduct and character to the colonial person which could be more correctly comprehended as the natural expressions of the colonial situation seen in its moment of time in the historical trajectory of Caribbean civilization. Colonialism, first Danish, then American, crippled the colonial in mind and spirit; to that injury was added the gross insult of the assertion that his deformity was the cause and not the consequence of his tragic situation. The fact that the Evans volume came with the support behind its investigations of Princeton University and the Social Science Research Council (both of which helped to finance the work) suggested that by the time the New Deal experiment ended, in 1940 or thereabouts, the Virgin Islands, like Puerto Rico, still had a long way to go before they could enjoy the full promise of American life.

32. *Ibid.,* p. 95, n. 3.

4

~~~

1941:
The War Period
and After

The twenty years between 1941 and 1961 constitute a sort of watershed between the depression of the 1930s and the expansionist economy of the 1960s based on tourism and a growing industrial sector. They covered, first, the World War II period, when extensive defense employment and abnormal tax collections temporarily solved the economic problem. At the same time, attention shifted to the strategic issues involved in mere physical survival as the German submarine command of the Caribbean passages opened up the grim possibility that the Virgin Islands could conceivably be threatened by the kind of occupation by enemy carrier task force that was to characterize the Japanese advance in the Pacific area. The years after 1945, secondly, constituted a difficult period of economic decline as the wartime prosperity evaporated, not unlike the doldrum period of 1880–1917; and the spate of Caribbean travel books and critical studies that appeared after the termination of the war—Blanshard, Brown, Roberts—all painted the picture of a Virgin Islands society in apathetic decline.[1] In retrospect, it is possible to see these years as a preparatory period in which the economy, perhaps only half-consciously, gradually came to concentrate, after some false starts, upon the tourist dollar as the answer to its problems, thus finally justifying those New Deal planners who had seen in their rehabilitation of Bluebeard's Castle as a new tourist hotel the single most important item of their program. Looked at thus, the period marked the completion of a

1. Paul Blanshard, *Democracy and Empire in the Caribbean* (New York: Macmillan, 1947), pt. 3, chap. 11; W. Adolphe Roberts, *Lands of the Inner Sea* (New York: Coward-McCann, 1948), chap. 8; and Wenzell Brown, *Angry Men—Laughing Men* (New York: Greenberg, 1947).

slow transformation of attitudes in which the upper-class group of the "old families," who had always lived on shipping and sugar, finally came to accept the truth that that era was over once and for all.

The war period, naturally, meant the bending of all energies, under Governor Charles Harwood's direction, to the new problems of the war effort. It was, first and foremost, quite simply a problem of survival, for the German submarine attacks in 1942 on the Aruba oil refineries made it brutally clear that the islands were in an active war zone, while the presence of the local bauxite transshipment plant made direct enemy attack always a distinct possibility. The situation was made even more perilous by the Vichy regime's control of the French Antilles; and the espionage affair of 1942, in which a ring of schooner masters in Honduras helped refuel German submarines after a pattern that could obviously be duplicated in any Caribbean island setting, further emphasized the real dangers. The general defense problem in the area, as the 1941 report of the American Geographical Society on *The European Possessions in the Caribbean Area* warned, was a dual one of, first, the proper defense of the shipping lanes and, second, the protection of the Panama Canal from seizure. The former problem was of peculiar urgency because of the existence in the region of strategically located islets, like Anegada, Virgin Gorda, Anguilla, and St. Maarten (all close neighbors of the Virgins group), which were likely to attract the eye of invaders. The occupation of any of those positions would immediately put the whole defense of the vital Anegada Passage, spanning the gap between the Virgins and the Leeward Islands group, into jeopardy; they were foreign possessions, and it was therefore imperative that none of them should fall into enemy hands.[2] Governor Harwood and his military advisers were clearly justified in taking a grim view of their duties and in making heroic efforts to get this view adopted by island populations traditionally unresponsive to the exhortations of their colonial administrators.

It was a herculean struggle. The routines of war and blockade—organizing vital supplies, civilian defense measures, and military recruiting and training—replaced those of socioeconomic reorganization. There was the task of putting the islands in a state of defense, in cooperation with the armed services and their contractors. There was the organization of the Home Guard, which later became the training ground for the first Virgin Islands contingents in active service on the war fronts. There was the problem of organizing food supplies for a population used to artificial reliance upon regular food imports from outside, made

2. Raye R. Platt, John K. Wright, John C. Weaver, and Johnson E. Fairchild, *The European Possessions in the Caribbean Area* (New York: American Geographical Society, 1941).

worse by the depletion of the scanty agricultural population as workers deserted to higher-paid jobs in the new defense projects. There were the innumerable new programs to be put into shape—the Civilian Defense School, the Police Training School run by the FBI, the government takeover of the West India Company to insure regular supplies of electric power, the local application of federal wartime controls (price controls and rationing, for example), and the setting up of local administrative machinery that was thereby necessitated. There was the job, never really successfully done, of persuading the local populace to take air-raid practices seriously. Not least of all, an entire range of local social services, never very good, had to be expanded, almost overnight, to meet the heavy pressure of the influx of additional population; for, again almost overnight, St. Thomas became a full-employment economy that attracted thousands of laborers from the outer islands in violation of the U.S. labor and immigration laws.

These efforts engendered further problems, many of them peculiar to the Virgin Islands situation. Alien labor, for example, rapidly became a heated political issue. The illegal entry of foreign workers, at first actively connived at by the federal Department of Labor, soon encountered the opposition, first, of the British colonial authorities who wanted formal contractual protection for their nationals and, second, of the local native workers who resented competition as the wartime boom began to decline perceptibly after 1943, not to mention the additional resentment generated by the fact that the immigrant was exempted from military service requirements. A home priority system was seriously frustrated by the local monopoly of import merchants whose greed drove them to the surreptitious import of luxury articles for the well-to-do local consumer on an active black market. The cost-of-living survey put out by the federal Bureau of Labor Statistics in 1944 indicated in its graphic figures the extent of that illegal economic activity: cooking utensils, tableware, and home furnishings practically disappeared, while living costs for the local wage-earning and lower-salaried clerical groups increased between 1939 and 1943 by some 37 per cent, as compared with 26 per cent in the continental United States.[3] The local Council for Civil Defense became involved in a heated controversy about slit trenches as a means of civilian defense during air raids, with the result that the local population was left to the "expert military opinion" that they should remain at home while under bombardment or retreat to the hills.

Conferences galore, with regional administrators of federal programs, Puerto Rican counterparts, and British officials in Antigua or Jamaica,

3. Bureau of Labor Statistics, *Cost of Living Survey, 1939–1943* (Washington, D.C.: Government Printing Office, 1944), reprinted in *Daily News,* May 2, 1944.

became the order of the day, with all of their attendant irritations and anxieties. The maintenance of public order became acute as clashes developed between American bosses and native workmen and between natives and American white servicemen. The answer to the latter problem, as the secretary of war saw it, was to send Negro troops to the islands, to "promote cordial and stable relationships between the Army and the people," as if the problems of the ghetto could be met by creating more ghettos.[4] The neglect of the local health and sanitation situation by the Department of the Interior—a long-standing complaint of Virgin Islanders—became even more acute with the added pressure of alien workers and their families. The accounts of the still continuing "night-soil" system, which finally received some attention only because of the strong complaints of the American military commander,[5] or the harrowing testimony in which Governor Harwood described to the House Committee on Insular Affairs in 1944 the truly appalling conditions in which patients were treated at the St. Thomas Hospital, with some of its worst passages reserved for the description of the care of the inmates of the psychopathic ward,[6] clearly show the continuation, after nearly thirty years of American rule, of social conditions which truly shocked American congressmen when they heard about them.

The real lesson of the wartime experience, however, far more lasting than the passing problems of wartime life, was that it frankly exposed the archaic character of American colonial government. True enough, the war justified the American prescience in buying the islands in 1917. But at the same time it threw grave doubt upon the applicability of the American system of checks-and-balances federalism to the governing of dependencies. The absence of a central Colonial Office forced the colonial governor to become, in effect, his own resident commissioner in wartime Washington, to the extent that local opinion came to resent his frequent absences from the island. Critics claimed that he was spending more time in the Stork Club with celebrities than in the Executive Mansion in St. Thomas, a sentiment made all the more bitter by the fact that Virgin Islanders have traditionally liked to see their governors in person. There was a fatal absence of effective coordination in a system founded on the tenet of divided powers. The governor, unlike his counterpart in

4. Secretary of war to Ashley L. Totten, president, American Virgin Islands Civic Association, July 6, 1942, printed in *Daily News,* July 14, 1942.

5. *Daily News,* Mar. 3, 4, 1944.

6. Reprinted in *ibid.,* Feb. 26, 28, 29, Mar. 1, 2, 3, 7, 8, 9, 10, 13, 1944. See also criticisms of the local wartime administration by the Virgin Islands Civic Association (New York), in *ibid.,* Feb. 7, 1942; report of the Municipal Council on local hospital conditions, in *ibid.,* July 15, 1942; and Edwin Todd, "The Insane and the Insane Asylum of St. Thomas," *ibid.,* Jan. 24, 28, 31, Feb. 2, 1946.

Jamaica or Barbados, was not the sole and unquestioned depository of the metropolitan power. On the contrary, the power was irrationally shared by a variety of insular representatives of federal departments, both civilian and military, who viewed themselves not as subordinates of the governor but as coequals clothed in their own independent federal authority. They were not always ready to bow to his local position and in cases of conflict were ready to appeal to their federal superiors against him.

The muddle between the Departments of Labor and Justice over the vexed question of the registration of aliens was only one example of the resulting difficulties that the situation created for the governor and his staff. The Navy and United States engineers on the islands tended to resent intervention by the local authorities in labor disputes; one commandant even suggested that the government secretary appear before an investigating board of officers for examination regarding his social views as reported in the press. The remark attributed at much the same time to the local director of the Office of Price Administration, speaking to his staff—"whoever is disloyal to me is disloyal to the President of the United States"[7]—illustrated the divisive pull between local and federal loyalties, making united effort all the more difficult. The rival jurisdictions alongside that of the governor were in a position of undertaking independent policies without any kind of consultation with local interests, although the governor was held responsible for these acts by local opinion—for example, the refusal of the armed services to drop their segregationist practices, or the highhanded way in which the Federal Works Agency took over the West India Company. Divided responsibility insured the defeat, or at least the inadequate implementation, of too many vital programs, such as the far-reaching plan, including government acquisition of land and purchase of agricultural products, proposed in 1942 by the Food Production Committee of the local Council for Defense. What this situation clearly needed was a theory of government that brought the branches together in a fused cooperative whole, not one that artificially divided them. It was ironic, speaking now of the internal relations between executive and legislature, that Governor Harwood should have opened the wartime period by privately obtaining from Washington an amendment to the Organic Act that absolved him from mandatory attendance at legislative meetings, on the basis of the supposed need to apply the "separate powers" doctrine to the colonial situation—a move that immediately earned him the vigorous denunciation of the Municipal Council.[8]

7. Jacob A. Robles, quoted in *ibid.*, Apr. 22, 1944.
8. *Proceedings of the Municipal Council of St. Thomas and St. John,* January 15, February 3, 1942 (microfilm, St. Thomas Public Library).

The Harwood governorship (1941–46) was important because it exhibited, on a tiny colonial stage, the essential unreality of attempting to meet twentieth-century problems with an eighteenth-century machinery of government. Governor Harwood, of course, was no Tugwell. His administration did not have to meet the deep ideological and political hostilities that beset Tugwell's New Deal liberalism in San Juan during the same period. On the contrary, the governor's conservatism made him the close friend of all the congressional forces that were against Tugwell. But that did not prevent the intrusion into the Virgin Islands situation of the sort of guerrilla warfare between congressional committee and administrative department sedulously fomented by the "separate powers" doctrine, its most notable expression, of course, being the notorious Robert Morss Lovett case of 1943.

Lovett's own account of that scandalous episode, along with a reading of the congressional hearings, makes it clear that the House Un-American Activities Committee was determined, possibly with the active connivance of Governor Harwood, to hound the government secretary from public life (because of his well-known liberal opinions) despite the fact that his long record in American civil liberties causes revealed nothing more subversive than a somewhat mild Jeffersonian liberalism. In fact, the committee was obliged to make as much as it could of an indiscreet letter written by him as far back as 1926 charging, in a somewhat anarchist sentence, that all governments were "rotten." The peculiarly vindictive character of the campaign was emphasized by the action of the House in finally ousting their victim by means of an objectionable rider to an urgent wartime deficiencies bill which the president signed under spirited protest (not to mention the fact that the rider in effect was a bill of attainder against a public servant without benefit of judicial proceedings or impeachment hearings and therefore both unconstitutional and an unwarranted encroachment upon presidential authority). The fact that the expulsion succeeded, notwithstanding a veritable barrage of protest—formal declarations of support from the two colonial Municipal Councils, dignified editorials in the St. Thomas press, public acclamation from associations covering almost literally all varieties of opinion in the territory, as well as the powerful dissents of both Secretary Ickes and President Roosevelt—was a graphic demonstration of the terrible vulnerability of the dependent possessions to all of the well-known weaknesses of congressional government. It was small consolation for Virgin Islanders to be told, when it was all over, that they deserved honorable mention for behaving with restraint and dignity in contrast to the vulgarity and malignity that marked the pages of the

Congressional Record.[9] It was, all in all, an early exercise in McCarthyite witch-hunting.

The Lovett case indicated that, in spite of the limited advances of the Organic Act in internal autonomy, the islands still suffered in the 1940s the varied abuses of congressional rule illustrated by the Pearson case in the 1930s. The office of governor remained as unrepresentative as ever, so that Washington connections rather than local popularity remained the real base of power of the incumbent. Thus Governor Harwood managed to stay on simply because he was one of the president's oldest political intimates, going back to the days when both had been members of the New York State Assembly. Even when a governor, like Harwood, managed to obtain handsome appropriations for the territory, people still felt that they were being treated as wards of charity and not as citizens entitled to what was rightfully theirs. One editor observed:

> We have become so deteriorated under this procedure that we can now judge the ability of our varied administrators solely by the appropriations they have been able to procure, while in Washington . . . little or no consideration is given to their true ability or experience in Virgin Islands affairs. This explains the appalling aimlessness, the total absence of any comprehensive plan or policy set out for these islands. We are simply the victims of political patronage, ever subject to the wiles and caprices of myriad personalities, whose tenure of office is controlled solely by the irrational laws of political expediency.[10]

Congress, on the whole, was apathetic, and at times openly hostile to local grievances. The crude arrogance of the remarks of Congressman John Dingell of the House Ways and Means Committee to the director of the National Negro Council in 1942 was not unrepresentative of the general congressional attitude: "At any time the people of the Virgin Islands do not want the protection of the American flag, I would tell them to leave. . . . If they do not like the American idea, living under the American flag, it is just too bad. They can just get out." [11] The ability to be heard in Washington continued to remain without fully defined forms, with the result that Virgin Islands interests were too often treated as if they were identical with Puerto Rican interests, a case in point being the unfortunate 1944 decision of the War Production Board to limit

9. For the Lovett episode, see Robert Morss Lovett, *All Our Years* (New York: Viking, 1948), esp. appendixes A-H; editorial, *Daily News*, Mar. 13, 1944; text of final court decision, *Robert M. Lovett* v. *U.S.*, in *Daily News*, June 4, 1946; and Milton Mayer, "Portrait of a Dangerous Man," *Harper's*, July, 1946.

10. Editorial, *Daily News*, Jan. 28, 1942. See also editorial, *ibid.*, Jan. 8, 1944.

11. Excerpt in *ibid.*, June 18, 1942. See also Ashley L. Totten letter to John Dingell, Apr. 22, 1942, printed in *ibid.*, May 14, 1942.

rum production. Unilateral efforts to remedy that defect, like the attempt of the local Legislative Assembly in the same year to set up an Office of Virgin Islands Delegates in Washington, were struck down unceremoniously by gubernatorial veto.

Nor, from the colonials' viewpoint, was the remedy to these problems the presence in Washington of liberal official friends, as distinct from congressional enemies. For, in terms of machinery, there was insufficient coordination between Government House in Charlotte Amalie and the Interior Department, and both Governor Cramer and Governor Harwood found that Interior officials fiercely resented their methods of ignoring protocol and seeking to deal directly with Congress and the president. And what passed for liberalism, from the figure of Secretary Ickes on down, was more often than not a vague claim of liberals that they "understood" Negroes in a way their Southern racist opponents did not. But it was rarely anything more than that. Not even Lovett, warmhearted humanist that he was, ever seems to have comprehended the harsh contradiction of first principle that existed between his liberalism and the colonial system he elected to join: the contradiction, that is, between a Jeffersonian liberalism that believed in the equality of peoples and a "Manifest Destiny" imperialism that in practice denied the equality.

The general outcome of all this, combined with the inevitable postponement of domestic reform programs that is always the price of war in democratic societies, was that the Virgin Islands entered the postwar period after 1945 as a colonial society with most of its major ills surviving in virulent, even aggravated, form. Both economic organization and social structure remained pretty much as before, with some modifications brought about by the post-1936 politico-legislative changes. The record of the fifteen years between 1945 and 1960, the immediately premodern period, is in essence the story of the gradual, frequently painful adjustment of those conditions to the general pressure of the new forces that had been let loose by the war.

In terms of economic structure the society remained a landlord-merchant oligarchy. The St. Thomas merchant import houses admittedly were at the mercy of the continental exporters, as indeed the wartime critical increase in freight and maritime insurance rates had shown. But, internally, they remained the masters of a marketing structure characterized by a high degree of monopoly control due to the continuing extraordinary dependence of the economy on imports. The added combination of importing functions with retail distribution reinforced the monopolistic condition, and there existed a low degree of real competition, with occasional exceptions, such as the grocery trade in St. Croix. The consumer remained the victim of all this—of high markups; of structural rigidity making the entry of new firms difficult, if not impossible; and of an excessive percentage of import charges added to retail prices due to the absence of any significant self-sustenance program in food production, this being the outcome of sugar landlordism in St. Croix, once the center, before 1917, of a flourishing fruit and vegetable economy. The existence of personal factors, as well as the fear of reprisals by merchants in a situation of close buyer-seller propinquity, made the average consumer even more of a captive buyer than he might have been in a pure price-behavior situation in which he could shift his purchases from store to store in response to the relative cheapness of articles. Both the New Deal and the wartime programs, moreover, being oriented to a public-works spending concept, in one way or another, had left essentially untouched this production-retail base of the local economy. Surprisingly, as the Guy Swope–Ashley Totten 1942 exchange of correspondence showed, although in the 1917–41 period the United States had spent the astonishing sum of some $13 million on the islands, social welfare problems remained in many ways worse than before and agricultural developments were a dismal failure. As for the unemployment problem, the war had solved it only temporarily, the only lasting benefit, perhaps, being the fact that the "spending solution" was finally taken out of the area of controversial public policy.[12]

In terms of social structure, the postwar territorial life was dominated as before by the Virgin Islands values of strongly entrenched social inegalitarianism. Dr. Albert Campbell's remarkable study of St. Thomas Negroes, the fieldwork for which had been done in 1940, and the findings of which were brought to the attention of Virgin Islanders by serialization in the local press, accurately portrayed for this period a society marked by the existence of class and color blocs with their accompanying snobberies.[13] With some modifying factors specifically Virgin Islands in character—the group of upper-class Danes, for example, whose more relaxed attitude toward color marked them off from the American group, or the declining group of middle-class Creole Jews whose class position and race membership gave them entry into the other white

12. For the Guy Swope–Ashley Totten exchange of correspondence, see *ibid.*, Apr. 1, 1942. For the wartime economy as a whole, see the illuminating *Report of OPA Activities in the Virgin Islands,* reprinted in *ibid.*, Sept. 15, 16, 18, 19, 1944.

13. Albert A. Campbell, *St. Thomas Negroes: A Study of Personality and Culture* (Evanston, Ill.: American Psychological Assn., 1943) , serialized in *Daily News,* June 9, 10, 12, 16, 22, 26, July 5, 7, 8, 10, 12, 1944.

segments—it was the typical West Indian picture of societal subgroups fighting a grim battle to "raise the color" as both a prestige mechanism and a lever of social mobility, and only united, in a completely negative sense, by the common deference which a white skin has historically commanded in the Caribbean. "The lower class person," observed Campbell, "tries to establish contact with the white marine for the same reason that the upper class person avoids such contact. Both are responding to the impelling need for social recognition and prestige which is the St. Thomian's inheritance from the bars of unstable and highly charged social stratification which have formed the island's history." But only a chosen few succeeded in that unlovely race. For the majority, the outlook was one of inevitable disappointment. Campbell concluded pessimistically:

> While some individuals live within a context of very limited aspirations and a few others are able to realise their ascendant ambitions, for the majority the situation is one of continual dissatisfaction and frustration. To this they react by attempting to establish status through available forms of emulation, by retreat from social relationships into egocentric isolation, by aggression against those with whom they have social contact, especially those who appear in the role of competitor, and by the formation of relationships of dependence toward the church, toward the administrators of the island's government, and occasionally toward individual members of the white race.[14]

This, altogether, was a social system of alternating privilege and poverty based on a dual value pattern of class and color, not always readily distinguishable one from the other. Two brief footnotes are worth making on the picture. First, there was clearly present a real feeling of shame, both of color and of culture, in the groups analyzed here. Nothing better illustrated its tremendous secret power than the furious outburst of middle-class indignation that followed the publication in 1944 of Jarvis' book *The Virgin Islands and Their People*, in which both local and New York groups denounced the author for his frank discussion of lower-class folklore beliefs and practices, including somewhat salacious obeah habits. That the local Legislative Assembly should have passed an intemperate resolution (with a single honorable dissent on the part of Valdemar Hill) condemning the book as immoral and stripping the author of his public teaching appointment indicated the presence of a cultural self-hatred and a sentiment of class contempt that made nonsense of the empty rhetoric about racial harmony in the colonial society. Not the least ironic aspect of the episode was that it proved the essential verisimilitude of the Campbell

14. *Daily News*, July 12, 1944.

analysis and, by implication, the inaccuracy of the harmony thesis that Jarvis himself had advanced in the very same book. Nor should the provocative fact be overlooked that the publication of the Campbell monograph, in many ways a far more damning portrait of the society than that drawn by Jarvis, passed almost unnoticed. What an outsider, who was white, American, and formally educated, could do with impunity was apparently forbidden, by the unwritten code of the society, to a local writer-teacher, who was colored and only self-educated.[15]

The second point is that the social situation was a potentially explosive one. This is to challenge yet another myth frequently met with in the literature on the Virgin Islands, clearly related to the myth of polyethnic harmony: in other words, the argument advanced by Jarvis that the mass of the Negro majority were "philosophical enough to accept the fact that they are ineligible for private social privileges that wealthy or official white folk enjoy," especially since, as the author implies, there existed no official segregation of the southern United States brand to sharpen class or racial feelings. Yet the episode, in 1944, of the Beatty case in St. Croix suggests that the pattern of easy social obedience, presumably part of the Danish cultural residue, could readily be upset if sufficiently provoked. The judicial acquittal of Beatty, a southern white gamekeeper, in the murder of a trespassing Negro hunter, and the jailing of two local newspaper editors, Canute Brodhurst and Paul Joseph, for criticisms of the Court's decision, set off a series of popular reactions that patently indicated feelings of class hostility of no small proportions. "What we are witnessing in St. Croix," editorialized the *Daily News* (not the most radical of the local newspapers in any sense), "is an upsurge of the economic slavery to which the masses have been chained for generations. There is a determined aggressiveness on the part of the poverty-stricken majority who want to move beyond the pale of economic distress. The present unrest reflects the impact of privation and suffering. It is a growing rebellion against overlords who dominate the island economically, politically and socially." It indicated "an ugly rift in their social fabric," for which, moreover, the official administration was in large part to be held responsible, since there had existed for some time a close coalition between the administrator, Harry Taylor, and the local "royal families," the Merwins, Skeochs, and Armstrongs. And that the St. Croix Mu-

15. For the Jarvis episode, see J. Antonio Jarvis, *The Virgin Islands and Their People* (Philadelphia: Dorrance, 1944) ; draft of legislative resolution, in *Daily News,* Dec. 18, 1944; *Proceedings of the Legislative Assembly of the Virgin Islands* (St. Thomas) , December 19, 1944; and Allen Grammer, "J. Antonio Jarvis, 1901–1963," *Virgin Islands View,* October, 1965.

nicipal Council had committed the tactical error of petitioning the president to recall the appointment of the judge did not diminish in any way the propriety of the charges.[16]

All this, in sum, was the legacy of the 1930s and the 1940s. But war breaks the crust of custom; and Virgin Islanders, whether they regarded themselves as American citizens or as a colonial people, fully shared in the great expectations set loose by the massive pro-democratic promises of the Allied powers during the war period. The postwar climate of opinion, emphatically radical, touched even Virgin Islanders, traditionally a conservative people. Nothing perhaps better illustrated the changing mood than the enthusiastic welcome that local opinion gave to the more progressive speeches made by the popular leaders—as distinct from the colonial officials—of the wider Caribbean area when they met as delegates in St. Thomas at the West Indian Conference of the Anglo-American Caribbean Commission in 1946. The local press fully applauded the insistence of Albert Marryshow that the real basis of social advance in the area would have to be the needs of organized labor, as well as the stern demand of Grantley Adams that all delegates to future conferences should be popularly elected representatives. And it was suggestive that of the two delegates who voted against postponement of action on Rafael Pico's daring request for the drafting of a charter of human rights and obligations for the Caribbean area, one of them, Roy Gordon, was the Virgin Islands delegate. Some of that press comment, striking a new note in Virgin Islands discussion, traditionally xenophobic, on the place of the territory in the larger Caribbean area, even supported the idea of a regional free-trade area. "After the delegates and Commissioners have been hob-nobbing for three weeks," one editor observed sharply, "it is still a crime for a poor farm boy from Tortola to take a job on an estate here, even though local labor is not interested in this type of work."[17]

But the dream of the Atlantic Charter, of a vast global wave of democratic confraternity sweeping the world, did not last long. The new

16. For the Beatty case, see editorial, *Daily News*, June 20, 1944; the full report of Judge Moore's opinion, *ibid.*, June 24, 1944; and a report of the proceedings of *The People of the Virgin Islands* v. *Brodhurst and Joseph*, in *ibid.*, June 28, 1944. Valdemar Hill correctly notes the significance of the Brodhurst case for the constitutional protection of free speech as guaranteed by the 1936 Organic Act (*A Golden Jubilee: Virgin Islanders on the Go under the American Flag* [New York: Carlton Press, 1967], pp. 77–78).

17. Reports on West Indian Conference in *Daily News*, Feb. 21, 28, Mar. 1, 2, 6, 8, 11, 13, 1946.

world was not around the corner. It had to meet, increasingly, the resistance of the old order. The swift collapse of the short-lived West Indies Federation (1958–62), which had been conceived in part at the St. Thomas 1946 meeting, dramatized in the immediate Caribbean environment the fragility of the concepts of international cooperation and rehabilitation based on social justice and economic reform, not to mention the concept of Pan-Caribbeanism, the *autentica conciencia pancaribe*. The domestic history of the Virgins society during this period is the record of the struggle of the local progressive forces to salvage what they could of social justice and economic reform in their own little bailiwick from the retrogressive pressure of the forces of inertia and tradition, both in Washington and Charlotte Amalie. Inevitably, then, the spirit of international awareness gave way, as it had done before, to an inward-turned localism. This process was accentuated by the restrictive pressures of the American immigration control legislation, which was so illiberal compared to the relatively easygoing immigration policies of the Danish regime. It was possible for some local residents to see that change as the replacement of an older, exciting cosmopolitan quality in the local life by a newer, less pleasing nationalism. "Fear," as Dr. Knud Knud-Hansen put it in his spirited address of 1942 to the Evangelical Lutheran church, "came in the jungle in the shape of Immigration Laws." [18]

The politico-constitutional aspect of the struggle centered, of course, around the prolonged efforts to eliminate the continuing vestiges of colonialism retained in the 1936 Organic Act. For although that long-overdue measure finally granted adult suffrage (with the single exception of an English-language literacy test which in effect disenfranchised a sizable body of resident Puerto Rican voters), it left practically untouched the undemocratic machinery of government. The various hearings and reports of congressional committees and of the Organic Act Committee of the local legislature pinpointed the leading reform items. These amounted, in effect, to four demands: an elective governor, a single legislature, a single treasury, and a resident commissioner in the federal capital. All of them were concerned with strengthening the bargaining power of the islands in the grossly unequal relationship between the popularly elected local parliament and the presidentially appointed chief executive. That required, above all, the effective unification of the islands. Thus a single legislature would force Virgin Islanders to work as a team, compelling them and their elected representatives to rise above their restricted concern with a

18. Address, March 31, 1942, reprinted in *ibid.*, Apr. 9, 1942.

single municipality, which was encouraged by the system of parallel government structures in St. Thomas and St. Croix. An elected governor and a resident commissioner would finally end the continuing humiliation of a system of territorial government that was in reality no system at all, for it was based upon the absence of any clear-cut territorial policy coming out of Washington. As a result of that absence of system, the islanders had to depend, as best they could, upon personal contacts made in the course of official relationships to get the things that should have been granted as a matter of course in terms of a planned future. It meant a personalized system of colonial rule. As one editor observed: "The recipients are often jockeyed into positions where they sometimes lose their self-respect as a people and enslave their future to gain immediate improvements from official friends who operate the political spigot." [19] It was hardly surprising that by 1954, when the promised revisions finally were granted by Congress, Organic Act Day, which had originated as a day of thanksgiving for the 1936 advance, had long since lost its fervor and meaning.

Yet those revisions, when they did come, were cold comfort indeed. For if 1936 was the Virgin Islands Magna Charta, 1954 was hardly the revolution. It was, rather, the counterrevolution. The Revised Organic Act of that year, which is still (1972) the basic constitutional instrument of the territory, not only left unchanged the governor's power of suspensive veto and the president's power of final veto, but actually reduced the previously accredited prerogatives of the elected legislature and increased those of the executive branch. The governor was granted fresh power to appoint administrative assistants for St. Croix and St. John without ratification by the local legislature; was given far-reaching discretionary powers to reorganize the entire administrative machinery; and was offered the additional aid of a new office of government comptroller which would hold the complete audit and settlement authority of all funds of the territorial government. The introduction of a unicameral legislature, seemingly a progressive move, in fact seriously limited existing legislative powers, including the right of legislators to set their own salaries, and was motivated more by considerations of financial retrenchment in government costs than of the extension of local autonomy. The idea of an elective governor was not even considered. The proposal for an elected resident commissioner—heartily endorsed by Representative Fred Crawford in his 1950 report

19. Editorial, *ibid.*, Nov. 26, 1946. See also the able series of articles by Valdemar Hill, "Whither Virgin Islands?," *ibid.*, June 14, 17, 18, 19, 1946. The text of the Organic Act of 1936 can be found in Luther H. Evans, *The Virgin Islands: From Naval Base to New Deal* (Ann Arbor, Mich.: J. W. Edwards, 1945), pp. 327–43.

to the House Public Lands Committee—was turned down. So was the recommendation of the extremely mild report of 1946 by the Organic Act Reform Committee of the local legislature that the presidential veto power should be replaced with the device of an annual congressional review. Taken as a whole, the Organic Act of 1954 was a piece of retrogressive congressional legislation which, in effect, as Senator Earle Ottley charged from St. Thomas, meant the virtual abolition of the territorial legislature and rested upon the assumption, as former Governor Morris de Castro (hardly a revolutionary) told Congress later, that the ills of democracy could be cured by less democracy.

The heart and center of all this, naturally, was the office of the governor. The political history of the period thus inevitably became a series of bitter and prolonged battles between the legislature and successive gubernatorial appointees, following the general West Indian pattern. The battles have by now become part of the local political folklore; first, with the Democratic nominees, Governors William Hastie (1946–50) and Morris de Castro (1950–54), and then with the string of Republican nominees, Governors Archie Alexander (1954–55), Walter Gordon (1955–58), and John Merwin (1958–61). Each of them arrived with the promise of a "new day" for the islands; each ended his term of office a sadder, if not wiser, man. Improvements were, of course, gradually made in the technique of nomination. Thus the Hastie appointment signaled an advance in that for the first time Virgin Islanders were invited to express their opinion of a candidate by being invited to testify at the congressional confirmation hearings, while the de Castro appointment was followed, again for the first time, by a full report from the new governor to his constituency on his activities in Washington. But those were marginal improvements only. They left untouched the basic flaw in the situation, the certainty of conflict between a weak legislature and an irresponsible executive; such a system was bound to produce discord and frustration as its natural products. The best of intentions, the most noble of imperial sentiments on the part of governors generally anxious to do well by the islanders, withered in the poisoned climate of the system. A local student of the system, who had worked within its framework, shrewdly observed:

In the heart of every legislator can be found resentment in some degree or other, which is a reflection of the sentiment of the people for the most part. Every governor is conscious of his almost absolute powers, a part of which is dressed up to appear milder than it actually is; while, on the other hand, every legislator is equally conscious of what the democratic rights of the people ought to be, but which rights are sadly missing. This arrangement of substance and shadow makes it only natural that the appointed governor is looked upon as the personification of all grievances. If the governor is competent it merely allays the situation for a while, and when he is obviously an incompetent administrator coals are added to the fire.[20]

One result of the system was a dangerous discontinuity of general policy, save what was imposed by the Interior officialdom. "Each new governor," the local press complained, "brings his own plans and policies. From Pearson to Hastie the policy of all the governors has been different. There has been no continuity in action based on an established plan. With each new appointment the islands are jolted by new approaches to old problems, some of them very costly and detrimental to the best interests of the inhabitants." [21]

What particular expression policy took naturally depended upon accidents of personality and current issues. The early Pearson regime had shown how easily a colonial appointment could become the graveyard of liberal reputations. Governor Hastie avoided a similar interment only because of his marriage to the daughter of the local Lockhart merchant family and his liberalism, which happened to coincide with the progressivism of the new brand of local political leadership based on the popular franchise; these factors gave him a position of insular strength which Pearson had lacked. But even Governor Hastie could not avoid unpleasant disagreements with the legislative majority over such issues as the implementation of an extended merit system of personnel administration based on the recommendations of the Public Administration Service of Chicago, the introduction of such a system being a prerequisite to the extension to the islands of such lucrative federal grants as those relating to child and maternity services under Title V of the Social Security Act. Success in channeling federal monies to the local scene could always guarantee immediate popularity for a governor. But, as Governor Harwood had found out, such funds could only alleviate the basic problem; they could not permanently resolve it.

Governor de Castro, by contrast, was caught up in the financial crisis brought about by the accumulating impact of postwar events, such as the closure of the submarine base and the end of the wartime demand for rum, which necessitated unpopular measures such as the suspension of the overtime provisions of the Wage and Hour Amendment Act. This general situation was exacerbated by the fact that, coming to the governorship from the field of administration, de Castro was the classical civil servant's governor, with all of the virtues and

20. Carlos Downing, "The Dilemma of the Virgins," *Daily News,* Jan. 18, 1958.
21. Editorial, *ibid.,* Jan. 12, 1950.

limitations of the civil service mind. His inaugural address, in which he spoke about the need for "intelligent planning" to combat "wasteful spending," with an eye to reducing dependence on the federal government, was bound to clash head on with a spending psychology that had been encouraged in Virgin Islanders by long-standing federal government policies. The almost immediate result was another typical budget struggle between governor and legislative councilors. Typically, as de Castro's local liberal backing waned, his congressional conservative backing increased. The final commentary on his period in office was Senator Butler's congratulatory letter of 1954 in which the powerful chairman of the senate Interior and Insular Affairs Committee apologized to the governor for believing that the Virgin Islander had been an unrealistic supporter of the "handouts" psychology and reiterated his own conviction that the parlous economic condition of the territory was not so much due to insufficient natural resources as it was to the lack of industry and initiative of the local population.[22]

The succeeding string of Republican-nominated governors during the 1954–61 period added to all of these normal difficulties the aggravating factor of the discrepancy between the new Republican climate of opinion in Washington under the Eisenhower regime and the prevailing Democratic sympathies of the islands. In one way, of course, it was not altogether a Republican-engineered change, since as early as 1946 the Ickes resignation (which lost to the islands one of their best friends at court, despite his irascibility of temperament) had signalized the return of "big business" to political power in Washington. What the unfortunate Alexander appointment did was to bring home to Virgin Islanders what that really meant. For if Pearson had been the Pennsylvania Puritan in the colonial Babylon, Alexander was a midwestern Babbitt who brought all the values of small-town America to the Caribbean. A contractor-engineer from Des Moines, Iowa, he seems to have collected his initial views on the island problems by reading an article in *Life* magazine, while his record as a past grand polemarch of the Kappa Alpha Psi fraternity enabled him to advance the thesis that the solution to the islanders' problems was for them "to go to work and tighten their belts." An openly contemptuous attitude toward the local people, a brash manner more befitting a gang foreman than a diplomat, and a complete inability to comprehend the subtleties

22. For Governor Hastie, see *Annual Report of the Governor of the Virgin Islands to the Secretary of the Interior, 1947* (Washington, D.C.: Government Printing Office, 1947). For Governor de Castro, see text of Inaugural Address, in *Daily News*, Mar. 27, 28, 1950; exchange of correspondence between the governor and the chairman of the St. Thomas and St. John Municipal Council, in *ibid.*, July 6, 8, 10, 1950; and Senator Butler to the governor, in *ibid.*, Jan. 28, 1954.

of West Indian social intercourse completed the picture. It was unfortunate, then, that his brief tenure coincided with the implementation of the new, unpopular Revised Organic Act (1954), leading to one of the bitterest executive-legislative encounters in local history, including dubious efforts by the governor to circumvent, by illegal devices, the confirmation powers of the Council. It was characteristic, finally, of the American business mentality that Alexander should have left behind him a minor scandal involving his use of the governor's office and its powers to further the financial interests of some of his business cronies from Des Moines with respect to a contract for the Charlotte Amalie waterfront highway project; this reportedly was the real cause of his being quietly relieved of his appointment by alarmed Interior officials. The slanderous picture that *Time* magazine constructed out of all this, of a "sluggish" and "backward" colonial people being brought smartly to attention by a hardheaded business executive, brought protests from Virgin Islanders as diverse in their political philosophies as Ashley Totten and Morris de Castro.[23]

Much of this, it is worth noting, belied the expectations that the way out of the general legislative-executive problem lay in the appointment of a native governor or, failing that, a continental Negro governor. Neither idea was sound. The record of the two native governors—de Castro and Merwin—rapidly disabused the territory of the validity of the first idea. Both of them were upper-class conservatives who preached the anachronistic virtues of a Herbert Spencer-like economic individualism. Both inevitably clashed with an electorate and a popular legislative leadership who had come to believe that the most important function of the governor was to lobby for increased federal appropriations. Both were lukewarm in their ideas for further local autonomy within the federal system; both were at best timid supporters of the concept of the welfare state. Both of them, it is true, had a personal identification with their people that no outsider could possess. But the colonial character of the office they occupied, as well as the divided loyalty that it necessarily caused, effectively prohibited the possibility of their gradual emergence as genuinely representative and

23. Hearings of the U.S. Senate Committee on Interior and Insular Affairs, printed in *ibid.*, Mar. 22, 23, 24, 25, 1954; the struggle over the implementation of the Revised Organic Act, in *ibid.*, Jan. 10, Mar. 16, Apr. 21, 22, May 6, 7, July 11, 1954; text of opinion of special counsel to the legislature of the Virgin Islands, in *ibid.*, May 5, 7, 1955; *Virgin Islands Report—Relative to Investigation and Hearings in the Virgin Islands with Reference to the Proposed Revision of the Organic Act and the Governmental, Economic, and Fiscal Structure in the Islands, with Recommendations on the Federally Owned Virgin Islands Corporation* (Washington, D.C.: Government Printing Office, 1954) ; and text of letter of Senator Butler to Governor de Castro, in *Daily News*, Jan. 28, 1954.

popular chief executives after the fashion of the American presidency.

The record of the continental Negro governors (Hastie, Alexander, and Gordon) was equally disappointing, especially to those analysts of the local scene who believed that the real problem was racial. The fact that both Hastie and Gordon were liberals with a fine record in the Negro civil rights movement did not diminish the fact that they both owed their appointments to a patronage system that was designed to pay off political debts and that was unofficially controlled, in the case of Negro assignments, by Representative William Dawson, the powerful vice-chairman of the Democratic National Committee. More particularly, however, there was the fact, so crucial to an understanding of the general relationships between Virgin Islands Negroes and mainland Negroes, that historically the attitudes of the two groups on the "race problem," because of a dissimilar development of race relations, have been peculiarly different. A colored majority in the islands did not need, like the colored minority in the United States, an aggressive race consciousness to feel their worth; thus they felt more kindly toward white persons, and correspondingly refused to accept the classification of Negro and white prevalent in the United States. The general result was that their internal politics were based on alignments difficult for a member of the NAACP (like Governor Gordon) to understand; for, as a visiting Negro correspondent noted ironically in 1946, the islanders would rally as quickly to Senator Bilbo as they would to Vice-President Henry Wallace provided the Mississippi racist offered them a panacea for their immediate woes. All of this was naturally difficult for the American Negro progressive to understand, and it is worth noting that it was spelled out in warning tones by a Virgin Islands publicist for Hastie as early as 1937 when he was initially appointed to his judgeship in the Virgin Islands District Court.[24]

Neither a native governor nor a Negro appointee from the States could, in and of himself, solve a dilemma that was overwhelmingly caused by the unworkable machinery of a colonial governmental system. He could not, in and of himself, add to the stature of the local government from a democratic viewpoint, nor could he eradicate the fatal dualism of his office. That could be seen from the fact that some of the most acrimonious executive-legislative vendettas of the period occurred under such appointees. The Gordon governorship witnessed a fierce trial of strength over the question of the gubernatorial veto, ending in a ludicrous situation in which, the insular Senate having overridden that veto, the president of the United States was called upon,

24. Geraldo Guirty, in *The Emancipator*, Mar. 10, 1937.

in effect, to determine the exact location of comfort stations in the Manning's Bay race track area of St. Croix. The Merwin governorship, in its turn, was hardly an exercise in mass popularity. The same period witnessed the resurgence of the method of the mass protest march on Government House on a scale not known since the struggle of 1935. The result, only too often, was that a governor, feeling he was not wanted, turned spitefully against the people he had thought, frequently with real sincerity, to serve. Nor were matters improved when the Interior Department elected to intervene to save its appointee. The crass intervention, indeed, of the unpopular Lausi-Edwards team in 1956 only served to underline the truth that no governor, however able, could be better than the Interior officialdom permitted him to be. The petulant letters that Secretary Seaton sent to Ron de Lugo and Valdemar Hill in 1958 show the depths of furious self-righteousness to which that officialdom could descend in its conviction that a generous guardian in Washington was being badly treated by impertinent and ungrateful colonials.[25] The postwar period thus ended, as it had begun, with the colony still denied the elective governorship which many of the insular leaders considered the only valid prescription of cure for their malaise.

Since politics is always a function of social structure, the social aspects of the political developments merit a special notice. For the Organic Act of 1936 not only brought civil government to the islands, but it also changed overnight the social basis of politics and government. The twenty-five years that followed its passage—or, to be more exact, the first elections to be held under its mass suffrage rules, in 1938—witnessed a quiet transformation in which politics, like education, became a new avenue of social mobility. A condition in which the combined voting lists of the islands contained the names of less than 500 qualified voters, roughly 1/35th of the population, and in which candidates for legislative office were frequently assured of victory on the strength of as few as twenty votes, was replaced with a system of wholly elected legislatures based on universal suffrage. The changes effected in Virgin Islands life were profound and far-reaching. They precipitated new

25. See, for all this, letters of Secretary of Interior Seaton to Valdemar Hill and Ron de Lugo, in *Daily News*, Mar. 10, 11, 1958, and text of radio address by Senator Earle B. Ottley, in *ibid.*, June 26, 27, 1956. It is worth noting that almost the only voice raised in Congress against the general attitude of the Washington bureaucracy to the Virgin Islanders was that of Representative Adam Clayton Powell. See his letter to Assistant Secretary of Interior Aandahl, March 28, 1958, quoted in Hill, *A Golden Jubilee*, p. 163.

relationships among politics, social class, sex, and color that have not yet perhaps run their full course. The main outlines, however, were fairly well defined by 1960.

Some of the changes were only minor. The elimination of the old Danish sex qualifications, for example, did not unleash a suffragette movement, and it was not until 1956 that the first woman legislator appeared in the person of Senator Lucinda Millin. Other changes were major factors in the gradually expanding democratization of insular life. A political career, to begin with, was thrown open to larger social segments, and the 1938 elections marked the point at which the older groups (the landed gentry, the town burghers, the government officials) gave way to the figures of the union leader, the newspaper editor, the college-educated youth, the smaller businessman and property owner. The Councils, then, mainly in St. Thomas but even in St. Croix, gradually became more representative of the population, which was reflected in the wider range of personality and individual idiosyncrasy of their members. A pen sketch of the St. Thomas Council in 1944 played teasingly on that theme, distinguishing between members like the rough-hewn Councilman Rhymer, who hated clothes, and those like Oswald Harris, "the man from the gut," who liked fine clothes so much that he was known to have changed suits three times a day, or between business-type members like Ralph Paiewonsky, replete with cigar and bankroll, and those like Roy Gordon, who frequently spent an entire morning composing a paragraph.[26] However, what might have become a new political individualism on the part of these new men, a mode of seeking entry into the reserved precincts of upper-class strongholds, was held in check by the growth at the same time of organized party politics. That was the story, over the years, of the Progressive Guide (the islands' first political group, founded in 1937), later transmuted into the Unity Party, which forced through the progressive legislation of the war years—the new school law, the Workmen Compensation Bill, and the Wages and Hours Act—and which went on to provide a younger, more socially minded popular leadership: Earle Ottley, Valdemar Hill, Omar Brown, Carlos Downing, Henry Richards, Oswald Harris, Roy Gordon. On some issues they were admittedly illiberal, as the shameful behavior of their legislative group on the Jarvis book issue of 1944 demonstrated. At their best, however, they brought a new note of social idealism and group responsibility into the territorial life. Whereas earlier governors could argue with some plausibility that their

---

26. "Clocking the Town" column, *Daily News*, Aug. 15, 1944.

legislative critics were only individuals, with no popular mandate, the post-1938 governors were denied that rationalization.

To put it another way, before the mass suffrage period the anti-colonial struggle was preeminently carried on by the lonely and isolated individual fighter, which was essentially the definition of the lives of Rothschild Francis, Hamilton Jackson, Lionel Roberts, and even the semi-legendary Romeo L. Dougherty, "The Sage of Union Hall Street," who, as one of the first Negro sports writers of national stature, used his influence early on to fight the racist government of the Navy. Later on the struggle became the charge of the organized political party espousing a coherent program and running electoral slates of candidates. The independent was replaced by the "machine," and Lionel Roberts' outburst of 1946 against the Progressive Guide type of "irresponsible and polluted politics," which, as he saw it, could only be ended by a return to Navy rule, was a *cri de coeur* of the old school of politicians against the new. The individual leader who had attempted over the years to lead by force of example or private personality—Alton Adams, for example, or Jarvis—was bypassed, sometimes unkindly, by the new collective forces. The same process also witnessed at this time the end of the era of the expatriate leader like Caspar Holstein, who for twenty-five years or so had used his wealth to help finance the early lobbying efforts in Washington after 1917, or Ashley Totten, who, for all of his authoritarian methods in the various organizations he controlled, had done so much in New York and Washington for the Virgin Islands cause.[27] Those outsiders had remained as real forces because they had been able to argue that the domestic leadership in the islands was either weak or socially reactionary. The rise of a strong democratic domestic political leadership finally terminated their influence, but not before the perennial exchanges between the "insiders" and the "outsiders" had contributed to Virgin Islands political literature some of its most colorful pages.

This transfiguration of politics was the surface expression of more profound subterranean changes, particularly in the areas of color relationships and education. The expansion of middle-sector opportunities in the economy created an enlarged colored middle class whose members were the fruit of the first generation of American-style schooling. The scale of the changes that they brought about by their elevation— which amounted to an almost complete turnover of personnel in the local "governing class," as distinct from the local "ruling class" in the

27. For Caspar Holstein, see obituary notice, *ibid.*, Apr. 8, 20, 1944. For Ashley Totten, see Ralph J. Bough, "Champion of Evils that Oppress Masses," *ibid.*, Mar. 20, 21, 1946, and editorial, *ibid.*, Feb. 1, 1946.

economic sector—can perhaps be gauged by the absolute ferocity with which the old white oligarchy resisted the changes. The wild charges of the continental "old hands" that were presented to Senator Butler's committee during the hearings on the revision of the Organic Act during 1953 and 1954 were typical. The resistance, of course, was that of a soured and malicious group of Negrophobes almost certain to fail, and their frenzied attempt in 1946 to sabotage the appointment of Governor Hastie was perhaps their last serious effort at direct political influence. That effort was so clumsy in its methods that the insular Chamber of Commerce felt constrained to cable Washington a strongly worded repudiation of its star performer, Leslie Hunt, as a representative of the business community as a whole, thus in effect disavowing its own official spokesman.[28]

This period witnessed, then, a distinctly visible change in the social and racial complexion of the political leadership. Equally dramatic was the entry of the same new group of native professional talent into the administrative machinery of government. Ever since the post-1919 political agitation had boldly attacked American imperialism in Haiti and applauded the struggle of the Indian Nationalist Congress against British imperialism, the idea of the seizure of local public administration by qualified local men had been a leading element in the propagandist literature; on a more narrow scale that, too, was the meaning of the early struggle of the Councils to retain their administrative commissions. At first, it was a claim put forward for the Virgin Islander who, usually without formal education, had done well in business. Later on, it became a brief for the college-educated professional person. As early as 1917 the American consul in St. Thomas had been a Negro, and even earlier, in 1904, Washington had appointed a Negro, Albert Van Harn, to the same post under the Danish regime. The rapid expansion of the bureaucratic machinery in the World War II period accelerated the process, as the new names in government service and appointments to all kinds of agencies and commissions showed: Jacob Robles as local OPA director, Malcolm Jackson as OPA rationing officer, Jarvis, Mylner, and Lockhart to the Selective Service Boards, and so on. As far as the ranking federal posts were concerned, the long tenure of Alvaro de Lugo in the St. Thomas postmastership established it almost as a Virgin Islands sinecure, and by the end of the war posts as assorted as those of legal adviser to the governor, commis-

28. Hearings of the U.S. Senate Territories Committee on the nomination of William Henry Hastie for Virgin Islands governorship, reprinted in *ibid.*, Mar. 23, 24, 29, 30, Apr. 3, 4, 5, 6, 10, 15, 16, 20, 1946.

sioner of finance, federal judge, government attorney, chief of police, and acting police judge were filled by colored persons.

The top posts, of course, remained immune to this nationalization process and continued to be filled by the "imported aristocracy" assailed by the critics. The appointment of Alexander as governor in 1954 served as a warning that Washington did not regard the appointment of a native candidate (as in the case of de Castro) as a binding precedent and that the office would continue to be used as an instrument for the payment of pressing political debts. Harry Taylor, as administrator of St. Croix, continued to hold his own as the most unpopular official in the islands, while administrator Arthur Hughes in St. John treated his appointment as a rest cure for an aging invalid. The strategic post of director of police remained more or less a continental stronghold, while the rapid turnover in leadership of the Department of Education, and sometimes the lack of it for years at a time, illustrated the chronic insecurity of a post that was subject to review by each new governor. Nevertheless, the principle involved here— that local talent should fill local posts—being thoroughly American, was certain to win out in the end, and by 1959, when Alton Adams came to assess the working out of the principle in practice, it was possible to claim that the local government was a remarkable tribute to the genius of the Virgin Islands career public servant: Roy Anduze, Percy de Jongh, Morris de Castro, Roy Bornn, V. F. Daniel, Dr. Axel Hansen, Calvin Wheatley, Mario Lewis, Pedrito Francois, Leo Penha, and many others. Thus was effectively ended the fiction that a Virgin Islands background was insufficient for the task of governmental administration, giving the lie to those outsiders, frequently aided by some natives, who had taken sadistic pleasure in belittling local abilities.[29]

All this, finally, must be seen within the context of the general economic problem which had been only temporarily relieved by the wartime prosperity. Official policy continued to emphasize welfare expenditure, leaving basically untouched the production system of private ownership. Agricultural reform, as before, lagged. One example was the new plan to develop cattle raising in St. Croix, as distinct from expanded crop production, which simply had the consequence of reinforcing an unequal distribution of land ownership without seriously increasing employment possibilities: the largest landowner on the island

29. Alton A. Adams, president, Virgin Islands Hotel Association, speech printed in *Home Journal* (St. Thomas), Jan. 17, 1959.

held approximately 10 per cent of the land but employed only 2 per cent of the working population, despite an imaginative cattle-raising program. A 1954 report estimated that some 40 per cent of the land in the islands was still owned by twelve individuals or firms, divided into special groups, indifferent heirs of old landed barons, and individuals who did not depend on income from their estates.[30] Nor was the Virgin Islands Corporation scheme, operating on a new federal charter after 1948, any real challenge to this situation, for it was run on private enterprise rather than on public service principles, with the result that the large property owners who wanted Congress to sell it to private capital were not in any sense endangered by its cooperative facade. By 1950, indeed, it was clear that the board of directors, responding to Washington pressures, was concerned primarily with making a profit so as to create a favorable impression on a conservative Congress. Another factor was that most of the key managerial positions were in Puerto Rican hands and the corporation appeared to be rapidly turning into an appendage of the Puerto Rican Reconstruction Administration, designed to provide employment for imported Puerto Rican workers who would eventually absorb any social effort which the company made. The provision of the new Organic Act of 1954 that guaranteed matching funds for the local treasury from the exportation of rum finally granted to the islands a privilege long held by Puerto Rico, and provided welcome fiscal relief, but at the same time it had the result, from the social viewpoint, of tying Crucian productive effort even more intimately to sugar. A sugar-based economy, furthermore, for St. Croix as much as for Puerto Rico, had to face the hard fact that any concessions from Washington, with respect to refining rights, for example, depended on the good will of the mainland sugar interests who reportedly, when united, could command 50 per cent of the votes in the U.S. Senate.

Inescapably, then, the territorial economy had to turn to the metropolitan economy. That, of course, had been the New Deal "pump-priming" policy. Its post-1945 expression, however, took on new forms. In the first place, the old idea of direct public-works relief expenditures was replaced with the new concept of sharing in the regional expenditures of the vastly expanded postwar federal administrative state, and especially of sharing in the massive expenditures of the Defense Department as New Deal America became, sometime after 1950 or so, the America of the "warfare state." The proper policy for

30. Report of the U.S. Senate Committee on Interior and Insular Affairs, reprinted in *Daily News,* May 10, 1954; and editorial, *ibid.,* May 11, 1954.

(116)

the Virgin Islands planners, it was felt by some Virgin Islanders who testified at various congressional hearings, should be one of actively soliciting Washington for the establishment of permanent naval installations and military training camps as an economically advantageous method of development, a policy already actively followed by cities in the United States. The Navy could thus be brought back to the islands, but without the danger of allowing their administrative affairs to revert to naval control. Second, there was a new emphasis upon the Virgin Islands economy as an integral part of the American social welfare state which, for all the American talk about the "folklore of capitalism," consolidated itself after 1945 as a permanent feature of the American way of life. Public policy in Charlotte Amalie increasingly became one of persuading Congress of Virgin Islands eligibility for a legitimate share of welfare-state benefits. To implement that policy it was necessary to create an effective public relations machine to withstand the attacks of congressional enemies who argued, more and more, that the territorial economy was a pampered economy. Such attacks were sufficiently persuasive that Congress set up, in the form of the new office of U.S. comptroller, a federal watchdog over all federal and territorial expenditures with no accountability to the local government or electorate.

It could be plausibly argued that all this amounted to a continuation, under more sophisticated forms, of the traditional reliance upon Uncle Sam with its resultant dependency complex, thereby perpetuating, as Lionel Roberts had warned earlier, the "dangers of a reverie still held closely to the bosom of our prominent citizens, that keep them in hopeless expectation, waiting for the return of the days that made St. Thomas a Singapore, of those of the former Danish Government by paternalism, or even the continuation of Federal Appropriation in large amounts." [31] That might have been so. But the fact is that by the time the decade of the 1950s came to a close the policies outlined here had become firmly entrenched and the Caribbean dependency was a fairly well-advanced specimen of welfare-state colonialism. Federal planning was consumption- rather than production-oriented, while revenue-earning capacity was increasingly that of the growing tourist private enterprise sector. Economic policy, in its turn, impinged on social structure. On one hand, the federal welfare spending program, combined with a matching local program, had the effect of strengthening and enlarging the public sector of the governmental and administra-

31. Lionel Roberts, Sr., "Educating the Masses," *ibid.*, Anniversary Issue, Aug. 1, 1933.

tive machinery, thereby consolidating the new power of the native middle-class groups of political leaders and government officials and their allies in the light-skinned professions. On the other hand, the growing importance of tourism helped create a new power bloc in the form of the white continental entrepreneurs in the hotel industry and its subsidiary services. Frequently at loggerheads with each other, those two groups, native and alien, possessed a bond of common interest in the power that they wielded over the variegated groups of the working population. That triangular arrangement of forces was to become, increasingly, the key to the Virgin Islands future.

Part Two

THE PRESENT

5

~~~

The Economy

It is evident, from all that has been said, that looked at in large historical perspective the Virgin Islands economy, as it stands today, is the end result of a set of general processes that have taken place over the last century and a half or so. The original grandeur of St. Thomas as the great commercial and banking center of the New World—even the Rothschilds had a branch office in the port—was based on conditions which, in the long run, were certain to disappear or decline in importance. Technological advances in maritime transportation, changes in the routes of ocean traffic, the development of South America, the growing use of fuel oil, the advent of radio communications, along with the disappearance of sugar and rum as exports, all combined to bring about the decline of that earlier commanding position. The one hundred and fifty years after Waterloo can thus be seen, in retrospect, as a prolonged period of steady erosion of the foundations of the islands' prosperity, attested to by the uninterrupted decline in commerce and population. A population which had already declined to 43,000 in 1835 had dwindled still further to 22,000 in 1930; in St. Croix alone a population, according to Oxholm's old map of 1799, of roughly 29,000 at that time had gone down to 13,000 by 1903. Islands like St. John, where sugar cane once flourished, became empty wildernesses, and St. Thomas itself became a relatively unimportant way station in world maritime trade.

The significance of this was not fully appreciated. The historic decline of the economy was the progressive product of world changes taking place relentlessly for a century or more. But local opinion preferred to believe that it was due to temporary conditions, such as Emancipation, or, later on, to U.S. ownership and congressional legislation. Local interests campaigned, therefore, for "remedies" that in fact were delusional—artificial props for sugar, new statute laws to favor rum production, the bringing in of a dry dock, or a change in coastwise shipping laws. They failed to see that the situation was one of endemic malaise due to changing global conditions, in which the contribution of U.S. control and legislation, and even of the world-wide economic depression after 1929, were minimal only, and certainly not the major operational factors. They did not fully appreciate that Virgin Islands economic history could be seen, in one way, as nothing much more than an irregular series of runs of good fortune, the result of a superficial play of forces over which the islanders had no real control, save for the fact that they could not help benefiting from its fortuitous offerings. They were blind, then, to the threatening implications of the general economic instability of the islands, and in large measure heedless of the irresistible succession of events which were ultimately to destroy the house of cards of their prosperity.

The real problem of the present-day economy is to determine whether it is simply the latest upsurge in the traditional "boom and bust" colonial economy or a new stage in economic development emancipated from the thralldom of the general phenomena here described. A proper analysis would have to determine, as far as it is possible to do so, the temporary symptoms and the permanent causes of the territorial well-being. It would seek to assess both the necessity and the natural limits of adaptation, in habits and attitudes, to the new conditions of the general character of the world economy. More particularly, since the local economy is more and more integrated with the U.S. economy, it would be obliged to determine what constitutes both the advantages and the hazards of that relationship, and if, in fact, there exist any viable alternatives within the general Caribbean–Latin American framework which Virgin Islands economic planning might seriously investigate.

The decade of the 1960s has seen the gradual emergence of an expansionist economy in the territory. Statistics in a series of strategic sectors—banking activities, flotation of general obligation bonds, tourist expenditures, cruise-ship traffic, house ownership, consumer expenditures, industrial location, Planning Board approvals of residential lots, levels of governmental activity in the public spending sector as evidenced in the growing numbers of purchase orders processed by the Department of Property and Procurement—testify to the astonishing explosion of economic prosperity that has taken place within less than a decade. An index from the federal government sector—the postal receipts at the Charlotte Amalie Post Office—further illustrates the commercial and residential growth accompanying all of this. It is interesting to note that that office may have a postal distinction in being the largest per capita user of airmail facilities within the federal system as a whole, a position enhanced by the fact that it is in addition a mail receiving point for the residents of the British Virgin Islands and a mailing point for tourist boats touching St. Thomas. It is a full-employment, even a surplus-employment, economy; so that whereas Puerto Rico (where the scourge of large-scale unemployment still remains) is a person-exporting economy, the Virgin Islands are a person-importing economy, as the statistics of alien workers in the leading employment sectors (some 30 per cent of an estimated work force of 45,000) graphically show. In an economy where, in 1966, only 0.23 per cent of workers covered by the unemployment insurance program were unemployed it is obvious that poverty, which does exist, is due to factors other than the unavailability of jobs. If, indeed, the statistics of the U.S. Census for 1960 and the more recent figures of the Virgin Islands Employment Security Agency are put together it is evident that there must be somewhere between 3,000 and 5,500 men and women workers following the Virgin Islands practice of "moonlighting," that is, working in more than one job. The main factor there, of course, is a relatively low wage level in an inflationary high-cost economy. But the practice indicates that the jobs are there, waiting to be filled. The general feeling of social optimism engendered by such an economy is evident in the extravagant self-congratulatory tone of the official literature.

The mainstays of this prosperity are tourism and tourist-induced services, government, industry, and agriculture. Of these, agriculture is the weakest, especially with the final termination of sugar-cane farming in 1965 when federal subsidies ended. The replacement of sugar with diversified farming built on the interinsular marketing of produce remains problematical, owing to the all but total absence of natural resources, inadequate moisture supply, a growing preference for imported canned foodstuffs fostered by the new supermarkets, and the traditional antipathy of the Virgin Islander to the land and the social values that historically it has stood for. After that comes the manufacturing sector, which employed, as of May, 1967, some 1,890 workers, primarily in textile factories and plants assembling watches, thermometers, and costume jewelry; these plants were attracted in part by a Puerto Rican–style industrial incentive program and in part by the duty-free provisions of the U.S. tariff legislation. In addition, there are the new Harvey alumina plant and the Hess petroleum refinery in St. Croix, which promise both to build up a heavy industrial base for the economy and to help St. Croix

(123)

recapture her old preeminence in the three-islands complex. The territorial government, in turn, looked at now as an employer, acts as an important income-creating component. Since it directly employs (as of May, 1967) a total of 5,593 work personnel, roughly one-quarter of the total labor force, and disburses a massive public sector expenditure, which increased from $10.1 million in 1960 to $27.7 million in 1965, it obviously constitutes a vital generator in a Keynesian economy. Whether it also constitutes, as many of its critics variously argue, a patronage spoils system of the old style or a socialistic public employment system of the new style is, from the economic viewpoint, irrelevant.

There is, finally, the lucrative tourist industry, which in 1966 broke all records by bringing to the islands more than 600,000 tourists, who spent something like $60 million on their various purchases. It is no accident that the Department of Commerce, which is the local administrative department that looks after the tourist promotion program, is the prime governmental source of fostering the local economy and that, by report, over 50 per cent of the revenues necessary for the operation of all local governmental activities is derived from the multitude of primary and ancillary businesses operating tourist activities. Tourism, in effect, is the main invisible export of the characteristically export economy of the territory. One statistic alone—the increase in hotels and guest houses, so much a part now of the local physical and social scene, from 11 in 1946 to 84 in 1962—tells the story. Many of the fortunes of the Virgin Islands class of "new rich" have been made, typically, in the tourist-generated fields of real estate and construction operations.

All this overwhelmingly influences how Virgin Islanders live and work. Their scale of occupational preferences indicates clearly that the most socially prestigious jobs are those in the governmental sector and the tourist-dominated trade and service industries. The fact that a large section of the labor force is employed in government offices might explain why no great advances have been made in the field of labor relations, and it might also explain the general immaturity of the labor movement in the economy. It is equally honorific to be a gift-shop clerk, a hotel receptionist, or an airline hostess (the leading airline serving the islands, Caribair, recently waived its trilingual requirements in order to recruit local girls who did not speak French). The taxicab driver enjoys a status peculiar to himself, all the more so since government regulations have frozen entry into the occupation, which in 1967 was limited to 819 badges in St. Thomas and 587 in St. Croix. The bartender also can always strike a good bargain for himself, and when Governor Paiewonsky sought to dismiss criticism of his administration by the president of the St. Croix Chamber of Commerce by remarking disdainfully that that particular continental had started his Virgin Islands career by working as a bartender at the Buccaneer Hotel he was not making a point likely to be supported by local opinion. There is clearly at work here a traditional prejudice which sees the overt prestige attached to particular jobs as being even more important than financial reward. Jarvis commented in 1944 on the great eagerness of comparatively uneducated women to become stenographers and clerks, and that the bias is not dying out is evident from the Job Opportunity Survey of 1958, which noted the almost complete absence of skilled workers in almost all job classes from machinists and chambermaids to automotive mechanics and carpenters.[1]

Some of this, it is true, is now changing with the advent of advanced industrial technology in the oil and aluminum sectors. There has been a noticeable increase in courses given in industrial vocational education at the Virgin Islands College campuses. College graduates are becoming interested in the industrial employment field, as well as in the burgeoning field of ecology control and environmental studies. The construction industry is giving rise (as in Puerto Rico) to workers who drive to work in their own cars and sport their hard hats off the job as status symbols. New jobs that involve something more than just sitting behind a desk emerge: telephone workers, electricians, boat mechanics, dental assistants. Too, as the Puerto Rican woman enters employment in the Crucian shops and factories she begins to break down (again, as in Puerto Rico itself) the oppressive psychological and social burden of male chauvinism, the Puerto Rican *machismo* syndrome. But before all this is accepted as proof that a fundamental reshaping of the islands' occupational structure is taking place, including the growth of an American-style labor aristocracy, certain considerations must be kept in mind. There is, first, the fact that, being capital-oriented enterprises, both Hess Oil and Harvey Alumina offer very minimal employment opportunities. There is, second, the fact that both of them actively discriminate against natives in their hiring policies: as of 1971, only 80 out of a total of 425 Harvey workers were natives, while natives constituted no more than 15 per cent of Hess's work force. There is, in the third place, the fact that at the middle and upper employment levels there is a decided preference for expatriate personnel; thus the Hess and Harvey compounds begin to look like examples of North American company towns, characterized by varying degrees of racial segregationist patterns, that have sprung up all over the Caribbean after the model of the bauxite company town of MacKenzie in Guyana. The impact of the Hess and Harvey complexes, this is to

1. Virgin Islands, Employment Service, *Job Opportunity Survey* (St. Thomas, March, 1958), pp. 17–19.

say, is still minimal. And, characteristically, the evidence for that conclusion was in large part presented by the 1971 report of a visiting subcommittee of the House Interior and Insular Affairs Committee.[2]

The bias, then, against manual labor still remains pretty strong. It is a bias, of course, that stems historically from the equation of manual labor with slavery. It survives today with almost all its old virulence because of an elaborate machinery of job selection which awards the socially degrading job to the alien and the socially elevating job to the native or the continental. This system helps to explain the continuing resistance to all programs of vocational education in the school system, which in turn helps to perpetuate the paradox in which a surplus-employment economy must continuously import its skilled labor. The growing importance of the tourist and industry sectors, together with the traditionally urban quality of Virgin Islands life—it is suggestive that so unimportant is the distinction between town and countryside that Charlotte Amalie is virtually St. Thomas and the two names are interchangeable in popular parlance—means also that agricultural labor is regarded as the most menial of all. That can be seen most graphically in the final collapse of the old dream of a prosperous Virgin Islands rural commonwealth, usually purveyed by American liberal reformers, summed up in the 1927 assertion of one of them that "The islands are not well served by a system of education that points the laborer away from the islands in the direction of Harlem. The negro has learned enough about politics, oratory, sociology and race equality to last him for some time. What he needs is an education that will assist him to raise vegetables and small crops against the time when the land may become available to him."[3] It would be difficult today to find an islander who would not scorn that idea. He is increasingly urban-oriented as the job structure becomes more sophisticated.

The whole employment situation, of course, is closely related to the commanding position of tourism. Geographic location, climate, scenic beauty, and imaginative leadership have helped shape a tourist boom of remarkable dimensions, thriving without the usual resort frills, gambling casinos, and superstar night-club entertainment of the Miami–San Juan type. Its economic basis, rather, is the duty-free shopping allowance which makes for bargains in perfumes, tobacco, and liquor, the latter a major business in itself. The majority of tourists are the one-day shoppers, streaming in from San Juan, Miami, and New York, and disembarking

2. Report of the visiting subcommittee, U.S. House Interior and Insular Affairs Committee, quoted in *San Juan Star*, July 30, 1971.

3. Thomas H. Dickinson, "The Economic Crisis in the Virgin Islands," *Current History* (December, 1927), p. 380.

from the cruise ships, drawn by the island advertising and constituting a type of "shopping bag" tourism that the luxury resorts contemptuously call the "sorry-no-vacancy" traffic. The result is a multimillion dollar tourist retail sales operation unequaled in the Caribbean, from which the gift shops rather than the hotels take the largest share. Like all profit-making tourist exercises, much of it is grossly exaggerated. The legendary scenery extolled by the lurid brochures is easily matched, and even surpassed, in other Caribbean islands; there is little of the pride of service so evident, by comparison, in the Barbados guest houses; while retail prices are comparable in most cases with some stateside levels, summed up in one postcard legend: "If it weren't for the booze, this would have been an expensive vacation." But for the average American tourist these are not consciously felt drawbacks, and he continues to feed the tourist bonanza. There is evidence that more and more tourists are from the American blue-collar class—policemen, firemen, postal carriers, members of the skilled trades categories—instead of the traditional white-collar class, while the Virgin Islands government's promotional activities indicate that in the near future larger numbers will come from the hitherto untapped market of the United States population areas west of the Atlantic seaboard.

Economic life and activity revolve increasingly around the art of getting the most out of the tourist dollar. The highest figures in the business establishments in the three islands listed in the *1965 Business Directory* refer to those enterprises serving in main part the tourist trade: 142 bars, 128 hotels and guest houses, 68 liquor package stores, 42 liquor wholesale stores, 83 gift shops, 59 night clubs, and 89 restaurants.[4] The same source lists some 145 real estate operations, which are capitalizing on the boom in land values by catering to resident continentals, many of them originally tourists (in 1967 a quarter-acre home site in a choice location in St. Croix could easily be valued at $20,000); while some 37 boat charter services, many of them centered in the St. Thomas Yacht Haven marina and anchorage area, look after the sailing and deep-sea fishing enthusiasts. Overwhelmingly, then, this is a service economy, as can be seen in the high percentages of the total labor force that are engaged in the wholesale-retail trade sector (3,445 employees) and the services sector (2,877 employees). Not unexpectedly, the figure of the tourist dominates the landscape, for there is little of the informal segregation that keeps the tourist in San Juan pretty much to the Condado "strip" area or in Jamaica to the Montego Bay area. Everybody, it seems,

4. Virgin Islands, Department of Commerce, Division of Trade and Industry, *1965 Business Directory* (St. Thomas, 1965).

just as in the Bahamas, gets into the act of making the islands into what the local auto license plates style a "vacation adventure"; and the essential respectability, even idolatry, of tourism is emphasized by the fact that ex-Governor Paiewonsky himself is a member of the leading local business family, of Lithuanian-Jewish ancestry, that owns and operates the prestigious Riise liquor complex.

Both the private and governmental sectors collaborate, not always amicably, to boost the tourist image of the economy. The Department of Commerce undertakes major promotional efforts, both locally and through its New York and Washington offices; solicits group visits and convention business; sends delegates to meetings of strategic bodies like the Caribbean Travel Association and the American Society of Travel Agents; organizes coups like the Governors' Conference of 1967; distributes portable Virgin Islands window displays, films to television stations, hotel rate-sheets, and individual items such as laminated vinyl passport cases; lobbies stateside newspapers for favorable mentions (the Washington *Daily News*'s inclusion of the St. Thomas Tramway in its *Guess Where* contest, for example) ; while various departmental officials take on a variety of exercises, from accompanying Emile Griffith, the Virgin Islands fighter, to St. Thomas for a local welcome following his middleweight championship bout, to conferring with NBC officials with reference to color television showings. Locally, the department does everything from operating its Visitors Bureau (it is local policy to think of tourists as "visitors") to persuading tourist shops to provide toilet facilities for shoppers. The office of the government secretary also participates in all this, and a frequent feature in local newspapers for years was a picture, presented with innumerable variations, of Cyril King, the photogenic secretary, exchanging ceremonial gifts with the captains of visiting cruise vessels.

The organized interest groups of the private sector add their own efforts. The Chambers of Commerce, sometimes meeting jointly, distribute their own literature; hold public hearings on items like interisland air fares, taxicab regulations, uniform traffic signs, and the notoriously bad service conditions of the Caribair airline; and lobby the Civil Aeronautics Board for more passenger and cargo permits for the Virgin Islands route. The Retail Liquor Merchants' Trade Association works, among much else, to prevent open price wars that might damage the tourist image, and to control the practice of liquor dealers' paying a secret royalty for every prospect delivered to their shops by tour operators from the airport or cruise-ship docks. The St. Croix Landmarks Society organizes tours through the elegant old homes of Christiansted and Frederiksted. The churches, in their turn, seek to mobilize public opinion against the idea of legalized gambling whenever that vexing question comes up, as it does frequently, lest the islands become another San Juan.

The Virgin Islands can be seen, at this point, as a prime illustration of the general character of Caribbean parasitical tourism. They belong to the Caribbean subgroup of pure tourist economies, like Bermuda and the Bahamas, which are dependent almost entirely upon their ability to sell themselves to the North American affluent societies. The general situation generates social problems of no mean magnitude, and it is worth noting that within recent years the churches especially, by means of successive consultations, have become particularly concerned with those problems. The tourist constitutes the only economic lifeline for these economies. They become, in effect, intensively organized advertising machines. Everybody becomes a tourist worshiper, just as in earlier years everybody in the old sugar colonies was a sugar worshiper. It becomes politically suicidal for anyone to openly oppose the sacred cow; so, in the Bahamian case, the new Pindling government seeks only to ameliorate the worst excesses of casino gambling and the more flagrant instances of real estate speculation rather than to eliminate the industry as such, while in the Virgins it is not the principle of tourism that becomes a political issue so much as some of its particular expressions: the quality of airline services, the availability of hotel space, the schedule of cruise-ship arrivals. The general framework of tourism, this is to say, is accepted by all. Even the emerging "black power" youth groups argue for tourism—but a localized, cottage-industry type of tourism that will place more emphasis on the principle of catering to the local Caribbean tourist. And even those groups that are more Marxist oriented readily point out that, in principle, there is nothing contradictory about a tourist industry within a socialist framework, as Yugoslavia proves. The situation, then, in the Virgins case produces intramural struggles, frequently of grim ferocity, among the various competing interests. There is the continuing squabble between government and the private operators as to who is responsible for maintaining standards of quality in the trade, as is illustrated by the fierce exchange over the critical Cornell report of 1967, which threw a sharp light on the essentially amateurish quality of the island tourist facilities.[5] There is the widespread dissatisfaction of all groups, including the local Senate, with the scandalous usage by Caribair of its long-standing virtual monopoly of the lucrative air run between San Juan and St. Thomas, despite the fact that the Paiewonsky family has been a leading shareholder in the company; this dissatisfaction has been only mitigated

5. Reported in *Daily News,* Aug. 1, 2, 4, 5, 1967; *Home Journal,* Aug. 1, 1967; *San Juan Star,* June 3, 8, 9, 1967.

by the fact that in recent years the monopoly has ended with the intrusion of competing companies like Prinair and West Indies Airways. There is the perennial complaint of the Crucian hoteliers that the Department of Commerce favors St. Thomas in its campaign to have the islands included on cruise-ship schedules, and the figures certainly indicate that the old rivalry between the two islands is taking on new expressions. There is the long-standing vendetta between the taxicab operators and the rental car agencies in which the tourist sometimes becomes involved as an innocent victim. There is, similarly, the feud between the old Virgin Islands Corporation and the St. Thomas Taxicab Association sparked by unpopular administrative decisions, such as the decision of the corporation to run the airport taxi concession itself. And, of course, there is the complicated guerrilla warfare among all groups—government, conservationists, airline operators, hotel men, federal officials—over the question of the proposed new jet airport in the magnificent lagoon area of eastern St. Thomas.[6]

But all of these differences yield to a united front when the total image of the economy is challenged, whether it is a question of Congress legislating to reduce the purchase exemptions for the islands, as in 1964; or, on a lesser scale, of the resident poet who writes with a fine eye of the aging St. Thomian dowagers who keep their gigolos;[7] or of the jaundiced English visitor who writes a critical book (like Philip Deane's *Caribbean Vacations*);[8] or, more generally, of a stateside press which makes naive assumptions about a "primitive" Virgin Islands when it laments the absence of "native" craft ware in the tourist shops.[9] "Don't stop the carnival" becomes the unofficial slogan of the society. For the Virgin Islands business community, as distinct from that in Puerto Rico, tourism is a complete commitment, golden eggs, as it were, laid in one basket. Nothing could better exemplify the difference than the fact that whereas in Puerto Rico the most scathing reports on the tourist trade, with all of its appalling vulgarity and cheapness, have come from the Chamber of Commerce, in the Virgin Islands, by comparison, comparable reports, such as

6. See the testimony of various citizens, for example, Isidor Paiewonsky, "Impact of New Jetport on Community," *Daily News*, Feb. 17, 1968; and Ronald Morrisette, statement presented to Special Committee of the Virgin Islands Legislature regarding the proposed new airport, in *ibid.*, Feb. 27, 1968. See also Isidor Paiewonsky, "The Case against a New Jet Airport for Saint Thomas," Focus Magazine, *Home Journal*, Feb. 18, 1968. For the vast literature of reports that this controversy has spawned, see those listed by Virgin Islands airport director, *Daily News*, Feb. 10, 1968.

7. Tram Combs, poem, in *Virgin Islands View*, June, 1965, p. 35.

8. Reviews of Deane's book, in *ibid.* (July, 1967), and *Daily News*, Mar. 25, 1967.

9. See *Daily News*, Jan. 11, 1964.

the 1967 one on hotels and guest houses, have been prepared by stateside university teams commissioned by the local government.[10]

The picture suggested by all this—the self-image of their tourist paradise that Virgin Islanders cherish—is that of a friendly holiday center that offers a "quaint" and "informal" vacation to the tourist. This, the tourist is told, is an alliance of "old Denmark" and American "hominess," quite different from the Miami–Las Vegas–San Juan circuit. He can bring his family confidently, for the earlier advertising style (to be seen in the old *Virgin Islands Magazine* of the 1940s and 1950s) which was addressed to single young men and women searching for a winter cruise-ship romance has been replaced by "family package" advertising, responding to the social changes in postwar America. It is a mass appeal to the mass audience; that is, there is little of the upper-class snob advertising, in the Noel Coward–*New Yorker* magazine style, that Jamaica promotes, and it is worth noting that, with the possible exception of the Rockefeller Caneel Bay operation, there is little of the genteel exclusiveness practiced in some of the other Caribbean resorts. "Formal dress" for the visitor means nothing much more than a jacket put on over a sport shirt and Bermuda shorts. It is quality, not size, that counts, so the advertising motif runs. Many of the Virgin Islands guest houses are run by enthusiastic amateurs, not slick professionals of the trade; the tourist can get his expensive night-club fare, if he wants it, in San Juan; and the official hostility to gambling keeps out the gangster element. All of this, finally, is presented in a suffused glow of tropical hedonism, replete with historically inaccurate hints about pirates, slave markets, and hidden treasure.

How much of this is hard fact, how much mendacious legend? After some fifteen years of organized tourism in the islands there now exists sufficient evidence to suggest there is in fact a serious discrepancy between the reality and the advertised image. That there is little desire on the part of local government leaders to keep out the "big business" elements of the international hotel syndicates is suggested by the presence of the huge tourist palace, with all of its pretentious and high-priced artificiality, such as the ubiquitous Virgin Isle Hilton and the new Caravan Hotel (the latter a glaring violation of local planning regulations, thereby frustrating a planned, consistent architectural treatment of the famous waterfront area in much the same way as, earlier, the St. Thomas skyline was assaulted by the hideous Teutonic lines of the building put up by

10. Cornell report, reported in *ibid.*, Aug. 1, 2, 4, 5, 1967; and *Home Journal*, Aug. 1, 1967. For the Puerto Rican case, see Chamber of Commerce, Tourism Committee, *Report on Tourism* (San Juan, 1966), reported in *San Juan Star*, Nov. 13, 1966, Jan. 18, 25, Feb. 8, 1967.

the North German Lloyd shipping line). What the literature terms "old world charm" is really little more than a thin veneer that covers an increasingly blasé operation conducted more and more by New York types like the fictional figure of the boorish Lester Atlas in Herman Wouk's *Don't Stop the Carnival*, who move in ruthlessly to make their money by gouging the unsuspecting tourist before the industry reaches its apex and then evacuate at the strategic moment, leaving behind a gaudy, unreal atmosphere and a permanently disgruntled local populace. The service motive gives way rapidly to the profit motive. As this happens there are signs that the American tourist, who generally is a shrewd analyst of the costs and benefits of what he spends, is becoming rapidly disillusioned and will very likely shift his patronage to the new European travel schemes, which have become no more expensive than the increasingly anachronistic (in terms of costs) Caribbean vacation tour.

Nor is the proof of all this simply the kind of novel, like the Wouk book, that employs the popular device of the imaginary Caribbean island to make its point. The professional travel writer, the stateside professional firm, and the local government agencies themselves have all contributed to the critical literature. As early as 1954 an official of the local Hotel Association reminded her radio audience of the harsh judgment on St. Thomas passed by the authors of the authoritative *Standard Guide to Mexico and the Caribbean*: "If you are looking for the exotic as found in Haiti, you'll be disappointed at the Americanness of things. If you want a lot of high life you'll also be disappointed. If you're seeking the cheap vacation, such as is offered by the British islands, you'll think the prices excessive. More small attractive hotels are needed." [11] The extensive survey by the local tourist director in the same year filled in the details. The report started out with a general warning:

> We have in this community many who think that tourism consists entirely of publicity and advertising—with emphasis on the former. They seem unable to appreciate that the most colossal publicity campaign in history could, of itself, never establish a resort on any permanent basis. Attracting visitors to a resort can never be more than half of the job. The other half is to make certain that the visitors are pleased with what they find here. If they are not it stands to reason that the more visitors we get the more adverse word-of-mouth publicity we will subsequently suffer.[12]

11. Mrs. M. Weber, radio address, January 26, 1954, printed in *Daily News*, Jan. 28, 1954.
12. Virgin Islands, Department of Commerce, Tourist Board, *A Survey and Report on the Tourist Industry* (St. Thomas, 1954), reprinted in *Daily News*, Aug. 18, 19, 20, 1954.

That many of the local hoteliers suffered from that publicity phobia was obvious from the myriad deficiencies that the report went on to list: failure to honor reservations, even when supposedly insured by deposit; unreasonable charges for extra services; lack of reasonable and courteous service; failure to pay commissions and make refunds promptly; the sizable sale, in some shops, of smuggled French perfumes and liquors; and a general feeling among tourists that they were not getting fair value for their money, to the extent that many travel agents—the vital key personnel in tourism—hesitated to book their clients into the islands. The continuing level of complaints about high prices in the shops was so serious, the report claimed, that the industry ought to consider obtaining competitive prices on a fixed list of items so as to make comparison feasible. The greatest single need, the report insisted, was professional hotel management:

> Beyond the house, or small guest house, the best intentioned amateur cannot hope to grasp the many facets of a smoothly efficient hotel operation. There must, after all, be a sound reason for the existence of hotel schools and the year of up-from-the-ground training which countries noted for their hotels, such as Switzerland, require. One of the most important hotel representatives in New York stated that he had never seen a resort so cursed with hotel amateurs as are these islands.[13]

What the situation cried aloud for, at the least, concluded the report, was the establishment, by means of a high-level government-hotel meeting, of a stringent code of hotel ethics to be enforced by real police power in the hands of the executive branch, perhaps by granting power to the government secretary's office to revoke hotel licenses on proof of serious deviations from the code. So long as such a police power was not present the current chaotic situation would continue, with the Hotel Association refusing to cooperate with other bodies, and with the Tourist Board, lacking any real authority, left with the unpleasant alternatives of doing nothing, even about serious matters, or of courting even more bitter enmity from owners and managers.

That the Tourist Board lost out in this struggle became evident later, not only by its own demise but also by the fact that the later Cornell study of 1967 reiterated the sharp observations of the 1954 report. Written by outsiders, of course, it lacked the authoritative tone of the earlier report, and was marked by the sort of naive observations that frequently come from visitors, even hotel-operation specialists. At the same time, it noted defects with candid honesty. Shop service in St. Thomas was courteous and not annoyingly aggressive, but restaurants

13. *Ibid.*, Aug. 19, 1954.

were relatively inferior. There was little professional entertainment, and many hotels used canned music systems indiscriminately. Most hotels had unattractive registration areas, used dirty and often out-of-date menus, concentrated on commercially frozen foods to the neglect of fresh native dishes, provided little if any radio and television services, served the little plastic containers for jam and marmalade that may be acceptable on planes but not at high-priced hotels, only too readily used paper napkins, and generally sported unbelievably skimpy interiors, usually highlighted by large calendars advertising airlines, beer, or real estate agents, and with so little furniture or so little public area comfortably furnished that there was nothing to do when it rained but go to bed. It painted, all in all, a pretty depressing picture. It can, of course, be properly argued—as some indignant hotel operators pointed out in their replies to the critics—that some of the deficiencies, such as water shortages or bad telephone service, are caused not by management inefficiency but by factors outside hotel control. It can even be argued that the report suffers from its unstated premise that the only admissible standards are metropolitan standards; in the sharp retort of one operator, "I'm not running either a Holiday Inn or a Waldorf-Astoria, and I don't intend to. That's not what my guests come to me for." The fact remains that where the small hotel charges anything but small rates, where everything is "informal" except the rate structure, the argument of informality falls to the ground. "Particularly in St. Thomas," the Cornell people noted, "a great deal is said about maintaining a fine informal atmosphere. In most places this is just an excuse for poor service and lack of facilities. It is to be noted that the service and accommodations in most of these places have been reduced to a standard which is convenient for the operator, and the deficiencies are excused in the interests of informality." [14]

The islands' tourist economy clearly faces a critical phase in its development. It is only recently that the reintroduction of direct air service from the mainland has promised a release from the precarious dependence on a feeder line like Caribair, which in turn is dependent on the major trunk carriers bringing in the tourists from the U.S. gateway cities. But the promise of the new service carries its own dangers. Such technological revolutions as the new supersonic airliners can take tourists away from the islands as easily as they bring them, and the new jumbo jets may do so, just as the steam engine in the nineteenth century eventually caused maritime shipping to bypass the Virgins group.

14. Cornell report, reported in *ibid.*, Aug. 1, 2, 4, 5, 1967; and *Home Journal,* Aug. 1, 1967.

No amount of advertising the islands as the one holiday area where "true democracy" exists (as suggested by the government comptroller),[15] or emphasizing the islands as part of a larger concept of the "American Caribbean," so presumably congenial to the American tourist,[16] can properly substitute for the revolution of attitudes necessary if the islands are to successfully meet the changing character of world tourism. A rejuvenated tourism, so its local champions demand, must do the following: deemphasize the shopping aspect of the trade, with its rabid appeal to human cupidity; capitalize on the one sure local asset, the "old world charm" of the Danish architectural legacy, by a bold program to preserve it from further commercialization through such devices as the restoration-incentive legislation used so successfully by the Institute of Puerto Rican Culture in its remarkable Old San Juan program; elevate the social status of tourism sector jobs by vocational training programs which will finally break down the traditional conviction of young native Virgin Islanders that the only desirable occupation is a government office job or a taxi franchise; and above all, perhaps, release the full potential of the private enterprise sector by putting an end to the politics-ridden interference of the Paiewonsky–Unity Party government machine, with all of its infirmities—its passion for empty publicity exercises, its favoritism, its organization of an overextended patronage public administration machine—to the detriment of genuine business enterprise. "New blood," the argument goes, "has no such infirmities, and as a healthy segment of professionally tourist-oriented businesses bring our islands to the forefront of the American Caribbean (potentially the favorite resort of 200 million Americans), the old ways will die, and the biggest losers will be those who think they are the smartest today—the poor fools who prefer a sinecure to a job, who dream of industry instead of *working* at tourism, or the simpletons whose education never differentiated between 'service' and 'servitude,' and whose self-defeating 'pride' results from ignorance and inadequacy, not competence and dignity." [17]

The weaknesses of this line of argument are painfully obvious. Its assumption that industrial development after the Puerto Rican "Oper-

15. Peter Bove to Governor Paiewonsky, quoted in *Daily News*, Feb. 7, 1964.

16. "The American Caribbean," *Virgin Islands View*, April, 1966.

17. Editorial, *ibid.*, June, 1967. For a typical expression of the continental professional tourist "expert" lecturing the natives, see speech by former entertainment director of La Concha Hotel, San Juan, reported in *San Juan Star*, Feb. 15, 1970. The assumption behind this sort of attitude is that everything must give way to tourist promotion—local politics, local government agencies, anti-American sentiment, and *independentista* activities.

ation Bootstrap" type is "unnatural" while tourism is "natural" is patently invalid when it is remembered that both forms of development rely on the profit motive and both promote economic subservience to large corporate outside interests. Its further assumption that the economic sector is "healthy" while the political sector is merely full of scheming politicians is so much a piece of romantic laissez faire theorizing that it hardly deserves attention. The anachronism of the thesis, it ought to be noted, is made even more emphatic in the Caribbean Lilliputian societies by the close relationship that exists, almost of necessity, between the political and economic subworlds. There is also an undercurrent of American chauvinism in the general argument, for it assumes, without openly saying so, that the "healthy segment of professionally tourist-oriented businesses" is to be seen as an expression of American drive and energy on the part of the continentals who own or operate most of those businesses, as against, by inference, the unproductive prejudices of the natives. Yet most of the practices condemned by the Cornell report refer, as a matter of fact, to continental hotels and guest houses, indicating, perhaps, that tropical laissez faire only too easily overcomes, in some American residents, the gospel of Yankee efficiency.

Nor is it too difficult to find American participants in the general tourist boom who allow the purity of their economic motives to become contaminated by political favoritism and corruption. The 1964 controversy about anti–"free enterprise" practices in the St. Thomas liquor business, for example, showed that if, on the one hand, native stores like Riise and Sparky's enjoyed an organized monopoly on the sale of liquor to the Navy clients of the Caribbean Frontier fleet, on the other hand, the Liquor Dealers' Association, composed in the main of continental businesses, exercised at the same time a price-fixing conspiracy, to the detriment of the small liquor dealers, like *Le Petit Parisien*, who find themselves pressured by the "Main Street Boys" when they seek to introduce competitive retail prices.[18] The minor scandal during the same year of the officially sponsored Virgin Islands exhibit at the New York World's Fair showed that if the local commissioner of commerce used the power of his political office to arbitrarily grant the printing and promotional contract to a favored client without calling for competitive bids, that client, at the same time, was a transplanted statesider resident in St. Croix with an unsavory record of sterile pub-

18. Hearings, Virgin Island Senate, reported in *Daily News*, Feb. 24, 1964. See also federal charges of price-fixing arrangements brought against local gift-shop association, in *Home Journal*, Sept. 12, 1969.

licity operations behind him.[19] The reprehensible practice of hotel over-booking, especially during the winter peak seasons, is yet a further example of how the Caribbean area hoteliers, most of them outsiders or resident *americanos*, allow public service to give way to private greed and self-interest; and there is as yet little evidence that they are prepared to give up the practice.

The argument that attempts to separate the political and economic segments of these tiny island societies into well-defined compartments is grossly unrealistic. The picture of Virgin Islands "politics" sabotaging the growth of healthy "free enterprise" business just does not fit the observable facts. It would, indeed, be more plausible to speak of the economic sector more and more setting the tone and direction of the governmental sector. The Paiewonsky regime (1961–69) was essenti-ally a businessman's regime; its policies were fundamentally pro-busi-ness oriented. Its obvious reluctance to seriously apply an official grading list for hotel operations showed that it would not try to upset the business community in any really important way, although it might indulge from time to time in petty harassment. Both government and business, as a matter of fact, saw eye to eye on the general desirabil-ity of capitalist-sponsored tourism. They tried to work together, as is evident, for example, in the particular problem of the distribution of advertising literature to cruise ships. The portrait of a general inter-play between government and business, each with its own developed philosophy, is far too sophisticated to fit the facts of insular life. What in practice takes place is an amazingly complicated charade of moves and countermoves, half in the open, half subterranean, in which the individual business seeks to get on the "inside track" at Government House, while government, and its agencies, uses its command of the bureaucratic process to penalize those who are *persona non grata*. Per-sonalities, all well known to one another, play a vital role in that game. At the same time the rules of the game are limited only by the occasional intervention of the federal government in Washington, and its local agents, operating as a third party.

The real point, of course, is that a tourism development program along professional lines, as requested by the critics in the Virgin Islands situation, could only have as its end result the sort of anticivilization that the model has produced in neighboring Puerto Rico. Virgin Is-landers like to tell themselves that they are not like San Juan; *san-juaneros* congratulate themselves that they are not like Las Vegas; but

19. *Daily News*, Apr. 4, 7, 8, 1964; text of radio address by government comptroller, in *ibid.*, Apr. 9, 1964; Governor Paiewonsky to Robert Lodge, quoted in *ibid.*, Apr. 10, 1964; text of Kimmelman-Lodge agreement, in *ibid.*, Apr. 11, 1964.

in reality all of them are traveling along the same road as they battle with increasing ferocity for the tourist dollar. The critical literature on the Puerto Rican case is already voluminous. The Chamber of Commerce series of reports in particular have listed the social evils more and more glaringly evident in San Juan: the growth of the huge tourist hotels and the neglect of lower-priced family hotels; a general slackening of service standards as the hotels become "as cold as a subway turnstile"; a progressive decay of the cultural relationship between tourists and residents; a general complacency in hotel operators bred by the traditional "free ride" in tourist development; the growth of organized international and interstate prostitution as the result of the tourist influx and the ease of movement and concealment provided by the relaxed tourist atmosphere; the vast increase in organized crime, along with growing evidence of Mafia infiltration, despite official protestations to the contrary; and above all else, perhaps, the massive deterioration in the tourist physical environment, evident in the way the once beautiful Ashford Avenue of the old Condado section has become, in the words of the U.S. secretary of the interior, a "blazing strip of vulgarity and tastelessness." Finally, all this produces a schizoid attitude in the local insular government as it is trapped between its eagerness to catch the tourist trade and its private sense of shameful guilt as it watches the erosion of its culture under the Americanizing pressure. This ambivalence of attitude is so profound that one outside observer has been moved to wonder whether it was not true that government officials "were out of sympathy with the tourist development and were permitting the quick-buck boys, the shabby profiteers who swarm so quickly around the smell of success and the sight of money to debase the island's beautiful tourist plant in a Machiavellian effort to discredit it." All in all, it is a damning indictment. Yet so pervasive is the climate of moral evasiveness generated by the appetite for the tourist dollar that the reports ended in a series of weak and vacillating recommendations posited on the facile assumption that the evils they listed could be seen somehow as accidents only and not as the central essence of tourism in a tropical business civilization.[20]

The close proximity of the Virgins to Puerto Rico, as well as their partial dependence upon the Puerto Rican tourist economy, makes this problem of more than just academic interest to Virgin Islanders. Two of the leading recommendations of a report made by the Puerto

20. Reports on the Tourism Committee, Chamber of Commerce of Puerto Rico, reprinted in *San Juan Star,* Nov. 13, 1966, Jan. 18, 25, Feb. 8, 15, 1967. The indictment of these reports is substantiated by the experience of other Caribbean resort areas based on full-scale casino gambling, as in the case of the Bahamas.

Rican legislature are certainly very much heard in the island debate on tourism: (1) that there should be a new public relations program undertaken to save the image of tourism, and (2) that the tourist industry on its private side should begin to assume a greater responsibility for self-regulation. Neither recommendation sounds persuasive. The first suffers from the Madison Avenue fallacy that the public mind can be successfully cozened by bright mendacious advertising, while merely to attend meetings of bodies like the Hotel Association or the Chamber of Commerce in the Virgin Islands is to feel the utter unreality of the second. It is true that there are many islanders who genuinely yearn for a clean and efficient, professional, service-minded tourist program. It is true, too, that there are a number of small places of quality that are a rare pleasure to stay in—the Villa Fairview in Charlotte Amalie, the West Indian-style guest house run by the Coulters in Frederiksted, the old Trunk Bay hostel, now regrettably gone, once run by the remarkable Erva Boulon, or the Miller Manor on Frenchman's Hill. But two comments must be made. Firstly, these smaller hostelries tend to cater to a small clientele of "regulars," and they receive scant consideration from a government eager to make the most of the "big money" enterprises. Secondly, and more generally, it is difficult for a genuine professional ethic to survive in an acquisitive society where hedonistic individualism and anxious social climbing run rampant, a difficulty compounded by the fact that the professional middle-class group in Virgin Islands society is in its first experimental generation of development. As yet, it survives precariously. It will only in time become a vibrant agent of social rehabilitation.

Meanwhile, as far as the tourist sector is concerned, the local government declaims loudly against the entry of the professional gambler but permits the open invasion of individuals whose social values are no less determinedly avaricious. It is perhaps even more true today than it was over twenty-five years ago that, as District Attorney James Bough put it, "I doubt if it would be correct to say that there exists a business philosophy in these islands; but if I must label the prevailing pattern which is the general characteristic of business here, I would have to say that it is a philosophy of indifference towards, and neglect of, the customer." That was in 1944. Yet the indictment was repeated, in even sterner language, by the president of the St. Thomas–St. John Chamber of Commerce in 1971.[21]

21. "Conclusions and Recommendations," Report of the Industry and Commerce Committee, Senate, Puerto Rico, reprinted in *San Juan Star*, Mar. 18, 1967; and remarks of James A. Bough, in *Daily News*, Jan. 22, 1944. See also remarks of president of St. Thomas–St. John Chamber of Commerce, in *San Juan Star*, Feb. 11, 1971.

The future of the tourist sector, obviously, depends on whether its architects are out, moderately, to make a living or, greedily, to make a killing. The economics of the governmental public sector are by nature somewhat different. A government structure of over 5,000 employees and with a $40 million budget, distributed throughout a dozen major departments, along with such local governmental entities as the Urban Renewal Board, the Housing Authority, the Water and Power Authority, and the Planning Board, and with the offices of the governor and the government secretary supplemented by additional federal appropriations, clearly holds a key position in the economy. Its revenue derives from a triple base: (1) local income taxes; (2) federal income tax schedules appropriated by congressional consent as local taxes; and (3) federal excise taxes collected on imports of Virgin Islands products to the mainland and rebated to the local government as matching funds. Added to this are such grants and loans as are made available to all of the states. Although tourism, based on the utilization of geography and climate as economic resources, remains the leading revenue source, the disposal of such a vast public budget (in comparative terms) makes the government a strategic instrument in the territorial economic development.

The disposal of that budget, in terms of public policy, is naturally the cause of intense controversial debate in the islands. The list of items passed during the 1966 legislative session indicates the quite remarkable scope of the areas covered by government spending: salary schedules for teachers, a new home for the aged, an interstate compact for educational interchanges between the Virgins and New York State, airport improvements, establishment of a Council for the Arts, protection of children against physical abuses, appointment of a commission on the status of women, fair labor standards for resident workers, participation of local sports teams in Central American and Caribbean games, purchase of the former U.S. Naval Submarine Base, moderate-income housing programs, management of properties taken over from the old Virgin Islands Corporation, cloud-seeding operations for weather control purposes, the construction of a golf course on the College of the Virgin Islands campus, and much else. In addition, there are the various advisory and promotional services of the government in its more specifically economic role: the Rum Council, supported jointly by government and rum distillers, which looks after the sale of rum; the Employment Security Agency, which offers, among other things, free job analysis services to interested firms; and the Department of Commerce and the government secretary's office, which share, not always logically, the supervision of the industrial development program directed to outside capital interested in locating plants in the islands. Not the least of the problems raised by this general activity is whether the tax-exempt tourist interests should begin to assume a portion of the advertising and solicitation programs carried on for so long by government.

It is generally agreed, by government and opposition alike, that there are serious and considerable deficiencies in the economic infrastructure. Gross underachievement in the various segments of the infrastructure— roads, utilities, housing, sanitation, service accommodations—is a major characteristic of the insular economy. In housing, a pattern of high rents and mortgage payments, along with a failure to develop extensive low-rent public housing schemes, means that large groups of people live in grossly substandard housing when, ironically, they could often afford better quarters if these were available. To take a ride, for example, on one of the rickety Manassah buses through the slum districts of Savan, Altona, and Frenchtown in St. Thomas is to realize with some shock that what the tourist brochures describe as bohemian alleys are really run-down and overcrowded areas only made tolerable because of a benign tropical climate. The situation is aggravated by a long-standing sanitation problem, with open gratings in streets along with the still widespread night-soil system (the use of pail privies) contributing to a serious environmental health hazard. There is also the intractable problem of potable water for the island communities due to the insufficient supply accruing from rainfall and underground sources, only partially resolved by the 1965 inauguration of a desalinization plant in St. Thomas. Drought and prolonged periods of water rationing are therefore not uncommon experiences for the Virgin Islands householder, forcing him to rely upon additional reserves brought in from Puerto Rico by the Navy and barging contractors. On occasion he must feel, like the Ancient Mariner, that he is tragically surrounded by masses of water he cannot use, while at the same time he must, by law, provide his home with a complete water system and in addition contribute by means of his tax obligations to an ever expanding community water system. The telephone service is notoriously bad, to the degree that complaints about cross-talk, wrong numbers, bad connections, and inefficient billing constitute a chief staple of local conversation; and it is ironic that the insular citizenry should suffer all these ills at the hands of a subsidiary of the giant International Telephone and Telegraph Company that was originally founded by the St. Thomas-born Sosthenes Behn. Finally, the high-priority need for an expanded and improved transportation system remains unmet, except for absolutely essential maintenance work on narrow roads and streets incapable of absorbing the rapid and uncontrolled proliferation of cars and the consequent growth of traffic congestion.

Some of these difficulties are the price Virgin Islanders must pay for the modernization most of them seem to want. If tourism, as a recent Hawaiian report approvingly quoted by a Virgin Islands survey puts it, is "a huge, rising market with the progressive increase developing out of the growth in the margins of discretionary disposable family incomes throughout the advancing national economies of the world," [22] it follows that the enormous pressures that it places upon the embryonic social service structures of the host economies must generate formidable problems of social planning. But there is little to suggest that those problems have as yet been realistically faced in the Virgin Islands case. It is true that the local administration under Governor Paiewonsky, born under the aegis of the metropolitan Kennedy-Johnson liberalism, paid lip service to the general idea of social planning during its period of office. But things, on the whole, are still left pretty much to chance. The machinery of state control is there, of course. But it is used with little imagination or purposeful direction. The Public Utilities Commission, the original creation of which occasioned a fierce political struggle, is mainly staffed by amateur businessmen, with the result that it is no match for the specialist talent which protects the ITT control over the local telephone service in order to insure the ITT grip on the lucrative overseas business. The local Planning Board has one trained professional planner, but too much of its time is spent on zoning matters, to the continuing neglect of problems that cry aloud for attention: the ugly proliferation of advertising signs and billboards, neglected maintenance of the traditional architectural flavor of the island towns, the increasing commercialization of beach areas, the glacial pace at which slum clearance takes place, the scarcity of architects and builders for low- and middle-income housing, the blatant violation of building codes, and much else.

Many of the offenders in all this are government agencies themselves; the scandalous failure to develop a planned control of continuing sea pollution, for example, is compounded by the irresponsible pumping of untreated sewage into the waters fronting Charlotte Amalie on the part of the Public Works Department. On the more general level of planning for an educational revolution geared to the imperative need for new manpower skills, the official educational program responds unimaginatively with a budgetary allocation that is less than the national average for the states and territories combined, along with a higher educational scheme (the College of the Virgin Islands) that trains its graduating classes to be academicians nursing the old anachronistic

22. Darwin D. Creque and Harry Goeggel, *A Study of the Tourist Industry in the Virgin Islands* (St. Thomas: Department of Commerce, 1964), p. 25.

predilection for unproductive white-collar jobs. Far too many problems of urgent social concern are left to be looked after, necessarily incompletely, by socially minded private citizens: Fred Gjessing and Isidor Paiewonsky in the field of architectural preservation, Angelo Marasco (following in the footsteps of Alton Adams) in the sphere of serious music appreciation, Bill La Motta in his long campaign to rehabilitate the status of the old Virgin Islands folk songs and colloquial tales, and George Seaman in his heroic struggle to protect the St. Croix deer herds against both an apathetic citizenry and an at times hostile government.

Part cause, part consequence of all this is the quite astonishing paucity of basic statistical information. Without such data the public policy-making process becomes far too subject to bias, prejudice, and favoritism. The economy proudly boasts the highest per capita income figure in the Caribbean. But in the utter absence of information on the distribution of personal income the figure becomes meaningless in terms of the relationship between economic development and social equity. The absence, in turn, of a price index makes it almost impossible to measure the overall annual flow of goods and services. The further absence of a cost-of-living index means that, although it is common knowledge that the dollar buys less in the islands than on the mainland, just what the differential is becomes a matter of heated opinion rather than verified fact, a situation only partially mitigated by the cost-of-living index prepared by the United States Civil Service Commission for the federal statutory salaried employees in the islands. There are no accurate statistical data on migration habits, the flow of tourist traffic, and the labor market. It can be argued, of course, that with reference to tourist traffic, for example, the deficiency is due to the fact that the islands are a part of the United States and therefore no tourist cards, visas, or other documentation are required from U.S. visitors, with the result that any local study must depend on figures supplied by airlines and steamship companies. But no such excuse is possible in the field of labor statistics; and, apart from the scanty information supplied by the local Employment Security Agency to the ILO *Year Book of Labour Statistics* and the wage orders issued by the newly created Wage Board, the exact nature of the insular labor force is largely unknown. It is, finally, an unending source of irritation, and sometimes of local humor, that no one seems to know the exact population figure, or the actual growth trends, of the territory as a whole, illustrated by the conflicting estimates issued, variously, by the U.S. Census Office, the local Bureau of Vital Records and Statistical Services, and Government House pronouncements. There is, at the least, a careless indifference to the statistical aspect of Virgin Islands government and, at the most, as some critics suspect, a deliberate conspiracy to suppress the publication of detailed information.

There are two general factors that aggravate the situation. The first is that, not to put too fine a point on it, Virgin Islands government is businessmen's government. There is an intimate connection between government and business, exemplified most obviously in the fact that Governor Paiewonsky was, during his governorship, a powerful figure in the old-established Riise liquor empire. The scandals of the connection were not of a Bahamian size, if only because a mass suffrage base had made necessary an alliance with the union-labor forces; also, as his early Progressive Guide political period shows, there had always been a strain of social liberalism in the governor's make-up, which accounts, for example, for his long vendetta with the Bourbonese conservatism of the Crucian "royal families." Even so, the insular officialdom wholeheartedly supports, now as it did then, the tourist-industrial island capitalism, sharing with the Main Street businessmen the sentiment, as one of them has put it, that St. Thomas is "a tremendous Department Store in which we are all concessionaires." Where there are differences between the two sides they tend to be differences of personality rather than of policy, as is evident in the 1965 exchange of public correspondence in which the owner of the L'Escale-En-Ville liquor store bitterly charged the governor with using the power of his office to persuade cruise directors to steer their tourist clients to his own family business.[23] The intimate relationships that prevailed between Government House and powerful tycoons like Sidney Kessler, O. Roy Chalk, Henry Reichhold, and Leon Hess, to name only a few, are well known, and the membership list of the Board of Overseers of the new College of the Virgin Islands exhibits the kind of socially prestigious reward that these "friends of the Virgin Islands" received for their services.

The mutually beneficial "deals" that are made in many cases are only a matter of hearsay. But at least one recent policy decision—to sell the majority of the public lands held in St. Croix by the Virgin Islands Corporation, the last surviving relic of the New Deal, to private interests, including the Harvey group—received sufficient attention to exemplify in some detail the surrender of government to the business ethic. That the alienation of the lands was decided on by a board of directors largely composed of outsiders, including some federal officials, without open bidding, did not of itself excuse the failure of the local government to undertake a serious fight in defense of the basic consider-

23. Donald Stanford, "Letter to Governor Paiewonsky," *Daily News*, Dec. 13, 1965.

ation that in a tiny 83-square-mile island whose growth is only just beginning government should seek to extend, rather than curtail, the public ownership of land, putting it to use in the developing construction of parks, recreational areas, agricultural enterprise, and public housing sites. The violence of Governor Paiewonsky's remarks in his exchange over the issue with the St. Croix Chamber of Commerce certainly indicated guilt feelings; but in any case his administration's earlier record in dispensing public lands to private owners—the questionable Recovery Hill and Sandy Point beach episodes, for example—sufficiently showed that Virgin Islanders will have to wait some time yet for the acceptance of the principle of land nationalization which is the only principle that makes sense in the minuscule Caribbean societies.[24]

The second aggravating factor to be noted is that the whole character of governmental activity in the islands tends to be promotional rather than informational. In part this is the result of a "pork barrel" politics feeding from the lucrative trough of the federal government, so that too many programs are organized with an eye to federal funds rather than to local needs; and in part it is the result of the frantic preoccupation with public relations which the pleasure-seeking character of a tourist economy so easily engenders. It produces, altogether, a Madison Avenue atmosphere, with tropical overtones. Vast ingenuity goes into the ephemeral task of entertaining the visitor, especially if he has money or readily usable political power. Governor Paiewonsky in his own person became almost a caricature of the peripatetic salesman, shrewdly deploying this combination of a wasteful political atmosphere and a public relations machinery in the service of his pet schemes. One year alone—1967—witnessed a "double feature" version of the show in the shape of the semicentennial celebrations and the annual Governors' Conference; and, indeed, the local organizers of the latter event were obliged to cut out some of the more grossly carnival items of the program and increase the working sessions because of the fear of some governors that their home state electorates might not take too readily to the spectacle of their chief executives enjoying a Caribbean winter cruise on a chartered liner. It is sometimes difficult to discover what work, if any, the government economist's office is doing, but it is only too easy to see what the Visitors' Bureau of the Commerce Department is doing. Everybody, then, struggles to get a prominent position in the general picture; thus, to cite a minor but revealing example, eight out of the twenty-three pages of an economic report by the local Development

24. For all this, see A. Bryant Henderson, "St. Croix Times" column, *ibid.*, June 4, 1964; John Hennessy, "The Story of the V.I. Corporation: The End of an Era," *ibid.*, June 12, 1964; *ibid.*, June 18, 25, 27, 1964.

Board are needlessly devoted to a series of biographical profiles of its members, some 50 per cent of them being, incidentally, government employees in one way or another.[25]

The general upshot is that most of the really significant analyses of the economy are undertaken, suggestively, by the federal offices involved with the territorial situation. Although the periodic reports of the U.S. comptroller's office are primarily concerned with the local administrative process, they frequently touch upon pertinent aspects of economic policy. A number of reports out of Washington over the years have pinpointed the salient problems, avoiding the bland optimism exhibited by the governor's annual reports: the OPA report of 1944, the Public Lands Committee report of 1950, and Dr. Moron's FHA report of 1965, to name only a few. More recently, the Interior Department has voiced concern about what is possibly the single most urgent problem of the islands' economy, the planned organization of a proper balance between the natural environmental factors and the growing pressure of tourism, industry, and urbanization. For there are clear signs that the massive despoliation of natural beauty that is already far advanced in Puerto Rico, as a result of governmental apathy, rapacious developers, the absence of any real planning as distinct from spurious planning, uncontrolled urban congestion, and private economic greed, is beginning to show itself in the Virgin Islands. There are also signs that the same sort of alliance between an accommodating government and the powerful American oil and petroleum industries that has already produced flagrant water pollution in Puerto Rico is beginning to take shape in St. Thomas and St. Croix, generating a permissive climate of opinion in which the drive toward increased material living standards is overstimulated by rapacious business interests rather than guided by standards of social justice. The Virgin Islands situation is perhaps even more desperate than that of Puerto Rico, since there is little evidence so far of the development of the kind of aroused public opinion which has grown up in Puerto Rico recently under the stimulus of the protests of university planning experts, private citizens' groups, *independentista* political units, and a handful of socially conscious government officials.

The single most striking feature of the Virgins economy is its satellite character. It has grown up over the last fifty years as a tropical extension, frequently artificial and always vulnerable, of the American capitalist economy. Its extraordinary dependence on imports, noted by the 1944

25. Virgin Islands Development Board, *Overall Economic Development Program* (St. Thomas, June, 1966), pp. 1–8.

OPA report, has intensified as the tourist industry, through the dispersion of its income into the local structure (it is estimated that the turnover of one tourist dollar results in approximately two and a half dollars of local income), has generated new demands for imported food and clothing, consumer durables, and materials and equipment required by trade and industry. The tourist industry itself is derivative, while a sizable portion of its receipts are returned to the U.S. mainland for the purchase of supplies and services and to those foreign sources from which the gift shops obtain much of their merchandise. All the instruments of U.S. power that have it in their hands to make decisions that can mean, almost literally, life or death to broad areas of the local economy—the Interior Department, the Civil Aeronautics Board, Congress and its committees—are insulated from local control because of the colonial status of the territory. The federal judicial power, likewise, can make or break local economic plans, as demonstrated by the Supreme Court decision of 1955 which struck down the local legislation setting up the postwar divorce "racket," since its frankly admitted character as a money-making device aimed at prosperous mainland citizens with marital problems exceeded the ambit of legislative power that Congress had delegated to the nonincorporated territories. This, in brief, constitutes an almost perfect case study of the colonial economy that produces what it does not consume and consumes what it does not produce.

The best example of this economic colonialism is in the industrial sector proper where a variety of developing industrial firms—in textiles, chemicals, and watches—operate under the protection of special-privilege incentives, both local and federal. The local incentives, mainly of a tax nature, are important. But it is abundantly clear, especially in an increasingly competitive field where nearly all Caribbean governments are following similar incentive legislation patterns, that in the Virgin Islands, as in Puerto Rico, it is the federal "loophole" legislation which constitutes the vital protective shield for their structure of business operations. The competitive environment is, indeed, the crucial factor. In the case of tourism there were already in 1964 some twenty-eight free ports in the Caribbean area, some with complete tax holidays providing exemption from tax obligations (as in St. Maarten) and some with completely duty-free imports (as in the "In-Bond" shops of the British islands), and many of those competing territories were burdened with a lower volume of expenditure in terms of wages, services, and social benefits.[26] Thus it is painfully clear that the industry must rely more and more upon the privileges, such as the tourist expenditure

26. "Case of Virgin Islands in Favor of Extension of $200 Exemption, and 48 Hr. Time-Limit Waiver," *Daily News,* Mar. 5, 1964.

exemptions and the forty-eight-hour time-limit waiver, granted by congressional legislation in Washington. The same is true, basically, of the various duty-exemption privileges of the U.S. tariff schedules, which permit the duty-free entry into the mainland market of goods assembled by Virgin Islands manufacturers containing not more than 50 per cent of foreign raw materials. The importance of these privileges can be readily appreciated from the fact that in 1964 approximately 9 per cent of 2,400,000 watch movements consumed in the United States were assembled by eleven watch manufacturing plants in the islands.

Yet the struggle to save the watch industry's position in 1965–66 was a graphic reminder of its thoroughly artificial basis. It had to meet head-on the challenge both of the rival mainland watch importers resentful of "undercutting" competition from island-based plants and of the Federal Trade Commission as its investigators uncovered the abuses of the "50–50" clause, especially those concerned with the "arms-length" dealings between mainland parent companies and their island subsidiaries. A typical example of this was the Janaco Corporation of St. Thomas, which allegedly purchased raw materials for its watch bands in the United States, shipped them to a Hong Kong firm for "processing," then received the processed parts back in the islands for "manufacture" and duty-free re-export to its parent firm, the Baldwin Bracelet Corporation in New York.[27] Responding to the pressure from the FTC, the local government appointed a fact-finding committee, whose general conclusion that the industry's rapid expansion rate "holds great dangers to the stability of employment in the Islands and to the Islands' commercial relations" was followed by the initiation of a self-imposed production quota calculated to discourage punitive congressional legislation (a distinct possibility in light of the observation of the House Committee on Ways and Means that the islands' watch industry was fast becoming an illegitimate operation using the duty-exemption privilege as a tariff-avoidance vehicle). The local quota statute, however, was declared invalid by the U.S. District Court in *Virgo Corporation* v. *Paiewonsky* as a violation of the local Organic Act; and only the passage by Congress of a federally administered quota finally saved the day. The entire story bears eloquent testimony to the ever present dangers, both judicial and political, that beset a local industrialization program dependent, in the final analysis, upon the good will of the various federal instrumentalities.[28]

27. *San Juan Star*, Oct. 29, 1962, June 21, 1966.
28. See, for all this, *Annual Report of the Governor of the Virgin Islands to the Secretary of the Interior, 1965* (St. Thomas, 1965), pp. 55–59; "Annual Report of the Governor of the Virgin Islands to the Secretary of the Interior, 1966," mimeographed

It has been the same story with tourism and the textiles industry: every so often the Virgin Islands government must mobilize its entire resources to fight off the respective mainland trade and manufacturing associations and their congressional friends. The most recent case has been that of the Hess petrochemical interests seeking to emulate in St. Croix the tremendous success of the Phillips interests on the south coast of Puerto Rico. What is involved, in both cases, is nothing less than the ability of "breakaway" oil corporations to obtain special permission from the Interior Department to ship their refined oil products into the mainland market, thus jeopardizing, as the domestic oilmen see it, the oil import quota system which over the years has been built up by the American "warfare state" as a national security mechanism. In that struggle the offshore dependency governments become little more than pawns, at best minor allies mainly for publicity purposes, of the big oil combines; the real struggle takes place in the national capital. It is worth noting that the favorable decision of the Interior people with reference to the Puerto Rican application has given rise to charges of gross favoritism; among other things, a number of Phillips board officers were heavy financial backers of the Johnson political bandwagon.

The intermixture of money, law, and politics is undoubtedly a growing phenomenon, one endangering the purity of the democratic process. A number of cases in recent years have shown how widespread it has become, giving rise to a corresponding mood of public cynicism about the honesty of government. Those cases have demonstrated how there grows up almost as a matter of course a mutually beneficial relationship between local officials and Interior Department officials, with some of the latter helping to direct lucrative contractual agreements to consultant organizations which they themselves join as officers on their retirement, and with much of the money being provided by the oil companies seeking lucrative concessions in the offshore dependency.[29] Equally marked is the practice, also widespread in Puerto Rico, whereby local officials, especially in the industry-fomenting agencies, use the business

---

version (St. Thomas, 1966), pp. 66–76; text of *Virgo Corporation* v. *Paiewonsky,* reprinted in *Daily News,* Mar. 25, 1966; and *ibid.,* Oct. 6, 1967. Where economic entrepreneurial chances are so dependent on administrative decisions, an entire politics of appeal to the courts on the part of disappointed applicants grows up; as an example, see *King Christian Enterprises, Inc.* v. *The Government of the Virgin Islands,* reprinted in *St. Croix Avis,* Mar. 30, 1965.

29. Front-page editorial, "Why Oil Quota Is Important to Virgin Islands," *Daily News,* Dec. 2, 1966. For the final affirmative decision of Secretary Udall and what it meant for the island economy, see *ibid.,* Nov. 4, 6, 1967.

contacts developed in their jobs to go into business enterprises themselves when they resign their governmental appointments. The special contribution that the local territorial government makes in these cases is to bring its own influence to bear upon Congress, usually employing variations on the general theme—always certain of a sympathetic congressional hearing—that a locally based industry complex will free the islands from the necessity of receiving "doles" and "handouts" from the federal government and thereby help the stateside taxpayer. In addition, the local legislature can with ease pass acts granting special favors to individual corporations, as the 1968 audit of the comptroller more than adequately documented. It is insistently clear, altogether, that in this kind of power play the local political forces remain perpetually, and often willingly, at the mercy of decisions taken by the private expatriate economic power. That power may even invade the local political jurisdiction. Witness the crass intervention of the Phillips interests in the Puerto Rican plebiscite campaign of 1967 by means of open letters written by prominent directors to political leaders emphasizing the scarcely concealed threat that a voting outcome unfavorable to them would involve their possible evacuation.[30] There is little reason to assume that the Virgin Islands will not become subject to similar interventionism, as the external economic forces that pay the piper seek, perhaps quite naturally, to call the local political tune.

If tourism is a perishable commodity and incentive-based industry dangerously fickle, it follows that a wise economic policy for the Virgins would concentrate on (1) internally, as wide a planned diversification as possible of economic enterprise, and (2) externally, a collaborative membership, as far as political status permitted, with the wider Caribbean economic community. In the internal field, the most conspicuous example of single-minded concentration upon one or two sectors to the detriment of others is, of course, the calamitous neglect of agriculture. The irrational dependence on imported fruits and vegetables, noted very early by the 1917 U.S. Department of Commerce investigators,[31] still continues; nor has much been done in the last fifty years to implement the opinion of a private report at that same time that if a land-

30. For this economic interventionism in the local political process, see the business-sponsored political advertisements in *San Juan Star*, July 20, 21, 1967. See also letter of Stanley Learned, president, Phillips Petroleum Co., to Rafael Durand, in *ibid.*, Apr. 14, 1967, and to Luis Ferre, in *ibid.*, July 21, 1967.

31. U.S., Department of Commerce, *The Danish West Indies: Their Resources and Commercial Importance*, Special Agents Series, no. 129 (Washington, D.C.: Government Printing Office, 1917).

clearing program were undertaken the entire acreage of St. John would offer splendid grazing facilities for local meat production.[32] Very little has been done more recently to meet the warning of experts that if the rapidly advancing urbanization of the agricultural areas of St. Croix— as the phenomenal rise in real estate values encourages many farmers to subdivide their holdings for other than agricultural purposes and as many old Crucian white families are willing to sell land to continental resident buyers which they adamantly refused to sell earlier to colored native sharecroppers—is not stayed the island will soon lose its most important asset for attracting tourists, as well as the opportunity to create a new pattern of independent commercial farm business serving the food needs of all the islands.[33] There is, admittedly, a problem of water supply. But it is not insurmountable. In the short run, it can be met by the usage of subterranean water supplies, a process already well under way in both Antigua and Puerto Rico. In the long run, it can be met by, first, desalinization of salt water, and, second, the condensation of fresh water from trade winds. The latter process is the subject of experiments now actually being conducted in St. Croix by Columbia University's Lamont-Doherty Geological Observatory.

As for the external field, the serious economic wastage involved in the excessively fragmented Caribbean tourist industry demonstrates the advantages that all of the competing islands would derive from a fully integrated regional tourist economy. It hardly makes sense, for example, that while hotel development in Antigua far outstrips tourist demand, in St. Thomas the reverse is the case. A united front would enable the region to operate as a single bargaining agent in such matters as its perennial struggle with the huge North American hotel corporations whose contractual demands—private beach sites, long-term leases, local government financing, and so on—become more and more onerous.

In the meantime, in the absence of such imaginative long-term planning, the Virgins economy is directed by an economic-political alliance eagerly exploiting everything exploitable in the compulsory bilateralism of the closed American economy. It constitutes a system, to quote Valdemar Hill, in which the islands and their limited resources, through local government and congressional benevolence, have become

32. *The Virgin Islands: A Description of the Commercial Value of the Danish West Indies* (New York: National Bank of Commerce, April, 1917).

33. James M. Blaut, Francis X. Mark, and Arthur E. Dammann, "Report to the Governor of the United States Virgin Islands on the Reconstruction of the Agricultural Economy of St. Croix," mimeographed (St. Thomas: Caribbean Research Institute, College of the Virgin Islands, June 15, 1965). See also Virgin Islands Employment Service, *St. Croix Agricultural Manpower Requirements Survey: A Summary Report* (St. Thomas, October, 1960).

a paradise of wealth for American capitalists and entrepreneurs and a source of income for poverty-stricken workers from the depressed British West Indian islands, while the native Virgin Islanders are stranded on the banks of the fast-flowing economic stream. The stream produces a general climate of economic opinion that sees everything in narrow terms of utilitarian advantage. Too many aspects of public policy are canvassed in terms of what they will do to accelerate the flow of the tourist dollar. An early example of this sentiment is shown in the 1950 report of the local Zoning and Planning Committee, which recommended the establishment (still not effected) of positive legislation to protect the local architectural heritage fashioned on the model of the legislation that protects the Vieux Carré section of New Orleans. The report emphasized:

> We cannot stress too strongly that the underlying reason behind these recommendations is economic. The Committee does not make these recommendations solely because they would like the town better if their ideas were followed. Rather they know that the only way to make the tourist prefer St. Thomas as a resort rather than other places is to preserve the oldworldliness and charm, call it quaintness if you will, of the island. A miniature New York or Chicago will not draw the travellers no matter how well it is done and, do not forget, the tourist industry is the money maker of the islands.[34]

The sentiment here noted was put even more emphatically in the astonishingly crass letter that the acting director of the Office of Territories wrote to President Wanlass of the College of the Virgin Islands concerning the effort of the college to divert jet traffic away from the immediately adjacent St. Thomas airport. He wrote:

> I see no more reason for the College of the Virgin Islands to object to the occasional whine of the jets coming into St. Thomas than I would were an individual student whose father is putting him through the College object to the loud whine of the cash register in his father's store. In each case it is the whine which is paying the bills. . . . Instead, I would expect that the classes at the College would use the brief period of forced interruption by each jet to give silent thanks that still another flock of sheep to be shorn has arrived safely at the fold.

Notwithstanding protestations to the contrary, it is not unlikely that the letter expressed pretty adequately the outlook of the political and economic forces that manage the Virgins economy.[35]

34. Report of the Zoning and Planning Committee, Department of Commerce, reprinted in *Daily News*, May 25, 1950.
35. Quoted in *ibid.*, Dec. 7, 1965; "The Political Observer" column, *ibid.*, Dec. 8, 1965; and editorial, *ibid.*, Dec. 9, 1965.

A blueprint for a more rational economic development in the islands would necessitate, clearly, a number of things. There is nothing inherently wrong in a tourist industry whereby the islands, after all, only exploit a natural and indigenous resource. What is needed is a planned direction which, among other things, will stimulate import substitution, so that local products are more fully utilized. There must be more emphasis on the cottage-type hotel industry in place of the mammoth hotel. There must be a more reasonable balance between agricultural and industrial development, so that the rich sugar lands of St. Croix, for example, already supporting a growing beef cattle industry, do not fall prey to the land developer and the building constructor; indeed, the chances of operating a successful agricultural program are becoming more and more marginal. Progressive governments in Trinidad and Guyana are already moving to assert more effective local control over the large outside business interests; there is no reason why a progressive administration in the Virgins should not seriously consider some of the devices that those experiments are suggesting: governmental share-ownership, joint administrative schemes, public stock offerings, stringent control over transfers of land ownership, even public ownership and administration in selected areas. Above all else, the political element in economic development must be made more pronounced. For development does not take place in a vacuum. It receives direction, shape, and quality from the political decision-making process. If that process so wills, development can do more than merely breed the acquisitive society. In the Virgins case its task, surely, is to break down the social class barriers inherited from the Danish tradition and to end the obsessive materialism brought in by the American tradition.

6

~~~

The Social Milieu:
The Native Virgin Islanders

The social structure of the Virgins constitutes what Porter, in his definitive Canadian study, has termed a "vertical mosaic," that is, a series of ethnic layers crisscrossing the other traditional strata of income, class, and occupation, with the added complication of color. It is, then, a socio-racial structure characterized by a number of fairly well-defined cultural groups, separate categories of high social visibility: native Virgin Islanders, continentals, French Americans, Puerto Rican Americans, and British West Indian aliens. Its definition in terms of the usual criteria of family, income, education, occupation, and religious affiliation is difficult because of the paucity of available statistical data (Weinstein was obliged to use the telephone directory as a guide to social-class membership) and the absence of a well-defined, sophisticated class structure. There is, for example, no refined aristocracy of inherited wealth to set the pattern at the top; there is at best only a handful of upper-class Danes who, although highly conscious of their social status, hardly constitute a patrician oligarchy. Thus the traditional vocations of leisure and philanthropy are filled by continentals who, like the Rockefellers, are too itinerant to become resident pacesetters of social life. Nor is there a long-established middle class highly educated in the Arnoldian, Anglo-American fashion; a four-year high-school education, after all, only became available in the 1930s and a local four-year college education only in the 1960s. Classificatory identification by occupation also is hazardous, if only because the tourist industry has played havoc with the customary reference points. Such lower-class jobs as bartender and taxi driver, for instance, are comparatively lucrative, while many continentals undertake jobs, in the service trades,

(154)

for example, that do not give them the financial reward their professional training merits.

Finally, there is no automatic correlation between social class and residence since, in the West Indian fashion, elegant concrete houses may stand cheek by jowl with wooden shacks. However, the absence of any planning for ethnically mixed neighborhoods has recently produced the phenomenon of class-segregated housing developments far removed from the older tradition of easygoing democratic neighborliness. Some thirty years ago Campbell's monograph could describe a social portrait of a series of ethnic nuclei caught up in a tremendously rigid structure, with very little give and take among them, in which the inevitable tension between structural rigidity and an individualistic set of values generated a pervasive psychological frustration and aggrandizement in the majority of the population (a rigidity which had the advantage, at least, of making the definition of class contours comparatively simple). However, the general picture has been profoundly altered by the subsequent development of new phenomena—the politically upward movement of the colored middle class; the growing political assertiveness of the masses, born of universal suffrage; the liberating effects of a first generation of school-educated children; and the slow growth of new social ideas. The mere pressure of numbers has led to qualitative changes. Campbell, for example, could describe the group of white resident continentals—apart from the Marines—as numbering no more than fifty in all, whereas today they must run into the many thousands.

The leading group in this pluralist matrix is, of course, that of the native Virgin Islanders. That the term "native" is enthusiastically accepted by the Creole group, whereas it is a term of racist opprobrium elsewhere in the Caribbean, suggests the deep power of the self-identification process. The term, as popularly used, refers to people, usually of mixed African-European ancestry, born in the islands or of Virgin Islands parents in the States. It is not, however, racially exclusive, since it includes the white Creole group of upper-class "old" Crucian families. To say, then, as a continental resident property owner has said, that native means colored, regardless of origin, and that a white man, even if born in the islands, is by linguistic definition a continental, can only be regarded as an expression of continental hostility or insecurity.[1] The term, in fact, is elastic. Whereas it is not

1. Howard A. Jackson, statement to Butler Committee, U.S. Senate, in *Daily News,* Mar. 17, 1954.

applied to French, Puerto Ricans, or continentals, even if their parents are born locally, it does extend to Tortolians and British West Indians, with whom there exists an extensive relationship springing out of the massive migratory movements of the Antillean region. These outsiders are accepted as family members and thus become natives after a passage of time: lower-class individuals after two generations, upper-class individuals after three generations, it is sometimes surmised. The continental Negro finds entry difficult, and even if he marries into a native family, as did Governor Hastie, it rarely means that he can carry the label. As a title of honor, it is granted reluctantly; thus Morris de Castro, although accorded full social prestige as a prominent member of the Jewish group—whose older residential mercantile families, mainly of Sephardic origin, are fully native—was always denied native status by the purists on the ground that he had come from the outside, having been brought to the islands by his parents as an infant.

The native group, then, is both class stratified and multicolored. The class composition runs from upper and middle to lower classes, covering the whole occupational spectrum from merchants, government officials, landowners, and professional men, through schoolteachers and small businessmen, to semiskilled and unskilled workers. The color composition is equally exhaustive, ranging from the white Danish families, most of them remaining from the Danish period, and white Jewish families, most of them descendants of the early Spanish and Portuguese refugee groups, through the groups of mixed blood, down to the more fully Negro proletarian types. Disregarding for the moment the question whether it is class or color that constitutes the major component of this hierarchy—which is part of the debate that flares up every so often on the respective merits of Danish and American rule—it is at least beyond argument that most Virgin Islanders accept the system, with all of its mechanisms of social competitiveness, emulations, and prestige-seeking. Outright challenge of the system tends, suggestively, to come from the more raffish elements of the continental group; there are few native *barbudas* or "counter-culture" people, although there are (what is quite different) many "hustlers" of the Trinidadian variety. There is, perhaps, more equation of social status with color in St. Croix than in St. Thomas, where socio-historical factors tended to perpetuate the old seignioral tradition, with the top families being almost exclusively white. But that is a subvariant only, just as is the long-standing mutual dislike of Crucians and St. Thomians: Crucians feel disdainfully that St. Thomas is too commercialized and a place where no one could really care to live, while St. Thomians respond with the contemptuous sentiment that St. Croix is "dead." Room is amply permitted for criticism of the social game by native commentators, as the popularity of satirical newspaper columns like the "Hait Boobie" column shows, with the proviso that such criticism not be taken to the mainland press, for everybody rallies in defense of the home society against the "outside" critic. There is, thus, at the most, a common allegiance to the idea of a hedonistic individualism in the native groups. The very variety of their family names, at the same time, bears witness to the tremendous scope of their ethnic and geographical background:

> The McCoys and the Sommersills,
> The O'Reillys and the Hewitts,
> The Canegatas and Prettos,
> The Teytauds and the Tuitts.[2]

The colored majority, then, is divided along class lines (with the ambiguities already noted), with each class marked by its own psychological traits and life-style. The upper class, whose economic privilege has been based on inheritance or personal achievement, has lived traditionally in luxurious St. Thomas hillside homes or Christiansted and Frederiksted town houses. It has its own separate cliques, going back to the Danish days when there existed a privileged subgroup of especially fine parentage and unusual ability whose social position was equal to that of the top layer of Europeans and who were, for example, on the preferred list of government balls and activities that excluded even the middle-class whites. Originally a landed aristocracy, and a strong force in island real estate, the upper class has been joined more recently by professional men trained in American universities, as distinct from the older tradition of attendance at European schools. Its earlier habit of racial exclusiveness and social withdrawal, which was based upon both an acute apprehension of discrimination at the hands of American visitors and a dislike of mixing with white tourists whose education and background it felt to be inferior, has also given way gradually to wider social participation. That process has been accelerated by (1) the social rise, into the top ranks, of dark-skinned professional men by means of college training and innate ability, frequently leading to intermarriage between the two groups, and (2) the internal influence of the mainland-educated sons and daughters of the aristocratic families. Both of those new groups, sometimes collaborating as like-minded persons, have brought with them new intellectual influences; their contact with American Negro groups, for example, has enabled them to think in terms of large racial issues rather than exclusively in the tradi-

2. Edward B. O'Reilly, "Down Memory Lane," *ibid.*, Mar. 1, 1954.

tional Virgin Islands terms of individual adjustment. The process, along with its accompanying conflict between, for instance, the parental "old folks" who had never allowed a white American to darken their doorstep and the daughters who have made white friends in the States and have begun to socialize with Negro friends a little lower on the local social ladder, is well portrayed, for all the maudlin sentimentalism of the story, in Helen Follett's semi-novel *Stick of Fire*.[3] The end result of this process has been that, although traditionally removed from political affairs, the members of this class are increasingly active in community functions, hitherto regarded as being beneath their dignity. They are seen regularly at the hotel fashion shows, Red Cross meetings, bar mitzvahs, the meets of the St. Croix Horse Show Association, and (a recent innovation) the dog shows of the elite St. Thomas Kennel Club; they are members of the Friends of Denmark and the St. Croix Landmarks societies; and one of their most well-known figures, George Dudley of the Lockhart business dynasty, for years has been champion prizewinner in the Carnival troupe competition.

This, altogether, is the prestigious world, partly upper class, partly upper-middle class, of the well-known Virgin Islands families: the Lockharts, the Lindquists, the Nelthropps, the Mooreheads, the de Jonghs, the Christensens, the Berettas, the Paiewonskys, the Sprauves, and others. They are divided, of course, by the usual social and political undercurrents. Perhaps the best-known example is the rivalry between St. Thomian Democrats and Crucian Republicans, the one personified in former Governor Paiewonsky, the other in Crucian "royal families" like the Canadays, who saw in the governor's social program, including the industrial intrusion into St. Croix, a conspiracy to destroy their "way of life," based as it was on colonial servitude and segregation by wealth. At its more strictly professional level the class has contributed vastly to the ethic of public service: to name only a few, Alonzo Moron, of Jewish-native parents, was a cabinet commissioner as early as 1932 and a reforming commissioner of education after 1960; Roy Bornn almost singlehandedly made the local social welfare system what it is today in the islands; Roy Anduze helped greatly to conquer elephantiasis and venereal disease as public health surgeon; Claude Markoe, of French Huguenot descent and a member of the Christiansted mercantile family, contributed to both the insurance and teaching fields; and Dr. David Canegata, the venerable patriarch of his illustrious Crucian family tree, gave fifty years of medical service. These names, of course, are those of the older men who now enjoy the status, accepted

---

3. (New York: Vantage Press, 1956), *passim*.

by all, of tribal elders in the society. They represent an older social tradition touched by the Danish forms of military hierarchy with rigid social classifications; and if it is not quite accurate to identify them, in Campbell's description, as a marginal group since they had repudiated any connection with the Negro race and still could not feel any secure identification with the white race, it is true, nonetheless, that their attitude toward "their people" tended to be imbued with ideas of European class paternalism. The second generation, their children, have escaped that marginality in some measure, and an entire body of families—Wheatley, Penn, Creque, Lewis, Penha, Nelthropp, de Lugo, Bough, Lawaetz—have given their sons to the sectors of politics and governmental service, forging a more direct and less seignioral relationship with the popular majority.

The middle class proper reaches out to include the administrative and secretarial echelons of the public service, skilled artisans, graduate nurses, social workers, salespeople, teachers, and shop proprietors. Most of them are high-school graduates. Many of them, as the Kunzer report of 1957 shows, are graduates from, in the main, the stateside Negro colleges: Tuskegee, Fisk, Howard, Russell Sage, and Hampton Institute.[4] In general, their skin color falls between that of the lower- and upper-class groups but has tended to become darker in the last twenty-five years. Their mark of differentiation from the lower-class group is less that of income than it is of job status; the base salary, for example, of a teacher with a bachelor's degree ($5,400 as of 1970) would be no higher than that of a heavy-equipment operator in the construction industry earning an hourly wage of $2.50 as set by the Wage Board. It is the public aspect of a job, what it involves doing in the public eye, that counts rather than its monetary or psychological rewards. Thus the maid who will feel immensely affronted if requested to feed the house pets can be matched by the departmental typist who will resent being asked to fetch the mid-morning coffee. It is the same sort of snobbishness which, as Jarvis noted, mistakes the appearance for the reality of social culture; thus a middle-class housewife would consider a large refrigerator in the dining room a more important badge of status than a flush toilet in the house. What is different today is that the economic base of that social disease has somewhat altered, being more and more a comfortable berth in a government department, made easier than in Jarvis' time by the quiet revolution which has turned the machinery of government almost completely into the hands of the colored middle-

4. Edward J. Kunzer, "Graduates from High School in St. Thomas and St. John Who Have Had Advanced Training Off the Island," rev. ed., mimeographed (St. Thomas Public Library, 1957).

class groups. The inordinate enlargement of officeholders that has resulted from that change, especially the creation of patronage employees (from less than 100 in 1961 to more than 800 in 1967), can be seen either as the growth of a political spoils machine, American style, or as the natural outcome of the world-wide development of the welfare state. There are elements of both in the phenomenon. But it can be seen, sociologically speaking, as an expression of the Virgin Islander's preference for an institutional rather than a private employer and, even more, as another device in his struggle to maintain his social position against the growing invasion of the non-native "outsiders." It is not so much a bogus state socialism as it is an expression of the inter-ethnic struggle.

It is not surprising, then, that an almost Augustan sinecure psychology has grown up in the ranks of the Negro governmental phalanx; and it is no less a respectable Virgin Islands elder than the irrepressible Alton Adams (in himself almost a territorial institution) who has castigated this exploitative attitude. Noting that his own generation of the Bornns, de Castros, de Lugos, and Daniels were men who, denied a college education, industriously worked out their own salvation by private reading, steady association with others, and a wise use of their spare time, he has sadly concluded that they have been succeeded by too many college students who "have risen and are still rising to high positions, governmental and other, merely on ladders of credits and diplomas, often amusingly displaying an air of offensive competence not in any way justified by actual achievement." [5] That it is not an inaccurate judgment can be seen, any day, in the ubiquitous figure of the Virgin Islands departmental bureaucrat, emphasizing his distinctiveness from others by a sartorial habit—neat shirt and tie, dark suit and fashionable briefcase—often comically inappropriate to a tropical climate.

The general class and race attitudes of the lower class mirror the influence of its historical subordination in a highly status-conscious society. Its members have inherited the sociological position of the slaves, only recently ameliorated by the emergence of the alien worker as the most lowly regarded of all groups in the society. It is increasingly difficult to speak of them as a group with distinctively sharp characteristics since they are more and more mixed up with their "down island" kinsfolk and, in any case, are giving way, numerically, to them: in 1965, for example, of the 1,141 live births registered in St. Thomas and St. John, 343 mothers listed the Virgin Islands as their place of birth while 649 mothers listed the British West Indies, 215 of those being from

5. Address, printed in *Home Journal*, Feb. 12, 1959.

Tortola.[6] The portrait of this class painted by both Jarvis and Campbell assumed environmental conditions of, first, mass unemployment and, second, gross educational deprivation, both of which are now more or less terminated. It is doubtful whether many individuals nowadays deprive themselves of food, as Campbell claimed, in order to buy attractive mail-order clothes. Nor is there today the startling contrast, also noted by Campbell, between the squalid condition of home interiors and the impeccable personal cleanliness of their owners, even in those working-class districts where water supplies must come from communal pipe stands. The aversion to any kind of work with the hands as being "slavery work" is still there. But it is breaking down; and the working-class native readily takes on the various jobs of the new economy—truck driver, printer, TV repairman, auto mechanic, and so on—especially if they are jobs that offer a relative autonomy. In a similar way, the old taboo that prohibited a middle-class or upper-class woman from doing her own shopping has quite disappeared with the arrival, in the last few years, of the modern supermarkets of the Pueblo style. Also, a generation of public school education has done much to soften social manners, and the uninhibited public obscenity and coarseness of behavior which Jarvis noted, with all the disdain of the schoolmaster, are much less in evidence today; where they do occur they are blamed, suggestively, on the alien.

Much, however, of the Jarvis-Campbell analysis remains true, within these altered environmental conditions. Class-consciousness is still part of the psychological make-up of the lower-class individual. He still continues to avoid, if possible, situations in which he may seem inferior, a difficult exercise since his class position forces him into many strained social relations. It is pride, rather than money, that drives him, and many continental employers have found how rashly imprudent it is to display impatience and anger in giving orders, for such attitudes only create angry resistance and eventual desertion of the job. An information sheet prepared for tourists by one of the business centers significantly includes a pointed warning on this score: "You will find our people friendly, courteous and hospitable. They are also sensitive and proud. Bear this in mind in your relations with them." There is, similarly, an excessive vigilance in the effort to avoid all situations that are potentially vulnerable or degrading, exemplified in the reluctance of school-leaving youngsters, as the 1954 report on the tourist industry lamented, to enter a career of catering to tourists. There is

6. Virgin Islands, Department of Health, Bureau of Statistical Services, *Vital Statistics, 1964–1965* (St. Thomas: Government Printing Office, 1966), table 15.

almost a paranoiac obsession with the outward insignia of well-being, a fear of relapsing into the sort of poverty out of which most Virgin Islanders have only comparatively recently emerged, after all; thus Weinstein reports that the disgrace felt in going barefoot is so great that taking patients' shoes from them is an effective means of preventing unauthorized departures from the hospital psychiatric ward.[7] Thus a social class that only a few years ago "sucked salt" is now determined to use its new prosperity for social leverage. Home interiors, even in the worst slum sections, will sport refrigerators, stoves, television sets, radios, and washing machines; the shanties survive less because of inability to pay higher rents than because of the old squatter system, long residence, no land title, and the shortage of low- and middle-income housing. Social recreations have also widened, and the lower-class person now attends the horse races at Sugar Estate and Flamboyant Park, takes the ten-dollar boat trip to Tortola, plans his week-end picnics at Magens Bay, and goes to his club dances at the various hotels (the recent dispute over the unwillingness of the management of the St. Croix by the Sea hotel to continue facilities for late-night parties by the local public indicates the existence of an affluent clientele willing to pay for its fun).

The complex interrelationships among the various segments of the three-tiered group of native Virgin Islanders have changed over the years only to the degree that a European-oriented class system has become an American-oriented system. The forms have changed, but the inner driving spirit remains much the same. Thus, the upper-class person still seeks to extract overt manifestations of social deference from those beneath him. Dress still remains the emulative device for all classes, who resist the habit of informality affected by the continentals. Habits of speech are similarly used as a mechanism for obtaining respect, so that whereas continentals invariably speak to each other in their offices on a first-name basis, the more formal titles of "Mr.," "Mrs.," and "Miss" are widely exercised in the government departmental offices among natives. There is, indeed, almost a pathological need for "respect," as is evident from the extrasensitive response to criticism, which frequently takes the form, at the lower social levels, of highly ritualized quarreling characterized less by physical volume than by an almost comic litigiousness; the ultimate measure against an opponent is not to strike him but to threaten to "give him a case," to take him to court. There is, significantly, very little of the Trinidadian *picong* (the habit of poking fun

7. Edwin A. Weinstein, *Cultural Aspects of Delusion: A Psychiatric Study of the Virgin Islands* (Glencoe, Ill.: Free Press, 1962), p. 115.

at others), and most continentals agree that natives possess little sense of humor. Indeed, the psychotic delusions among hospital mental patients, cited by Weinstein, indicate a pervasive social morbidity, which might be traced, historically, to the general fact that Virgin Islands cultural patterns have been shaped by the psychologically stringent norms of the Protestant-Puritan ethic, first through the Danish instrumentality and then through that of the United States. There is, in fact, something of a combination of Ibsen and Cotton Mather in the Virgin Islands character.

Such a society is inevitably characterized by (1) a marked deficiency in any positive sense of community spirit and social obligation, and (2) a spirit of keen suspiciousness, even overt hostility, between social classes. The first characteristic is best expressed, perhaps, in the exaggerated individualism of the Virgin Islander. He does not identify, as Weinstein has shown, with the leading institutions of his society: government, family, church. He has little sense of occupational vocation as a force shaping his life attitudes. The resident Catholic priest, who is socially minded, might occasionally preach a homily of Catholic socialism to his parishioners,[8] but the message will rarely be heard in the midst of a spirit of social careerism in which the participants, as one of their own number bitterly noted, will only mix with the clergy if they can exploit the clerical social graces, and in which, therefore, the Horatio Alger philosophy of life gives way to Henry James's "bitch goddess Success."[9] At the middle- and upper-class levels the thing to do is to seize upon honorific positions, in the spirit of a local politician's comment at an earlier period upon the then superintendent of social welfare: "He has more titles than Ickes, and like a typical Virgin Islander every position that passes by he grabs." At the lower-class level the desideratum is a job with the minimum of social control and the maximum of social maneuver, ideally exemplified in the status of the taxi driver. The comparison with the Port of Spain "pirate" taxi in the Trinidadian shiftless society comes to mind. Yet it is indicative of Virgin Islands anti-social values that whereas the "pirate" taxi is a sort of social mean in Trinidadian life, in which civil servant and dockhand, both pedestrians, will jostle and talk with each other in a raucous, democratic fashion, the Virgin Islands taxi caters almost exclusively to the tourist traffic. The rest of the population, if they are poor, walk or ride the private concessionaire buses, and, if they are well-to-do, drive their own cars. Only the introduction in recent years of the public taxi, the Puerto

8. Rev. Fr. Francis Meehan, Superior, St. Patrick's Church, Frederiksted, "Christianity and Democracy," *Daily News*, Aug. 30, Sept. 7, 1944.
9. Letter by "Observer," in *ibid.*, Sept. 22, 1942.

(163)

Rican *carro publico,* providing cheap interurban transportation, is beginning to change this picture. There is also at the same time a marked group preference in vehicular traffic. The taxi driver, thinking no doubt of the tourist preferences, usually sports a large American car, preferably "with the breeze" (air-conditioned) ; the continentals prefer small foreign cars; the French use pickup trucks; and the vacationing college boys and girls have taken over the small, colorful runabout.

It is essential to note the peculiar quality of this Creole individualism, which is not so much utilitarian as hedonistic. It is less the economic individualism of the Calvinist commercial virtues than it is the typically West Indian solipsism of the "spade," the "saga boy," the "limer," with its roots in the preindustrial colonial experience. It is powerfully narcissistic. If, then, the Virgin Islands continental is a heliophile, the native is a heliocentric, believing that the universe revolves around him and his works. He is proud of the record number of public holidays (twenty-three in all, including some like Supplication Day and Organic Act Day not observed in the United States) of his society, and defends them against American critics who want to "import some of the features of the ulcer circuit to the tropics." [10] This does not mean, of course, that he is lazy, and it is a palpable error to say that he is; popular dicta, like the saying that "Tortolans work and St. Thomians steal," are clearly libelous. It is true, at the same time, that the traditional laissez faire economic virtues are not the sacred images that they are in the American folklore of capitalism. Work, thrift, the "eye on the main chance" are not much esteemed for their own sake. The energy that continentals invest in their recreational activities is a continuing source of amusement to the native onlooker. Despite the jealousy with which rank, especially in the middle-class groups, is guarded, there is little of an exclusive professional identification, as is evidenced by the widespread habit of "moonlighting," in which a person may hold two or even three jobs at the same time; there is a well-known young native, for example, who works in an administrative capacity in the Labor Department, is a leading columnist for the *Home Journal,* and sells insurance in his spare time.

What this social temper produces, at the working-class level, is the figure of the young Virgin Islands "sport," casually dressed, with his dark sunglasses and transistor radio as status symbols, "hurrying" to get a car in order to "set up" his Saturday night dates, knowledgeable about volleyball and softball, sufficiently uninhibited to be able to shuffle happily

10. Editorial, *ibid.,* Feb. 25, 1965. For full list of Virgin Islands holidays, see *ibid,* Jan. 8, 1964.

by himself in front of the bar juke box, but not so forgetful of his Virgin Islands fear of making a fool of himself in public as to become drunk or objectionably rowdy. As a general comment on the phenomenon being discussed here, it is worth noting that despite the fact that the local journalistic literature is full of the "black bourgeoisie" ideology in praise of the energetic Virgin Islanders who have "made the grade" in the white American world—the Jarvis writings are full of this theme and Jarvis himself founded the *Daily News* in the 1930s as a vehicle for this Booker Washington gospel—the individual who gets the popular applause is not so much the self-made businessman as the keen-witted sharpster who "gets away with murder." Living on one's wits, in fact, is a common mode of survival in Virgin Islands life, as it is in Caribbean society in general. "The Horatio Alger tradition of bootblack to corporation president," concludes Weinstein, "may be closer to reality in the Virgin Islands than in the continental United States, but it is not sentimentally cherished." [11]

Interclass relations do not approximate to a higher social good either. There is, as already noted, a common allegiance to the individualistic ethic. But there is little that is more positive. The various grades of the native group are held together at best by a certain mutual disdainful tolerance, at worst by a venomous mutual antipathy. The native whites have throughout adopted the face-saving rationalization that the Americans since 1917 have "spoiled" the workers, who once provided them with a docile servant class. The lower-class colored native has retained much of the older tradition of mutual aid in his relations with his fellows; but his attitude to the brown-skinned middle class and the light-skinned upper class still remains one of suspicion, since those classes, it is believed, "have forgotten where they came from." There is a general reluctance to give a man his due, and the rise of individuals to economic affluence or social prominence is usually attributed ungenerously to questionable dealings or sexual favors. Everybody will unite on occasion, of course, to pay homage to the popular "native son"; but the homage is usually accompanied with the assertion that, as in the case of the much-respected native pharmacist Oswald Heath, he is a "gentleman of the old school" who is dying out in this "commercial minded, money grubbing age." [12] Feelings of class envy, of course, are softened somewhat by social mobility generated by educational opportunity, and the progressive social elevation of succeeding generations of dark-skinned natives over the last fifty years has done much in this

11. Weinstein, *Cultural Aspects of Delusion*, p. 64.
12. Editorial, *Daily News*, Apr. 21, 1964; also *ibid.*, Apr. 15, 1964.

respect. The case of the Amadeo Francis family is perhaps represent-ative: the grandfather was a policeman under the Danish regime; the father was a schoolteacher under the new American regime; and the son, the Amadeo Francis now domiciled in Puerto Rico, is a well-known figure in the upper echelons of San Juan public administration. At the same time, however, that elevating process, insofar as it helps reinforce new social inequalities based on income, also serves to reinforce the social contempt for manual labor. A characteristic expression of that contempt can be seen in the snobbish taunt of the local native press against its critics among Harlem Virgin Islanders to the effect that "Even though the municipality is impoverished for skilled workmen in all crafts and there are opportunities in other lines of business these underground politicos still work in subway exchanges in the day, live in conditions unknown here and administrate the islands from cook-shops as a sort of indoor pastime." [13] The proper retort, of course, was to point out, as did Ashley Totten, that some of those cooks were paid higher wages than most native officials in the islands.[14] Humble social beginnings are thus a matter of embarrassment rather than of pride. A leading colored official of the Chamber of Commerce is popularly referred to as the "pants presser" as a mark of ridicule, while it is not difficult to encounter negative comment on the early origins of the Paiewonsky family fortune in, according to popular legend, the illicit liquor industry of the Prohibition era.

Virgin Islands social life can be seen as a series of concentric circles, both of social and ethnic group, that surround but only marginally touch one another. The top white stratum keeps pretty much to itself, relying more, perhaps, on its caste status than its class power. Senior cites the case of the richest man in St. Croix who was not accepted socially by the Crucian "royal families" because he was an immigrant of Eastern Mediterranean stock.[15] Both the middle- and lower-class native worlds are closed cultures and there is little Negro solidarity to overcome the mutual suspicion between "brown" and "black." The middle group, in particular, like their Barbadian counterparts, are characterized by the habit of social withdrawal, and an invitation to visit their homes is more likely to come from those of its members who have lived for some time in the States. Their deep sense of cultural shame, so vividly

13. Editorial, *ibid.*, Feb. 1, 1946.
14. Letter in *ibid.*, Mar. 13, 1946.
15. Clarence Senior, "The Puerto Rican Migrant in St. Croix," mimeographed (San Juan: Social Science Research Center, University of Puerto Rico, 1947), p. 17.

emphasized in their treatment of Jarvis, is only slightly ameliorated by their more recent espousal of "culture," which in fact amounts to little more than a willingness to enjoy the Carnival *bamboula* and *quadrille* dances and a continuing vigilance against "dirty" calypsos. These attitudes are the result, in part, of the ethnic marginalism of the group, and, in part, of the social ostracism they have suffered at the hands of the more socially favored. The general attitude of the white elite was summed up, early in the American regime, in the slanderous assertion by the white Danish Crucian Halvor Berg to the congressional hearings of 1926 that a large Negro population like that of the islands could not be relied on to carry on for themselves since they lacked "certain essentials." It speaks volumes, then, that about the only united front all these groups can put together is the essentially negative front against the continentals, summed up pretty adequately in the splendidly haughty observation of one island aristocrat quoted by Jeanne Harman: "After all, my great-grandfather and my wife's great-grandfather were educated in Europe. Half of these Continental Americans don't even know who their great-grandfather was, much less where he went to school—if he did." [16]

It is equally significant that the only breaches in this hostile barrier occur in those small social subworlds where special considerations prevail: the Jewish Synagogue, of whose congregants the majority in 1967 (some 70 to 80 families out of a total of 102) were recent stateside immigrants, whose names—Kimmelman, Kessler, Machover—figure equally with the older native names—Sasso, de Castro, Robles; and the Danish community—an estimated total of some 15 families in St. Thomas in 1967—which also includes the older native families like the Mylners, Magnussens, and Jensens, and the newer arrivals like the Nielsens and the Dithmers.[17]

Despite the official portrait of the society as, in Eldra Shulterbrandt's eulogy, "people living in dignity and mutual respect for one another and with a common goal of creating and developing a better life, each having an opportunity of sharing in the fruits of his labor, in accordance with his ability and regardless of the roots from which he sprang," [18] it is, on the contrary, a parallelogram of informally organized segre-

16. *The Virgins: Magic Islands* (New York: Appleton-Century-Crofts, 1961), p. 149.

17. For the Jewish congregation, see Isidor Paiewonsky, *Jewish Historical Development in the Virgin Islands, 1685–1959* (St. Thomas: Isidor Paiewonsky, 1959) ; and interview with Mrs. Roth, Jewish Synagogue, St. Thomas, September 7, 1967. For the Danish group, see *Familie Journalen* (Copenhagen), quoted in *Daily News*, Virgin Islands Golden Jubilee issue, Apr. 3, 1967.

18. "Quo Vadis?," in *50 Years* (St. Thomas: St. Thomas Friends of Denmark Society, 1967), pp. 61–62.

gationist entities pregnant with feelings of jealousy, hostility, and even fear. It is true that the divisiveness is offset by pride in being a "native Virgin Islander" in its more positive sense. But that term also has a negative meaning, used as a sort of personality test to differentiate its possessor from the alien components of the social mix. The body of island superstitions, although now much attenuated by the spread of education, indicates, in its excessive preoccupation with the hazards of pregnancy, sickness, and death, a general feeling in the masses of defenselessness in an unfriendly world. The available defense mechanisms in their struggle have not been plentiful at any time; and it is worth noting that the abuses committed against the more vulnerable of the poor have frequently been exposed not by a protective native force but by the occasional outside force: the visiting reporter like Bill Frank, who wrote scathingly of the atrocious conditions of the old detention center for juvenile delinquents in the ancient dungeons of Fort Christian,[19] or the stateside institution like the famous Carville Center in Louisiana, which campaigned for nearly twenty years for the closing down of the Christiansted hospital for Hansen's disease patients with its slave-camp conditions.[20] Even Jarvis, for all his heroic struggle to project his people as an object of serious and sympathetic study, could write, with anthropological naivete, about their "childish simplicity and credence" and assert, like the most hidebound reactionary, that "even in their saner moments they have the mob spirit." Even the area of recreation, which could conceivably be a common meeting ground for everybody, yields in part to the habit of mutually convenient separatism, so that there are bars, like the Moon Glow restaurant, that cater mainly to aliens; those, like Duffys, looking to the teenage children of St. Thomas' "best" families; and those, like the Powder Horn Tavern, attracting a mixed crowd of young Negro "bucks," professional civil servants, and the more democratic continentals (formerly the clientele of the Grand Hotel Gallery before it became a popular luncheon rendezvous for the tourists). Similarly, in Virgin Islands clubland, places like Don's Alley in the rundown Pollyberg area are preferred by the "counterculture" crowd; places like the St. Thomas Club are not patronized by the natives; and places like the Fallen Angel and Eddie's Back Street Club draw a mixed continental and native islander crowd.

Myth and reality are especially interwoven in the literature that deals with the upper-middle colored group of native Virgin Islanders.

19. "Frankly Speaking" column, *Daily News*, Feb. 1, 1964.

20. Article on Hansen's Home in St. Croix in *Home Journal*, July 16, 1958, reprinted from *The Star*, official publication of Hansen's Disease Hospital, Carville, La. See also Dr. William J. Fordrung, letter, *Home Journal*, Mar. 12, 1958.

Most commentators on this group have emphasized the qualities of superlative self-confidence and relaxed social poise growing out of their special status in the Danish class-color spectrum. The qualities are there, beyond doubt. But there are signs that they are being slowly undermined by feelings of insecurity as the non-native groups begin to press against them both in numbers and economic power. Much of their private conversation turns around the fear that they are "losing out" to the American invaders, that they are being pushed to the wall, that they are losing control of the economic foundations of their way of life. In the words of one of their versifiers:

> We are now caught between two massive jaws—
> The alien and their fairer counterparts.[21]

Added to this there is a gnawing suspicion of missed opportunities, of lucrative economic enterprise neglected by natives and seized upon by continentals, a sentiment perhaps justified in the light of the fact that tourism was, in fact, a viable exercise first grasped by the expatriate force before the local group overcame its innate isolationism sufficiently to become aware of the possibilities. The result, altogether, is an almost paranoiac anxiety, a feeling of unpleasant social claustrophobia in this group. Much of the local politics, which is frequently a running battle between a Creole-controlled machinery of government and a continental-dominated economic sector, is to be understood in the light of this. The Virgin Islands diaspora also begins to feel the pressure, and editorials are written in the Virgin Islands New York press on the need, for example, to organize an annual homecoming tour in order to offset the growing influence of Puerto Ricans and British West Indians. The resettlement program of the insular government, seeking to bring the exiles back home, can be seen as a further expression of this struggle for ethnic survival, corresponding to the land-selling policy of the Crucian white oligarchy with an eye to building up in St. Croix, through "new blood," another white-Bermuda situation.

Yet even here the myth-making propensity is evident. For to speak of their economic patrimony being "lost" to them is to assume that the native group originally controlled the economic sector, which, historically, is doubtful. The economy, in its heyday, was controlled mainly by outside forces and their local agents. With economic decline, it is true, the big warehouse stores vacated by evacuating foreigners were taken

---

21. C. L. Emannuel, "Reflections on the Semi-Centennial," *Daily News*, Virgin Islands Golden Jubilee issue, p. 15. For similar complaints from the British Virgin Islands, see Noel Lloyd, "A Lack of Vision," *The Island Sun* (Roadtown), Mar. 9, 1968.

over in part by clerks and small businessmen, who partitioned the large rooms and the covered archways, producing the small, hole-in-the-corner shops characteristic of the island town scene in the 1920s and 1930s. They came to represent, certainly, a vital Creole business element of native merchants, especially in the grocery and dry-goods fields. But the second generation, their college-educated sons, failed on the whole to carry on the entrepreneurial tradition, deserting it for more pleasing vocations, especially in the continental United States; and they were replaced by the subsequent economic invasion of continentals. The upshot of all this has been that, as of today, with few exceptions, such as Joe Alexander, Alexander Moorehead, and Peter Christian in St. Croix, and Charles Hay, the Paiewonskys, Lockharts, Heaths, and Anthony Quetel in St. Thomas, the business economy is one of expatriate ownership and management. The process continues apace; the older generation of businessmen (like David Chinnery, who worked his way up, in the legendary Alexander Hamilton tradition, from hired store clerk to successful ownership of his own store) is giving way to the younger generation of energetic teachers and educators (like the Lincoln-Oberlin-educated Phillip Gerard), who are moving into the new field of local higher education.

This, then, is not the catastrophic revolution of ownership the Creole myth likes to embroider upon. The degree of change, at the same time, has been sufficiently large to make native Virgin Islanders feel that they are displaced persons in their economic society. Their injured pride seeks compensation; and it is not by accident that the most socially pretentious of the personal profiles in the unofficial *St. Thomas Directory* that Lis King put together in 1962 are of prominent natives: Alton Adams, the Bornns, Henry de Lagarde, Cyril King, Aubrey Ottley, the Paiewonsky brothers. It is, perhaps, the chief weakness of the Campbell and Weinstein analyses of the Virgin Islands character that, although their treatment in terms of psychological categories improved upon earlier analyses couched in terms of racial categories, their preoccupation with psychological phenomena led to a comparative neglect of the economic power structure which creates the major properties of the social experience. How the socio-psychological traits of this group will develop in the future will depend, very much, upon whether or not they are allowed a "place in the sun" in the general economic development of the society.

How valid is it, in the light of all this, to speak of a Virgin Islands "culture"? The recent establishment of a Cultural Center, based on the thesis that "The people of the Virgin Islands are a mixture of subcultures in the process of becoming a fully participating part of today's world while still valuing their own uniqueness and heritage," [22] makes it a pertinent inquiry. The spurious quality of the legendary Danish culture has already been noted, amounting as it did to little more than a sort of genteel patrician pose nicely summed up in an American observer's notice that "The attitude of the Petersons [as Virgin Islands Danes] toward the less fortunate Negroes, and their concern for their problems . . . was just as simple and natural, within cultural limitations, of course, as toward their upper-class colored friends who dropped in for afternoon coffee." [23] It is difficult, then, to accept the pleasing conceit that the Danish-American Victor Borge, who keeps a Crucian residence, somehow personifies that culture when, in fact, he is as American, in the social values he embodies, as Herman Wouk. Nor has the Jewish impress been any more noticeable, because the group is very small numerically, having been reduced to a mere handful of families by 1900, and the continental group is preponderant in its presently revived state; these two factors have precluded the growth of a strong creolist Judaism. It is significant that the history of the group written by its local historian, Isidor Paiewonsky, says little, if anything, of the problem of the relationship between Jewish cultural traits and the historical development of St. Thomian capitalism.

It is equally difficult to discover much that is truly indigenous in the Indian and Negro sectors of the islands' cultural landscape. Apart from the St. John petroglyphs and a few scattered artifacts from the St. Thomas and St. Croix kitchen midden sites, there is little left of the original culture of the Taino-Arawak Indian groups. Of the later popular Negro culture many of the traditional African forms, in dance and song, for example, have disappeared, as have also the older crafts, despite the effort of the New Deal cooperative schemes to adapt them to the embryonic tourist trade. Boat-building is now a dead art. There is something left, it is true, both of basketry and of hat-making, but neither perhaps is economically feasible in the light of mass-production competitive goods; there are a few remaining furniture makers of the old Danish tradition; while on a somewhat more optimistic note there are still some four families of jewelry makers practicing their traditional trade, especially the creation of gold and silver bracelets. In

22. Virgin Islands Council on the Arts, "The Arts in the United States Virgin Islands," a study report by Ruth S. Moore, mimeographed (St. Thomas: Caribbean Research Institute, College of the Virgin Islands, 1967), p. 1; see also the supplement, "Arts in the U.S. Virgin Islands," by Ruth S. Moore and David M. Hough, 1967.

23. Helen Follett, *Stick of Fire*, pp. 70–71.

the field of the verbal arts there is, as is well known, a large body of folktales and stories collected over the years by, variously, Florence Meade, Elsie Clews Parsons, and Jarvis, further enriched by the *adivinansas* and *aguinaldos* perpetuated by the older elements of the St. Croix Puerto Ricans, with possibly some early French influence emanating from Vieques island. The 1967 report of the newly formed Virgin Islands Council on the Arts indicates a reviving interest in this cultural heritage.[24]

Yet none of this amounts to much when certain critical conditions are brought to mind. The folktale lore has so many generic similarities with that of the other islands that it is obviously a general West Indian rather than a particular Virgin Islands phenomenon, just as is the tendency toward proverbial utterances; even the Negro dialect of the Virgins shares with others a general base in early eighteenth-century English, traditionally the language of trade and piracy in the West Indies. Much of everything else—clothing styles, dance, theater, crafts like cabinet-making, architectural styles—was copied from the Danish-Nordic model. Religious life, shaped by European missionary effort, gave rise to "white hymns" rather than a hymnology of local origin. The poetic literature put out by the local versifiers—Cyril Creque, J. P. Gimenez, Aubrey Anduze, and others—has been couched in a feeble neo-Tennysonian Gothic style, quite ignoring the possibilities of the rich, picturesque speech of the masses. It is even possible to discover German folklore, Shakespearean tales, the Uncle Remus stories, and garbled biblical stories masquerading as original island stories. The painters who are invoked in the Virgin Islands cultural pantheon turn out to be artists, like Pissarro, Durant, and Prud'homme, who were born there but did their work abroad in exile, or, like Melbye and Visby, were expatriates living for brief periods only in the islands.

All this has been reinforced, in the post-1917 and especially the post-1945 period, by the inundation of any genuinely authentic local cultural survivals by (1) the West Indian influence, and (2) the massive

24. For all this, see Folmer Andersen, *Notes on St. Croix* (Christiansted: St. Croix Museum Commission, 1954); Florence Meade, "Folk Tales from the Virgin Islands," *Journal of American Folklore*, Vol. XLV, no. 177 (July–September, 1932); St. Thomas and St. John Municipality, Department of Education, Summer School, 1929, "Collected Folklore of the Virgin Islands," mimeographed (St. Thomas Public Library); Elsie Clews Parsons, *Folklore of the Antilles, French and English* (New York: American Folk-lore Society, 1943), pt. 3; J. Antonio Jarvis, *The Virgin Islands and Their People* (Philadelphia: Dorrance, 1944), chaps. 7, 8, 10; Virgin Islands Council on the Arts, Study Report and Supplement; J. C. Trevor, *Aspects of Folk Culture in the Virgin Islands* (Master's thesis, Emmanuel College, Cambridge University, 1950); and W. Bryant, "Ceramic Periods of St. Thomas and St. John Islands, Virgin Islands," *American Studies* (Pan-American Philosophical Society), 4, 1962.

Americanizing process in every aspect of insular life. The West Indian influence is there most notably in calypso, so that even the versatile Bill La Motta, whose dream has been to "give the world a true, unadulterated version of calypso that is indigenous to the Virgin Islands," has admitted that the calypso form is in fact a Trinidadian import. The same West Indian influence can be seen in the fact that the steel band invasion from Trinidad produced some fifteen local bands in the period 1954–60.[25] The American influence, of course, is utterly pervasive; even Jarvis, at the moment of bitterly complaining about the inexpert rendition of Stephen Foster songs during a Negro History Week program, could only suggest that they be replaced not by authentic island songs but by the Negro songs, mostly Negro-American style, of Marian Anderson.[26] Virgin Island culture, in brief, is overwhelmingly derivative in character. Thus most of the fare offered by the quite numerous theatrical and choral groups today is, of sheer necessity, of Euro-American content.

The recent development, then, of public discussion about island "culture," also taken up by the Department of Education, must be seen as a movement interesting in the main because of the social considerations motivating its champions in the middle-class native sector. It is, to begin with, fashionable. It is also a social weapon: defiant assertions about local culture, like the defense of "dear old Denmark," can be used in the social war against vulgar continentals, just as in Trinidad and Guyana assertions about Indian caste are used as weapons by East Indians against offensive Creole Negroes. Nor does it require much mental effort, for it is easy to talk airily about native culture without knowing much about it, just as many people speak authoritatively about Jarvis as the grand innovator of the movement without in fact having really read his books. That explains why it was outside and not inside forces—the Danish National Museum after 1919 and the Royal Academy of Fine Arts after 1950—that cared sufficiently about the preservation of the Danish architectural heritage, in the face of the potential threat posed by a mass American tourist traffic, to undertake an exhaustive codification of it.[27] Vast ingenuity is expended in identifying cultural resources and in drawing up impressive blueprints for their preservation and strengthening; and granted the paucity of such resources this leads

25. "Music Lecturer," *Home Journal*, Aug. 11, 1967; and "Artist Strives to Keep Local Flavor in Songs," *Daily News*, Jan. 8, 1965.

26. J. Antonio Jarvis, lecture on theme of the Negro, printed in *Daily News*, Feb. 18, 1944.

27. Inge Mejer Antonsen, "Researches on the Domestic Culture of the Danish West Indies," from *Dansk Folkemuseum oz Frilands-museum*, 1966 (microfilm, St. Thomas Public Library). See also synopsis of the Royal Academy report in English, "Three Towns," *Virgin Islands View*, March, 1968.

to blatantly deceptive claims. When, for example, governmental subsidies are granted to groups which are largely continental in membership, the question arises as to whether this is not simply a scheme in which the local government officialdom caters to "continentals-come-lately" and "imported artists." A similar skepticism arises when a listing of cultural facilities includes the four radio stations and the five newspapers of the islands, most of which are actively engaged in the dissemination, in one way or another, of cultural pollution from the United States.[28] It is difficult, after all, to believe that the few native foods like fungi and whelks even begin to match the culinary richness of East Indian foods in Trinidad or that the few stories that the linguistic anthropologists are able to collect begin to rival the wealth, say, of St. Lucian popular folklore. The whole thing becomes even more ludicrous when the right-hand drive habit is invoked as local culture.

The government-sponsored *kulturkampf* sort of program, in brief, must be seen, for all of its real merit as an effort to bridge the gulf between government, the public, and the arts, as another play in the interclass, intergroup competition. It facilitates the social power of the native professional class. For whereas the old Pearson "social uplift" program was manned by the white federal expert, this later program is manned by the local community leader, the local educational official, the local leading citizen, along with, of course, the ubiquitous stateside consultant. It lacks the élan of a war of liberation against the colonial power, pitting the native culture against the metropolitan culture. It evinces, indeed, a fatal ambiguity about its ultimate goal; thus, a list of famous Virgin Islanders of the past drawn up by a local educator is so indiscriminate in its selection that it includes at one and the same time the names of the Crucian Negroes who led the 1848 and 1878 revolts and the name of the slave, Mingo Tamarind, who helped his masters to put down the slave insurrection of 1733.[29] A similar ambivalence of first principles is to be seen in the "Project Introspection" report of the Department of Education, which properly noted the profound cultural ignorance of the Virgin Islands schoolchild but failed to draw the lesson that this had been brought about by first a Danish and then an American school system that have throughout denigrated things local and elevated things metropolitan, the typical legacy of colonial education. This ambivalence can perhaps be explained by the

28. Virgin Islands Council on the Arts, Study Report, p. 19; and Virgin Islands, Department of Education, "Project Introspection," Application for an Operational Grant, ESEA Title III, mimeographed (St. Thomas, June 8, 1967), p. 2.

29. Alexander Henderson, "Famous and Important Virgin Islanders of the Past," mimeographed (St. Croix: Department of Education, 1966).

assumption of the same report that the purpose of future policy is not so much to reconstruct the despised insular culture as to give Virgin Islanders a greater participation in the metropolitan American culture, many of them being presently possessed of feelings of resignation and negative perceptions of themselves for having been forced to live on the periphery of that culture.[30]

What has really taken place, of course, over the last fifty years is the tragic deculturation of the island peoples under the Americanizing pressures. It is possible, thus, to see the social history of St. Croix, as DuBose Hayward's account in his semi-novel of 1938, *Star Spangled Virgin*, portrays it, as the inundation of a peasant folk-culture, marked by strong feelings of social deference, by a wave of officially sponsored "self-improvement" programs in the name of a "Noodeal" some of the islanders might have imagined to have been a real person out of Washington. Some of this, of course, is a true cultural assimilation in which American forms become creolized, so that, for example, baseball has become a fully indigenous sport. Much of it, however, is cultural subjugation, with much being needlessly destroyed by the American contempt for the past. Whereas older folk—the remarkable Mrs. English, for instance, of the St. Croix office of the Department of Education— watch with regret the passing of the older folkways, such as the old estate queen competitions, many working-class islanders have become so culture-alienated that they speak with disdain of "that 'Nancy foolishness." Cultural spontaneity has not, of course, been completely crushed, so that if the old queen songs catalogued a century ago by Thurlow Weed have now disappeared the habit of mass musical activity still manages to express itself, although somewhat differently, in the popular choral and instrumental groups of the present day. The old Danish custom of free Saturday likewise survives, for the attitudes toward work and leisure it embodies, in the Virgin Islander's passion for public holidays. Even so, the American cultural impress becomes daily more emphatic, and it is suggestive that some of the most vividly imaginative stories to come from Virgin Islands schoolchildren lately, in the form of the recently published *Donkey Wings and Other Things*, have been made up by boys and girls from St. John, the island least touched by that impress.[31]

The main Creole elements seek, generally, to forget a native heritage of which they are on the whole ashamed. They turn with fury on any one of their own who seeks to enshrine that heritage; and the comment

---

30. "Project Introspection," p. 5.
31. *Donkey Wings and Other Things*, by fifth- and sixth-grade students of Julius Sprauve School, St. John, 1964, ed. Doris Jadan (St. Thomas: Island Press, 1964).

of an old friend on Jarvis' book of 1944—"The book has a grievous fault. It is too damned factual"—tells much about the general hostility of the society to serious examination of the skeletons in its closet. There is probably much truth, then, in the opinion of those critics who feel that the newly developed fashionable interest in Virgin Islands culture is not to be seen as a genuine conversion of attitudes but as simply a self-interested response of the mulatto elites to the fact that in the last few years lucrative federal funds have become available for such exercises, and both of the reports so far published have been, in fact, papers prepared as conditional requirements for the receipt of such funds. It is still pertinent, then, to quote Jarvis' bitter observation that "Superficial culture is the badge of the aristocrats, an occasional mask for the middle class, and a book of amusing pictures to the masses."

What has actually occurred in the islands, under the dual influence of Americanization and tourism, has been the growth of what one mordant French critic of U.S.-oriented tourism in the neighboring French Antilles has termed a *folklore imposé*.[32] A spurious culture of "quaint" and "charming" things is invented to please the tourist palate. A local variety of calypsonian emerges who is, generally, a pale echo of his Trinidadian model. The tourist hotels tout bizarre concoctions of luridly named cocktails that are purveyed as "Virgin Island drinks," whereas in fact most drinks served in local homes are based on the West Indian rum and coke, gin and soda pattern. Most bizarre of all, the local annual Carnival is widely publicized as "the purely local, wildly colorful, West Indies equivalent of Mardi Gras,"[33] whereas in fact it is not to be compared to the tremendous bacchanalian events of Port of Spain, New Orleans, and Santiago de Cuba. Originally started in 1912 by George Levi and Valdemar Miller as something to contain the high spirits of clerks and young businessmen, it has become, over the years, more and more an organized parade of floats in the American manner and less a mass "jump up" in which all participate. There are, it is true, still the donkey races of St. Croix and the Christmas Festival parades, with their steel bands, clown troupes, and marching columns. But comparison with descriptions of earlier events like the old Christmas merrymaking choral bands and the Fourth of July celebrations of thirty and forty years ago, with their massed crowds of "jumping jacks," masked dancing troupes, and "scratch" bands, suggests that a

32. Jean Raspail, *Secouons le cocotier* (Paris: Robert Laffont, 1966), chaps, 22, 23.
33. Associated Press report, *San Juan Star,* Mar. 25, 1967.

talent for mass spontaneous celebration has somehow been lost along the way.[34]

A variety of socio-cultural processes has contributed to all this. Economic greed has much to do with it; St. Thomas Carnival is increasingly a commercialized event geared to the tourist trade. There is something in it, paradoxically, of the breaking down of class barriers, for the older events, being segregated between the popular street celebrations and the Grand Hotel dance for the members of the American colony, high Navy officers and their wives, and the official English aristocracy from the British Virgin Islands, at least permitted a degree of uninhibited hedonism less likely now to occur as the present-day Carnival events are organized by committees of continentals and upper-class natives. There is, too, the sharp difference between the Danish and the American colonizing habits. While the Danes left the populace pretty much to themselves, the Americans, with their general education and their genius for collective organization, have studiously brought the masses into their conformist cultural network. Whereas, then, it is possible to write novels on the Danish period, like Michael Rasmussen's *The First Night*, which take as their basic idea the fact that Danish "law and order" hardly went beyond the town environs, it would be impossible to so write about the American period where, despite certain resistance, the whole of the local life has become encased in the American cultural envelope.

The sum total, then, of the historical aggregates of experience that make up the culture of a given set of people is, in the Virgin Islands case, at once pronouncedly imitative and derivative. Its power to differentiate itself from the metropolitan culture has been inhibited by the absence of both a distinctive linguistic base (like Spanish in Puerto Rico) and a powerful indigenous tradition of local Creole groups with distinctive life-styles (like the French and Portuguese Creoles in Trinidad). The island societies, as a result, have been, and continue to be, culturally absorbent. Virgin Islanders were taught to play cricket after 1865 by the prominent English businessmen residing in St. Thomas and St. Croix, and in turn were taught to play baseball by the first set of Navy officers and men after 1917. In terms of personality traits this has produced a noticeable docility in the native which is much wider in the waveband of social behavior that it covers than the narrowly racial expression—"raising the color"—noted by Campbell. The semi-militaristic character of both Danish and American naval rule encouraged the

---

34. See articles by R. A. Sell, *Houston Chronicle,* reprinted in *St. Croix Tribune,* Aug. 24, 25, 1922, and in *Virgin Islands View,* December, 1965.

docility. This marked trait was noted, before anything else, by the American visiting writers after 1917, such as Nies and Sell.[35] The latter wrote:

> These people have been brought up under a government that was largely paternal; they do not possess initiative to any extent. However, they are sober, peaceful and industrious; they speak good English, 95 percent of them can read and write, 99 percent of them belong to church and they are really religious. They get along well with one another, there have been but two murders committed on the island of St. Thomas in the last five years. Their aptitude, industry and adaptability as servants have won them a reputation in New York City.[36]

It is the portrait, essentially, of the respectable colonial, and it is significant that the virtues here singled out for praise are still the virtues lauded by the American literature of the present-day period. Whether the native Virgin Islanders can produce a viable cultural nationalism out of all this depends, surely, upon their capacity to recognize that what to the outsider and the continental are laudable traits are, in fact, the mark left upon them by Danish-American colonialism.

35. E. H. Nies, letter, *The Emancipator,* Jan. 30, 1926; R. A. Sell, article, *Houston Chronicle,* reprinted in *St. Croix Tribune,* Sept. 14, 1922.
36. Sell, *St. Croix Tribune,* p. 5.

7

~~~

The Social Milieu:
The Continentals

The place of the resident white groups in the segmented Caribbean societies, as Hoetink has pointed out, has been curiously neglected in Caribbean studies, with attention habitually being fixed upon the more "exotic" groups.[1] The neglect is somewhat more pardonable in the case under consideration here since, unlike some other Caribbean societies where the whites constitute the oldest segment, in the Virgins the continentals are very late arrivals, their "invasion" of the islands having picked up momentum only in the last fifteen years. Although exact statistical information is unavailable, educated guesses estimate their numbers to vary between 9,000 and 13,000. But they are, of course, a minority group; the 1965 live birth statistics list the smallest number, 99 births, as belonging to parents in the white group, although the figure would naturally include children born to white Creole parents.[2] Both by reason of skin color and economic activity the continentals are conspicuously visible. Earlier on, they were identified mostly as single individuals, persons like Charles Edwin Taylor in the Danish period and Frederick Dorsch in the early American period. Today, however, they form a distinct social and ethnic collectivity. The problem of their relationship to the host society becomes, then, less and less individual and more and more institutional in character.

As a generalization, it is possible to argue that the American exodus

1. Harmannus Hoetink, *The Two Variants in Caribbean Race Relations: A Contribution to the Sociology of Segmented Societies,* trans. Eva M. Hooykaa, Institute of Race Relations (New York: Oxford University Press, 1967), p. 59.

2. Virgin Islands, Department of Health, Bureau of Statistical Services, *Vital Statistics, 1964–1965* (St. Thomas: Government Printing Office, 1966), table 4, p. 15.

(179)

to the Virgins is, historically, a particular aspect of American romantic escapism. America, in its historical beginnings, was the paradise regained, the lost horizon, the rediscovery of innocence. As that dream waned under the pressures of colonization the salvational role was transferred to the American West, which in its turn became imbued with all of the romantic properties that the settled parts of the new republic had lost. And as, in turn, the West inexorably became "civilized," the romantic component of the conquering white power had to turn elsewhere for its psychological compensations. Such compensations, after 1898, were provided by the new colonial empire. An American colonial administrator, Ernest Gruening, thus noted, in an article in the *Nation* in 1931, that Puerto Rico had been acquired at that time in the period of American romantic thought which was epitomized in music by Sousa's marches, in literature by Richard Harding Davis' adventurous gentlemen, and in art by Remington's frontiersmen. The acquisition of the Virgins in 1917 gave a new lease of life to that romanticism, although it should be noted that their role in that respect goes back much earlier in American culture history, certainly to the celebrated poem of the 1770s, "The Beauties of Santa Cruz," in which the colonial poet Philip Freneau invited his fellow-Americans to find solace in tropical islands where snow and frost were never seen.

The various elements of the American exodus to the islands after 1917 can be classified, in part, in order of their arrival. A seniority system so arranged would put the "hill crowd" first: retired military and naval officers and foreign service officials with a liking for the tropical life, not unlike the "old hands" of British India, along with the very rich on retirement. The most famous of the latter category certainly was Arthur Fairchild, who created out of the old Louisenhoj estate a tremendous Gothic-Italianate castle and whose sense of public philanthropy lives on in his gift of Magens Bay to the local municipality, in much the same way as the Bliss Institute in Belize City commemorates a similar eccentric millionaire who fell in love with British Honduras. His successor, Joe Green, has capped it all with an extensive art collection, and, along with others like Ed Bindley and Bill Clarenbach, runs the local Navy League organization, a not insignificant task in a society where sailors are still viewed with some suspicion from the old Navy regime days. After this group comes the motley crowd of artists, footloose wanderers, unregenerate individualists, and disbanded servicemen who came in the post-1945 period and whose struggle, half heroic, half comic, to cope with the peculiar difficulties of tropical adjustment is described somewhat archly in Jeanne Harman's book, *The Love Junk* (1951). Next in line are the refugees from the American gray-flannel-suit belt who fled to the islands as a sort of tropical middle-class sub-urbia, a movement at once more ostensibly professional and more deliberately organized than the preceding migration waves. There is, finally, a growing international social set centered around Little Dix and Caneel Bay, the quality resorts built up by the Rockefellers; that American family empire, with its strongly entrenched corporate family sense, has bought up vast tracts of Caribbean real estate as a long-term investment policy.

The life of the American colony is made up in large part of the relationships among these varied constituent elements. If one looks at the archaeology of the migration it is pretty clear that by now the early "Greenwich Village crowd" period is over. However, there exists a quite distinct literature on the period; all of the novels, for example, that use the St. Thomas setting as an exotic background for murder and interracial sex, replete with stateside gangsters, "hippie" artists, philandering tourists, and malevolent natives, adding up to something like a melodramatic Bogart-Hemingway movie, tend to view the conti-nental as a transient: R. H. Barbour's *Death in the Virgins* (1940), Richard Ellington's *Stone Cold Dead* (1950), Robert Dietrich's *Steve Bentley's Calypso Caper* (1961). All of them manage, collectively, to portray the continental as a marginal type—the gay divorcée, the gang-ster's moll in search of respectability, the rich escapists drinking them-selves to death; and all activity is centered around certain key spots—the Normandie bar, the gambling clubs, Frenchtown treated in the Erskine Caldwell manner. There is still something left of this kind of life, but it is increasingly on the defensive as it is replaced by the residential, hard-working, family-style life of, first, the middle-aged or elderly refugees who initially came for retirement and were then drawn into active work because of the obvious money-making possibilities, and, second, the young married couples concerned with settling down in a serious way. The theme of the Wouk novel *Don't Stop the Carnival* (1965) is, sug-gestively, that of the more exotic subgroups of the homosexuals, the bearded artists, and the girls home from college, and so is unrepresenta-tive of the present-day continental life style. Generally, continentals must be seen as the Caribbean variant of the general theme of the explo-sive flight to the suburbs that took place in American society during the 1950s.

The occupational sphere of the American colony as it now stands is a combination of the orthodox and the unorthodox. It is orthodox in that many of its members have simply brought their skills with them: builders, stenographers, doctors, therapists, accountants. The growth of satellite industries has brought in managerial and technical personnel, with their families, who take up where they left off in the States; a representative figure would be Guy Sideboard who, as a trained horologist, was sent down in 1961 by the Benrus Watch Company to head its new island plant. There is, however, an unorthodox aspect: coming to any economy in which the occupational spectrum is narrow compared to the stateside communities from which they migrated, the vast majority of the permanent American colony have had to turn to new jobs, tourist-derived situations, or service jobs created out of sheer inventiveness. Since only a small percentage are senior retired citizens, that has been the situation confronting most new arrivals. They have had to make do in an economy which, in Mrs. Harman's observation, is just civilized enough to have some of all of the necessities of life, just isolated enough not to have any of them at the time they are needed. A large number of these residents find employment as clerks in the gift shops of Charlotte Amalie and Christiansted. Some open guest houses, restaurants, and bars, often on a shoestring. Others have gone into real estate, a field that has attracted a major New York clothing manufacturer and a large circle of former Madison Avenue advertising executives. Some become practicing journalists, like Victor Gilbert; or rare book dealers, like the poet Tram Combs; or move on from bartending to become, like the late Allen Grammer, editor-publisher of a successful local magazine. Others exploit the opportunities latent in the tourist trade, like the Harmans, who originated the first glass-bottom boat tour business; while yet others cash in on rising consumer demands, like the two young Cleveland men who, noting that all the ice cream in St. Thomas was shipped in from Puerto Rico, set up a successful ice cream business.

There are certain features about the sociology of all this that are worth noting. In the first place, as these new worker types replace the escapist beachcomber type seeking relief for his pychosexual problems, they come to constitute a functionally operating group, less and less inclined to take the merely romantic view of their socioeconomic role.

In the second place, a sort of primordial pioneer instinct seems to assert itself in which the newcomer, faced with the grim choice of finding some quick means of steady income or leaving, addresses himself to the task with zest and energy, very much like Crevecoeur's new "American man." So there are scores of working husband and wife teams who have successfully carved out a new life for themselves on the basis of those virtues alone, and they have no false pride about the kind of work they must undertake. Whether it is Seth and Laura Larrabee operating their surrey tour business; or Carl and Honor Tranum running their car rental service; or Tom and Marnie Ford plying their vacation cottage service in St. John; or the Joseph Byers and their remarkable transformation of the Yacht Haven marina; or (turning aside now from the married couples) Frank Burke and Alex Forbes who between them did so much to found the charter boat business—all of them work with a driving enthusiasm. Being from middle-class America, they possess the American conviction that life means work. They are, perhaps, psychologically incapacitated to adopt the beachcomber values.

In the third place, there is a remarkable capacity to shift work roles. A former stockbroker works as a real estate agent; a film producer clerks in a store; a magazine editor repairs refrigerators. Although it would be socially fatal for one of them to become, say, a street cleaner, there are dozens of ex-white-collar persons from the mainland who work, variously, as carpenter, short-order cook, shop mechanic, bartender, and cab driver; and frequently they work for colored employers or supervisors. Some of them, of course, relish the status traditionally awarded to certain roles—the expert cook-dietician Sid Rogers, for example, now chef for the Carousel Restaurant, who plans to write a book on the favorite recipes of European crowned heads. Some of them, too, strike it rich, like the former Greenwich Village bartender Hugh Duffy, who turned guest-house owner-manager. All of them, however, are evidence, as they see themselves, of the continuing validity of the American success story. Duffy's remark—"This is a wonderful place for failures. The place is loaded with them, only they're not failures down here. Every one is a success here who was a failure back home. For me, and others like me, this place is a money machine"[3]—is a characteristic expression of this continuing temper of economic individualism. There are similar personal success odysseys among native Virgin Islanders, such as Louis Shulterbrandt, the son of a local cigar-maker, who became assistant to Governor Paiewonsky. But it is the continental group rather than the native group which takes a sentimental pride in the phenomenon.

For a group of its size, it contributes a vast amount of personal talent and social energy to the community. It has a large proportion of writers, painters, musicians, and art specialists; of the more than one hundred persons listed in those categories by the Arts Council report the majority most certainly are continentals. Some writers, like Wouk, come with reputations already established. Others come as novices hoping to find creativity in tropical serenity; their saga, often tragicomic, can be read in an account like Robb White's *Our Virgin Islands*. Most of the artists are the amateurs of the Island Art Club. Others, like Larry Gluck and Bill Tolsch, not to mention Jim Tillett and his Tutu art center, are professionals making a living at their craft. In other fields

3. Hugh Duffy, quoted in John Donovan column, "As Others See Us," *Daily News,* Jan. 4, 1965.

a quite phenomenal energy expresses itself. There is, for example, Bill Zuber, whose skill as a continental angler and sports fisherman created almost singlehandedly the present status and popularity of big-game sports fishing in St. Croix, while captains like Jack Carstarphen have done the same for the art of charter sailing; both illustrate, incidentally, the fact that Virgin Islanders on the whole are not a sea-oriented people. Or, to cite from yet another field, there is the late Jayne Miles, whose superb skills made the Virgin Islands community ballet-conscious for the first time. It is, all in all, a contribution that gives the lie to the myth of tropical enervation. It is also remarkable proof of a quiet social revolution in which the old taboo against manual work of the older Caribbean class-color-work structure on the part of the white resident has to a large extent broken down. White continentals in the contemporary Virgins will do the kind of work which in other islands, where the European stamp is more marked, would be viewed, even today, as a grave threat to the foundations of the social order.

This slice of island existence is increasingly family-oriented. In the early 1950s there was hardly a single married couple with children; today they are legion. Even the life of the most carefree element of the colony, that of the "boat crowd" of the Yacht Haven community but gradually spreading eastward to the Red Hook area, is geared to child-raising. Some of the childless yacht-owners do a lucrative trading or chartering business "down the islands," where, incidentally, they can escape the jurisdiction of the U.S. Coast Guard service. But most of them live the year around in the marine community, trailer-camp style. A typical early-morning scene, with children being prepared to meet the school bus and wives joining a taxi pool for shopping in town, illustrates how rapidly the American family unit domesticates even the hardiest of pioneers. The pressures of family living thus create for the continental group as a whole the general problems of stateside life and the typical responses to them: the private school, the car pool, the PTA.

That, indeed, is a point that deserves further comment. The truth is that as the Swiss Family Robinson quality of island life begins to wear off the peculiar difficulties begin to make themselves felt. The leisure activities of modern living, American style, are still there, of course: the boating, the participant sports like golf, centered around the championship Fountain Valley golf course in St. Croix, the civilian flying craze based on the accredited flying schools at Isla Grande in nearby San Juan. But it all comes at an increasingly onerous price. An inflationary living-costs structure means food bills between 15 and 20 per cent higher than in the States; terrifying rentals that start at a monthly $250 and are more likely to reach $400; and expenses so generally high that the travel literature advises prospective newcomers that the absolute minimum is a joint $10,000 annual income earned by a young, able couple, both of whom are able to work and, preferably, are childless. The local aphorism—"luxuries are cheap, necessities expensive"—sums up a frustrating situation in which the ability to buy cheap liquor and cigarettes, not to mention Russian caviar, Danish hams, French *pâté de foie gras*, and Swiss cheeses at inexpensive rates, does not help compensate for expensively priced meat, eggs, milk, and fruits. Tourist-oriented shops show a relative paucity in the more prosaic items, so that things like stateside-quality men's suits are almost non-existent. Prolonged exposure to continentals in complaining mood suggests that, beyond all that, they feel that their children's education suffers, they miss cultural events of real quality, they are unendingly tortured by poor appliance service, and they feel, generally, that the massive abundance and convenience of American living cannot be equaled. It is hardly surprising, then, that many of them lead mercurial lives in the islands and contribute to the high turnover in the American colony. The complaint attributed to one long-time resident in the Wouk novel sums it all up fairly accurately: "We're moving to La Jolla, California. I mean this is the finest little island in the Caribbean, but there comes a time when you start thinking of those mainland amenities, you know? Like decent roads, movie houses with good movies and seats that don't tear up your fanny, shops with real food in them, courteous service, mechanics that can fix things, you know, I mean a plumber, an electrician, just normal workmen who show up on time and do things fast and right." [4]

There is much glib talk, especially by the professional image-makers, of the "integration" of the continentals into the local society. Apart from the difficulty involved in purporting to integrate the continental U.S. resident into a society which itself—as already noted—has little distinctive cultural identity of its own and is increasingly a carbon copy of the continental system, there is the added difficulty that the American resident himself evinces little interest in being so integrated. To begin with, he has to meet the barrier of the social pride of the aristocrats, both white and colored, who feel that they have nothing to gain from close contact with the newcomers. He will receive a more friendly welcome from the less staid lower class, but even then it is an amused tolerance, not a democratic embrace. The middle

4. Herman Wouk, *Don't Stop the Carnival* (New York: Doubleday, 1965), p. 281.

class, in turn, adopts a polite attitude, but offers nothing more. This is not to say that he cannot "break through," for he usually possesses most of the attributes of Virgin Islands upper-classness: a good education, the ability to dress well, and, not the least important, a command of "good" English. Nor is there, as in Puerto Rico, a language barrier to keep him at arm's length. But American casualness and what islanders consider lack of manners (the traditional complaint of European travelers about their American cousins) inhibit complete assimilation. This in turn generates resentment, compounded by the bitterness that many continentals feel at being dubbed continentals, a psychological burden many of them seem unable to bear with composure. They feel it somehow unfair that they will never be accepted as "true Virgin Islanders" while the accolade is readily conferred upon natives who—like the famous songwriter Bennie Benjamin, for example—have spent the best part of their lives and careers abroad.

So, somewhat understandably, the American resident retreats into his own social ghetto. Whether it is the result, over the last fifty years, of his own American color prejudices, as distinct from a Danish pattern which drew rigid class lines but flexible color lines, or whether it is a defense mechanism against the local barriers noted here, is perhaps less important than the fact that the informal segregationism presently exists, with tacit acceptance by most concerned. That most Virgin Islands social entertaining is done at home facilitates the habit, so that it is easy to come across continentals of ten or even fifteen years' residence who do not have close native friends. The ultrademocratic character of continental cocktail parties, so frequently noted, with wealthy dowagers and down-at-heel bohemians mixing freely, can thus be seen less as real social egalitarianism than as the natural response of a minority group to the social chilliness of the host society, closing its ranks under the pressure. There are entire neighborhoods, like Water Island and Judith's Fancy, which, being in the main composed of well-to-do retired mainlanders, take on at least the appearance of white residential districts. There are dining places, like Yacht Haven and Galleon House, the Café de Paris and the Left Bank, to which natives will rarely go; on the other hand, they will eagerly patronize places like the Rix-Ski restaurant, which serves native dishes, for reasons as much cultural as gastronomical. There are, finally, fairly well-defined areas of neutral ground, where mixing, polite but not intimate, takes place between all.

The three islands, with their different stages of modernization, accurately reflect the different stages in the mixing process. The most mixing is found in St. Thomas, the most developed economy. There is somewhat less mixing in St. Croix, where the set of American estate overseers established a rigid pattern of prejudice after 1917, with their refusal to understand real Crucian patois and their organization of a "white man's burden" life-style centered around their Jim Crow Tennis Club; this pattern, somewhat attenuated, was later taken over by a wealthy retired American set. The least mixing of all takes place in St. John, where the bizarre combination of a thousand or so peasant laborers and fishermen and a handful of escapist American property owners has produced a sort of tropical village paternalism, with native class deference on the one hand and American "pink gin and verandah" living of the old prewar West Indian style on the other; it is nicely summed up in Charlotte Dean Stark's *Souvenir of St. John,* in which the author, like a sort of West Indian Agatha Christie, pinpoints the quaint charm of the village life. If this type of inward-turned expatriate settlement life is ever apt to encourage the sort of tropical disintegration of Robert Louis Stevenson's Polynesian stories, it would be most likely to occur in St. John, where the touch of the outside American "master culture" is least heavy.

The problem is best understood, perhaps, by viewing the continental as caught up in the dilemma of cultural marginality. He is at once an "insider" and an "outsider." As "insider" he seeks to "adjust" to Virgin Islands experience, often with real sincerity. That can be seen in the way in which, as a transplanted statesider, he so frequently takes on an attitude of fierce possessiveness toward "his" island, so that it is somewhat astonishing to find him absorbing the traditional interisland prejudices, adopting the Crucian disdain for St. Thomas or the St. Thomian contempt for St. Croix. He writes the advertising literature, like Jeanne Harman's *Here's How: Your Guide to St. Thomas* and the David Antoniak publications, *St. Thomas Holiday Island Guide* and *St. Croix Guide,* in which there creeps through a note of curious anxiety, courting the prospective new resident with the usual "island in the sun" rhetoric but warning him against too great expectations: "Most Continentals—those expatriates from the American scene—work as hard or harder here than they did in the citadels of commerce stateside. If you're coming for the life of *dolce far niente,* you'd better have a steady stream of coupons to clip or a rich uncle." [5] Along with that veiled warning to the beachcomber, there goes another warning to the tourist, who, of course, is always the necessary but unreliable "outsider." Imaginary conversations between continental

5. *St. Thomas Holiday Island Guide, Summer 1967* (St. Thomas: David Antoniak, 1967), p. 65.

salespeople and tourist shoppers are, interestingly enough, a staple of the local journalism, in which the naive or stupid questions of the tourist, based on gross ignorance of Virgin Islands geography and sociology, are parried by the replies, sometimes defensive, sometimes sarcastic, of the expatriate resident.[6] This at times becomes a shrill admonition to the tourist to behave himself. He is reminded that the noisy, garishly dressed, selfishly bartering tourist is a menace to the American image abroad: "I am an American, clear to the bottom of my thongs, born and reared in the Western United States. I now reside in St. Thomas and I care what these people think of people from the United States. . . . I call upon every American who visits these islands to remember that each of us is representing a country, a great country. We want people to know the continental U.S. at its best, not its worst." [7]

This is the "insider" complex, the mild disease known as being "island happy." It is, clearly, just another expression of the antagonism between the white man living in the tropics and his compatriot who remains in the "mother country," so well known a feature of Caribbean social history. But in the contemporary Virgin Islands case it does not become the gross disease of *tropenkolder*, extreme tropical derangement, because the continental is at the same time an outsider retaining much of the outsider complex. Like the continental in the much larger Puerto Rican American colony, he is always within easy access of Miami and New York. There is, indeed, much steady commuting on the part of the more well-to-do residents. The high turnover rate precludes the growth of an inner-regarding settler group in conflict, actual or potential, with the "home" government. It is true that the more liberal-minded individuals will write indignant letters to their congressmen about the archaic colonial attitudes of Congress, but this is not very different from what they would have done had they been writing from a stateside address. They will criticize the "ugly Americans," but they themselves still remain, in their own eyes, Americans living abroad. They see themselves not as creolized Americans in a different Caribbean society but as denizens in the American Caribbean. The self-congratulatory tone is consequently well pronounced in their outlook: "The American flag means American-trained doctors, American school system, food inspected under United States public health standards, American courts, American goods, American

6. For an early example of imaginary conversations between continental salespeople and tourists, see *The Emancipator*, May 2, 1923.

7. June Read, "An Open Letter to U.S. Visitors," *Daily News*, Mar. 12, 1964.

postal system, customs, protection by the military. Residents who wish to can take their problems to the United States Congress or even to the President for redress." [8]

What grows up, then, is not so much a settler mentality as the well-known enclave syndrome of the Malta-Gibraltar-Bermuda-Ulster variety. Whether consciously or only half-consciously, the continental thinks and acts as an ambassador of American life. For him (as indeed for most natives, too) the chief street of Charlotte Amalie, Dronnengins Gade, is Main Street, and he exhibits the Main Street mentality. He clings to the cultural lifeline with "home" by means of stateside papers and magazines, including the Sunday *New York Times,* airmail, for one dollar. He tends to adopt the local upper-class attitudes to the native masses, seeing them as children-people who are enjoyable but unreliable. In his economic life he defends the traditional Calvinistic economic virtues at the very moment when they have become largely anachronistic in the American planned corporate capitalism. In his political activities he reproduces a typical stateside civics, the suburbanite homeowner preoccupation with property rights and tax rates. He becomes not so much a Virgin Islander as a "friend of the Virgin Islands"—the pose adopted, for example, by the Rockefeller chieftains in their St. John National Park stronghold. Even the home he builds tends to be North American rather than tropical in style; for although the wealthier immigrant will frequently construct remarkable tropics-oriented houses—of which there are some fine examples in the islands—the householder of average income will build the usual concrete house, with Miami blinds and protective encasing, with furniture and kitchen cabinet units culled from the inappropriate models of *House Beautiful* magazine. He will feel liberally self-righteous, especially when he has stateside guests, about the fact that he has Negro neighbors. But, as already noted, he rarely has an intimate friendship with them. "If there is a funeral," in the words of one continental, speaking of her colored neighbors, "we send flowers, and we smile politely at each other in the street. I don't dislike their faces, and I hope they don't dislike mine." Even the "way of death" of the group is stateside-directed. When the size of the group was smaller, twenty-five years ago, it was considered a duty on the part of all whites to attend the funerals of other whites who died in the islands, and the custom was for the bodies to be sent "back home." Now it is a common practice for deceased continentals to be buried at sea, and local opinion tends to see the practice as throwing

8. Jeanne Perkins Harman, *The Virgins: Magic Islands* (New York: Appleton-Century-Crofts, 1961), p. 268.

doubt upon the continental claim to be "one of us." Exceptions to the practice are so rare as to be openly commented on, as, for example, when Mrs. Caron, the mother of Leslie Caron, the actress, was interred in St. Thomas in 1967.

The resident American becomes, in sum, a culture carrier of American values. Like the resident Englishman in the former British colonies, the American is bound by the intransigent superiority complex of Anglo-Saxon civilization, which makes it difficult, if not impossible, for him ever to shed in any real sense his conviction of the innate sanctity of all things generally Anglo-American. The fact, of course, that the Virgin Islands colonial mentality of the natives tends to share that conviction makes a genuine creolization of attitudes all the more unlikely. The outsider component of the immigrant self, then, tends to overshadow the insider component. The primary identity is with the ancestral culture, not with the new society. Despite the propagandist note about the islands forming a part of the Old World in the New, along with the accompanying theme of their continuing peaceful coexistence, the American resident, if pressed hard enough, will admit the palpable absurdity of the claim. The colony, it is true, has had its fair share of radical or alienated *norteamericanos* who bring their disaffection with them. But apart from the general embarrassment involved in trying to "go native" in a society characterized by weak community organization and fragile institutional identities, such types have had to meet the combined hostility and persecution of both the native top class and their own more "respectable" compatriots. The autobiographical account of one of them—Elizabeth Hawes's *But Say It Politely* (1951)—in which the author, a radical-minded erstwhile trade union educational organizer, describes her encounter with the light-skinned oligarchs and racist Americans in the St. Croix of the late 1940s when that society was still playing the faded Barbadian colonial piece, illustrates how readily the vindictive fury of the insular conservative establishment is turned against the expatriate maverick who attempts the *vie de Bohème* with the wrong people.

This is a well-known phenomenon throughout the Caribbean area. There is ample evidence on the various methods that the new governments of the ex-colonial Caribbean nation-states are willing to employ in order to rid themselves of "undesirable" persons, whether coming from the former metropolitan societies or from other West Indian societies. The Walter Rodney case in Jamaica—in which the Jamaican government in effect ousted a "black power" non-Jamaican faculty member from the university by refusing to extend his work permit—has shown how the methods can be used against radical university faculty members. The recent case of the VISTA workers in the Virgin Islands, in effect deported because of their efforts to organize alien workers, is evidence of a similar pathology in the islands' ruling group. In the particular case of the Virgins, furthermore, this repressive tendency is augmented by the anxiety of the residential continental bloc as it strives to keep on good terms with that group. The continental wants, above all, to be accepted, to be liked, to be protected, if necessary, against "black power" militancy. He wants to prevent the growth of a negative image of himself, such as that expressed in a 1950 local newspaper editorial that he and his like were "a collection of society rejects and plain stinkers who have not been a particular asset to the place which they left. . . . They show themselves up as four-flushers, professional malcontents and ready tools for community trouble." [9]

The continental segment of the society, all in all, is characterized by both a minimum acculturation and a maximum ethnic identification. Its geographical immediacy to its continental sources helps promote both phenomena. There are differences of interest and attitude between its various constituent elements—the adopted St. Thomian as against the adopted Crucian, or the retired professional group apprehensive about the growth of a tourist industry that "spoils" the islands, or the middle-aged entrepreneur as against the beachcomber type ("they destroy each other," in the phrase of one continental informant). But they are not differences sufficiently profound to create rifts in the common ground of continentalism. The vertical thrust of that concept is not seriously compromised by horizontal divisional lines. It constitutes, in effect, an invisible ghetto. So, even the "old hands," the Americans of lengthy residence, who feel—as against the motley crowd of tourists, yesterday's newcomers, and transients like the stateside schoolteachers annually recruited by the Department of Education— that they "know" the Virgin Islands, may know them in superficial senses only: through the limited medium of servant-employer relations or on the basis of pub crawling through the town bars. Their reiterated slogan—"we love the islands"—thus takes on the air of democratic sentimentalism so typical of many Americans abroad. What is more, that sentimentalism seeks approval from others so eagerly that it rapidly generates anger, resentment, and frustration when met with native frigidity or, at best, armored politeness. That can be seen clearly

9. Editorial, *Daily News*, Aug. 9, 1950. See also editorials in *ibid.*, Aug. 11, 12, 1950. This prejudice against the "wrong sort" of stateside visitor or resident has more latterly been directed against the "counter-culture" youth and the "black power" militant types.

enough when the American colonial enclave psychology is compared with that of the British in the British Caribbean area. "On first acquaintance," observed an American traveler in 1936 of his fellow-Americans in Puerto Rico and the Virgin Islands, "we become warmly personal, and then paternal. The British are different. They are coldly impersonal; they go out to rule and nothing swerves them. In their code there is always socially an abyss between natives and rulers, yet they will die for each other. Time and time again, in our colonies, we have seen the American contact grow into something like a canker sore, a form of social indigestion, as it were, from too much sweetness." [10]

Nothing illustrates this better, perhaps, than the relative paucity of the contribution that the continental residents have made to the intellectual culture of their adopted society. The island historians have been local names—Jarvis and Paiewonsky. American historians failed to take up where Westergaard left off in 1917. The accumulated work on Virgin Islands ethnology and archaeology has been done by visiting American scholars, not resident continentals—Fewkes, de Booy, Quin, Meyerhoff, Kemp. The sole exception has been Folmer Andersen, who, as manager of the Bethlehem Sugar Factory in St. Croix between 1916 and 1931, built up and catalogued a splendid archaeological collection later purchased by the St. Croix Museum.[11] No American governor, not even Pearson, who had the intellectual equipment, collected bibliographies or wrote scholarly books on his colonial district in the manner of Lefroy, Burdon, Olivier, and Burns in the British Caribbean area.

The American continentals in the Virgins have been business-oriented in the main, with all of the cultural philistinism of the business mind. They could argue in defense that the native community has been equally philistine. That is true. But the communities in which the British governor-scholars did their work were also philistine, exhibiting the same general anti-intellectualism of the colonial society. There are, happily, recent signs of improvement. The liberal magazine, *Virgin Islands View,* and at least three bookshops of quality are operated by continentals, thus carrying on the tradition started by the ubiquitous pioneer Jarvis in his old Art Shop of the 1940s, while the new College of the Virgin Islands, by means of its faculty and visiting public lecturers, has introduced at least the beginnings of a new intellectual liveliness in the society. The resident poet Tram Combs has helped put

10. Henry Albert Phillips, *White Elephants in the Caribbean* (New York: Robert M. McBride, 1936) , p. 155.
11. Folmer Andersen, *Notes on St. Croix* (Christiansted: St. Croix Museum Commission, 1954) .

St. Thomas on the serious poetic map.[12] But how far any of this can go to impregnate a community generally preoccupied with tourist money-making and tropical outdoor living remains to be seen. Virgin Islands society is still pretty much what it was in the words of a local newspaper editorial back in 1929, prompted by the news that a continental in St. Croix had bought up all the rare books and documents of the defunct Athenaeum: "We crucify our prophets, mock intelligence, smile at pretence and uphold ignorance." [13] It is problematical whether that condition can be changed by a minority group most of whose members are business people primarily concerned with making money but who affect an air of largesse and condescension. Their presence would seem far more likely to provoke negative rather than positive responses, which in turn give rise to a sado-masochistic conflict of cultures retarding maturity for all involved.

As a highly operational group the continentals are clearly of some importance as an integral element of the Virgin Islands economic power structure. They are concentrated, as already noted, in the entrepreneurial sector. Yet before the data on that fact are elaborated it is worth noting that the occupational seclusion, strong as it is, does not preclude presence in other sectors. The old continental monopoly in the political-administrative sector has disappeared, so that whereas in the 1940s fifty to one hundred white Americans monopolized all the prestigious positions—governor, government secretary, CCC directors, municipal doctors, government engineers, and agency heads—in the 1960s there were only a handful of them in that sector: Henry Kimelman as one-time commissioner of commerce, Peter Bove as the U.S. comptroller, Fred Berger and Daniel Ambrose as special assistants to the governor, Bruno Neumann as economic advisor, Howard Blaine as deputy commerce commissioner, and scattered specialists and administrative assistants in various departments. Mrs. Ruth Jones is U.S. collector of customs, an appointment partly explained by her special status as the wife of J. Raymond Jones, the powerful New York Negro political leader of Virgin Islands origin. There are openings in the broadening field of public service; in 1967 there were seven resident statesiders on the Board of Trustees of the College of the Virgin Islands

12. Tram Combs, *Pilgrim's Terrace: Poems American West Indian* (San German, Puerto Rico: Editorial Nueva Salamanca, 1957), and *Saint Thomas: Poems* (Middletown, Conn.: Wesleyan University Press, 1965).

13. *The Emancipator*, Aug. 12, 1929.

and twelve on the local Economic Development Board. The faculty body of the College has added to the roster of new stateside residents, while the president, Dr. Lawrence Wanlass, serves widely on various public bodies, including the Virgin Islands Council on the Arts. The group is even represented in politics, the preserve of the educated native Virgin Islander, with two of its leading businessmen being senators in the elected single-chamber legislature: Senator David Hamilton of St. Croix and Senator Ken Alexander of St. Thomas, the latter a leading figure in the French-Alexander real estate family operation. There is, finally, a subgroup of residents with special expertise in the communications fields of radio, television, and the press—Margot Bachman, Helen Auble, Francesca Greve, Katherine Bailey, Mrs. Guy Qualls, Betty Austen—some of whom enter government service, such as Bryant Henderson, who was at one time a journalist-photographer in the St. Croix Office of Public Relations. It is clear that with the novelty of tropical residency passing off, the type of inner-regarding continental who merely wants to get away from it all is being matched by an outer-regarding type who brings the best of American community consciousness to the island life.

The American presence in the islands, even so, is above all an economic presence. The two major sections of the economy, as noted by the 1963 federal Census of Business, are the retail trade and the selected services areas.[14] Of the 545 active unincorporated business establishments in the retail trade area there were, at that date, 160 food stores and 161 eating and drinking places, along with 68 dress and apparel shops and 44 gift and novelty shops. Of the 214 establishments in the selected services area there were 89 hotels, tourist courts, and camps, 10 laundry plants, and 19 beauty shops. The effective majority of most of these categories are owned or managed by continental interests, with a variety of legal arrangements. The well-known Main Street names—Bolero, Caron, Little Switzerland, L'Escale en Ville, Sebastians, Tropicana, Casa Venegas—are continental-owned or managed. So are the vast majority of the tourist hotels—1829, Galleon House, Queen's Quarter, Shibui, Club Comanche, to name only a few. Many of the dress shops are run by continentals, following the pioneer work of Elizabeth Kiendl in introducing functional ready-to-wear island styles to the continental market. There is, of course, still a handful of English and European names, relics of the earlier cosmopolitan economy when English concerns, for example, operated the cable company, the floating dock,

14. U.S., Department of Commerce, *1963 Census of Business* (Washington, D.C.: Government Printing Office, 1963).

and the Royal Mail Steam Packet company. But the dominant stamp is American.

This is not to say that there are no important native economic interests. There are a few native families, usually of the "whiter" variety, that have successfully held their own: the Lockharts, with their liquor and real estate interests (the latter including the old Grand Hotel, originally built by the patriarch of another Virgin Islands family, Jean Baptiste Anduze, in 1843), and the Paiewonskys, whose wealth is of more recent vintage, going back to the 1930s, and whose present holdings include the Riise liquor and rum manufacturing enterprises, real estate and commercial building operations, and the two Charlotte Amalie cinemas, all of them managed in the old-fashioned family style.[15] There are also large Crucian business families like the Penthenys, as well as the de Chaberts, who have recently gone into the new food market business. In St. Thomas, there are other, somewhat smaller native owner-operators: the Chinnerys, in the grocery and restaurant business; George Conrad, in the Scandinavian Center gift shop; Mrs. Corbiere, in the Peppermint Shop (candy); and Miss Zeathea Armstrong and Attorney Eustace Dench, in the Virgin Islands Apothecary (by a quirk of definition Miss Armstrong is generally identified as a native Virgin Islander although in fact she is a long-time Negro stateside resident who was born in Brooklyn).

These, however, are exceptions. The general picture is that of an economic sector mainly continental in its personnel and a political sector mainly native in its personnel. The majority of the personnel of the Chambers of Commerce, as well as their leading officers, are continentals. It must be noted that a series of basic operative trends is at work currently to make this distinction even more emphatic. The Victorian family-style business firm readily gives way to more efficient, institutionalized firms, so that when the head of a one-man operation, like Manassah Francis, the St. Thomas bus operator, dies there is frequently no one to replace him. In recent years, then, there has been a noticeable tendency for such operations to sell out to larger impersonal units operated by groups of continental businessmen—the sale of the David Chinnery grocery store, for example, to the Lucy's Markets corporation, or that of the International Plaza complex from Leayle Levi to another group of investor continentals, or finally of Lockharts to the Arthur Witty interests. Along with that process goes one of even further alienation whereby (1) continental-owned businesses amalgamate to form

15. U.S., Congress, Senate, Committee on Interior and Insular Affairs, "Holdings of Raphael Paiewonsky in the Virgin Islands," in *Nomination for Governor of the Virgin Islands: Hearings*, 87th Cong., 1st sess., March 10, 11, 14, 1961, pp. 33–34.

even larger operational units, and (2) Danish-owned operations sell out either to resident continental interests or to corporations in the continental United States. An example of the first category was the 1967 merger of the Atlantic Trading Corporation and the General Trading Corporation, the business name of the operators of the Bolero shops; and an example of the second category was the sale in the same year of Vitraco, the large building-equipment company owned by Jorgen Fog, to the American Standard Plumbing Manufacturers. Another example of the contraction of the Danish economic interests was the recent decision of the old and long-established West India Company (whose president has always been appointed from Copenhagen and who has traditionally occupied the imposing Danish "Embassy House" overlooking St. Thomas) to relinquish some of its widespread operations—its various automobile franchises, for example—in order to concentrate on its more profitable dock area operations, thus still further emphasizing the American economic hold on the economy.

Perhaps the most suggestive trend of all is the growing importance of those business corporations that are domiciled outside the islands proper: the Hilton hotel chain, Sears Roebuck, the Puerto Rican–based Pueblo supermarket chain, as well as the Puerto Rican Swiss Chalet hotel-restaurant firm. This situation underlines even more emphatically the satellite character of the insular economy. And not the least important of the consequences of that satellization are, first, the sharpening influence in the insular policy-making process of the wealthy American business tycoons (either domiciled in the islands or in the continental United States) who became close friends of Governor Paiewonsky during his period of office—Harold Toppel, Roy Chalk, Leo Harvey, Leon Hess, and Sidney Kessler—and, second, an incipient rift, both of economic interest and social attitude, between the "small business" element of continentals and the new "big business" element.

Perhaps the best-known example of how these economic developments generate new social group alignments is that of the Rockefeller-sponsored National Park area in St. John. There was much resentment generated, in the beginning, by the sometimes questionable methods, including the bait of fabulous prices, used by the Rockefeller lieutenants in their gradual purchase of the park area lands, leading to the destruction of the small-property structure of the island. At that time, it became a melodramatic struggle between the small property holders and the Rockefeller corporate oligarchy, leaving behind many deeply felt animosities. At the same time, it has to be noted that in turning over the area to the federal park authorities for conversion to a national park the Rockefeller family saved the island from the sort of ruthless private development that has spoiled so many of the islands to the south; and it is significant that it is not too difficult to find profit-minded members of the Cruz Bay commercial group who would have been happy enough to undertake that sort of spoliation. This, on any showing, is a vast achievement: it keeps St. John as a permanent resource tool for the growth of a legitimate tourist development program. What alienation still remains is due to the feeling of the local population that they are cut off from the park authority. The feeling could possibly be assuaged by measures that would bring the islanders into some kind of joint administration of the park.[16]

The American residents clearly are a mixed crowd, with the business person the most in evidence. In a society where there has always been a dearth of social entertainment they work hard to relieve their frustrations, both at private pleasure and at community-oriented service chores. But it is private pleasure rather than public service that is the main preoccupation, for, socially, they tend not to have a large civic sense. A native business leader, speaking in his capacity as outgoing president of the St. Thomas–St. John Chamber of Commerce, has recently emphasized that failure. His remarks were rather bitter:

> We must face the fact that, in general, the recent white arrival from the U.S. mainland has not been a good neighbor. Lacking roots in this community, he finds little in common with native Virgin Islanders and makes no serious effort to bridge the cultural gap that separates us. He is one of many migrants from many places and has little sense of responsibility to this community and not too much sense of common purpose even with other whites, except in search of congenial and social companionship. . . . It would be difficult to find a mainland city the size of St. Thomas where the business community is as disorganized and as lacking in civic spirit as our mainland white-dominated business community here.[17]

The continentals' political sense mirrors that social exclusivity, for they keep in close touch with their federal officials and congressional representatives, usually by way of correspondence, and they tend to see the local situation as a competition between "bad" Virgin Islands politics and "good" public administration citizenship after the American

16. See various reports by Walter Priest and Ronald Walker, *San Juan Star*, Sept. 7, 8, 21, 1962. See also testimony of St. John residents in "Report of the Commission on the Reapportionment of the Legislature of the Virgin Islands," mimeographed (St. Thomas, 1967), pp. 149–203. The increasing appearance in the local press of laudatory pieces on the big-business continental names in the insular economy is noteworthy; see the piece on Leon Hess, *St. Croix Avis*, Jan. 4, 1967.

17. Henry Wheatley, speech reported in *San Juan Star*, Dec. 14, 1971, pp. 30–31.

liberal-reformist fashion, with all of the oversimplification that such a view implies.[18] Economically, there is a great deal of private wealth involved; the recent sale of the Estate Contant in St. Thomas by its local continental owners Michael Resche and Irving Patron for a reported sum of $405,000 speaks for itself. That sort of wealth inevitably breeds for its owners a certain reputation for sharp practices, and Virgin Islanders speak quite openly and with amused cynicism about the mutually beneficial arrangements supposed to have been made between the former governor and his American friends, or about the fact that in an economy where there are no professional investigating teams most commercial fires seem to take place, suspiciously, in continental-owned establishments on the verge of being transferred to new ownership.

In terms of socio-cultural attitudes, finally, the American presence has helped to create a schizoid situation. The native wonders why the American resident has left a prosperous continental economy for an underdeveloped Caribbean island economy; the continental wonders why the native ever wants to leave his paradise. The one wants to modernize his community; the other wants to retain its "old world charm." The one seeks to escape the burden of the colonial society; the other seeks to escape the burden of the Roman decadence of the metropolitan imperial society. The local press is frequently full of the type of *cri de coeur* indicative of this sharp conflict of outlook and prejudice: "Any stranger coming to live among us finds St. Thomas a heaven, while we to the contrary believe it is a hell"; [19] or, "We are ignorant enough to be ashamed of ourselves, while the stranger wishes he was like us. Will this mock-social condition ever be modified?" [20] The psychological sickness all this exhibits, on both sides, can perhaps be ended only when the metropolitan-colonial relationship which originally spawned it is ended.

18. For example, Thomas De Witt Rozzel, letter, *St. Croix Avis,* Jan. 29, 1965; and Victor Gilbert, columnist, *ibid.,* Feb. 26, 1965.
19. Editorial, *The Emancipator,* Aug. 14, 1937.
20. *Ibid.,* Aug. 1, 1931.

8

~~~

The Social Milieu:
The French
and the Puerto Ricans

The most conspicuous cultural groups in the Virgins mosaic, after the natives and the continentals, are the French and the Puerto Ricans. Both of them are immigrant groups: the first is composed of descendants of immigrants from the tiny French island of St. Bart's in the *départmente* of Guadeloupe, who originally came to the Virgins in the period after 1850; the second is more recent, and began emigrating as a result of the recruiting campaign undertaken by the Crucian cane growers in the Puerto Rican island of Vieques after 1927. The French tend to be segregated in the two St. Thomas settlements of Northside and Carenage (Frenchtown), while the Puerto Ricans are overwhelmingly concentrated in St. Croix. Every mediocre novel and every travel guide written on the islands mentions the French, known by the derisive nickname of "Cha-Chas," largely because of their immediately recognizable exotic characteristics. But there is a marked scarcity of detailed sociological analysis of either French or Puerto Rican groups, with the exceptions of Wenzell Brown's perceptive discussion of the St. Thomas French, Senior's 1947 monograph on the Puerto Rican migrant, and the more recent work of Morrill and Dyke on the Northside community.[1] Metropolitan French scholarship on the French Antilles has evinced little curiosity about the Virgins offshoot, while Puerto Ricans in Puerto Rico similarly exhibit a marked lack of interest in their confreres in the neighboring islands.

1. Wenzell Brown, "Cha-Cha Town," from *Angry Men—Laughing Men* (New York: Greenberg, 1947), reprinted in *Virgin Islands View,* June, 1966; Clarence Senior, "The Puerto Rican Migrant in St. Croix," mimeographed (San Juan: Social Sciences Research Center, University of Puerto Rico, 1947); Warren T. Morrill and Bennett Dyke, "A French Community on St. Thomas," *Caribbean Studies,* V, no. 4 (January, 1966), 39–47.

It is even possible for a popular Puerto Rican family journal to publish an article about St. Thomas as if it were still a somnolent backwater, and to omit any mention of the island's Puerto Rican citizens.[2] Because both groups are U.S. citizens, and therefore not separately listed in official statistics, it is difficult to estimate their numerical strength with any accuracy. It is generally agreed, however, that something like 15 per cent of the St. Thomas population and 35 per cent of the St. Croix population are Puerto Rican; this would mean, if the St. Croix total is set at 35,000, some 12,000 or more Puerto Ricans in that island.[3] The French population is usually listed at about 1,500. Morrill and Dyke estimate a total of 915 persons in the single Northside community, with a possible margin of error as high as 10 per cent.[4]

Both of the French communities are derived historically from the post-1850 movement of fishermen (of the Gustavian district) and farmers (of the Lorient district) to St. Thomas from the French island of St. Bart's, thus constituting a further example of the Caribbean migratory cycle. The sole importance of the St. Bart's point of origin, from the Virgin Islands viewpoint, is that it has given them their French contingent. Otherwise, it is simply another half-forgotten islet that enjoyed a brief notoriety after 1789 as a haven for refugees fleeing from the revolution in the French islands and as a neutral port during the Napoleonic Wars. The St. Thomas French, however, have maintained close contact with the island throughout their exile, and retain strong affection for it. There has been a steady though small influx of later migrants, especially young adult males; group excursions to St. Bart's to attend a funeral or a wedding or to see friends and relatives is still a widespread practice; and there are many residents who visit the ancestral home regularly each year. The regular small-boat traffic between the two islands, moreover, facilitating access to the plaited woven grass from St. Bart's which for so long has been the major raw material ingredient of the Frenchtown basketry culture, has also made for continuing mutual contact.

That contact, along with other factors—the merely surface character of Danish rule, the comparatively recent advent of American influence, and the relatively isolated geographical position of the Virgins—helps to explain the retention of the French culture pattern noted by all

2. "Saint Thomas, Calipso y Licor," *Boricua* (San Juan), Aug. 1, 1967.
3. For the St. Croix figures, see *Home Journal*, Aug. 6, 1967. For later population figures of the 1970 federal census, see report in *San Juan Star*, Nov. 14, 1971.
4. Morrill and Dyke, "A French Community," pp. 39–42.

observers. Like all the other "poor white" groups in the region, in Barbados and the Bahamas, for example, the St. Thomas French were characterized by features that facilitated their acceptance by the host society; that is, they were at once culturally different, racially disparate, and socially inferior, while their occupational specialization, in fishing and farming, did not place them in a competitive relationship with the St. Thomian Negro majority and its urban-oriented life-style. The social distance between the majority and minority groups was exacerbated by geographical separatism, since the French congregated, almost ghettolike, either in the isolated hillside settlements of the northern slopes or in the "Cha-Cha" village of Frenchtown, which comprises several hundred boxlike houses a few miles from the heart of Charlotte Amalie. This isolationism was only broken, interestingly enough, by the peculiar status of the Normandie bar, which traditionally has been the social center not only of the villagers but also of the island population as a whole, so that it has always been possible to meet a cross section of St. Thomian life there. Brown's description of 1947 still viewed the French as a collection of humble fisher folk and land toilers, resting without resentment at the bottom of the Virgins rigid caste system, racially inward-turned, speaking an archaic seventeenth-century French patois, marked by signs of consanguine degeneracy, profoundly religious, and carrying on, in a quite astonishing manner, the traditional values of the old Breton-French peasant society. In the same year Michael Rasmussen's novel *The First Night* portrayed the "Cha-Cha" community, with gross exaggeration, as a people filled with social docility and Negrophobic feelings, to the extent that they permitted themselves to be dominated by a wandering white Russian adventurer who established over them a private tyranny, replete with bacchanalian orgies, brute violence, and the *droit de seigneur*. Fantastically absurd as the picture is, even today one can look at Frenchtown, physically dominated by the doll-like edifice of St. Anne's Catholic church in an almost feudal manner, and half believe in its faint possibility.

This would certainly be to misread the picture, however. What may be construed as French timidity is, in fact, as Jarvis noted, merely a protective coloration of a group of people who, under provocation, were fully competent to stand up for their rights. For all of their cultural traditionalism, their quiet growth over the last twenty years testifies to their basic adaptability to changing conditions; and indeed the general picture painted by the earlier observers is today almost completely anachronistic. The age-old physical isolation, to begin with, no longer exists now that the business expansion of Charlotte Amalie has brought the town, with its new developments—the harbor highway, the Hilton hotel, the Antilles Airboats station—to the edge of the old village. A regular bus service makes the walk into town no longer necessary. New concrete houses testify to the recent affluence of the leading French families, although a number of these dwellings are occupied by "outsiders," while a large Negro sprinkling is also obvious. In the half-resigned words of one older resident, "You can hardly call it Frenchtown any more." The Northside community, because of its topographical character, retains something of the older isolation, yet even there a certain amount of residential penetration, usually of American continental professionals renting from French landholders, has taken place.

Yet such changes are likely to take place in any community that accepts in its value patterns the desirability of progress. They are more important as surface phenomena of the more profound structural and cultural changes that have taken place over the last generational time period. There has been, for example, a fundamental shift in the economic culture. Subsistence farming (Northside) and fishing for market sale (Frenchtown) have declined, the first in response to the increasing unavailability of land as it became concentrated in the hands of a few large holders and to the growing habit of speculative sale to real estate men and developers, the second because of changes in the market structure, most notably the fact that the special demand of the new hotel–guest house trade required regular supplies of large catches and refrigeration equipment generally beyond the financial resources of the average fisherman. In 1966, only one Northside man had an income derived entirely from farming; yet even then it was a case of commercial farming, not of traditional subsistence farming.[5] There may be some forty fishermen or so in the Frenchtown area, but half of them were cited, in 1967, as visiting St. Bart's fishermen,[6] and most of them in any case fish only to supplement the family larder. The once flourishing hat and basket weaving trade, operated as a domestic house industry, has declined as the grass supply from St. Bart's has become depleted and as the old cooperative system has been destroyed by competition from the new American stores in town. It is an ironic commentary on those defenders of Virgin Islands popular arts and crafts who see weaving as a "local" product that, as Jarvis put it, people who had not even heard of Hawaii should have been trained by Americans in the 1930s to manufacture hula skirts of bull-tyre palm.

There are still a number of truck farmers doing a limited delivery business of fruits (not so much ground crops) to a round of selected

5. *Ibid.*, p. 43.
6. Interview, Frenchtown resident, Theodore Danet, November 10, 1967.

customers. However, the major income source has shifted to wage labor, especially for unskilled and semiskilled workers in the tourist-stimulated building trades, and to salaried employment for the younger and better-educated men and women as clerks, secretaries, bookkeepers, and sales personnel in the business sector and to a lesser degree as employees in the territorial and federal government agencies. If, then, the history of French farming efforts can be invoked to expose the myth of the impracticability of field work in St. Thomas, and if French maritime prowess can be invoked to emphasize, by contrast, how empty is the fear of the physical environment that characterizes so many native Virgin Islanders (the plot of an early novel, *Death in the Virgins,* made much of the ability of its Frenchtown murder suspect to swim the St. Thomas channel from Hassel Island), these· efforts are of lessening validity as French homogeneity in occupation and social class becomes diluted.

It is, indeed, the general trait of homogeneity stemming from the French immigrants' protracted history of social and geographical isolation and their inbreeding habits that is now breaking down—at different speeds at different levels, of course. The traditional absence of class consciousness, for example, is giving way to new formations of income differentiation, especially as the children of the wealthier trader-landowner element enter the modernizing salaried group; informants in 1970 listed working sons and daughters as, variously, nurses, clerks, mechanics, hotel waiters, secretaries, and teachers. One Frenchtown store owner listed three sons and one grandson as clerical workers in the West India Company, all following in his footsteps of thirty years' service with the same company. The leading Frenchtown merchant, Anthony Quetel, of the Quetel clan, listed four sons and four daughters, among them a registered nurse, a doctor, and a staff member of the local Department of Public Safety, and all educated at college in, variously, Connecticut, Wisconsin, and Puerto Rico. The Northside patriarch leader, Joseph Sibilly, included in his family a principal of the local parochial school, a supervisor in the Public Works Department, an Army captain, an engineer in the local Housing Division, and a grandson who was an officer in the local branch office of the Chase Manhattan bank. While there has been a history of informal educational segregation, in that most French children have been educated in the Catholic schools, a new educational experience at stateside academic centers is clearly producing an educated, privileged elite group. This results, in turn, in a gradual loss of the older patois language form as English becomes increasingly both the language of domestic life and the prestige language of business activity. The situation is reinforced by the fact that there is apparently little parental pressure on the parochial schools (controlled by continental priests) to introduce French as curricular subject matter. The sentimental regard for patois is there—"the kids should hang on to it, good French or bad French." But everything conspires to reduce its functional importance. So, there is no concession to French in religious services, radio and television programs, or the press; the prayer candles and religious picture series in the church carry English titles; and while the business places in the old Honduras section may continue to sport French names—the Normandie, Le Chateau Blanc, and so on—the language heard in them is the "calypso English" of all popular Antillean street life.

Other areas of French life testify to a similar erosion of the old ways. The distinctive dress—high poke bonnets and long cotton dresses for the women, wide-brimmed straw hats and trousers rolled halfway up to the knee for the men—is now seen only on elderly people; the Council of the Arts investigators in 1966 could locate only one woman still wearing the traditional headgear of the married women, the *caleche,* or shoulder-length headdress of plaited straw covered with white cloth, resembling that worn by the Breton peasant women. Usually there are modifications of the older sartorial style—long plaited hair, modified straw hats, blouse, skirt, and white apron. Even the French physiology is changing somewhat; Brown asserted in 1947 that he had never known a French resident to become fat, yet today the younger merchant sons who are taking over the family businesses from their fathers, in the Quetel and Danet families, for example, tend to look more and more like well-rounded, prosperous, bourgeois Main Street businessmen. It is sometimes asserted that, being Catholic, the local church and church-run schools help to accentuate French separation from other groups. But, on examination, the Catholicism turns out to be nominal only; the priests, as continentals, are frequently the cigar-smoking, extravert type who talk with their young male communicants more about baseball than theology; while, for example, the announcements in the English-language church bulletins that warn against young ladies' neglecting to wear some kind of head covering at masses and devotions suggests that the clerical influence has to fight against modernizing tendencies even in the traditionally devout female following. Weinstein has noted that the French, suggestively, do not structure their environment in terms of religious categories or employ religious symbols as modes of adaptation to stress, as do both Puerto Ricans and lower-class natives.[7]

Finally, although in the past the French community did not participate in politics, after 1938 that phase was succeeded by the development,

7. Much of the information in preceding paragraphs is based on interviews of the author with French residents during 1967, 1968, and 1970.

under Progressive Guide influence, of the group as a dependent-client entity, supporting its country member in the new electoral system, Omar Brown, and working through its own party intermediaries like Theodore Danet. More recently the group has emerged as an independent entity, with the two major political parties equally well represented, and even providing its own local candidates. It is worth noting, in this respect, that as early as 1942 it was the habit of candidates at election time to write indignant letters to the press protesting the continuing use of the opprobrious epithet "Cha-Cha," which was seen by local press comment as an obvious pre-election trick that the French ought to disavow.[8] It is true that the French still lack complete political assimilation, so that, for example, they do not write letters to the press as regularly as do other groups. But such letters do now tend to appear, one of them, interestingly, from a "St. Thomas Frenchman" taking the left-wing mayor of St. Bart's to task for that dignitary's criticism of President de Gaulle.[9]

It would be easy to exaggerate the significance of all this. It is clear that the French are in a transitional stage with their cultural distinctiveness slowly disappearing under the weight of the modernizing influences, the fate of all exclusive minority cultures in the American unitary society. However, it is possible to argue that in many areas—child rearing, the status of parental authority, family organization, attitudes toward illegitimate children—there still remains a very real and stubborn Gallic tradition. The traditional festivals—St. Anne's day, Bastille Day, the Christmas day parade—are still held. The client-patron relationship still perpetuates itself, especially among the mountain French where the rural tradition, as distinct from the commercial tradition of the waterfront French, keeps social and economic paternalism strong. So, it is possible to talk with Joseph Sibilly in his uplands *finca* and gain a distinct picture of a paternalistic community leader, helping to support widows, renting land for tiny, superficiary houses at a modest rent, granting land gifts to the church, and generally serving as an intermediary between continentals and natives, even claiming to control the voting habits of his French people, all based upon his early acquisition of extensive land holdings in a strategic mountain location.

Most important of all, French separatism continues to be founded upon an intensely felt racism. There is an elaborate set of beliefs about Negro character and physiology, all of them uncomplimentary. Where intermarriage with an outside group takes place it tends to be of upperclass French with white continentals; the marriage of a Frenchtown girl with a resident continental Negro who has a managerial position in one

8. Roy Gordon, letter, and editorial, *Daily News*, Sept. 14, 1942.
9. "A St. Thomas Frenchman," letter to mayor of St. Bart's, *ibid.*, Dec. 18, 1965.

of the town supermarkets is the exception, not the rule. There are, of course, anomalies in this area: the high degree of interracial mating, especially in the Frenchtown community as distinct from the more conservative Northside community, is evidenced in the numbers of mulatto children born to French women; also, Mr. Sibilly himself, although generally accepted as being socially "white," is in fact a light-skinned Negro of Guadeloupan ancestry. The sense of racial kinship, even so, is still highly pronounced, as can be seen in the keen awareness the French have of their origins. There is a local tradition that they are descended from escaped prisoners of the Cayenne penal colony, consigned there for political offenses but coming from "good families" in France. The general sentiment can be summed up in a remark made in private to a visitor by one of the French store owners, speaking of racial inter-marriage—"I don't like it, but you can't say anything, I keep it to myself."

How long, and how successfully, these more intractable elements will hold out against complete assimilation is, perhaps, only a matter of time. The general climate of opinion in the French communities is one of apathetic resignation to the inevitability of change. Frenchtown civic organizations make their appearance, seeking to improve the image of the community, which in itself can be seen as a capitulation to the operating value structure of the mainstream culture. The home interiors of the reasonably well-to-do resemble more and more those of the native middle class. There are even Virgin Islands French citizens, like the businessman Edward Greaux, who reside and work in town and appear to have little real relationship with the parent community. Nor is there any real sense of French nationalism to offset any of this, comparable, say, to the Indian nationalism which since 1947 has made itself felt in the East Indian groups of Guyana and Trinidad. The influence of the French consul in Charlotte Amalie on either Frenchtown or Northside is quite negligible. He is, in any case, a domiciled *metropolitain* from Paris, head of the Caron business establishment and quite removed from the French folk-people; it is significant that when he elected to give an address to the local Rotary Club on "The French Influence in the Virgin Islands" it turned out to be in fact a discursive treatment of the general French presence, historically, in the Caribbean and a eulogy, in part, of Frenchmen of St. Thomian descent like the Deville brothers, who made a name for themselves in the French natural sciences during the nineteenth century but who could hardly mean anything to the French people of the present-day Virgin Islands society.[10]

10. Claude Caron, "The French Influence in the Virgin Islands," mimeographed (July 13, 1967).

The Puerto Ricans, by reason of their numbers, cultural habitat, and economic activities, constitute a situation of an entirely different order. A conservative estimate of the incidence of first-generation Virgin Islanders who are of Puerto Rican descent would be around 25 per cent, with the figure significantly higher for St. Croix alone.[11] Unlike the ghetto distribution of the French settlers, the demographic pattern of the Puerto Ricans indicates a fairly widespread penetration in both urban and rural areas. The original wave emerged from the decaying economies of the Puerto Rican islets of Vieques and Culebra, and the number of immigrants increased significantly after 1927, when U.S. immigration legislation was applied to the Virgin Islands. Whereas in the first generation there was a heavy percentage of field workers among the new migrants, who replaced Crucian workers deserting the land because of the equation of rural work with low social status, the second generation has moved into a more heterogeneous employment pattern. The social defenselessness of the immigrant subculture, so marked in the French population, has been offset in the Puerto Rican case by the geographical proximity of the mother country. There has been little inclination in San Juan to interfere in Virgin Islands affairs in order to protect the Puerto Rican "nationals" in the neighboring islands, although there are records showing that in 1922 the Puerto Rican trade union leader Santiago Iglesias opposed schemes for recruiting Puerto Rican cane-cutters for work on the Crucian estates on the ground that there existed no proper guarantees of protection.[12] Even so, the nearness of "home" has always meant a lot to Puerto Ricans in the islands, and that sentimental attachment, along with easy communication links, has led to a continuing keen interest in affairs, and especially politics, in San Juan. The importance of the Puerto Rican ties have been openly recognized by the Virgin Islands host society in the form of the establishment by the legislature in 1964 of an official Puerto Rico–Virgin Islands Friendship Day.

It is generally agreed by most informants that there exists a sophisticated degree of occupational heterogeneity among the Puerto Rican group. Constituting perhaps 50–60 per cent of the total is the broad base of field workers, unskilled laborers, farm hands, garbage disposal and road gangs (it is not unusual to meet Public Works trucks operated by Puerto Rican scavenger hands and a native driver), merging into the group of semiskilled workers such as cab drivers, plumbers, carpenters, bricklayers, and fishermen. A large percentage of the staff workers of

11. Jean Larsen, "The Cruzan Kiva" column, *West End News* (Frederiksted), July 11, 1967.
12. Remarks of Santiago Iglesias, reported in editorial, *St. Croix Tribune*, Dec. 13, 1922.

the new Christiansted Pueblo supermarket are Puerto Ricans, while some 75 per cent of the skilled labor force of the watch assembly plants are Puerto Ricans also, especially girls, whose manual dexterity is highly prized. Then there is the lower-middle-class group of teachers, nurses, artisans, small traders, technicians, and clerical workers, many of them the sons and daughters of the original migrants who made their mark in the fields of retail grocery and food merchandising. Most of these are successful high school graduates and are to be found in both the private and public employment sectors: social welfare workers, bank clerks, newspaper columnists, commission agents. They have even entered areas, such as the police, that migrant groups rarely penetrate: in St. Croix there are 15 Puerto Rican patrolmen out of a total of 68 force members.[13] Above this group, finally, there are the higher-income elements, the thriving merchant group, such as the Suarez and Miguel families in Frederiksted and the Cumpiano and Belendez-Sola families in Charlotte Amalie. A striking embodiment of older Puerto Rican business wealth is the figure of Antonio Gonzalez, the barefoot proprietor of a Company Street dry-goods store in Christiansted and the reputed owner of vast real estate holdings on the St. Croix south shore. To all these must be added the newly emergent subgroup of Puerto Rican college-educated professional persons: Felix Bello, for example, who is assistant attorney-general in the St. Croix district, and Luis Diaz, who is the Christiansted port director of the U.S. Customs Service. The next stage in Puerto Rican development, some informants opine, is in fact the enlargement of the professional group, as yet very small; even Mr. Bello can hardly be regarded as representative, being viewed by some older Puerto Rican residents as a "Johnny-come-lately" trying to recoup his political fortunes in St. Croix after an abruptly terminated political career as assemblyman in the San Juan municipality. Even so, the occupational variety is impressive, ranging from hotel owners, and a handful of lawyers and engineers, to store managers, public accountants, and Spanish-language TV commentators.

Certain features of this general picture stand out prominently. In the first place, the Puerto Rican group is a predominantly Crucian phenomenon, adding tremendous impetus to Crucian economic growth: in 1965 only 29 mothers of new live births in St. Thomas and St. John quoted Puerto Rico as their birthplace, while the figure rose to 166 in St. Croix.[14] Second, it is a family-oriented settlement, for although in the beginning there occurred, as in most migratory movements in their early

13. Interview with St. Croix police lieutenant, Christiansted, November 7, 1967.
14. Virgin Islands, Department of Health, Bureau of Statistical Services, *Vital Statistics, 1964–1965* (St. Thomas: Government Printing Office, 1966), tables 13, 15.

stages, a high sex imbalance, with more men than women (as is now the case with the West Indian alien movement), the high degree of family solidarity in Puerto Rican life, with families rapidly joining the parental pioneer, soon reasserted itself in the new environment. Even where there is a consensual marriage pattern, the loose-jointed out-of-wedlock system, it is not so much distinctively Puerto Rican as a pattern that historically has characterized both native and Puerto Rican lower-class cultures. There are other cross-cultural similarities in, for example, the patterns of divorce, desertion, and family size. These, however, do not completely overshadow the intense family-based identification of the Puerto Rican Virgin Islanders, evident in their Catholic puritanism, their overprotectiveness of women, and the fact, in itself interesting, that the hard-pressed foster-home program sponsored by the child welfare division of the Department of Social Welfare has been least successful with Puerto Rican households, where the blood relative is made more welcome than the alien child. Third, despite what some observers note as a unifying sense of national identity in the Puerto Rican elements, they constitute a highly structured social-class phenomenon with some deficiency only in the upper-level echelon of the professional salaried group. It is true that, as with the East Indian group in Guyana, there is a legend of Puerto Rican wealth based on a "rags to riches" reputation. Both Schroeder, in his early description of how the Puerto Rican street peddler rose by hard work to a status of relative affluence as a store proprietor,[15] and Jarvis, in his astonished description of the same metamorphosis,[16] tended somewhat uncritically to support the legend. Field trips undertaken through the narrow back streets of the two St. Croix townships or into the back-road country districts, however, indicate that this affluence is by no means the destiny of the majority of Puerto Ricans.

The history of the Puerto Rican influx over the last thirty years or so has witnessed a gradual transition from an initial hostility on the part of the Virgin Islands host society to a remarkably amicable acceptance. Clarence Senior's early study, *The Puerto Rican Migrant in St. Croix* (1947), dramatically annotated the early phase. The first wave of Puerto Ricans, settling as they did into jobs on Crucian cattle ranches, sugar fields, and stores, came initially into an economy that was only slightly better off than the decaying Viequan sugar economy they had left; inevitably, there was a conflict of cultures characterized by innumerable mutual antagonisms. In the virtual absence of a middle class these

15. Cited in Senior, "The Puerto Rican Migrant," p. 18.
16. J. Antonio Jarvis, *The Virgin Islands and Their People* (Philadelphia: Dorrance, 1944), pp. 58–59.

antagonisms were mostly among the working class. Senior noted five main areas of anti–Puerto Rican complaint: unsanitary habits; troublesome behavior; clannishness; attempted monopoly of livelihood sources; and "white superiority" beliefs. They were summed up in the prevalent half-bitter expressions: "The Puerto Ricans take our jobs"; "The Puerto Rican is haughty"; "The Puerto Ricans are a thankless lot and like to fight"; "The Puerto Ricans are too forward with women." Puerto Ricans, naturally, responded in like manner: "Crucians are filthy"; "The Crucians are two-faced and hypocrites and talk about the Puerto Ricans"; "They laugh when the Puerto Ricans speak English"; "They do not visit us unless on business matters." In such an atmosphere it was easy for rumor to insinuate that there was a concerted Puerto Rican plot to "run the Crucians off the island," which was in turn answered by ineffective "Buy Crucian" campaigns. With the single exception that Crucians were prepared to admit the superiority of Puerto Rican work habits, it was a generally negative picture. Nor was that offset by any large-scale Puerto Rican participation in community organizations. There was a sort of forced participation in the compulsory Selective Service system. But in all other areas—church life, the school system, civic organizations, politics—there was hardly any attempt to bridge a gulf made wider by the language barrier. The solution to it all, according to Senior, apart from a long-term program of planned economic growth, could be an attempt to copy the Danish experience in agricultural development, co-operative enterprise, and adult education (since things Danish still had some prestige left in the insular life). "Neither the caste and class-ridden mores of slavery and post-slavery days," he concluded in the best Jeffersonian liberal style, "nor the economic and social thinking on the continent, colored so deeply by gigantism, provides a feasible pattern of life for St. Croix." [17]

In opting for a forced industrialization sponsored by huge American corporations, St. Croix of course has turned its back on Senior's prescription. At the same time other factors have helped to take the sharp edge off the cultural friction that he described. Biological and cultural integration—already under way in the 1940s, as Senior noted—has proceeded apace. That process, combined with the new economic prosperity, has produced a whole new parallelogram of Crucian–Puerto Rican relationships. The differences between the two peoples have gradually given way to the far larger body of things they hold in common. Children, mixing in street and school, began to learn each other's language, as later did the adults, so that it is possible today to listen to conversations in shops

17. Senior, "The Puerto Rican Migrant," *passim.*

and bars in which both Puerto Rican and Crucian participants will switch, frequently with apparent arbitrariness, from one language to the other, with no loss of mutual comprehension. A mixing of cultures has taken place. The Puerto Ricans, for example, finding that the West Indian calypso was rhythmically compatible if not lyrically comprehensible, took over that musical form as soon as their command of the new language made it possible, for there is a common style of social satire in the calypso and the Puerto Rican *decima*. There is a high level of effective intermarriage, and at the middle-class level this tends to mean that English becomes the language of family intimacy, with the children learning Spanish from the grandparents. The old-style seclusion of the Puerto Rican woman has given way, too, to modernizing tendencies, and the group of working mothers in the local economy—a widespread phenomenon, according to a recent preparatory study [18]—has its fair share of Puerto Ricans. The traditional overprotectiveness continues, however, and there is still a common prejudice among Crucian men that it is better to marry a strict family-type Puerto Rican girl than the "loose" Crucian girl. But in a social economy where women workers comprise some 75 per cent of employees in all of the tourist-related occupations many Puerto Rican wives contribute substantially to the family income, which means that the husband gradually loses his authority to dictate his wife's extrafamilial activities. If, too, the wearing of mini-skirts and pants is an index of feminine emancipation, then many Puerto Rican women in Crucian society are in successful rebellion against the traditional Puerto Rican theme of strong male authority.

The erosion of Puerto Rican cultural distinctiveness has gone so far, indeed, that one Crucian observer has referred to the resultant mix as "Puerto-Crucians." [19] "We have proven to them," in the words of one successful Puerto Rican entrepreneur, "that we are not exactly a second class people." [20] "We are all integrated now," is the rather defiant assertion of a leading Crucian newspaper publisher, himself an acclimatized Jamaican whose daughter-in-law is Puerto Rican.[21] Increasingly (except, perhaps, among the older people) the feeling of in-group solidarity, that "we must all hold what is ours," is replaced with the sentiment that "we are all in the same boat." Evidence abounds, certainly, to support this optimistic view. There are no separate Puerto Rican teams in the island sports activities. Where there is an element of segregationism, sig-

---

18. Virgin Islands, Department of Labor, Division of Special Projects, "Interim Report: Survey of Working Women, 1967," mimeographed (St. Thomas, 1967).

19. Jean Larsen, "The Cruzan Kiva" column, *West End News*, Oct. 29, 1967.

20. Interview, A. B. Suarez, Frederiksted, November 6, 1967.

21. Interview, C. Brodhurst, editor, *St. Croix Avis*, November 8, 1967.

nificantly, is in those tourist-oriented sports—golf, yachting, scuba diving —that tend to be monopolized by the wealthier continentals. It would probably be impossible today for any legislative member to say, as did a member of the old St. Croix Municipal Council in 1940, that Puerto Ricans ought not to be allowed to enter the territory to bring diseases with them and expect free medical treatment.[22] From time to time there are allegations of discriminatory treatment. But the evidence on that score is equivocal. The case of Norma Polanco, for example, who was invited to participate in the Miss Virgin Islands contest and then was inexplicably dropped, could be cited as prejudice against a Puerto Rican candidate; but it could just as legitimately be seen as an expression of the well-known St. Thomian prejudice against Crucians.[23] The hostility that has been shown by Virgin Islands political leaders toward the figure of Dionisio Trigo is almost certainly not because he is a Puerto Rican but because he is the chief executive officer of the thoroughly unpopular Caribair airline organization. A local Puerto Rican columnist, to take a final example, has cited as evidence of general discrimination against Puerto Ricans in the public service the case of a Puerto Rican woman employee who, on coming over from San Juan to join the staff of the governor's office, was put in charge of rent collections instead of being treated as the intellectual she was; but this is clearly less a case of ethnic prejudice than an example of the notorious irrationality of the Virgin Islands machinery of government.[24]

One sure test of a minority group's sense of insecurity is whether it feels impelled to organize itself as a consciously ethnic bloc in community activities. The Puerto Ricans in St. Croix certainly felt so in the earlier period of the 1940s and 1950s, when various attempts were made to organize the "Puerto Rican vote" in local politics. It is well established that this vote was thrown behind a local politician in the 1944 council-manic election on the basis of his promise to have the unpopular health ordinance, requiring Puerto Rican immigrants to pass a health check, modified. Later on, in the 1950s, the Peoples' Party was started by resident Puerto Ricans in St. Croix and returned the first Puerto Rican candidate, Candido Guadalupe, to the insular Senate in 1958. At much the same time a group of Puerto Rican notables banded together to further the gubernatorial candidacy of John Merwin; and one of the group's leaders has since described how, once successfully nominated to the office, Governor Merwin failed to honor a pledge to give him a

22. St. Croix Municipal Council, *Proceedings,* quoted in *ibid.,* Jan. 19, 1940.
23. Letter by guardian of Miss Polanco, *West End News,* July 6, 1967.
24. J. E. Carrero, column, *ibid.,* Sept. 21, 1967.

handsome appointment in the local police system.[25] But political separatism has yielded, since then, to political assimilation. Both of the Puerto Rican politicians in the pre-1970 insular legislature, Senators Aureo Diaz Morales and Santiago Garcia, were members of the all-island political groupings, while a recent Puerto Rican political aspirant has opined that, at best, he could only hope to get some 35 per cent of the Puerto Rican vote, since "Puerto Ricans never act together." [26] There is, in brief, little of the sense of bitterly felt discrimination which drives the New York Puerto Rican community to a Tammany Hall type of ethnic bloc power play. The 1970 elections, again, innovative in so many ways, brought into political prominence Spanish-speaking legislative politicians—Hector Cintron and Jaime Garciaz—who were at once young, forward-looking professional persons and members of the leading political groups. It is true that talk about organizing a separate Puerto Rican party perennially flourishes, especially in St. Croix. But Puerto Rican opinion there is sharply divided on strategy—whether, that is, they should organize a full-fledged Puerto Rican party or simply a political bloc supporting Puerto Rican candidates within the existing party structure. It seems safe to say, in any case, that the power of the American system to absorb its minority groups will make it difficult for the Virgin Islands Puerto Rican minority to opt out in the manner, for example, of those *independentista* groups in Puerto Rico itself that argue for the strategy of electoral boycott. The truth is that social mobility and economic success have been easier for Puerto Ricans in St. Croix than in the mainland cities; their alienation is correspondingly less pronounced. It will take much more than the dissatisfaction they feel at the moment to give rise to the separate evolution of political organizations.

Few things, perhaps, illuminate so well the prestigious status of Puerto Ricans in the Virgin Islands community as the consideration awarded to their language. There is little, if any, of the unconcealed disdain with which the language is treated in the continental American society, summed up in the remark of an upstate New York bar owner, speaking of migrant Puerto Rican farm workers: "This is America, and they don't speak American. So they get nothing to drink. Not here. Let them go to North Collins [a nearby town]." [27] It is, perhaps, the distinctive trait of Caribbean civilization as a whole that it has always been capable of a higher cultural hospitality. So, St. Croix makes gracious

25. *Ibid.*, June 6, 1967.

26. Interview, Assistant Attorney General Felix Bello, Christiansted, November 7, 1967.

27. Quoted in "Puerto Rican Migrants Face Difficulties," *New York Times*, July 17, 1966, pp. 1, 60, an article on Puerto Rican migration in upper New York State.

concessions to the intruding language. The Lutheran church in Christian-sted uses a book of meditations, *Luz Cotidiana,* for its Spanish-speaking communicants; both of the Crucian newspapers, the *St. Croix Avis* and the *West End News,* carry Spanish-language columns on social and po-litical gossip; the St. Croix Festival and Cultural Organisation appoints a special assistant for Puerto Rican affairs; while the courts provide an interpreter, whose services eight out of ten Puerto Ricans who appear before the courts elect to use, according to a local law officer, despite the fact that many of them are adequately bilingual. There is, obviously, a large body of official and semiofficial opinion which welcomes the Puerto Rican presence as an integral component of the insular main-stream culture. It is suggestive that, back in the 1950s, when a local anti–Puerto Rican movement developed to forestall a reputed plan of Puerto Ricans to take over control of the islands, its leaders were taken severely to task for their ill-conceived goal and were reminded that Puerto Ricans were not foreigners but as much American citizens as Virgin Islanders themselves.[28]

The Puerto Rican picture, even so, is not completely positive. In the area of language, for example, there is a dark side, especially in the status of Spanish in the insular school system. Whatever the linguistic democracy of the church or the saloon bar may be, it is regrettable that there does not yet exist a truly bilingual educational system. Puerto Rican children are introduced to English as a native language, not as a second language; furthermore, they are frequently taught by "teachers' aides" whose own command of English is extremely faulty. The aware-ness of the cultural fact that, for the Puerto Rican child, especially in the St. Croix schools, English is a second language has barely penetrated the consciousness of the Education Department. This is in part a conse-quence of the fact that Virgin Islanders have tended, over the last seventy years or so, to lose the polylinguistic gift that they used to possess, and it is possible today to encounter native faculty members at the College who will balk at using non-English reading materials in a proposed Caribbean Heritage course. The Puerto Rican child becomes the person who is hurt most by this shortsightedness. Nor is this situation much offset by the recent decision of the local legislature to publish some government publications in Spanish in order to help those citizens whose English is faulty.

There is, on a wider island scale, the tremendously intriguing question of what will happen to the Puerto Rican role as the "black power"

28. "Political and Economic Security or Demagogy?," reprinted from *The Civic* (New York), in *Daily News,* Feb. 14, 1956.

ideology becomes more pronounced in the native Virgin Islander groups. There is already a local white backlash to that phenomenon. There could also be a Puerto Rican backlash. The return to ethnicity is an increasing movement on the continental American scene, even among the older European stocks. The Virgins Puerto Rican group could follow suit, especially if the "black power" message fails to take into account the polyglot character of the Caribbean plural society. Crucian society, much more than St. Thomian society, is a race-color-class mixture. There has always been a three-way movement of persons between Vieques, St. Croix, and Puerto Rico proper which keeps the home spirit alive, and there is evidence that the growing nationalism of the San Juan *independentista* groups is making inroads among the Puerto Rican teenagers of the St. Croix high schools. The future of Crucian society will very much depend upon whether it is the magnet of social class or that of ethnic identity that appeals the most powerfully to the younger Puerto Rican element.

The startling contrast between the French and Puerto Rican situations is painfully obvious. In part, it is a matter of size. The Puerto Rican element has been large enough to exercise real bargaining power in its relations with its host society. The French, by comparison, have been a minuscule group, so bereft of independent power that their relations with the host society have always been essentially unequal, with the minority's fate being dependent on the amount of condescending good will existing at any given moment in the majority attitudes. In part, it has been a difference of economic role, for whereas the French have been at best marginal to the major economy, the Puerto Ricans entered directly into it; and there is a sense in which the Puerto Rican businessmen of the early 1930s made credit a household word for Virgin Islands consumers accustomed to the niggardly business practices of the native stores. Whereas the Puerto Ricans have been absorbed into the host society, frequently on their own terms, the French have been submerged, suffering the stigmata of cultural inferiority historically assigned to all such groups.

Yet perhaps the real secret of Puerto Rican success has been the fact that, although *émigrés,* the Puerto Rican newcomers have remained under the peculiar spell of their home society in Puerto Rico, which, despite its continuing colonial character, is a remarkably strong, viable human organization with a high awareness of cultural identity. From the very beginning Crucians were visibly impressed by the deeply felt homesickness that this engendered in their Puerto Rican neighbors. It meant that the Puerto Rican migrant could effectively adjust to the new environment but at the same time retain his passionate attachment to the "mother country." The attachment, moreover, was expressed through a medium—that of the collective opus of Puerto Rican romantic music put together by the great Puerto Rican composers Juan Morell Campos, Pedro Flores, Rafael Hernandez—which Crucians, like all West Indians, could instinctively appreciate, and even assimilate. To be Puerto Rican, whether physically located in the island or not, is to be the willing prisoner of that nostalgic musical opus, the *lamento borincano:*

> Adios, Borinquen querida,
> Adios, mi diosa del mar;
> me voy, pero un dia volveré
> a buscar mi querer
> a soñar otra vez
> en mi viejo San Juan.

It is, all in all, a powerful migrational mystique which afflicts the Puerto Rican emigrant everywhere, as much in Christiansted as in New York. In the Caribbean case it visibly enriches Crucian life, for it is not an archaic art form artificially kept alive by the organizing commissars of the emergent state apparatus of "culture" development but a vibrant element in the daily life of a volatile populace.

9

~~~

The Social Milieu:
The West Indian Aliens

Perhaps the single most remarkable fact of the Virgin Islands way of life is that its economic base, in the form of the majority of the labor task force, is alien; that is, it is constituted of non-American immigrants settled, legally or illegally, in the various island communities. Initially coming from the neighboring British Virgin Islands and then, later, from the more distant Leeward Islands group, they have been, historically, refugees from the desperate poverty of their Caribbean background, responding to economic opportunities in the more affluent American possessions. They provide a further example of the general metastasis of West Indian populations, of the vast, silent, and often underground cyclical movements of uprooted peoples in search of jobs. It has been largely an economically motivated phenomenon, with few of the political motives that have characterized, by comparison, the Haitian exodus to the Bahamas or the Cuban exodus to Puerto Rico. But these immigrants at the same time constitute, as do those other groups, a potentially acute minority problem for their host society, for if in the neo-Hellenistic Virgin Islands society the continentals play, as it were, the role of the Romans (from the viewpoint of the native Virgin Islanders), the alien laborers and their families play the role of the barbarian helots. The cultural, economic, and social consequences of their presence are felt daily and ever more acutely in the spirit of Virgin Islands life.

The historical background of the alien influx relates to the fact that the U.S. Virgins have constituted the economic magnet of the entire northern Antillean chain of territories. The area as a whole, indeed, forms a natural labor market entity. The exchange of goods and services, and, within the last four decades or so, of human beings, has been a leading feature of its existence. Two particular aspects of the phenomenon are worth emphasizing, as a sort of prefatory note to the analysis of its consequences.

In the first place, it has been a comparatively spontaneous movement in response to economic pressures, that is to say, a semivoluntary uprootedness as distinct from the earlier completely forcible uprootedness of the slave trade. Many of the migrants support children and aged parents back in their home islands—Tortola, Anguilla, St. Kitts, St. Maarten, Nevis, Montserrat, even Trinidad—and much alien income leaves the Virgins in the form of remittances home, although its statistical amount is unknown. However, there is little of the romantic nostalgia for the *patria madre* so eloquently evident in the Puerto Rican migrants. Nor is there any recognizable return migration pattern, similar to the wave of returning Puerto Ricans from the continental United States described in José Hernández Alvarez's monograph, *Return Migration to Puerto Rico* (1967). There are, of course, the regular visits home to bury a parent or bring back yet some more children. But the average alien seeks to become permanently integrated into the host economy. The American dream may have faded for other immigrant groups, but for the West Indian in the Virgins it is still a real thing. Their migratory movement is a response, more or less voluntary, to the promise of American life. It should also be noted, as a matter of interest, that the West Indian influx predates, historically, the transfer of 1917. Of the 120 residents, for example, of the Herbert Grigg Home for the Aged in St. Croix, a not insignificant number of 29 are old folk who had come to the islands during the Danish period.[1]

The other particular aspect deserving notice is that the legal status—or, more correctly, the absence of legal status—of the alien has been problematical from the start. Generally speaking, the immigration function, that is, the general control of alien admission, has been divided among the three federal departments of State, Labor, and Justice. Yet strangely enough the first large influx, during the Second World War period, was a thoroughly laissez faire episode, with none of the incoming migrants being processed with work permits; they entered as "visitors," found jobs, worked without interference by immigration officialdom, and were even permitted voluntary departure, thus removing the onus of illegality from their employment. The federal machinery was only brought into play once the wartime boom ended, and much of the social history of the aliens after 1945 was that of a cat-and-mouse game, with immigration officials scouring the islands for aliens in hiding; there is

1. Data obtained from visit to Herbert Grigg Home for the Aged, Kingshill, St. Croix, September 5, 1967.

in fact a growing popular literature describing the tragicomedy of the hunt.[2] The abolition of the old 29-day visitor's permit has helped to regularize the position somewhat, but there still remain the many injustices inherent in the subsequent bonded labor system, an ad hoc program, with no basis in law, instituted by the U.S. Department of Labor. It is difficult to avoid the conclusion that the U.S.–Virgin Islands authorities have made things easy for the alien worker when they have needed him and moved to harass him once his presence became embarrassing. He has become, increasingly, the victim of a combination of official neglect and public hostility, and it is only comparatively recently that any institutions of insular life, such as the College of the Virgin Islands, have begun to show any keen and sympathetic interest in his problems.[3]

These two factors—the voluntary character of the migration and the often questionable legal status of the individual immigrant—perhaps help to explain the surprising docility of the West Indians and their generally unrebellious attitude toward their frequently infelicitous conditions of life and work. The more negative aspects of the contract are apparently offset by the fact that there is a job to be had, and that the financial remuneration is frequently handsome, for wage and hour matters are statutorily regulated (with the single exception of domestic workers, who come under federal provisions). On the whole, the migrant is only conditionally present in the economy, being a bonded worker at the pleasure of the employer and a nonpermanent alien at the mercy of the immigration authorities; these factors naturally discourage him from undertaking any sort of active protest against the more onerous conditions of his stay, even if he does find them difficult. His general attitude is either one of philosophical and good-tempered acceptance of the good with the bad or a sullen and suspicious regard of any visitor —welfare officer, academic researcher, census gatherer—who tries to pry information from him. To the degree that he adopts the latter attitude there is a regrettable loss of the warm and contagious bonhomie so

2. See, for example, Eilenne L. Parsons, "What Do You Keep in Here, Mrs. Keggler?," *Virgin Islands View*, August, 1965.
3. For the reports sponsored by the College of the Virgin Islands, see "The Alien Worker and His Family," mimeographed (St. Thomas: College of the Virgin Islands, January, 1967); *Aliens in the United States Virgin Islands: Temporary Workers in a Permanent Economy* (Washington, D.C.: Social, Educational Research and Development, Inc., January, 1968); *A Profile and Plans for the Temporary Alien Worker Problem in the U.S. Virgin Islands* (Washington, D.C.: Social, Educational Research and Development, Inc., 1969). See also *How-to-Do-It: A Booklet for Aliens in the United States Virgin Islands* (St. Thomas: College of the Virgin Islands, February 1, 1968).

characteristic of the West Indian in his home habitat, almost as if emigration has stripped him of part of his being.

It is difficult to put together an exact statistical picture of the alien presence, for a number of reasons: not all the foreign-born are aliens; many aliens are integrated in native homes—men with native girls, girls with native men; the absence of a housing registry makes it impossible to use occupancy indices as a guide to population figures; and there is widespread evasion in declaring the alien person—many aliens, in the phrase of the officer in charge of the 1960 census program, left by the back door when the census enumerators appeared at the front door. As of mid-1967 the local government's Office of Statistics and Economic Studies estimated a total of 13,000 aliens—8,000 in St. Croix and 5,000 in St. Thomas–St. John; on the other hand, the local office of the Bureau of Immigration, a year earlier, estimated a total of some 14,000. There is no doubt, however, of the vastly accelerated growth of the alien population. The Governor's Annual Report for 1926 estimated that 21 per cent of the then total population of some 23,000 people were British Virgin Island aliens. A 1965 report on St. Croix alone estimated a total population at that time of 21,761, with aliens representing 23.9 per cent of the figure. The live birth statistics tell a similar story, for beginning in 1961 the number of listed foreign-born parents exceeded the number of native-born parents; most of them were from the British West Indies, with Tortola predominating. The proportion of foreign-born to native-born mothers has continued to rise annually, although after 1965 there were fewer Tortolan-born mothers than those from the other British islands. Some of the foreign-born parents, of course, are naturalized citizens. But most of them are aliens, with or without resident visas (a recent study indicates only some 423 aliens with permanent residency in St. Croix), who seek the benefits of United States citizenship for their children.

Whatever the correct figure at any given moment may be, the statistics as they stand indicate several considerations. First, the Virgin Islands population is rapidly changing in its basic character. Second, as far as the alien component is concerned, the newcomers are not transients, "visitors" or merely contract labor, but a visibly integral part of the community, intermarrying and establishing permanent households, indicating altogether a determination to stay. Third, the aliens constitute a vital element in the economy, since so far no other effective way of recruiting the economy's supplementary labor force has been established; only limited success has attended the efforts of the local Labor Department and the Virgin Islands Employment Service to recruit American workers from Puerto Rico and the mainland, most of whom are deterred in any case by the massive housing problem that awaits most newcomers to the islands. Finally, of course, the average alien is lower-class, poor, colored, and generally unskilled, in contrast with the class of European and American business and professional aliens who resided in St. Thomas and St. Croix during the Danish period and who, interestingly enough, enjoyed the alien franchise granted them by the Danish Colonial Law of 1906. The comparison indicates the vast transformation that has taken place in the character of the alien over the last sixty years or so. It is a far cry from the Charles Edwin Taylor type of European gentleman-alien, cultivating the upper-class values of the old St. Thomas Athenaeum Society, to the West Indian proletarian-alien of the present-day period, desperately trying to hold his own in a bitter struggle for survival.

Characteristically, the alien workers are at the very bottom of the Virgin Islands economic and social ladder. That is clear from the profile of alien employment. The largest number are employed, mostly as un-skilled laborers, in the construction industry; the next largest group perform domestic work in private households; a less numerous group work in the service and trade sectors; while the 277 aliens who, as of 1966, were governmental employees worked mainly at the menial and dirty jobs like the night-soil collection brigades.[4] Thus the average alien is forced to take what is available to him: the job vacated by an upward-bound local worker, or the job everybody else refuses to do. He accepts willingly, in large part because of the rewards of a wage structure hand-some in comparison to anything he has known in the West Indian economy. The angry response of the local political leaders to the sur-prise directive of the U.S. Department of Labor in 1967, which raised the wage rate of the 2,700 alien domestic workers of the economy to a variable minimum of $100–$148 a month, unsettling as it did the secondary economy of the working housewife dependent on maid service, demonstrates how real the protection of the federal bureaucracy can be in the struggle between native employer and alien employee.[5] But another reason why the alien worker accepts his working conditions is that in many other ways he is far from being a free agent. His certification, although approved by the Virgin Islands Employment Service and ac-cepted by the U.S. Immigration Service, is not a contract in the full sense of the word. It guarantees little beyond the prevailing wage rate. His

4. "Aliens Admitted to the Virgin Islands, July to September 1966," Attachment B, in "The Alien Worker and His Family."

5. "Record of Proceedings and Debates, Seventh Legislature of the Virgin Islands of the United States," January 18, 1967, mimeographed (St. Thomas, 1967), pp. 22–25; *Daily News,* Jan. 19, 20, 1967; *Home Journal,* Jan. 19, 20, 1967.

employer is not required to house him. He can be arbitrarily farmed out to other jobs, especially in construction, or shifted to a higher job classification without increased pay. If he objects, he can be threatened with deportation, a form of intimidation widely practiced. He is therefore more than ordinarily willing to accept "under the table" arrangements with the employer, to the detriment of the normal collective bargaining process. Thus he performs almost all of the productive and menial work of the economy, but as a bonded worker he is not allowed to freely seek employment. If, as frequently happens, he comes in as a short-term visitor on a no-work basis and then proceeds to violate the conditions of his entry, he becomes even more vulnerable to intimidation. It goes without saying, naturally, that all this severely militates against any possibility of trade union activities on the part of the alien worker. There is a large file of cases in the San Juan office of the regional authorities of the National Labor Relations Board that deal with the victimization of union-minded workers, many of whom were deported to their island homes long before their cases were finally adjudicated.

It is not surprising, then, that the alien laborer is subject to some of the most flagrant general living conditions existing anywhere under the American flag. An alien residence census in the Crucian population concentrations has classified "houses," either built or rented, into three categories: (1) residences constructed from plywood board sheets or a combination of sheets and wood recovered from packing cases; (2) old plantation barns, warehouses, and dilapidated brick structures "patched up" to provide housing; and (3) an amazing assortment of unclassified decrepit frame buildings, galvanized shacks, and in some instances crudely constructed concrete structures. Of these, some 90 per cent, many of them illegal "squatter" structures, had electricity installations of questionable design and materials, while 96 per cent of them had no indoor running water or other plumbing facilities, the most prevalent means of sewage disposal being the antiquated pit privy system; all of these conditions added up generally to an overcrowding situation so immense as to constitute a serious threat to health and general welfare.[6] A visit to St. Croix will testify to the essential correctness of that indictment. The Crucian rural landscape is dotted, all over, with small clusters of this kind of housing—behind a small gas station, around the base of an old sugar mill, on the edge of idle estate land, and sometimes even in decaying, abandoned slave quarters.

6. "A Study of the Alien Residents, St. Croix," Phase 2, "Alien Residence Census," mimeographed (St. Thomas, October, 1965).

In addition to these makeshift assemblies that proliferate all over the islands' landscapes, there is the separate category of housing provided by some employers of large cadres of alien workers. But much of it, following the bad example set earlier by the now defunct Virgin Islands Corporation, is esthetically displeasing. A visit to the temporary block housing provided by the Harvey and Hess companies in St. Croix will show that although superior to the old "Vicorp" villages—which can be seen in the Bethlehem and Machuchal areas—it is essentially of the steel-made trailer camp variety, constructed with no physical or community relationship to either existing housing or planned future development, and apparently concerned only with the consideration of proximity to the site of employment. Aliens, of course, not being in practice eligible for public housing projects, must do the best they can in the private housing developments. Yet even there, as surveys of areas such as the Golden Rock development have shown, slum conditions rapidly make themselves felt, under the population pressure, even in the newest of structures. It is hard to believe, looking at all this, that rent control laws and building and housing codes exist on the Virgin Islands statute book.

One of the single most antisocial features of the alien situation is the prevalent rental exploitation. Entering an economy which is a classic example of the truth of Henry George's land economics, the alien becomes its first victim. He must pay exorbitant rents for jerry-built housing. To meet his rental obligation he must crowd as many bodies as possible into the rented quarters, usually family members or friends from his home island who masquerade as "visitors"; the many stories circulated of units that are used in shifts by several groups of tenants are reminiscent of those heard about tenement house occupancy in New York City at the turn of the century. The big real estate and housing operators now entering the economy are responsible for much of this exploitation; the testimony of long-time shack tenants before the Rent Control Board in 1967 demonstrates how a large corporation like Harvlan in St. Croix is prepared to use the terroristic economic device of massively accelerated rents in order to get people off property it wishes to exploit more profitably. However, those individual property owners who are only too ready to make the most of this human misery must carry some of the blame. The deputy regional administrator of the federal Department of Housing and Urban Development, in a spirited attack upon this exploitative situation, has ventured the opinion that if the presently available legal tools for its correction were fully utilized by the local government forces the income of many Virgin Islanders on various social levels would be reduced, rental income being the item that is most often

(223)

"forgotten," or at least "adjusted," at income tax time.[7] Forced into the sort of substandard housing that is organized on the basis of private greed, the alien worker can find no consolation in being told that although there are no legal barriers to his eligibility for inclusion in the various low-income housing programs undertaken by both the local and the federal governments there are in fact operative practical barriers, because priorities are assigned to both natives and resident aliens before bonded non-resident aliens can even begin to be considered, and thus he should look to private nonprofit organizations, such as cooperatives and church groups, to provide nonprofit rent supplement housing for him.[8]

It seems at times that the whole of Virgin Islands society is engaged in a conspiracy to make life hard for the alien stranger at the gate. If he comes from the British Virgin Islands he must undergo an onerous and humiliating encounter with the U.S. immigration officials at the St. Thomas quayside, standing in line endlessly in a hot tropical sun while his interrogators sit in shaded comfort on the boat. He must pay income tax to the local treasury, but if he sends remittances to children or parents back home he cannot list them as deductible dependents for tax purposes. He must go through endless paperwork in order to regularize his status, which becomes an additional area of exploitation: native clerks and stenographers charge excessive fees to do the work, and there is at least one former judge of the Municipal Court, well known in social circles, whom local rumor points to as having made a small fortune over the years in processing, frequently fraudulently, papers for alien clients. Employers complain that, because of the feudal semi-slavery of work conditions, only untrained employables come to the Virgins to work, in spite of the money advantage; yet little is done to improve the conditions so as to encourage the intake of more skilled workers. Many employers themselves contribute to this situation by their practice of requesting certification for more workers than they need, with the surplus being casually left to fend for themselves.

Yet there is more to it even than this. The exploitation of the alien

7. Alonzo G. Moron, "Housing for the Alien in the United States Virgin Islands, 1966," in "The Alien Worker and His Family," pp. 17–25. On the failure of the Virgin Islands public taxation system to compel the more affluent elements to make a fair contribution to territorial revenues, see U.S., Congress, House, Subcommittee on Territorial and Insular Affairs, *Memorandum on Organization and Management with Reference to the Virgin Islands* (by Director, Office of Territories, Department of Interior), in *Election of Virgin Islands Governor: Hearings,* 90th Cong., 1st sess., serial no. 90–15, 1967, pt. 2, pp. 719–21.

8. Thomas R. Blake, planning director, Virgin Islands Planning Board, in "The Alien Worker and His Family," pp. 26–31.

has been compounded by a vast indifference over the years on the part of the Virgin Islands government as a whole. The essence of the problem—a rapidly increasing population accompanied by very little planned effort to accelerate welfare facilities and services to meet the explosion—has failed to elicit an imaginative response from official leadership, either political or administrative. That can be seen from the gross anomalies characteristic of the relationship of the alien to the public service regime. He is the mainstay of the economy; he pays taxes, and without him entire areas of activity, from public works operations to the hotel trade, would collapse. Yet what he gets in return by way of welfare aid and social services is scanty to a degree. His employer must pay unemployment tax, but he cannot collect unemployment benefits. The local Employment Service office gives him no help in finding a job, unless he is a permanent resident alien. He and his family can benefit from certain limited services offered by the Department of Social Welfare, such as the child adoption program, the foster home program, the financial assistance program to the needy, and others. But, as with the day-care program, the alien must pay the full board fee for most of these services; he is not eligible for the surplus foods program; he, or his employer, must meet the expenses if he requires treatment under the cancer care program; and he is generally excluded from the regular public assistance program. It is true that both the hospital and the social service case-load programs are overburdened by a tremendous pressure of alien patients and clients; but nevertheless the alien must bear the expenses as best he can. It is not unknown for hospital staff to refuse a birth certificate to an alien mother until she has paid the full fee.

In the field of education, alien children, until only very recently, have not been eligible for entry to the public school system. Thus there has grown up an unofficial, third, alien–parochial school system, with second-rate standards, which in any case is restricted to children whose parents can afford the rather high fees required. Unequal access to the public school system has also generated the phenomenon of the private home nursery, in which a single, sometimes elderly, woman looks after the infant children of alien neighbors who are also working mothers. Such nurseries are quite unregulated by any sort of inspection system, and the possibility of the emergence of Victorian-type Dotheboys Halls run by unconscionable "educators" is apparent enough. Not the least tragic of all Virgin Islands figures is that of the working mother, usually alien, who—single, divorced, separated, or widowed—must provide everything for her family on an average income that rises only slightly above the national poverty level. The only solution, as a recent report has indicated, is governmental provision of day-care centers throughout all the island communities to guarantee adequate care and supervision for the preschool children of this important group of people.[9]

The social consequences of this unequal availability of public services, which turns the bonded alien into a second-class citizen, can be seen at every turn. It has produced the characteristic types of sociocultural maladjustment: the alien schoolchild turned truant; the abused or neglected alien child, frequently abandoned by parents who make emergency trips to look after other children left behind in the home island; the adolescent girl who becomes pregnant out of wedlock by an alien and is frequently a bonded "companion" of the man without any guarantee of security; the young male alien worker whose natural sexual problems are not in any way helped by bachelor-oriented housing arrangements; the alien maids and gardeners who have live-in housing arrangements with their employers that do little to meet the problem of social relationships, not to speak of sexual relationships, with fellow nationals; the pregnant woman who comes to the territory, technically as a "visitor," in order to guarantee American citizenship for her child; and the diseased person who for want of proper medical attention contributes to the recent resurgence of venereal disease, from which it was once assumed the islands had been fully freed by the earlier work of Dr. Roy Anduze and his colleagues. So endemic and widespread are all these problems that they have evoked the angry criticism of both congressional leaders and federal administrators in the national capital. The acting director of the Office of Territories of the Interior Department wrote to Governor Paiewonsky as follows in 1965:

> One of the few things wrong with the Virgin Islands is a complex of problems, two of the parts of which might be labelled "alien labor" and "low wages." Six, eight, ten alien laborers sleeping in a room in a chicken house, away from their families, or when they manage to bring them in under circumstances of questionable legality having them be an impossible burden on the social services of the community, while they are paid sweat-shop wages by enterprises that never had it so good—this does something to the quality of life in the islands that is not compatible with the Great Society.[10]

9. For all this, see C. Warren Smith, "Principles of Health Services to Alien Workers," Arthur A. Richards, "Education of Non-Citizens," and Macon C. Berryman, "Welfare Services and Aliens," all in "The Alien Worker and His Family." See also Walter S. Priest, "The Alien: Problem Man in St. Thomas," San Juan Star, Sept. 4, 1963, and the two reports by Social, Educational Research and Development, Inc. (SERD), cited in note 3 above.

10. John Kirwan to Governor Paiewonsky, August 12, 1965, text in San Juan Star, Oct. 17, 1965. See also the sharp criticism in Look, March 10, 1970, and the angry reaction of the Virgin Islands resident commissioner in Washington, quoted in San Juan Star, Feb. 28, 1970.

This is a harsh but thoroughly justified charge. In return for a federally permitted alien labor program the Virgin Islands assumed responsibility for protecting alien interests. Until only very recently, certainly, the territorial government has done little to honor that obligation. It has done hardly anything, as its own planning director has admitted, in the way of undertaking those long-range, detailed studies of the actual situation without which no rational planning can be done, so that there is an astonishing dearth of material on the topic as a whole. Most of the officials concerned with various aspects of the problem —social security benefits, education, unemployment insurance, employment opportunities—seem not to have thought critically in any way about the moral implications of the separate programs for citizens and non-citizens that they administer. It is true that the record is not one of complete inactivity. Since 1962, the local government has made determined efforts to overhaul the antiquated insular minimum-wage structure in order to provide coverage where Fair Labor Standards Act protection fails to reach. More latterly, efforts have also been made to liberalize various eligibility criteria for certain social services, while in 1967 Governor Paiewonsky began to push hard for a "permanent solution" to the situation in the form of a program to convert the bonded alien into a full-fledged permanent resident alien (the alien enthusiasm for this program is curbed only by the fact that one condition of the acquisition of permanent residence status is acceptance of U.S. military service obligations).[11]

But certain things must be noted about these efforts. In the first place, much of this activity has been a belated response of the local governmental bureaucracy to insistent federal pressures which, given the colonial character of the island territories, cannot be ignored. It is no accident, for example, that in the record of the 1967 Virgin Islands College conference on the problem of the alien—which unanimously recommended a radical revision of all public services on the basis of equal use by citizen and non-citizen alike, so that, in Eldra Shulterbrandt's apt phrase, all agencies cease referring to an "alien problem" and deal with human beings—the finest expression of fierce indignation came from the late Alonzo Moron, the remarkable Virgin Islander who, as a federal housing expert, had done so much to prod his fellow islanders into recognition of their obligations to their alien guests. Second, there has

11. *San Juan Star*, Apr. 15, July 16, 1967; and "How a Bonded Worker Becomes a Permanent Resident," Focus Magazine, *Home Journal*, Aug. 13, 1967. For the matter of minimum-wage legislation, see Valdemar Alexander Hill, Jr., *Minimum Wages in the U.S. Virgin Islands, 1938–1968* (San German, Puerto Rico: Inter-American University, 1968).

been, and still is, a gross discrepancy between the money, imagination, and effort that the Virgin Islands governmental machine has devoted to furthering the interests of the local business community and what it has been prepared to do for the alien interests. John Kirwan, in the same letter to Governor Paiewonsky already quoted, said:

> I know that the problems on the $200 duty allowance, and the liquor exemption, and the watch and woollen problems are technically the concern of the Customs Bureau, and the Commerce Department, and the Treasury Department. Yet the pressure from the Virgin Islands people, legislature, and government upon such agencies has been unremittant, creative, and successful. The Virgin Islands just wouldn't take "no" for an answer in those cases, and couldn't care less what the regulations, the old law, or the old established limitations were. If they got in the way of progress they had to go, even if it meant months of footwork here in Washington, and a series of new laws from the Congress.[12]

The contrast, Kirwan went on to note, between that record and the reluctance of any Virgin Islands lobby to persuade the Congress to raise wage levels in the territory—by means, for example, of eliminating the Virgin Islands exemption from the federal minimum-wage legislation, which only benefits employers battening on the underpaid alien worker —throws serious doubt upon the willingness of the territorial leadership to move with any urgency or determination in the cause of the alien. Nor has there been—and this is the third point—any visible effort on the part of the local government to utilize its tax powers to raise more revenue for alien services, a scandalous dereliction of duty in view of the fact that the territory, with all its affluence, is one of the most lightly taxed areas under the American flag. The result of that fiscal conservatism is an ever widening gap between the low wage and living-conditions level of the bottom of the work force and the increasing affluence of the entrepreneurial segment of the tourist and export industries.

Short, then, of active federal intervention to protect him—a sort of active colonial trusteeship which Washington has neither the spirit nor the machinery to indulge—the alien worker can hardly expect much positive action on the part of the local Virgin Islands Establishment to alleviate what amounts to a modern variant of indentured labor. It is easy to see what must be done. What the assistant director of the local Employment Security Agency has called a "full service plan" must be set up, putting the recruitment of the overseas worker on a rational basis and envisaging his integration, as an equal, into the domestic labor force. That could be accompanied by a shift in recruitment methods to

12. Kirwan to Paiewonsky, August 12, 1965.

the labor departments of the islands from which the worker originates. One gross defect of the present recruitment system is that the British consular office in Charlotte Amalie knows nothing, officially, of new arrivals yet is expected to help in the human problems that are produced by the irrationality of the system; what is more, that office, under the jurisdiction of the San Juan consulate, is pathetically understaffed, possesses no kind of revolving or benevolent fund for use in distress cases, and is generally ignored by the Virgin Islands bureaucratic machine.[13] There is a crying need for a revitalization of the old Inter–Virgin Islands Conference as a method of resolving the difficulties (which go back to the passage of the McCarran Act of 1950) created by the strict application of federal legislation designed, in effect, to break the traditional economic and family relationships that have grown up between the British Virgins and the American Virgins over the last 200 years. It is worth noting, in that respect, the opinion of a knowledgeable observer that the Conference meetings, of late, have achieved almost nothing, tending to be more a high-level social event—"a social club not even well directed"—than a serious effort to solve the matter.[14] The whole bureaucratic process of dealing with the alien, which in any case is essentially an international problem, not an exclusively American one, needs both simplification and humanization, along the lines suggested as far back as 1943 by the Coert du Bois memorandum to the Anglo-American Caribbean Commission of that period. It is intolerable, for example, that an alien desiring permanent residence status must still undertake a costly trip to distant Barbados to finalize his papers. It is time that both Charlotte Amalie and Washington come to a full and generous recognition of the fact that although the alien has come for essentially selfish reasons his contribution to the society cannot be denied.

In the meantime the alien takes his place in the complex of Virgin Islands social relationships. His is a recognizable subworld, but it is far from being homogeneous. There is a certain linguistic homogeneity, due to the overwhelming preponderance of persons from the English-speaking islands. But even there internal divisions appear between that

13. Interview, Henry O'Neal, officer in charge, British Consular Office, Charlotte Amalie, December 7, 1967.

14. Interview, St. Thomas informant, December 9, 1967. For the history of the Inter-Virgin Islands Conference, see Norwell Harrigan, "A Study of the Inter-Relationships between the British and United States Virgin Islands," mimeographed (St. Thomas: Caribbean Research Institute, College of the Virgin Islands, 1969), pp. 186–93. See also text of proposed contract to protect aliens, report of Inter-Virgin Islands Conference, in *St. Croix Avis,* Feb. 16, 1965.

majority and, for example, the Negro immigrants from the French islands, who, interestingly, have little to do with the established citadel of the white Frenchtown community. The French person from St. Maarten who speaks English will feel that it makes her somehow superior to the French immigrants from Martinique and Guadeloupe who lack that facility. There are similar divisions, both of economic status and social attitude, among the British West Indian majority. The historically earlier relationship between the American and British Virgins, resulting in intimate kinship relations, makes the Tortolan resident feel socially superior to the more recent arrivals from the other islands. Representative of the first-generation immigrant who resents the social manners of later arrivals is the case of a woman who came from Roadtown in 1923 and is a permanent resident. She runs singlehandedly a kindergarten school for alien children, sells ice to her alien neighbors because "they all live five or six to a room and not one of them is going to buy a 'fridge' to serve the others," and in general feels that aliens are "lucky to be here." Such a person, amateurly entrepreneurial, who spends $42.50 monthly to send her child to the Anglican school, can afford to be nonchalant about government services ("going to hospital is a joke"), whereas a neighbor, who rents a barracks-style shack on Kessler-owned property and who has had three operations since 1960, will feel openly grateful for St. Thomian medical aid.

There is a general sentiment of relief at being able to get regular employment. Whether, however, the relief is accompanied by home-sickness or not will depend on the earlier experience in the home island. Thus, speaking only of Antiguan immigrants, a girl who came from the depressed urban life of St. Johns and now works as a Christiansted barmaid will have no regrets at all, while a hard-pressed mother of eleven children who came from an Antiguan rural district will miss not only the free educational facilities for her children but also the piece of land and fishing boat that used to supply her with food. Most of these people have a harsh struggle for survival. Witness the young mother who, with an aged parent and five children to support, earns a monthly $100 as a bonded maid, out of which she must pay $60 for her water supply, or the older woman who earns only 95 cents an hour as a hotel dishwasher but must pay a total of some $230 for a ten-month school period for each child at the Seventh Day Adventist School, or the cab driver who must register his car fictitiously in the name of a Crucian friend and who must fight the increasing competition of the big continental rental car agencies, or the pregnant female visitor who is driven to play a cat-and-mouse game with the immigration authorities and her sponsor in attempts to conceal the pregnancy.[15] All of these people have freely elected to start a new life in the American tropics, but few of them would be likely to agree with a Virgin Islander, himself exiled in Barbados, who a generation ago assured their predecessors that "You live in a more Utopian atmosphere than any other people in the whole sweep of the Caribbean." [16]

The psychiatric aspect of this struggle must not be overlooked. A defect of Weinstein's analysis of psychotic reactions and obsessional anxiety states in the territorial population is that it arbitrarily puts native Virgin Islanders and aliens into the same cultural category and thus overlooks the special factors in the alien situation that can seriously affect the alien's mental health. Unlike the locals or natives, the off-island immigrant (in many ways like the retired continental, another group overlooked by the Weinstein analysis) must bear the stress and anxiety that stem from the unexpected discrepancy between his dream of the American Virgin Islands as a land flowing with milk and honey and the shock of the confronted reality. Officers of the Mental Health Division— one of the few government agencies that treat citizen and non-citizen patients on an equal footing—have listed the factors provocative of stress and anxiety in the alien psyche: the forced separation from families and friends; the loose sexual liaisons with native men or women; the uncertainties surrounding pregnancy; the ever present possibility of loss of a bond, or the threat of non-renewal when the time is up; and the general hostility shown by the more prejudiced sections of the native community.[17]

There is ample evidence to document the power of that last item. If, indeed, anti–Puerto Rican sentiment has declined over the last twenty years or so, it is due in large part to the fact that the Puerto Rican has been replaced by the alien as the malefic scapegoat of the society. A superior-inferior relationship is exploited to blame him for practically every social ill. As far back as 1928, members of the old Council, even the progressive colored members, were sounding the alarm: "Alien votes are non-American, and so are appointed members." They were also calling attention to the consequences of lower-class immigration: "The aftermath is a cosmopolitanism which has corroded our entire system.

15. Much of the information in this paragraph is based on interviews of the author with West Indian aliens during 1967, 1968, and 1970.

16. Albert A. Guiler, letter in *Daily News,* Apr. 24, 1942.

17. Eldra L. M. Shulterbrandt and Leta Cromwell, "Mental Health and the Alien Worker," in "The Alien Worker and His Family," pp. 48–49.

The remedy is nationalism, we must feel as one people."[18] This has by now become a veritable hue and cry. It is a widely felt belief that the alien is mainly responsible for all crimes committed in the islands, and the press references to "alien criminal elements," never really spelled out in detail, are so frequent and numerous that their citation becomes superfluous. Alien cab drivers generally feel that there is police discrimination against them: "There are some police who seem to think an alien shouldn't drive a taxi." There is, even more, active police resentment against the alien presence as such: "Ah, so you want to live like a king in St. Croix?" There are signs, beyond that, of informal segregationist tendencies: aliens and natives frequently patronize different bars, native girls refuse to dance with alien men at dance halls, native and alien cab drivers prefer separate pick-up areas in the Christiansted plaza. It becomes a popular assumption that the alien is fair game for any trickery, so rackets that exploit his defenseless position abound. An extortion racket in which natives charge aliens excessive amounts for filling out permanent residence papers—$75 and more, with employers collaborating to deduct payments from wages—is one of the latest reported.[19] The domestic service racket, of course, is endemic, in which hundreds of women, including both native Virgin Islands girls and alien girls, are transshipped at exorbitant charges to the U.S. labor market; stories illustrating the details of this traffic have been frequent in the Virgin Islands press for years.[20] In natural response to all this, aliens have as little as possible to do with the official institutions of the society; they rarely use library facilities, for example, unless they are seeking specific information on technical immigration and status matters.[21]

On this entire topic much care has to be taken to penetrate the pervasive fog of prejudicial stereotypes. The relationship between crime and immigration, for instance, is extremely difficult to establish. There are no adequate police statistics. It is widely believed, indeed, that many offenses fail to get on to the records. There can be little doubt, however, that the laxity of immigration officials has permitted an influx of alien persons with criminal records. How far that makes the alien the chief cause of a rising crime rate is problematical. Puerto Ricans on St. Croix are more than adequately represented in the Richmond Penitentiary population. A number of rape cases have involved vacationing mainland whites as attackers. Yet it becomes only too easy, under the pressure

18. Remarks, Councilors Corneiro and Moorehead, report of *Proceedings of the Colonial Council of St. Thomas and St. John,* October 11, 1928, in *The Emancipator,* Nov. 10, 12, 1928.

19. *West End News,* Aug. 31, 1967.

20. For examples, see *Daily News,* Feb. 19, 21, 1955, and *Home Journal,* Dec. 7, 1967.

21. Interview with the librarian, St. Thomas Public Library, December 7, 1967.

of a rising public concern approaching panic about the changing crime picture, to believe (1) that the alien is the villain, and (2) that cases of personal assault are racially motivated. It is at least verifiable that a new mood of fear has appeared in the continentals, especially in St. Croix, with a number of them beginning to carry guns on their persons in the old American vigilante manner. It is equally certain that most of them are more than willing to exaggerate the racial element and play down the class element in the general environmental picture of white affluence and black poverty.

Yet this situation has not, as yet, led to an open and mutually hostile confrontation between the alien mass and the native resident population. What takes place, in fact, is a tug of war between conflicting considerations. There is a latent prejudice against the outsider. But economic considerations, the fact that the alien worker, like the Puerto Rican worker in the New York megalopolis, is ready to accept the menial jobs the home worker disdains, act as a constraint on the prejudice. There is also the fact that both alien and native working classes belong to the same category of Caribbean Afro-American proletarian masses, and thus it behooves the Virgin Islands society, from a cultural viewpoint, to seek to assimilate the alien Negro, with all his close ties of race and kin, rather than the white continental. It is this consideration, clearly, that facilitates intermarriage between the two colored groups; the fact that in 1965 some 54 out of a total of 249 divorces in the islands related to unions of which only one party was a native indicates widespread sexual intermixture of a formal kind.[22] This, in turn, facilitates friendly welcome, summed up in the philosophic observation of a St. Thomian carpenter: "A man cannot be born all over the world. He must be born in a certain place. And he must go to find work elsewhere if it need be." It produces, with some significant frequency, the appearance of zealous pleas for racial fraternalism in the face of common difficulties. James Bennerson's fine contempt, in his *West End News* column, for the native who demanded "if these people become citizens, who will be the maids and gardeners?" is as good an example as any:

Pal, our parents were maids and gardeners and before World War II some of us were of the same occupations. We have moved up the labor ladder ourselves and our children some day may be flying around in outer space. Fellow, you are sick; for let us be frank, these people are of the same background as you and I, plus they are racially the same. Do you mean you will want to see such a large segment of our race (12,000 aliens in the Virgin Islands) relegated to

22. Virgin Islands, Department of Health, Bureau of Statistical Services, *Vital Statistics, 1964–1965* (St. Thomas: Government Printing Office, 1966). p. 85. See also Harrigan, "A Study of the British and U.S. Virgin Islands," pp. 167–71.

domestic work? Also do not forget some of these people are citizens of free, unfettered and independent nations. We might have to appeal to these nations sometime in the future for some kind of assistance. . . . Let me prove how much we are brothers to the Antiguans, Kittitians and others from the neighboring islands. Let the average Antiguan, meaning physically, any you walk down any street in Mississippi, Alabama or Georgia and the bulls decide to burst black heads; I'll bet a plugged nickel that they would not know who is Crucian or who is Antiguan but they will go up against both your heads with equal speed and with no question as to who come from what island.[23]

Passages such as this indicate the existence of a large reservoir of potential good will. The alien West Indian in the Virgin Islands, unlike his counterpart, say, in the United Kingdom, is not a member of a racially disparate and visibly differentiated minority group. He enters a society that is as ethnologically Caribbean as the one he leaves. But there are two considerations that seriously condition that situation. The first is that the alien has been made welcome, overwhelmingly, because he is useful in a full employment economy, where the economic roots of prejudice are much weakened. But any interruption in economic expansion, with a possible decline in employment opportunities, could very rapidly engender demands for the repatriation of alien workers, as was indeed the case in the years after 1944 when the war defense boom in the islands began to falter. There is little evidence that the native working class, who were in the front line of that earlier antialien campaign, have subsequently learned much about working-class solidarity. Despite the fact that the aliens have crowded into the unions, bringing with them a strong pro-union bias from their British background, the leadership has remained native and, what is more, strictly amateurish. There has always been a high and rapid turnover in union leadership of native middle-class types who use the posts as steppingstones in their own careers; the present union officers are generally ignorant of both modern union administrative methods and the special West Indian background of their rank-and-file membership; and there is as yet practically nothing being done in the field of labor education. It is true that the Paiewonsky administration courted the aliens, as could be seen in its support of permanent residence for them, just as earlier there was talk of "Ottley's Tortolans." But this was so obviously a politically-motivated interest that it must have constituted at best a weak reed to lean on. Some close Washington observers of the island scene, indeed, have been puzzled by the tendency of the labor-oriented majority faction in the local legislature to fight zealously for the interests of the business groups and to sit idly by in the presence of the interests of the alien

23. "Back at the Old Stand" column, *West End News*, July 9, 1967.

group: "It is ironical thàt the very legislature which some unthinking and ill-informed parties in Washington thought would be irresponsible and radical would turn out to be so statesmanlike that forebearance and restraint seem to be its outstanding characteristics." [24]

The second consideration is that, although very little race-based hostility has been shown toward the alien, he is exposed to social snobbery and cultural contempt, as evil in their own way as color animosity. Derogatory social qualities are not only generally attributed to aliens but are actually brought out in them by the fact that they are compelled to live in social conditions of substandard quality. They are criticized, without logic, for both their alleged social impertinence and their equally alleged clannishness. Held against them is the very fact, culturally understandable, that they play, instead of baseball, cricket and more latterly soccer football—despite the fact that the doyen of Crucian cricket, going back to the Danish-European days before 1917, is an elder statesman of native stock no less revered than Dr. David Canegata. In the eyes of the natives they are rude, wild, fierce; it is alleged that they fight too much, a criticism that goes back to native feeling against the so-called cane wars that the earlier group of off-island laborers indulged in during the 1950s; and they are seen as uneducated people coming from a British colonial background that is regarded by natives as inferior to the American background. In addition, they suffer opprobrium not only from the native and continental segments but also, to add insult to injury, from their more established compatriots, who, like first-generation arrivals everywhere, resent the influx of newcomers whose traits may be evaluated as lower and who it is feared may adversely affect the status of the earlier groups now somewhat accepted after their own rough passage. Thus it is not uncommon to hear children in the streets taunting others with the opprobrious epithet "garrot," which has replaced "Cha-Cha" as a general term of abuse in island social intercourse and is directed particularly at aliens; that is to say, a term traditionally directed at the French minority has been replaced with a term directed at the alien West Indian minority. Perhaps most poignant of all, the alien labor army, as it huddles in its dilapidated, unpainted shacks, frequently cheek by jowl with the massive, luxurious, glassed-in palaces of the tourist trade, comes more and more to symbolize the new and increasingly acute social inequalities of the community.

To sum up, the alien situation constitutes a major social disease in Virgin Islands society. "It is not within the nature of a democratic so-

24. Kirwan to Paiewonsky, August 12, 1965.

ciety," stated the first Social, Educational Research and Development, Inc., report, "to contain large numbers of people who have few social, political or economic rights." "A final point," stated the second SERD report, "is the general alienation of the alien community as a whole, and in terms of their roots in this community. It seems to us that organizations such as labor unions, the churches, alien organizations, poverty programs, etc., must make a special effort to improve the quality of contact between the alien and non-alien communities." [25]

So far, however, little has been done along those lines. In 1969 the legislature established a Special Commission on Non-Citizens, which has yet to show what it can do. Only too often the Virgin Islands ruling mandarins assume that problems of this order can be solved by a high-powered conference of experts, almost as if the publication of a series of high-minded resolutions that usually follows such a conference in itself meets the issues at stake. More important, certainly, is the emergence during the last few years of alien-oriented private groups, seeking to do something concrete but inevitably limited in funds—the Alien Interest Movement, Citizens–Non-Citizens, and the United Alien Organization. Groups like the Antigua Progressive Association have also appeared, seeking to promote exchanges between West Indians both within and outside the territory. But the potential leadership that could grow out of these organizational efforts is severely hampered by two factors. There is, first, the readiness of the local political class to deport, under various guises, any stateside individuals who, by associating themselves with the alien cause, become suspect as "troublemakers." There is, second, the reluctance of many aliens themselves to court the prominence of a leadership position in any alien body lest it expose them to the attention of the same local authorities. In both cases, there is at work the repressive psychology of a native governing class deeply intolerant of criticism. It is a temper that bodes ill for the future of civil liberties in the territory.

The alien, then, must continue to protect himself as best he can in a host society that needs him but does not want him. That he prefers to be called "off-islander" rather than "alien," in itself a small matter, speaks volumes for the sense of insecurity that haunts him. It is not too much to say that there is a clearly distinguishable arrogance in the attitudes of superiority that the native black brings to the alien black. That, in turn, is compounded by the myth, propounded by both government and employers, that the alien is some sort of migratory worker, here today, gone tomorrow; and the myth serves as an alibi for inaction.

25. *Aliens in the United States Virgin Islands,* p. 2; and *A Profile and Plans,* p. 87.

It is, altogether, a potentially explosive situation that cannot lie dormant forever.

In the last resort, there is the ultimate sanction of deportation. The illegal alien, naturally, is always subject to that sanction. But because, technically, it is the job and not the worker that is bonded, the bonded alien is also subject to deportation if and when he leaves the job for which he has been originally hired—which frequently happens. Many aliens, then, live with the daily fear of being detected. It is not an empty fear. A roundup of aliens by U.S. Immigation Service officers can net as many as 3,500 persons within three or four weeks, most of whom will be summarily deported to their homelands. It is not surprising that a rich folklore has grown up around the personalities of those officers, all of them white and all known personally to the local population. A cat-and-mouse game develops. An accumulation of police cars in a neighborhood, or the recognition of an immigration official traveling on a country road he would not normally frequent, or the knowledge that the immigration offices are working overtime is enough of a clue to send dozens of aliens into temporary hiding in the house or in wooded areas nearby. It is not unknown for populations of whole villages to spend the night sleeping in abandoned canefields or in broken-down automobiles along deserted roads until the danger passes. The whole process constitutes a shameful commentary on American democracy. Not the least distressing aspect of it is that, when wholesale deportation takes place, as it does periodically, there is hardly a voice from native Virgin Islander, continental, or Puerto Rican groups raised in protest.

The Virgin Islands situation has obvious importance as a case study in the sociology of migration. It bears out in many ways the theoretical premises first established by Ravenstein in his celebrated paper on the laws of migration presented to the Royal Statistical Society in 1885.[26] The dominance of the economic motive—what that paper termed the desire inherent in most men to better themselves in material respects—is clearly present in the West Indian arrivals. That motive is also there in the continentals, but in a less crude form, since the appeal that the business opportunities of the island boom offers them is mixed with considerations of climate and retirement prospects. There is the further difference that the West Indian alien movement is basically characteristic of the classic migratory rural-urban movements of the

26. E. G. Ravenstein, "The Laws of Migration," *Journal of the Royal Statistical Society,* LII (London, June, 1885) , 241–301.

nineteenth century, in which the rural masses responded to the magnetic pull of the big industrial cities, whereas the continental movement is characteristic of a more modern pattern at once interurban and educationally and occupationally highly selective. They are all newcomers, as indeed everybody has been in the history of Caribbean population movements, with the exception of the original Indian inhabitants. But West Indian alien and American mainlander have come basically for different reasons. In a sense, the one is a forced movement, the other a free movement. In a highly formal sense the West Indian migrations— including that to Britain since the 1950s—can be classified as a free movement, as distinct from such forced movements as that of European Jewry in the 1930s from Nazi Germany. However, they are forced in the sense that they have been caused overwhelmingly by poverty and unemployment in the sender-societies. Economic pressure of that kind is as essentially involuntary as the different type of pressure that has produced the prototype of the political refugee. To see the migratory process in terms of an economic determinism, in which the migrant responds to the fluctuating supply-demand character of the international trade economy, is to miss completely the human dimension of it all. The formidable literature on the terrible homesickness that assaults the Puerto Rican emigrant in Harlem and the West Indian emigrant in the English industrial centers describes the spiritual amputation that takes place as the Caribbean peasant-worker decides to make the break from the ancestral homeland, a break that is at best semi-voluntary in terms of the propulsive motives that go into the decision. The sociology of West Indian migration, thus, is the sociology of suffering. It only awaits a West Indian literary genius from Antigua or St. Kitts or Tortola to put the particular Virgin Islands variant of the general experience into some recognizable form.

10

~~~

Family, Color, and Community

The astonishing compression of richly diversified detail within narrowly circumscribed boundaries which is so marked a trait of all the segmented Caribbean island societies is nowhere more pronounced in the particular case of the Virgin Islands unit than in the twin areas of family organization and color relations. Sex and color have always been closely intertwined, frequently in explosive fashion, in Caribbean society. But in the Virgins the connection has been made much more complex by the existence, side by side, of different classificatory systems and different universes of moral judgment relating, respectively, to the various cultural groups: natives, off-island aliens, continentals, French, and Puerto Ricans. The result is that any discussion of problems—color as a component of social status, the status of women, attitudes toward marriage, the parent-child relationship, the correlation of sex and social role, the family as an instrument, negative or positive, in community building—must assume that there exists no single overriding Virgin Islands value system to confer either unity or simplicity on the observable data. Whether, in turn, observable structural changes are working toward cultural and racial homogenization is not so much a matter of deductible fact as it is a variable dependent upon which particular framework of reference among the various groups is being employed. All the key words that proliferate in the highly charged Virgin Islands debate—*prejudice, immorality, integration*—mean different things to different participants. The absence of a common universe of discourse is related, naturally, to the profound differences that have characterized the historical evolution of social structure in each one of the participating groups. The island society, in brief, has not been an isolated and inward-turned community

(239)

slowly and imperceptibly building up a powerful sense of meaningful communality on the twin pillars of stability and continuity, but rather an outward-confronting, tropical state of nature successively shaken by the rude, elemental force of invading immigrant peoples bound together, at best, by fragile and tenuous relationships.

Traditionally, of course, the Virgin Islands Negro lower-class family has been part of the general matricentric societies of the West Indian area; it is characterized as, typologically, a consensual union of working mother and absentee father. In the Virgins, as in the general area, that type of familial unit, so inimical to any sense of family pride or solidarity and productive of profoundly weak parent-child relationships, goes back to its roots in the slave period, where everything about slavery—the female slave as the linchpin of the regime, inheritance through the female line, with paternity counting for little, the promiscuity of planters, the fact that, in Nabuco's Brazilian phrase, "the most productive feature of slave property is the generative belly"—combined to grant the colored woman an independent status denied to her male partner. This background produced at least two features of cardinal importance: (1) the low prestige of the marriage tie, as compared to the Western monogamous tradition, and (2) an excessively liberal (to American continental eyes) attitude in native Virgin Islanders to sexual life in general, including as it does the distinct pattern of serial monogamy in which a woman will live with and bear children to several men, apparently without any real conflict emerging from the plural relationship. Both of these features have managed to survive the various attacks launched on them by American puritan morality since 1917. In fact, a leading story of local folklore deals with the famous "parade of the married folk" organized by the Americans at one time in St. Croix and laughed out of court by the huge counter-demonstration of the unmarried majority; the story is the central episode of at least one novel on the islands, Du Bose Hayward's *Star Spangled Virgin*.

That these features have survived is not so much proof of any ethno-historical continuity in the insular life as it is of their continuing functional use in new conditions, for the prevailing socioeconomic conditions perpetuate and encourage a general collection of attitudes and preferences illustrated by the following examples: there are "grandmother households," or family units without resident paternal heads; the average Virgin Islands woman has little of the deference that the American housewife gives to the male breadwinner; the Virgin Islands male on the whole is prepared to accept more willingly the financial responsibilities of paternity than of marriage; there exists, generally, in both men and women, a quite remarkable tolerance of extramarital activities on the part of companion or spouse; Virgin Islands men, unlike American men, show very little prejudice against the figure of the professional woman in business or government; the general attitude behind all this, as Weinstein puts it, is that sex is not so much bad as merely dangerous. It is not simply a matter of "immorality," as the pietistic Catholic French in Frenchtown or the more Catholic-traditionalist Puerto Ricans in St. Croix are likely to think as they profess their open contempt for what they regard as the gross sexual laxity of their Negro neighbors. It is, rather, that with slavery gone other peculiar institutional factors have grown up to give new support to the traditional matrifocal tendency and its corollary, productive of so many other phenomena, the absence in social mores of a strong male model.

The remarkably free status of the Virgin Islands woman, both within and outside the family grouping, is thus the end result of a number of factors. There is the general fact that, this not being a traditional subsistence culture, men do not obtain prestige as food gatherers; nor, on the other hand, is the economy an advanced technology in which superior skill and education could give men an advantage over women. Women suffer few, if any, civil disabilities; the U.S. Department of Labor's 1948 bulletin on the legal status of women in the territories and possessions reported that, in the Virgins as in the other territories, women benefited from a progressive attitude in the statutes.[1] More important, in native Virgin Islands families almost all women work professionally. An interim report of the local Division of Special Projects in 1967 indicated that perhaps the majority of St. Thomas women worked away from home, with the heaviest concentration (leaving out the special category of alien women workers in domestic service) in clerical positions, the public and service industries, and the tourist trade; some 68 per cent of them had children at home, which made mandatory, according to the report, the immediate institution by government of adequate day-care centers, at present still almost nonexistent.[2] It is clear that the female worker has been given a new lease on life by the preference of the tourist trade and light industry for women, by the general sexual imbalance in population figures, by the general hedonistic atmosphere generated by the tourist-

1. U.S., Department of Labor, Women's Bureau, *The Legal Status of Women in the United States of America as of January 1, 1948: Reports and Summary for the Territories and Possessions: Alaska, Hawaii, Puerto Rico, Canal Zone, Virgin Islands* (Washington, D.C.: Government Printing Office, 1951), p. 1. For section on the Virgin Islands, see pp. 67–77.

2. Virgin Islands, Department of Labor, Division of Special Projects, "Interim Report, Survey of Working Women, 1967," mimeographed (St. Thomas, 1967).

playground syndrome, and, not least of all, by the availability of alien domestic help. Women, consequently, make as much money as men in most of the occupations open to them. At the lower-class level, indeed, the custom of women working is so well established that it is the policy of the local Department of Social Welfare to help its clients find jobs rather than to subsidize them to stay at home with their children. With few exceptions, then, women in general do not acquire their major status through the social position or the economic power of their husbands but rather through their own accomplishments. Their names, in the field of public administration, for example, testify to their eminence: Enid Baa, Eldra Shulterbrandt, Mrs. Greaux. There are entire governmental units—the Public Library, the Department of Education—that are virtually feminine domains.

There are, of course, exceptions to the generality here noted. Many native men marry in the States and return to have their households function on the American middle-class model, with the man as nominal head. Yet, on the whole, native family organization is marked by a clear absence of the nuclear family, headed by recognizable male authority, which is the main feature of both the French and Puerto Rican family systems. The picture that emerges is that of the strong Virgins woman, more emotionally dependent on brother and son than on father or husband, owing loyalty to consanguineal kinsmen rather than to affinal kin, undertaking a myriad assortment of transactions outside the household directly rather than going through a male intermediary, and channeling the entire system of household life, from visiting patterns and emotional bonds to eating patterns and sleeping arrangements, along female lines. In this system, the man plays a secondary role throughout. His use at times seems to be little more than that of sexual service. He inhabits a universe of open boasting about sexual conquests, more particularly of fathered children, for there is a recognizable fertility worship in his value system. He becomes a participant in the elaborate game of sexual begging, and much of his small talk consists of stories of his prowess; it appears in fact to constitute a sort of compensatory consolation for his removal from the center of household power. His womenfolk, in turn, reinforce all this by the low esteem in which they generally hold the male sex as a whole.

This is more than a matter of domestic matriarchism. For the Virgins woman has managed to penetrate areas and institutions that elsewhere in the Caribbean are still male preserves. It is not easy to forget that two of the most famous riots in the islands' history, those of 1878 and 1892, were led by women. As far back as 1922 an American correspondent, watching a St. Thomas labor union parade, quoted a bystander as remarking: "The women are the Union here. In most instances each one of these women supports a man." [3] Eminent women have likewise played their part in the exile community in New York. Geraldo Guirty has noted them in the series of articles in which he has paid homage to their memory. There was Elizabeth Hendricksen, who learned her socialism early at the old Rand School of Social Science and then used it, as one of Ashley Totten's lieutenants, in the service of the islands' working classes. There was Redalia Matthews, whose New York home for years was a shelter for visiting delegations from the islands to New York and Washington. There was, finally, Aminta Burnet, descendant of one of the old French-Jewish families of St. Thomas, who valiantly fought the color bar in the New York City public school system and contributed her legal talent to the cause of the many Virgin Islands societies in the city.[4] It only requires, today, successful entry into the political field, hitherto almost wholly a male sanctuary, to complete the picture. Work still needs to be done on behalf of whole groups of island women, especially those of the despised minorities. There is, for example, the exploitation, over the last few years, of the Cuban and West Indian girls imported as prostitutes, who are brought into St. Croix to serve the male workers of the industrial trailer camps there. Clearly, the role that the Virgin Islands woman (meaning not only the locally born woman but also the domiciled alien woman from the British islands, both of them being culturally identical, especially at the lower-class level, as the widely used phrase "cousin family" indicates) has carved out for herself goes back in large part to her personality type; for such an achievement would hardly have been possible had she been either the protected young woman of the French family system or the idealized mother figure of the Puerto Rican system.

Much of American professional comment has tended to view all this in terms of family disorganization. Professional economists, for instance, speaking at the 1968 conference on the family in the Caribbean at the College of the Virgin Islands, saw the socially ill-defined role of the Virgin Islands man as inimical to economic growth and development, and so, by inference, undesirable. The propensity of the male to escape from family responsibilities, it was argued, leads to a general reluctance to accept job responsibility.[5] Although not couched in morally pejorative

3. R. A. Sell, *St. Croix Tribune*, Aug. 24, 1922.
4. Geraldo Guirty, "Tribute to Virgin Islands Women," Focus Magazine, *Home Journal*, Mar. 10, 1968.
5. *The Family in the Caribbean: Proceedings of the First Conference on the Family in the Caribbean* (San Juan: Institute of Caribbean Studies, University of Puerto Rico, 1968), pp. 42–44, 80–81. For a different theoretical interpretation of the family, see Lionel Vallee, "The Negro Family of St. Thomas: A Study of Role Differentiation" (Master's thesis, Cornell University, 1964).

language, the argument is in fact not very much different from the indignant criticisms launched in the earlier period by the American moralists against the "easy life" of the native populace. It is, in fact, the same assumption, that the values of the American Protestant work-ethic are at once morally superior and socially desirable. The argument fails, frankly, to appreciate that the local worker, of both sexes, operates within a value system of quite different character. Work is related more closely to status than to income; informal American methods are frequently seen as infringements on personal dignity; and the whole psychology of incentive is so different that the American-type rewards—leisure, play, promotion—are not necessarily seen as being in any way related to the successful accomplishment of tasks. It is thus profoundly erroneous to suggest that the Virgin Islander is lazy. He works well on the condition, absolutely essential to his sense of well-being, that a good personal relationship is established with him. The everyday language of social intercourse emphasizes this ingredient of "niceness." The remark of a St. Thomian woman on her alien neighbors—"If they treat us nice we treat them nice"—or the remark of a young teenager—"I'm a straight, nice behavior boy"—sums up the general attitude. The American urge to "make the grade" is thus tempered by a civilized insistence on the social quality of economic effort. Nor should the religious aspect of life, which is still strong, be overlooked. "Together with a Sears Roebuck catalogue," the *Daily News* told its stateside readers years ago in a special issue put out for the Democratic National Convention in 1944, "you will find a Bible and Sankey's Sacred Songs in almost every home in the Virgin Islands." [6] The ends of Virgin Islands life, in brief, are far more variegated than those contained in the American credo of economic individualism.

This variance in attitudes and values can be put in a slightly different fashion. The American system eulogized by the visiting economist is that of a vibrant corporate capitalism posited on the career-oriented goal of personal elevation within the system. Virgin Islands life, on the contrary, is that of a far less sophisticated society which, for the vast majority of its working folk, means not so much the pursuit of a clearly defined career as a harsh struggle for survival, "hustling," that is, in the Trinidadian manner; and it is suggestive that the Trinidadian calypso, with its savagely cynical attitude toward the problems of daily island life, strikes a responsive chord in the Virgin Islander's heart. For most Virgin Islands working people the problem, then, is not the long-term one of career organization, but the short-term one of mere survival

6. *Daily News,* Overseas Issue for Democratic National Convention, July 19, 1944.

from day to day, Within that struggle, the extended kinship relations of the family can be seen not as a barrier to economic development but as a protective cushion against the cruel buffetings of the daily encounter. It is true that those relations are slowly being eroded as the American-style transformation of the insular economy proceeds apace, just as in the case of the Hawaiian Islands the old habit of *aloha* is being reduced to the status of an empty tourist slogan under the pressure of a similar transformation. But they still function effectively as relations; and families manage to look after those individuals—the aged grandmother, the widow, the young unmarried mother—who tend to be overlooked in Western-type societies founded on the principle of economic rationality.

That this is so in the Virgins is most graphically shown by the tragedy of those groups which, for one reason or another, are denied the protective shroud of the West Indian family structure. Preeminent among those groups is, of course, that of the West Indian bonded aliens, along with illegal aliens. Their status, or rather lack of status, has been documented in shattering detail in the 1968 and 1969 reports put out under the auspices of the College of the Virgin Islands.[7] Everything about their condition conspires to break down the family. The typical male alien is young, unmarried, and denied access to most social service benefits. If he has left a wife, or consensual wife, back in his home island, he is sooner or later driven to set up a second family in St. Thomas or St. Croix; and the pressure of the two-family situation leads to acute financial and psychological problems. If he remains single, he is likely to live in the sort of isolated company barracks, like those of the Harvey Alumina complex in the desolate scrubland of the Crucian south coast, where all the problems of the young male worker separated from his family become hopelessly intensified. If, alternatively, he sets up house with a local girl, he is driven into the appalling shack housing to be seen in the Machuchal and Bethlehem areas of St. Croix. If, in addition to all that, he is an illegal immigrant, he is constant prey to the fear of a brutal police roundup, accentuated by the fact, as aliens will readily testify, that whereas in the other West Indian islands the police try to keep marital squabbles a domestic and private matter, in the Virgins they will do all they can to persuade a local woman to betray her alien consort.

The female alien worker, usually in domestic service, does not fare much better. She becomes little more than an indentured servant ex-

7. *Aliens in the United States Virgin Islands: Temporary Workers in a Permanent Economy* (Washington, D.C.: Social, Educational Research and Development, Inc., January, 1968); and *A Profile and Plans for the Temporary Alien Worker Problem in the U.S. Virgin Islands* (Washington, D.C.: Social, Educational Research and Development, Inc., 1969).

(245)

ploited by her employer. The complaint of one of these women in the 1969 report sums it up for all: "Aliens should be treated better, especially maids. No where to live, and quite a lot of work. Some employer just step out the underwear and leave it for the maids to take up. The maids have to bathe cats and dogs and if one don't treat these animals as human beings they are fired. Think of that."[8] Totally excluded from participation in the local community, almost completely ignored by the federal agencies, ostracized by the local population (it is a commonly held belief, although lacking any statistical proof, that most of the prostitutes operating in the island bars and clubs are off-island girls), it is hardly surprising that the average alien suffers from deeply felt personal and social dislocation. He shares a common life-style with the lower-class Virgin Islands person, of course, summed up in the title of one of the popular Puerto Rican records: *mucho trabajo, poco dinero*. But the mark of the undesirable immigrant still lies heavily upon him.

Yet it is perhaps the child and the adolescent, of both native and alien family situations, who carry the heaviest burden of all. For although those situations exhibit, as has been argued, basic values relating to sexually ascriptive roles that are not necessarily negative because they run counter to the North American Protestant family ideal, it is true that they are weak at the point where they seek to provide a role for the child. Deprivation of a mother due to migration, or of a father due to the habit of absentee paternity, contributes to damaging the child's development, while the anxiety created by that deprivation is rarely counterbalanced by any sort of real mental stimulus either in the home or at school. Jarvis noted that children in the islands are seldom collectors of shells, stamps, insects, and such, so that unlike, say, the American or the English child, they rarely enter into those worlds of romantic associations. But even this cannot be seen exclusively as the fault of the family system. For the family unit does not exist in isolation; it is penetrated at every turn by the societal environment. The absence of intellectual stimulus, then, is not so much a consequence of the child-raising patterns of the Virgin Islands family in which, traditionally, the child has been trained to be quiet, obedient, and well-behaved, as it is the consequence of the powerful anti-intellectual character of the colonial society. An American pedagogical theory may be tempted to view those patterns as repressive or authoritarian; a stateside educator's document such as Robert Dalton's *Mothers and Children,* written for the local Division of Mental Health, derives its pessimistic conclusions from the temptation of the author to see native child characteristics through

8. *A Profile and Plans,* quoted in synopsis of report in *Daily News,* Sept. 27, 1969.

the prism of American educational theory. It is at least arguable whether the Virgin Islands parent's insistence on good manners, decorous behavior, and respect for elders is intrinsically less admirable than the continental parent's predilection for more permissive behavior patterns.

What is at work here, clearly enough, is not anything so simple as the positive or negative elements of the native and alien family structures. It is, rather, a crosscurrent of conflicting general culture patterns. The male pattern does indeed help to damage the native and alien child. But the real, more persistent damage is perpetrated by the conflict of culture patterns, of which the family pattern is only one element. The continental parent sees the native parental role as backwardly semi-Victorian. The native parent at the same time sees the alien parental role as unduly harsh. Both native and alien parents, in their turn, see the continental parental role as unduly permissive.

It is the Virgin Islands adolescent, perhaps, who more than any other single person in the society feels the onerous pressure of the culture conflict. He, or she, has been brought up in a society in which adolescence has been a brief period without clear identity, facilitated by (1) the ease with which the young person has been able to find paying jobs, and (2) the early period of motherhood for girls, unaccompanied by any sense of social shame. There has been little of the cult of youth so pronounced in American life, so that, for example, young people's organizations in the island towns have tended to be ancillary adjuncts of institutions such as the church, young people are not recognized by the commercial culture as a special consumer group, and there is little, if any, tradition of successful bachelor life. Growing up in this tradition, the adolescent of the present period is increasingly confronted with the new American stateside style. Favored drugstore or restaurant hangouts begin to make their appearance; Charlotte Amalie High School, like any American high school, begins to cultivate its own special teenager identity; the Sunday supplements of the local newspapers begin to solicit the views of selected teenagers in special interview columns; and even a local "counter culture" makes its appearance, evident in the open sale of the New York *Village Voice* in the local newspaper shops.

The adolescent is assaulted, especially by an Americanized school curriculum, with new, stateside codes of behavior. Thus, a booklet put out by the local Department of Health seeks to instill in its young readers the secret of social popularity in the best American style, outlining "the basic social skills that can help you to get along with others." Those skills include, among other things, the art of controlling temper, of seeking cheerfulness and serenity, of developing a pleasing personal appearance, and of being "sincere." This catalogue of virtues obviously comprises the bland, mindless, extravert personality of the American popularity cult. Everything odd must be carefully suppressed: "Try hard not to be grouchy, moody, or over-sensitive. Nobody likes to be humbugged by a constantly complaining and argumentative person, so watch out for these tendencies." Even more objectionable, however, is the fact that this advice runs counter to the local cultural environment of the Virgin Islands youngster. According to the new rules, he is warned to say nothing about other persons unless it is something pleasant, as if that were possible in a small island society which, like village society, thrives with tropical virility on the habit of fierce gossip fiercely enjoyed. Or it can be broadly hinted that the local speech habits are something to be apologetic about: "There's certainly no reason to be ashamed of our softly melodic calypso accents. Just be sure that you don't use calypso as a cover-up for bad English." [9] Trapped in this tension of competitive culture patterns and culture models it is hardly surprising that Virgin Islands youngsters, such as those of the newly emergent graduating classes of the College of the Virgin Islands, exhibit feelings of ambivalence and embarrassment toward their parents and the parental background. It is perhaps the chief task of that new education to help them toward an awareness of the truth that the crisis of their family is, in microcosm, the crisis of their society.

It is almost official dogma in the islands that color, as a problem, does not exist. Even an observer as perceptive as Weinstein tended to accept the dogma at its face value. It would be more true to say that there is a color problem but that it is not couched in the harsh, polarizing terms of the North American white-black confrontation. The trajectory of race relations took a different direction in the Virgins, as already noted, than in the continental society. The classificatory system of the color spectrum, to begin with, was not the simplistic American one but the pluralistic West Indian one, a fact noted by the first of the American visiting correspondents after the transfer. A 1922 report thus noted that the local children were divided by local opinion into the well-known shades of "black," "red," "high yellow," and "Cha-Cha"; "red" referred to white persons, mostly of Danish stock, who through intermarriage retained a "black" trace that might reappear in future generational stock, and "high yellow" referred to persons with mainly white characteristics who also contained pronounced "black" elements.[10] In a community as tiny as

9. Virgin Islands, Department of Health, Division of Mental Health, *You and Others* (St. Thomas, January, 1967).

10. R. A. Sell, article in *Houston Chronicle,* reprinted in *St. Croix Tribune,* Aug. 25, 1922.

this everyone's racial ancestry is known, so that there is little of the racial ambiguity that has permitted the special art of "passing" in the larger American society. What, then, Adolph Sixto succinctly told local newspaper editors in 1923 is as apposite today (1972) as it was then:

> We have no interest in knowing who you or they were, and since every living son of St. Thomas, notwithstanding his present circumstances, is nothing more than a goat skin's aristocrat and cannot therefore afford to personally criticise another without affecting the skeletons that may be in our homes and cause their bones to rattle, I would suggest that you stop this kind of personal and disgusting newspaper abuse.[11]

Finally, since the Virgins have always been a black majority community, the local colored person has rarely had the sense of being an aggrieved minority, as had the American Negro; the result of that difference is that the American Negro has rarely been a welcome person in the islands, whether he has come, as in the 1950s, as a "carpetbagger" hanging on to the coattails of an appointed Negro governor or, as in the 1960s, as an ambassador of the more militant civil rights movement on the mainland. The message of Martin Luther King, not to speak of the message of Eldridge Cleaver, is clearly anachronistic in a society where the governing class, especially in politics and administration, has been overwhelmingly black for the last two decades or so. A political-constitutional system in which the two leading power figures are a native professional man as governor and a native colored political leader, in the person of John Maduro, as president of the local Senate, is clearly operating on principles profoundly different from those prevailing in the continental United States.

However, it must be strongly emphasized that the Virgin Islands are in no way an ideal racial democracy. The well-known West Indian "white bias" is there and produces the same schizoid personality traits as elsewhere. The prejudice might even go as far back, historically, as the ethnocentric tendency of the ancestral white society of Elizabethan England to find blackness repulsive and whiteness angelic; at least it was possible as late as 1965 to find a bulletin note in the mainly colored Moravian church in Charlotte Amalie in which a description of the five liturgical colors of the church festivals called white the "color of perfection, of peace, nourishment, holiness, and joy," and black the "color of the depths of woe, sorrow, utter darkness." It is still an ingrained attitude in the masses that to be black is to suffer the most grievous disability of all, even though the feeling may be disguised beneath a ribald street humor about color: the spectacle of a very dark Virgin Islands man

11. *The Emancipator,* Aug. 1, 1923.

calling out from his bar stool to a passing colored woman, "Hey, black woman, why you so black?," illustrates the point. The Virgin Islands concept of what constitutes a successful person reveals the same bias; the people take as a model someone like Raymond Jones, the Virgin Islander who rose to the top of Harlem politics by tacitly accepting and working with the New York white power structure, or someone like Emile Griffiths, the fighter, who is certainly no Muhammed Ali in his political beliefs but rather embodies all of the respectable social virtues Virgin Islanders admire in their native sons. The absence of any visible sanctions against skin color only makes the invisible ones all the more onerous. Inevitably, all groups involved in this situation develop their various myths to make it more tolerable; the black bourgeois elements cultivate the pleasing fancy, for example, that they are descended from royal and aristocratic African forebears, "Guinea's captive kings," while the local white elements pretend that they, in turn, come from an upper-class European background. For the proletarian majority, however, such myths are less easily sustained, and theirs, of all the segmental experiences, is the most cruel. The *cri de coeur* of one of them, roughly penciled in a local church hymnal, sums it up essentially for all of them: "Dear God, here I is an my children, jes slaves. Look on us with pity and give us Freedom, dear God, please to give us Freedom." [12]

This race-relations picture, so typically West Indian, has of course been enormously complicated in the Virgins case by the introduction, after 1917, of American racist attitudes. It is important to note the ambivalence of those attitudes. From the very beginning the American spirit was at once enchanted and vaguely disturbed by the miscegenative character of the native populations. There was a mixture of Puritan shame and reluctant surrender to temptation in the observation of an early visitor in 1917, speaking of his first encounter with the strikingly handsome *sangmêlée* women, that there was about them "the same sense of a breeding and a tradition we knew nothing of, exotic and fascinating, and at the same time vaguely shocking, like the first taste of a mango." [13] The American beachcomber type has tended throughout the years since to yield to the temptation. Yet, on the whole, as the continentals have become a more settled and internally organized group it is the sense of revulsion that has become more and more pronounced in their attitude. It is at least suggestive that the revulsion should have been the leading theme of two novels written about the islands, R. H. Barbour's *Death in the Virgins*, written in the 1940s, and Herman Wouk's

12. In flyleaf of hymnal, Moravian Church, St. Thomas, November 17, 1966.
13. Wilbur Daniel Steele, "At the Ocean Cross-roads," *Harper's Monthly Magazine,* October, 1917, p. 684.

Don't Stop the Carnival, written in the 1960s. The heroine-figure of the first novel is an American woman driven into shock by the belated recognition of the fact that she had unwittingly married a Haitian man with colored background, while the hero-figure of the second novel is a New York Jewish liberal who cannot stomach the fact that an American woman resident of the islands should have elected to become the mistress of the colored governor.

In the earlier period, when the small American colony was on the defensive, even the less sophisticated types would make a special effort to be racially tolerant, summed up in the words of one of them at the time: "I'm no bleeding-heart liberal. As a matter of fact, politically, I've been called to the right of McCarthy. I honestly don't know if I could live in a stateside town where seventy-five percent of the people were colored, where in every part of my life—medically, socially, in day to day activities —I associated with Negroes. Here, I don't give it a second thought. Except maybe to mind my manners a little more than I did at home— because the people emphasise politeness more."[14] But that period in the history of the American excursus into the islands, essentially pioneer in character, is over. It was a period in which the American liberal escaping to the islands felt that all that was called for was to adopt the "right attitude" toward Negroes, which immediately placed Virgin Islands Negroes in a special category for whom certain attitudes were deemed appropriate. It was a period, even more, when the *avant-garde* of Americans had no choice but to socialize with the local population. But with the mainstream of the American invasion already under way by the 1950s these considerations became less compelling, so that today the newcomer no longer has to associate with the locals. As his own, growing group becomes more elaborately structured and the rules of social conduct become more clearly defined, the compulsion to engage in a meaningful dialogue with St. Thomians or Crucians becomes less imperative. The end result of this process is the increasingly sharp segregationism that characterizes the native-continental relationship in the present period.

Much of this, of course, is softened by the fact that color is not by any means the sole component of social status. The fact that its members are white, for example, does not automatically confer social prestige on the local French group. The Negrophobia of that group, at the same time, is inhibited by the fact that, economically, they are lower class.

14. Jeanne Perkins Harman, *The Virgins: Magic Islands* (New York: Appleton-Century-Crofts, 1961), p. 267. For a satirical native comment on these continental attitudes, see Joyce La Motta, "Some of My Best Friends Are Liberals," *Virgin Islands View*, March, 1967.

They are economically vulnerable, which makes it difficult for them to be outspoken. Some of the more sophisticated members of the group can stand aside and see the dilemma objectively. As one of them graphically puts it: "It's like being in the South in America, but because they (the French) are not rich they can't act it." Racial prejudice is thus to some degree attenuated in its public expression by social position. That there is in turn a certain mobility in terms of wealth and power means, too, that native colored persons can and do gain access to the local commanding heights, so that they at once gain compensation for the liability of their color and are able to enjoy a life-style similar to that of their white neighbors: in the West Indian saying, "money whitens."

Yet when all this has been taken into account there remains the fact, starkly obvious to all save the professional optimists, that the society is based upon a set of elaborate disqualification exercises in which color almost certainly plays a major defining part. "If you're light colored," in the words of one of the victims, "you can pretend you're just browned by the sun, or you're a Puerto Rican, perhaps even a Hawaiian. But when you're black likewise, you're black, and no fooling. And you don't try to wangle an invitation to the parties of the upper crust, white or colored; you wait and let them invite you, which they rarely do." [15] That was written in 1956. But the passionate speech of Judge Moore in 1962 on racist attitudes in St. Croix demonstrates that they still persist. The report, in 1969, of the discriminatory practices permitted in the Hertz rental car agency in St. Thomas makes it clear that the supposed distinction between white attitudes in St. Thomas and white attitudes in St. Croix, with the former allegedly more liberal—an essential point in the argument of Judge Moore's speech—is largely imaginary.

For the colored bourgeoisie there is always the consolation of their control over the political and governmental machines, and that this means much is evident in the exaggerated respect for the dignity of those offices that they demand from their social inferiors. Yet political control without economic power is ultimately delusory, and there is a growing awareness that a situation of black political power and white economic power—which is in essence the Virgins reality—means the effective loss of the local economic patrimony to outside forces. As a long-time white resident put it, "They're becoming a minority in their own bailiwick, and if they start losing political control they are not going to like it." [16]

15. Helen Follett, *Stick of Fire* (New York: Vantage Press, 1956), p. 91.
16. Quoted in James Ramsey Ullman, "Cruzan Days," *Caribbean Beachcomber* (San Juan), January-February, 1968, p. 52. The Judge Moore speech of 1962, referred to in the text, was reprinted in Virgin Islands, *Legislative Record*, sess. 1962, February 19, 1962. For the Hertz rental car agency hearings, see *Daily News*, Jan. 31, Feb. 1, 1969.

All this helps to explain the emerging ferment of "black power" talk in the islands over the last few years. Public Safety Commissioner Felix' remark of February, 1967—"I feel that St. Croix is adequately situated south of St. Thomas. But you and I, and all of us, who are serious and fairminded, will hate to see it be known as the Deep South" [17]—probably set off that ferment, referring as it did to the resurgence of racist patterns in Crucian society. From the debate accompanying that ferment a number of salient points emerge. First, there is a belated recognition by native Virgin Islanders that the tourist-based economic development of the last fifteen years or so has had the end result of reproducing in the island economy the old, traditional closed racial composition of the West Indian business community. The lines drawn between employers and employees, or between big business and small business, increasingly coincide with the lines drawn between white and non-white. The 1967 struggle between the taxi drivers' associations and the continental rental car agencies was only one example of this. The taxi drivers' news sheets emphasized the economic and social aspects of the struggle: "It's clear, gentlemen, the battle lines are drawn. It's Rentals and Associates against cabbies, big against small, or rich against poor. Call it what you will, it is clear that this is a fight for survival. . . . What we now have we will keep. If it ever changes hands it must be to our children and no one else. This, we repeat, is the only factor of the tourist industry that is in the hands of locals or natives and the big boys now feel they want in and we must get out." [18] But it was just as clearly a battle line drawn along racial lines as well. In the second place, a new note of almost desperate anxiety is beginning to make itself felt among the native groups. They are asking whether they are destined to be an extinct breed. They revive the debate, which goes back for decades in Caribbean life, as to why the Negro, as they see it, seems to have no aptitude for the entrepreneurial life; and they are insisting that it is time that what colored businessmen there are should either become race conscious or hand over—as a local radical newspaper editorial put it over thirty years ago—to a new generation of the black proletariat conscious of race, creed, and color.[19]

Even a new attitude toward the American connection, so traditionally sacred in Virgin Islands life, is beginning to be heard by the younger radicals in local politics. The traditional alliance with liberal friends in the States is also called into question, since it is beginning to be recognized that the old liberal gospel of integration really meant the willing-

17. Quoted in *St. Croix Avis*, Feb. 9, 1967. See also *ibid.*, Feb. 11, 12, 1967.
18. Virgin Islands Taxi Organization, *Newsletter*, December 5, 1967.
19. Editorial, *The Emancipator*, Sept. 21, 1935.

ness on the part of the black man in that alliance to renounce his own local cultural originality. The observation of the above-mentioned radical newspaper, back in 1926, that some eight hundred Haitians fought on the side of the colonists in the American Revolutionary War in order, ultimately, that the American racist South could be enabled to carry on its Ku Klux Klan activities, would have been regarded as a lunatic belief by most Virgin Islanders at that time; today, on the contrary, it is likely to win the approval of a growing section of the electorate.[20] It is easy to see how the "black power" ideology will increasingly appeal to this new awareness in the more articulate local groups, and how it will place new strains upon the structure of interracial community. Granted the special juxtaposition, for example, of the black worker group and the Creole-continental white Jewish group, the stage is potentially set for the growth at any time of a black anti-Semitism or of a Jewish Negrophobia, or both; this possibility seems all the more likely when it is noted that the St. Thomas synagogue has no black Jews in its membership who could act, theoretically, as friendly broker between the two groups.

The third and final point to note is the almost predictable response of the islands' power structure, both white and colored, to the question of race. Anger, fear, even panic, have all played a part. The top groups have always borne down harshly on anyone daring to question the image of multiracial harmony so carefully put together by the mass media and government publicity. The angry response of the Senate to the Felix speech was symptomatic. Also, the same groups have always been peculiarly inventive in the creation of scapegoats. It has become a fixed article of faith that the aliens are responsible for most crime (however true that may or may not be in fact) and now for the infiltration of what is regarded, in part, as an alien West Indian ideology. Or if the alien is not to blame, it is either the socially dissident type of the continental group, or professional black "agitators" down from New York, or even returning natives who have picked up "dangerous ideas" during a mainland residence. Senator Ottley's speech of May, 1968, with its reference to "emotionally disturbed" extremists trying to seek revenge for their real or imagined grievances, set the tone, exemplifying as it did so perfectly the myopic *insularismo* of the island psychology. The same can be said of Governor Evans' later references to the *New York Times* series on race relations in the islands. In both cases there is the cultivated myth that tensions are imported from racially restless sections of mainland society. It overlooks the fact that there are a number of local groups

20. "A Vicious Dissembler," *ibid.*, Oct. 11, 1926.

actively agitating against conditions: for example, a local chapter of CORE is demanding, among other things, the reversion to public owner-ship of beaches and roads alienated to private concerns, and there are radically minded groups among the college student body. To spend an afternoon with the young volunteers who man the Alien Interest Movement's small and crowded office in Raadets Gade in Charlotte Amalie, helping aliens with advice on all of their problems, is to be made aware of the fact that there exists sufficient explosive social ma-terial for the more militant type of activist to ignite should he elect to do so; it is to the credit of the volunteer groups that they have chosen, instead, to undertake quiet, practical work of help and advice, often, to the extent that they can get it, with the cooperation of government agencies.[21]

On a more theoretical level, it is sometimes urged that the "black power" theme is locally irrelevant because there already exists a solidly entrenched black governing class. That argument, also frequently heard in the similar Jamaican and Trinidadian situations, overlooks the crucial fact that, in contrast to the black governing class, there is, in the Marxist sense, a white ruling class with an equally firm grasp on the means of production within the economy. Another argument is that with the growth of sociocultural assimilation in American life, and the con-comitant disappearance in the mainland city politics of the older racial blocs, like the Polish enclave in Chicago or the German enclave in St. Louis, the phenomenon of beleaguered ethnic minorities is on the way out; and the inference is, as some Virgin Islands editorialists have argued, that Negroes and Puerto Ricans will disappear in the same way. Yet the massive evidence of the 1968 federal Civil Rights Commission report is there to disprove that particular illusion, showing that it is the ultimate, irrevocable barrier of skin color that makes the black American ineligible for salvation through the mechanism of the "melting pot" theory.

The theory of Virgin Islands exceptionality breaks down in the light of all this. In the area of race relations, as in other areas, the native leadership is trapped within its American connection, for it seeks to maintain that connection and yet to insulate its society from penetration by the explosive ideas raging within the metropolitan center. That pene-tration is certain to grow more sharp with time, with all of its intima-tions of racial conflict. The Virgin Islands can still revert to their earlier

21. Senator Earle Ottley, speech, special session, Virgin Islands Legislature, re-ported in *San Juan Star*, May 7, 1968. For Governor Evans, see *Daily News*, Oct. 1, 3, 1969. See also extended remarks on the race issue in editorial, *ibid.,* Oct. 2, 1969. For the local CORE body, see statement of demands, *ibid.,* Jan. 6, 1970. See also remarks of Roy Innis, CORE leader, in *ibid.,* Mar. 27, 1969.

Negro militancy, finely summed up in the "Queen Mary" song of the Christiansted "fireburn" of 1878, with its inflammatory picture of the Crucian Negro Joan of Arc being waited upon by captured white servants:

> Fan me, buckra Missy,
> Fan me till de break o' day
> Me pon me way to Bassend
> Me goin' burn all de way.

The fragmentary character of island life has already been noted, in which any community spirit that exists is continually being placed under acute strain by an undeclared state of social civil war in which the complementary-competing groups vie with one another for either supremacy or prominence. But it is worth recapitulating what this means for the future of the society. Emphasizing the publicity which attends everything in this kind of small-island existence, a local observer has aptly seen St. Thomas as a multitiered stage in which everybody is an actor in a stark drama, the basic theme being the acquisition of wealth and its concomitant power. "This intense and at times abrasive inter-action of people constantly on stage makes strong leadership a matter of necessity instead of a mere luxury. While Crucians regale in frac-tionalism along every conceivable line, with sixteen different schools of thought on everything, from making *tisane* to torching crabs, they in effect have as much cohesiveness as a handful of dry sand." Since St. Croix—this observer's argument continues—is at best a mirror of St. Thomas, exhibiting merely the spin-off of a power structure perfected on the St. Thomas stage, it is in Charlotte Amalie where the serious drama is conducted.[22]

The actors of the drama emerge, as this portrait unfolds, with all the brutal clarity of an Elizabethan play by Webster or Marlowe. There is the native, who, having spent most of his life in an endless, redundant summer and having left land speculation to the American hustler and now regretful of missed chances, is resigned to the fact that his best efforts will bring little lasting change or improvement. At one time capable of living with himself, he is now so intent on accumulating material acquisitions that he is losing sight of who he is and where he is going. The fact that he was born on the island no longer confers on him any prerogative; he is caught up, as one of the lesser actors, in the American mainstream as it has come to the islands, along with its seduc-tive material wealth and profound racial warp. After him, there is the

---

22. Jean Larsen, "The Cruzan Kiva" column, *West End News*, Sept. 3, 1967.

continental, working with frenzied excitement and building impressive monuments of entrepreneurial skill in his desperate efforts to flee from himself. If he is still of working age, he seeks fresh escape in routines of hard play. If he is retired, as many are, he lives an existence in which he joins committees, builds nonprofit organizations, and helps organize Carnival, thus effectively re-creating the very life-style from which he is supposed to have escaped. He is, instinctively, in the American fashion, a genuinely friendly person, anxious to make a good impression, so that he is first puzzled, then angered, by the reluctance of the native to respond. There is, finally, the alien off-islander, playing a passive role in the drama, willing to absorb the humiliating nature of his status in the society because of the economic advantages residency gives him; but in the long run, he is an unintended affront to the democratic principle since he is one of an unenfranchised group, cut off almost entirely from any participation in the political-constitutional processes.[23]

The end result is a society whose members are united, in a negative sense only, by the fact of their geographical residence in the island setting, but who are divided by color, race, religion, and culture. The continentals are seen as middle-class persons who, translated to a class-color situation, give themselves aristocratic airs. "On the continent they would have been well sunk in the heart of the middle class. On St. Croix they could give themselves all the airs they liked, have their little Tennis Club and believe themselves the aristocracy. . . . They were not in the least the type to be taken up by the upper classes anywhere, being largely bereft of humor, wit, and gaiety, and not being rich enough to buy their way in. They felt themselves far above the 'lower' classes anywhere, and, of course, above all Crucians."[24] In turn, the continentals build up their own hostile image of the native Virgin Islanders, who are seen as aloof, withdrawn, unfriendly, lacking the warmth and spontaneity that should accompany tropical sun and sea; and it is not unusual to find the local press carrying admonitory letters to the natives, urging them to throw off their exaggerated reserve. Of all the groups, the closest ties exist between the lower-class natives and the lower-class off-islanders, founded on generations of interisland visiting, interisland intermarriage, interisland sharing of social services, interisland religious life and organization; these were recently described in the first exhaustive analysis ever to be made of the structure of relationships between the British and the American island groups.[25]

23. *Ibid.*, July 23, 1967.
24. Elizabeth Hawes, *But Say It Politely* (Boston: Little, Brown, 1951), p. 33.
25. Norwell Harrigan, "A Study of the Inter-Relationships between the British and United States Virgin Islands," mimeographed (St. Thomas: Caribbean Research Institute, College of the Virgin Islands, 1969).

The dominant social climate, consequently, is that of a rampant individualism. A Tortolan political leader has recently summed up that temper as he sees it in the British Virgins. But the portrait stands equally well for the American Virgins. "We don't have a boy scout group," he writes, "because every boy wants to be scoutmaster, we don't have a community band because everyone wants to be bandmaster, we do not have anyone in the Police Force (the Police Force is imported) because everyone wants to be Police Inspector, and for the same reason we do not have a political party because everyone wants to be a party leader and no one wants to be instructed. This is a cancer we have to destroy." [26] Until the cancer is indeed destroyed the society will remain one in which no group, except in very formal terms, accepts responsibility for its shaping and reconstruction along lines directed toward real community. It remains, then, not a nation but a segmented society.

This situation was in its essence noted by all the historians, Creole and foreign alike, who have written on the islands. Virgin Islanders who eulogize Knud-Hansen, for example, as a protagonist of the Danish culture fail to appreciate the fact that his autobiographical volume, *From Denmark to the Virgin Islands,* was a bitter indictment of the Danish regime from the viewpoint of a medical man with a keen sense of social humanism. Likewise, there is at the present time a tendency to elevate Jarvis into a national hero and to play down his bitter criticism of the shortcomings of his society. But perhaps some of the most acute observations on the malaise of the society were made by the most famous of all Virgin Islands clerics, the Anglican minister John Levo, in his two books on the Virgins, *The West Indian Adventure* (1929) and *Black and White in the West Indies* (1930). It was the central thesis of both books that the reconstruction of Virgin Islands society would have to come from an acceptance of the cardinal truth that racism of any kind was not innately rooted in people: "In the West Indies the extremist on either side has little weight. The relation between the two races is largely determined by social and economic facts, not by inveterate hatreds, nor by oratory, nor printed propaganda, nor any other forms of emotional appeal." The "white man's burden," then, had been a legitimate phrase to the degree that it had meant a sincere effort on the part of the white rulers to grant to the black ruled everything of value in European civilization. But that in any case was now of only historical value, for the region was entering into a new democratic age. In that new period, the natural leadership of the islands, Levo urged, had to be that of the educated colored groups:

26. Noel Lloyd, remarks in *The Island Sun* (Roadtown), June 4, 1966.

Socially and culturally they have sympathies with the white, racially with the simple colored folk. They are a bridge between the races, and can feel and act for both. The future of the West Indies and of race relations there are in their hands. . . . Their position, education, and wider experience make them the natural spokesmen of their race. When circumstances prompt them to open advocacy they are usually temperate; for although the West Indian loves politics, he seldom produces demagogues. The colored men of greatest influence are those who show a sense of sober responsibility, and an aptitude for service rather than for eloquence.[27]

In one way, of course, this was an accurate prophecy. West Indian society after 1930 or so, including that of the Virgin Islands, was in truth the emergence and victory, at the political level, of the colored middle-class group Levo had in mind. Yet as that victory has become consolidated the emptiness of too many of the assumptions of the Levo argument has become painfully clear. Its note of social class paternalism, perhaps valid enough in 1930, has become a synonym for class tyranny in 1972. Its distrust of demagogues was grievously misplaced, for it was the demagogue leader (men like Rothschild Francis and Morris Davis in the Virgin Islands struggle) who, much more than the temperate citizen, made the change possible. Worst of all, perhaps, the argument was psychologically weak, for it underestimated the authoritarian streak that is so prominent in the colored middle-class personality and so especially pronounced in its Virgin Islands prototypes. For, made to feel inferior by the continental, the Virgin Islands middle-class person tends to seek compensation in the exaggerated deference that he demands from his black social inferiors, engineered as that deference is by an elaborate art of social bullying. That explains why, in the strictly political field, the Ottley political machine responds as neurotically to the appearance of "black power" groups like the Black Cultural Organization at the College of the Virgin Islands as comparable black middle-class governments have responded over the last few years to the growth of black student radicalism in the various centers of the University of the West Indies in Jamaica, Trinidad, and Barbados. Levo wanted a new liberal social order for the black common folk to whom he had devoted a lifetime of Christian struggle both in Tortola and St. Croix. But it is doubtful if, in the changed spirit of the 1970s, that end can be fulfilled by means of his doctrine of racial accommodation.

Racial assertiveness rather than accommodation is likely to be the order of the day, although the Virgins colored leadership is still fixed,

27. John Ernest Levo, *Black and White in the West Indies* (London: Society for Propagation of Gospel in Foreign Parts, 1930), p. 15. For Levo, see Knud Knud-Hansen, *From Denmark to the Virgin Islands* (Philadelphia: Dorrance, 1947), chap. 12.

in its assumptions, in the accommodationist mood. It is suggestive that, in a whole generation of local newspapers from 1930 onward, there is only one reference to the remarkable Virgin Islander, Dr. Edward Wilmot Blyden, who in the last century became the intellectual spokesman, in his writings, of a gospel of negritude which, despite its Victorian Christian overtones, anticipated the later black revolt of the mid-twentieth century; and that reference, inevitably, was in Jarvis' newspaper, the *Daily News*.[28] The recent revival of interest in Blyden's career and his writings comes from English and American academic sources, not from the Virgin Islands. [29] Blyden wrote, with astonishing prescience:

> We must show that we are able to go alone, to carve out our own way. We must not be satisfied that, in this nation, European influence shapes our polity, makes our laws, rules in our tribunals, and impregnates our social atmosphere. We must not suppose that the Anglo-Saxon methods are final, that there is nothing for us to find for our own guidance, and that we have nothing to teach the world. There is inspiration for us also. . . . The special road which has led to the success and elevation of the Anglo-Saxon is not that which would lead to the success and elevation of the Negro, though we shall resort to the same means of general culture which has enabled the Anglo-Saxon to find out for himself the way in which he ought to go.[30]

This is a note, with its bold attack upon Eurocentric culture and thought, which is still almost unheard, let alone heeded, in the circles that shape Virgin Islands education and culture. The direction in which social change will go within the period of the next generation will thus depend on whether the pivotal agencies propelling that change will shape their policies on Levo's doctrine of racial accommodation—which for all its original spirit of Christian humanism has really now outlived its purpose —or will move on to accept Blyden's doctrine of racial assertiveness. The very fabric of Virgin Islands society could depend on that decision.

It might appear that this segmentation of Virgin Islands society could have been offset in some way by the healing ointment of a creolization process in which all the different groups could have been welded to-

---

28. May 27, 1955.

29. Edward W. Blyden, *Christianity, Islam and the Negro Race* (1887; reprinted Edinburgh University Press, 1967); and Hollis R. Lynch, *Edward Wilmot Blyden, Pan-Negro Patriot, 1832–1912* (London: Oxford University Press, 1967).

30. Blyden, *Christianity, Islam and the Negro Race*, pp. 78, 83. For this note in recent Virgin Islands radical literature, see publication of the Organisation of Afro-Caribbean Consciousness and Unity, cited in *Daily News*, Feb. 15, 1968, and issues of *The Black Revolutionary*, published by the Black Cultural Organization, College of the Virgin Islands, St. Thomas.

gether as they came to identify themselves with the island society. That
has been a process, after all, peculiar to Caribbean society, whereby immigrant groups have come to accept a body of values and behavior patterns
indigenous to their new terrain and, if only half-consciously, have turned
their backs on the memory of the ancestral homeland, whatever it might
have been. A novel by Jean Rhys is perhaps the most effective statement,
beautifully rendered, of that socio-psychological experience.[31] The history of that experience is writ large in the societies of the Hispanic
Caribbean—Cuba, Puerto Rico, Santo Domingo—and, to a lesser degree,
in the history of the French and English territories. Why has it not
developed in the Virgins? It cannot be a matter of race, for white groups
throughout the region have been as fully creolized as others. Nor can
it be a matter of language, for linguistic pluralism can often go hand
in hand with nationalist assimilation; indeed, what Fishman and his
associates have aptly termed "language loyalty"[32] among immigrant
groups in the United States has left behind vast non-English language
resources in the republic that have not stood in the way of the Americanizing process. Nor, finally, can it be a problem of the presence in
Caribbean societies of seemingly unassimilable ethnic groups (which is
the basis of the thesis of the "plural society" as advanced by certain
sectors in Carribbean scholarship), for in fact societies characterized by
even marked degrees of heterogeneity can often show equally marked
success in developing an overriding consensus of common national
identity.

In the Virgins case some of the answers to the problem have already
been suggested. There has been a deeply felt clannishness on the part of
the native Virgin Islanders that has discouraged the creolization process
in the immigrant groups. The commercial character of St. Thomas,
leading to a high turnover rate in the out-groups, has also discouraged
the process, since creolization, by definition, is closely related to prolonged residency. Puerto Ricans have creolized well, the French less so.
With regard to the continental influx (which, perhaps, is the heart of
the matter), other factors have been at work. There is, as already noted
(see pp. 187–89), an insider-outsider ambivalence which militates against
complete assimilation. There is the bias of race, although many individual continentals valiantly strive against it. Perhaps most insidious
of all, however, is the spirit of American cultural imperialism. The
American in the Caribbean, as much as the Englishman, seems morally
incapable of becoming creolized, weaned from the conviction of belong-

31. *The Wide Sargasso Sea* (New York: Norton, 1966).
32. J. A. Fishman et al., *Language Loyalty in the United States* (The Hague:
n.p., 1966).

ing to what Kiernan has called the "lords of human kind." He is unlikely to become anything else, or even to want to become anything
else, because what he already is seems to him to be the pinnacle of
human perfection. He may not possess the effortless habit of authority,
the calm assurance that by nature he belongs to a ruling class, which
has so characterized the Englishman in the Caribbean colonial empire.
But he is nonetheless, in his own estimation, a superior being; and the
conviction works against any real possibility that he can ever see himself
as a coequal citizen in a Caribbean polyglot society. It irks him to be a
passenger; he feels he ought to be in the driver's seat. A final example
of this habit of group separatism is the fact that the resident Americans
have become a vocal and articulate group who, by their insistence,
manage to receive all kinds of services—housing, telephone installation,
sanitation collection, and so on—that are denied to the native Virgin
Islander because of his traditional social meekness and fear of exposure,
which make him a much less demanding client. Until the American
learns to join and remain in the Virgins society on the terms set not by
his own group but by the larger society itself, his type can only do
irreparable damage to the growth of real community.

It is true that in recent years an encouraging growth of genuine
community consciousness has taken place, through the formation of a
number of socially minded civic groups. Bodies like the VISTA group,
the Alien Interest Movement, and others have begun to appeal to a
sense of social shame about the conditions of life and work of the alien
labor masses. Religious leaders like Rabbi Murray Blackman and Father
Charles Hawes have begun to shake the long habit of neglect of the
alien problem on the part of their churches. Virgin Islands youth, especially at the college, have taken the lead in similar issues; the Action
Coalition group is a case in point, with its militant stance on matters
as various as education for the alien child, the injustices of the federal
Selective Service system, and the appointment of a local native to the
position of government secretary.[33] Groups like the Black Cultural
Organization have begun to emphasize the link of a common cultural
heritage between Virgin Islanders and the eastern Caribbean societies,
a link that hitherto has not been sufficiently recognized because of geo-

33. See the letter of the Action Coalition group in correspondence column, *Daily
News*, Oct. 27, 1969. For the Alien Interest Movement, see its report to Acting Governor King on alien communities, cited in *ibid.*, Apr. 11, 1969, and its statement in
support of the federal Department of Labor minimum-wage levels for alien workers,
cited in *ibid.*, Jan. 13, 1969.

graphical accident and colonial separatism.[34] Issues that have tended to
be swept under the carpet by a repressive political oligarchy now receive
widespread attention, mainly because of the aroused civic spirit engineered by these groups. So, only a few brief years ago, it was possible for
the Virgin Islands Establishment to silence critics by devious means,
and get away with it. Today, that is increasingly difficult to do, as is
witnessed by the furor aroused by the dismissal and transfer of VISTA
volunteers because of their involvement with the alien issue. The newly
organized teachers' groups have managed to dramatize the scandal of
the local public school system, with all of its glaring deficiencies, in a
way that would have been unheard of just a few years ago, when it was
still possible for commissioners of education to rule in the old autocratic
colonial fashion.

All this is encouraging. Yet it is clearly only a beginning. It is restricted, so far, to zealous and enthusiastic minorities. Most of the major
ethnic groups, by comparison, still tend to think in terms of their
separate interests rather than in terms of a felt sense of Virgin Islands
nationhood. The socially conscious businessman, black or white, is a
rarity. The "black power" slogan, despite the rhetoric which denies its
applicability to the island scene, by its very nature encourages an
inverted racism as a response to white racism; and it is worth noting
that the white racism is sedulously cultivated by the ingress of tourists,
most of whom, oddly enough, are white. The Creole Jewish group, in
its turn, keeps to itself. Its members, indeed, are not averse at times to
exploiting the theme of anti-Semitism for their own purposes. One leading newspaper noted how Governor Paiewonsky, on the eve of his
resignation, sought to retain his occupancy of the governorship by
persuading influential contacts in Washington to put out the inuendo
that to dismiss him would be interpreted as anti-Semitism in the Jewish
community at large.[35] The resident white continentals, in their turn,
despite individual exceptions, are certainly intensely chauvinistic, even
if not racist, in their attitudes. It was certainly pleasing to most of them
that as late in the day as 1969 President Nixon was prepared to nominate
one of their own number, Peter Bove, as the new Republican governor,
despite the fact that the precedent of appointing a native person seemed
to have become solidly established, and that Bove could hardly have
been said to be immensely popular in the islands.[36]

34. For the Black Cultural Organization, see interview with Alexis Weatherhead,
Home Journal, Aug. 29, 1969.

35. See report by Washington Bureau, *Daily News,* Apr. 21, 1969.

36. For the Bove nomination episode, see island press throughout March, 1969.
See also Eneid Routte, "Peter Bove: A Vermont Yankee in St. Croix," *Sunday San
Juan Star,* Dec. 26, 1971.

The ultimate test of effective community in this sort of society is, of course, that of racial intermarriage. The Danish practice in the area of interracial sexual drives has already been noted. A volume of stories written by a Danish resident at the turn of the century and published posthumously in 1969—Lucie Horlyk's *In Danish Times*—illustrates how tolerant Danish attitudes on the matter could be.[37] American attitudes, on the contrary, were never so benign. They continue, today, to stand in the way of anything like a widespread habit of racial intermarriage. A recent sampling of opinion on the matter by a perceptive continental observer suggests the presence of profound psychological resistance to the mere idea. "I could be attracted to white guys here," stated a native woman, "but I simply won't let myself. I have the distinct impression that a white man wouldn't value me or take me seriously. He doesn't in the States; why should he here?" "I've reached the point," observed a native male, "where I don't want to go out with white women any more. In the beginning I suppose my desire for them was mostly curiosity. But a lot of these tourist chicks come running down here on a fling and they think a black man's here for them to use. There's a sign on them which says 'look at me, I'm liberal,' but when it's all over they shake hands and are as businesslike as a Cuban prostitute. No thanks, not for me." If these expressions are in any way typical they bode ill for the growth, within any time period worth considering, of styles of interracial sex based on feelings of mutually accepted equality.[38] And without such a foundation in an area of relationships so strategic there can be little hope of a broader sense of community making itself felt.

37. Ed. Betty Nilsson (Stockholm, 1969).
38. Ellie Heckert, "Color Blind from Birth," *The Nation*, October 14, 1968, reprinted in *Daily News*, Nov. 15, 1968.

11

~~~

Religion, Education,
and Communications

For historical reasons religion and education have always been closely connected in island life. The history of education for more than a century after the establishment of the first Moravian mission in St. Thomas in 1733, with the Lutherans following in 1757, was the history of the religious missions. The story of the early missionaries, who were martyrs at once to a hostile climate and a hostile plantocracy (some died just a few months after landing), reflects the full impact of their Christian sacrifice: the Catholic Father Kendall; Pastor Johannes Kingo, most notable, perhaps, of all the Lutheran workers; Leonard Dober of the Moravian Brethren; and the Lutheran Pastor Stoud, whose history of brief devoted service to the Christiansted congregation can be read on one of the beautiful memorial tablets that line the walls of the Christiansted church. The list of Lutheran ministers and missionaries to the islands over some two centuries testifies in some measure to the historic continuity of Danish Lutheranism and its tremendous service to the religious and educational life of the colonial dependency.[1] It is true that all of the churches compromised on the issue of slavery. At the same time they brought a note of thought and culture into the anti-intellectual colonial society. Certainly the Lutheran Church, the state church in Copenhagen, did far more than the Anglican Church managed to do in the British islands. Levo, himself an Anglican priest, made the

1. Jens Larsen, *Virgin Islands Story* (Philadelphia: Fortress Press, 1950), app. A. For the Catholic contribution, see Joseph G. Daly, "Archbishop John Carroll and the Virgin Islands," *Catholic Historical Review*, LIII, no. 3 (October, 1967), 305–27. See also Patricia Shaubah Murphy, *The Moravian Mission to the African Slaves of the Danish West Indies, 1732–1828* (St. Thomas: Caribbean Research Institute, College of the Virgin Islands, 1969).

(265)

trenchant remark that "The Church was the timid satellite of the upper classes, and neglected the white labourer at home and the black one abroad with an equal impartiality." [2]

The legacy left by the missionaries is the respect with which the churches and their leaders are traditionally treated in the present-day society. Religious, as distinct from racial, discrimination is practically unknown, although a public figure, like President Wanlass of the college, might occasionally have his religious affiliation sardonically noted, in this particular case because his Mormon faith made him suspect to those who knew something about the Mormon theological teaching on the subject of the Negro.[3] The astonishing number of public holidays, including at least four religious holidays not observed in the States, such as Holy Thursday and Supplicatory Day, also testify to this religious heritage. The legend supposedly relating to the St. Thomas Reformed Church— Protestant in its teaching, Presbyterian in its government, Dutch in its national origin, biblical in its emphasis, English in its language, and American in its support of equal rights—aptly sums up the astonishing variety of the heritage.

There is, even so, a negative side to the heritage. For most of the main churches the islands still have a missionary status. The Lutheran Church is part of the Caribbean Synod, with synodical headquarters in San Juan; the Moravian Church is also part of the Caribbean Province, which extends down to Trinidad; the Pilgrim Holiness Church is ruled from a superintendency located in Barbados; the Catholic Church is attached to the Metropolitan See in Washington, D.C.; while the Methodist Church is also part of a Caribbean district that includes the Leeward and Windward Islands. While a Caribbean regional boundary is certainly better than an overseas metropolitan boundary, the fact remains that religious institutional control, along with the power to appoint respective priesthoods, lies outside the local territory, so that there is a noticeable lack of a local pastorate. The Catholic cathedral of St. Peter and St. Paul is run by the American Redemptorist Fathers. The Episcopal Church waited until 1953 before appointing its first native Virgin Islander, Kenneth Barta—who traces his genealogy some nine generations back to a settler who arrived in St. Thomas in 1685—to its ordained priest-

2. John Ernest Levo, *The West Indian Adventure* (London: Society for Propagation of Gospel in Foreign Parts, 1929), p. 29.

3. For Rabbi Moses Sasso's fifty-year leadership of the St. Thomas Hebrew congregation, see *Daily News*, June 17, 1964. For the equally long service of Catholic Bishop Edward J. Harper, see *ibid.*, May 29, 1964. On the matter of President Wanlass it is perhaps enough to say that any public official who is a Mormon in any Caribbean society today is sooner or later certain to invite confrontation. For a typical statement of Caribbean black attitudes to the Mormon Church, see *Ascria Says* (Georgetown, Guyana), I, no. 1 (January, 1970), 3–4.

hood. A recent tabulation of pastoral and ministerial occupancy in all of the organizations appearing in the religious directory of the local Sunday press—in all, a total of seventeen, ranging from the Apostolic Faith Church to the Seventh Day Adventists—suggests that at least fourteen of them, the effective majority, are looked after by non–Virgin Islands clerics.[4]

It is worth noting the relations between religion, social class, and color in this general situation. There is, naturally, no rigid caste barrier that determines church membership. The day, too, is certainly long departed when pews in the Lutheran Church were rented out to the prominent families of both the English and Danish congregations. At the same time, there exist subtle social pressures that serve to produce a pattern of informal religious segregation. It is a segregationist pattern, moreover, that tends to be racial rather than social; the membership, for example, of the All Saints Episcopal Church in Charlotte Amalie certainly manages to include most of the social strata of the town, as does the Methodist Church, situated even more centrally in the Market Square area. What appears to have happened is a selective process whereby parishioners decide to attend those churches where they feel most at home, that is, where members of their own ethnic group form a comfortable majority. So the Jewish Synagogue, by definition, presents a white face, reinforced by the fact, or so it is believed, that the congregation is open only to members whose parental background is pure by Talmudic law; and local authorities will cite the case of the denial of membership to the famous Virgin Islands painter Camille Pissarro, one of whose parents was Catholic. Thus, too, the Episcopal, Baptist, and Methodist churches are all overwhelmingly colored, as well as alien, in their memberships. The Methodist persuasion, indeed, goes back in its foundation to the influx of workers from Anguilla and Tortola, who resisted all efforts to be assimilated into the Moravian and Lutheran folds during the period after 1890. The continentals, in their turn, have patronized the Dutch Reformed Church, to the extent that it has developed a reputation as being a haven for whites. The list of vestry members of the Episcopal Church in St. Thomas who are Convocation delegates includes a heavy native professional group at the top of the structure, including such prominent persons as Bertha Boschulte, Dr. Warren Smith, Attorney Almeric Christian, and Jane Tuitt. The whites stay away, for a variety of reasons. There is no reason, socially, for them to go. In the sharp words of one ecclesiastical dignitary, "There is no social clique they can belong to . . . they worship at the beach . . . most continentals don't come to the Episcopal Church because they find the

4. See "Religious Directory," in *Home Journal,* Mar. 24, 1968.

services too high and the color too black, but mainly the latter reason." [5]
A combination of tropical hedonism and color animosity is hardly
conducive to the cultivation of religious, not to speak of Christian, habits.
An informal apartheid thus characterizes the Virgin Islands religious life
almost as much as it does the economic life.

For the working-class population, church membership and attendance
play important social roles. In a society largely bereft of social entertainment—the few movie theaters constitute a dismally low-quality circuit—
going to church is a crucial social function. The island children on their
Sunday perambulations to church or chapel, immaculately dressed, usually in white, illustrate the extent to which religious activity is an
important source of identity for their parents. It is clear that the habit
of sartorial ostentation serves to sustain feelings of pride and self-respect,
a practice that goes back to the Danish period; the visiting Thurlow
Reed, in his vivid description of the songs and dances of the estate Negro
populations in 1845, noted the same phenomenon, summed up colorfully
in the words of some of the Christmas anniversary songs that he managed
to transcribe as he listened to the black "ladies of the garden" teasing,
with obvious sexual undertones, the white English and Danish gentlemen of the great houses, the "lions in the wood":

> We wear the best shaleys—we sport the best de lanes,
> We wear the best muslins—we do not spare the cost.
> Here is our Queen—she wears the best of linen
> She sports the best of Cambric and doesn't mind the cost.
> Our gents smoke the best segars—they sport the Otto of Roses,
> For they have pockets full of doubloons.[6]

That pride in dress is still there, although the splendidly Rabelaisian
dance and song tradition that Reed described seems to have quite disappeared. The pride survives, in one way, in the weekly turnout at
church and chapel services. That the rich spontaneity has disappeared is
apparent in the highly formal character of most local religious services.
There is little of the rich public emotionalism, the "soul brotherhood," so
pronounced in the Negro Protestantism of the American South. This
may possibly be due to the fact that in recent decades the most emphatic
religious influence, leaving aside for the moment that of popular Ameri-

5. Interview, Father Richard Abbott, Charlotte Amalie, March 21, 1968. The list of
vestry members of the Episcopal Church is taken from the church notice board, as of
March, 1968. See also critical remarks of Rabbi Blackman and Bishop Mills on the
attitude of the churches toward social issues, cited in Jack Star, "Virgin Islands:
Shame in the U.S. Tropics," *Look*, March 10, 1970.

6. "Letters from the West Indies," excerpt in *Virgin Islands View*, December, 1966.

can revivalism, has been that brought in by the alien populations shaped by the more formal English religious tradition.

That, indeed, is a point that has to be underlined. Virgin Islands religion, today, is overwhelmingly alien West Indian religion. Methodist, Pilgrim Holiness, Jehovah's Witnesses—all of these congregations are almost totally alien in their composition. Only a cursory acquaintance-ship with aliens demonstrates that they entertain a vast contempt for what they regard as the awful irreligiosity of Virgin Islanders. "If you go to Seventh Day Adventist church," in the words of one of them, "you will only find three or four Crucians in the mix; if you go to Anglican church, if there are three Crucians there ain't four." So much is this the case that certain denominations almost wholly concentrate on services for the alien communicant; thus the Seventh Day Adventist Church, apart from its well-known medical services, helps to bond its members and has also interceded (until recently, when conditions changed) with the public school system at the tenth-grade level for possible entry of its alien students into the system. So keenly appreciated are those services that it is not unusual to find parents who are Catholic or Moravian sending their children to an Adventist school. While it is true, then, that the Virgin Islands churches, possibly because of the Erastian charac-ter of the church under the Danish regime, have not undertaken, like Negro churches in the United States, an active leadership role in any civil rights movement, at the same time the social service record of the more heterodox churches, mainly for the alien, constitutes an admirable example of practical Christianity. A generation ago Elsie Clews Parsons did not find it difficult, when collecting local folklore traditions, to gather together popular stories satirizing ministers of religion; that was a time, after all, when a parson like Father Levo was a beloved Jesus-figure in a church almost completely bereft of any social gospel element.[7] Today, on the other hand, it would be rare to find an alien, especially an alien mother, who did not have profusely grateful things to say about those denominations that have been especially helpful. In a society whose major institutions have either ignored or neglected him, the alien has found refuge in these socially conscious churches. Until the permanent commission for aliens recommended by the 1968 report becomes a work-ing reality, with real powers to do something, the alien will continue to look to those churches for aid and comfort.

Any visit to a meeting conducted by one of the more pentecostal denominations will sustain this conviction. A class meeting of the Pilgrim

7. Elsie Clews Parsons, *Folklore of the Antilles, French and English* (New York: American Folk-lore Society, 1943), pt. 3, pp. 331-32.

Holiness church in Charlotte Amalie reveals a group of alien young people valiantly attempting the extemporaneous exposition of difficult Old Testament passages under the affectionate guidance of a young continental pastor. The young girls, giggling with embarrassment, yet clearly sincere, struggle to make sense of the messianic prophecies of Joel and Haggai, and to understand the historical difference between the Minor and Major prophets, on which topic they will be required to present a short paper at the following meeting.[8] At a Jehovah's Witnesses storefront church in Christiansted, there is a similar cross-examination of its young members, at once gentle and rigorous, led by a "brother" hardly older than themselves, upon the set task of the evening. It takes three electric fans to make the small, hot room, with its religious slogans on the wall printed in both English and Spanish, at all comfortable; but it is transparently clear that a vital Christian spirit is at work. The impression gained by such visits is overwhelmingly one of a democratic congregationalism, in which the friendly relationship between teacher and students is not distorted by ritual or ministerial authority. As these ordinary people struggle to express themselves over the abstruse problems presented to them by the lesson—ranging from the question whether Adam exercised free will in his choice of Eve, through the problems of Archbishop Usher's biblical chronology and St. Paul's attitude of neutrality in politics, to the nature of the Roman Empire and the full meaning of the liberty proclaimed by the Liberty Bell in 1776—it is obvious that, despite their mostly stereotyped answers, learned by rote from the fundamentalist literature of the tracts usually printed in Chicago or Los Angeles, they are learning somehow to speak their minds and, even more, to understand something about the nature of Christian liberty.

It is, of course, a message of passive obedience, essentially quietist, in matters of the social order, not unlike the Moravian message earlier on in the matter of slavery. It is respectful of the civil authority. The observation of a Tortolan cab driver, addressed to the territorial legislature—"My good Senators, our Creator was born in Bethlehem. Did he stay there all the time? He, too, travelled to different countries, thus becoming an alien"—shows how easily the alien mind turns to biblical analogy and also how willing it is, so far, to appeal for justice in respectful terms. The young Baptist preacher, in yet another gospel hall meeting, who used the text of the rich young man in the Scriptures to tell his alien congregation that the "citizenship of Heaven" was far more important to them than "the citizenship of the United States so many

8. The descriptions in these paragraphs of local religious life are based on visits of the author to various groups during 1967, 1968, and 1970.

of us are looking for," was giving characteristic expression to that temper of social quietism. In one way this is to be expected, in light of the fact that the main influence on this popular religion is that of the aggressive American revivalist campaigns that have inundated the whole Caribbean area in recent years. Dozens of brash, religious executive-preachers cast in the Billy Graham mold invade the area, including the Virgins, every year; and the spectacle—among many others that could be cited—of a visiting choral group of white, clean-cut American collegians from some obscure college in South Dakota singing songs of evangelical uplift in the circle of Emancipation Gardens in Charlotte Amalie to respectful, awed audiences of the colored poor is a sort of Uncle Tom's Cabin vignette it would be hard to imagine taking place anywhere else in the contemporary United States. The intellectual content of this religious imperialism is grossly low, for Americans, as a people, are for the most part theologically Victorian. If, then, there is ever to be a revolt of the alien masses, it will hardly be under the inspiration of this particular influence.

At the same time, there is a strong democratic influence at work. The newer denominations have made the alien their peculiar cause, and they offer him a chance of democratic participation in classroom and service. By contrast, none of the older established churches in the islands has spoken out boldly against the shameful treatment of the alien population; although it is only fair to add at this point that the Anglican bishop, the Right Reverend Cedric Mills, was a hard-working member of the Special Commission on the Status and Problems of Non-Citizens in the Virgin Islands that was set up by the local legislature in 1969. But that is a notable exception. Moreover, these older churches are still somewhat bureaucratic structures; it took the local Catholic church, for instance, a full century or more before, under the liberalizing influence of Vatican II council, it created an advisory diocesan board with equal representation of the laity. Oscar Lewis' documentary study of another Caribbean depressed group in neighboring Puerto Rico, *La Vida,* shows how broken and schismogenic family life may become when its traditional Catholicism is not tempered or fortified by more positive social factors. The religious ideology of the Virgin Islands alien, by contrast, with the backing of his gospel churches, manages to give him a personal dignity and a sense of rational control over his environment denied to the socially dispirited members of the Rios family, the central figures in the Lewis book. It is for much the same reason, perhaps, that there has not as yet emerged in the alien congregations any kind of radical messianic cultism such as that described in Leonard Barrett's recent study of the Jamaican Rastafarian movement. Yet such a development cannot be dismissed as impossible. The alien will not forever accept a situation in which he is increasingly important numerically (the 1968 report pointed out that the total number of aliens is now larger than the total number of Virgin Islanders who voted in the 1966 election) but is still expected to patiently accept the collective civil disabilities that at present stultify both his social and his spiritual life. Living a democratic life in his church, he will sooner or later demand a democratic life in the state.

The special character of Catholicism in St. Croix deserves a final note. Whereas Catholicism is a minority faith in St. Thomas, it is probably the majority faith in St. Croix. It is, naturally, overwhelmingly Puerto Rican, although there does exist an interesting group of Roman Catholic Crucian natives of middle-class professional background. If, then, there is a popular traditional faith in the islands, as distinct from the Protestant sects, it is Crucian Catholicism. It has its middle-class clients, of course, as is shown by the frequent High Masses celebrating wedding anniversaries of well-known families. But it is also deeply rooted in the life of the Puerto Rican poor. The church celebrates the popular religious holidays, including the festival of the *Reyes Magos*. It incorporates the popular rhythms into its new, permissive services. Furthermore, in addition to maintaining its more traditional lay groups like the Knights of Columbus, it takes on a tone of real social obligation, as is evident from the remarkable work of Sister Marthe and her helpers in the Catholic Action Center in Christiansted, concentrating as it does on Puerto Rican poverty groups. It is true that the "social gospel" aspect has not produced, Camilo Torres fashion, the type of radical, *independentista* priest already appearing in Puerto Rico proper, or even the priest who goes beyond the pre-Vatican II theology. But it may only be a matter of time before such a type does emerge in St. Croix. As in Puerto Rico, there is both an official and an unofficial Catholicism. The official faith centers on the church, in which membership cuts across social class lines. The unofficial faith, tolerated by the church, constitutes a sort of cultural penumbra, a parasitic growth of popular spiritualistic beliefs, as can be seen in the enormous variety of *oraciones* by means of which the Puerto Rican seeks semiorthodox, semioccult aid in love, sickness, family affairs, struggles with neighbors, business dealings, and even the turn of the San Juan lottery (heavily sold in the islands). These beliefs are also evident in the pre- and post-death rituals of Puerto Rican family life, such as the *velorio,* or wake, that celebrates the recently dead. There is also a widespread use of talisman objects, sometimes cleverly disguised as ornamental jewelry. These unofficial ceremonies, including weddings and confirmations, exemplify the fact that if religion has been an opiate of the Puerto Rican people (for there is still much of the famed social docility of Puerto Rican life in the Crucian groups) it has also been a consolation.

The island public school system, reshaped along American patterns after 1917, inherited the principles of freedom and opportunity established by Governor von Scholten's introduction of compulsory public instruction in 1839 as part of his slavery emancipation design. On no single topic do islanders wax so enthusiastic as on that of the educational advances of the last fifty years under the impetus of the American passion for public education as the basis of popular democracy. Vastly increased expenditures on the schools; the almost complete conquest of illiteracy; the drastic reconstruction of curricula; the introduction of the American-type senior high school (1929) and junior college (1963); the gradual extension of the various federal educational grant-in-aid legislative acts to the islands, including the important and far-ranging Higher Education Act of 1965; the elaboration of Governor Pearson's pet idea, free adult education; the accreditation of the secondary schools—these advances and many more have been amply documented by proud Virgin Islanders, with much justification. After 1917 local candidates could enter stateside colleges, and the Kunzer report of 1957, on the advanced off-island training of local high-school graduates, demonstrates how much local education has been served in the last thirty years by the welcome given those graduates seeking to become professional workers by, especially, the leading Negro colleges on the mainland.[9] So, today, the Department of Education is among the most powerful departments of the territorial government. The American belief in the omnipotent power of education to solve all social problems has long been a fixed article of faith in the communal psychology.

After 1917, too, the figure of the teacher began to receive increased social prestige, though not necessarily increased financial reward. Jarvis was, above all else, the teacher supreme. In that earlier period there were famous teachers of the old school who spanned both the Danish and the American regimes: Edith Williams, who started in the Moravian town school in St. Thomas and taught generations of islanders, and Benjamin Oliver, who brought a fierce passion for education and a hatred of mere social privilege in the world of the school out of his early training at the famous Mico College in Antigua.[10] The Virgin

9. Edward J. Kunzer, "Graduates from High School in St. Thomas and St. John Who Have Had Advanced Training Off the Island," rev. ed., mimeographed (St. Thomas Public Library, 1957).

10. See note on Edith Williams, *Daily News*, Jan. 7, 1944, and on Benjamin Oliver, *ibid.*, July 1, 1942.

(273)

Islanders of today, of course, are more likely to remember those notable figures' successors, who, once teachers and high-school principals, have gone on to make their mark in politics and administration: Bertha Boschulte, Ulla Muller, Jane Tuitt, Louis Shulterbrandt. If, all in all, the Platonic dictum is correct, that the most important minister in the state is the minister of education, no single process has Americanized Virgin Islanders and their total life-style so much as that of the educational revolution set in motion by the new American educational officials after 1917 and carried on by their Virgin Islands successors.

Going to school in the islands today is almost like going to school anywhere in America. So it would seem. Yet there are urgent and peculiar differences that belie that superficial likeness. Much of the old colonial authoritarian character of education remains; a Department of Education that is run by an executive-appointed and legislature-approved commissioner and a presidentially-nominated governor (until 1970) is not much more democratic in its structure than the old colonial ex-patriate director of education ruling native teachers with an iron hand. The results of this have been disastrously plain for years. The Department has been too full of political intrigue, and over the years only an occasional brave teacher, like Ray Moorehead in St. Croix, has been willing to fight it. The desideratum that might end some of this—a real Board of Education, with members who would be appointed for defined irrevocable terms, restricted as to political activity, fully qualified educationally, and responsible solely to the public—has never existed and does not appear to be a likely phenomenon in the near future. Complaints by teachers and other interested citizens have too often been dismissed by departmental officials as the work of outside "cranks." The recent affair of the newly built St. Croix High School is a case in point: the complaints of the staff about the appallingly bad conditions of the new plant, including leaking roofs, bad acoustics, inadequate air-conditioning fixtures, uncontrollable noise conditions, serious drainage defects, and much more, were finally conceded to be justified, thus exposing the incapacity of the Department even to build a physical plant properly adjusted to a tropical environment. Other conditions have aggravated the education problem. Too many native-born teachers, particularly men, have sought other work after a short exposure to the heavily female hierarchy of the Department, while many of the younger teachers have chafed under the direction of older administrators brought up in the authoritarian tradition.

The most grievous evidence has been, until recently, the depressed condition of the teacher, which has been fully documented in innumerable reports, very few of which have gone beyond the Department's filing cabinets. Reid noted in his 1941 book how the earlier recommendations of the 1929 Hampton-Tuskegee report for improving the training, pay, and working conditions of teachers had been ignored; since 1921 there had been no attempt to raise salaries, to fix a uniform schedule, or to provide pension rights, all of these matters being left to the discretion of individual commissioners. The Robinson report of 1954 repeated all this and stated that of the 83 per cent of the teachers who were native-born personnel at that time, over 70 per cent had had no college training of any kind, placing the islands in a position even worse than that of Virginia or Mississippi. The 1963 report of the New York University School of Education showed the extent to which these conditions managed to persist into the 1960s. Although couched in diplomatic terms, the report scored the almost intractable problems: disorganized and excessively bureaucratic operations, inadequate fiscal accounting, small and overcrowded schools, lack of parental interest, political meddling, an expenditure per pupil that ranked the system thirty-seventh among the mainland states, and visible reading disabilities in the school population as a whole; and, with particular reference to the status of the teacher, poor training, low salaries and low morale, dissatisfaction over promotion policies, and an alarmingly high turnover in personnel. It will clearly require years of serious remedial effort—which is admittedly already under way—to revolutionize the system. Granted, too, the character of small-island politics, it will take perhaps even more than time to eliminate the social pathology that surrounds the system, that is, the temptation of reform-minded members, especially teachers or junior administrative personnel, to remain apathetic for fear of triggering disadvantageous consequences or even inviting malicious reprisals.[11]

Two special problems have emerged over the years as the harvest of this dismal record. The first is the rise of the private school as the result of parental reaction to the low standards of the public system. The second is the hired stateside teacher who is brought in, as yet another off-island type, to help solve the problem of teacher recruitment. The private school came into existence because the Virgin Islands lack the

11. For all this, see *Report of the Educational Survey of the Virgin Islands*, authorized by the secretary of the Navy and conducted under the auspices of Hampton and Tuskegee Institutes (Hampton, Va.: The Press of the Hampton Normal and Agricultural Institute, 1929) ; Charles F. Reid, *Education in the Territories and Outlying Possessions of the United States* (New York: Bureau of Publications, Columbia University, 1941) ; William H. Robinson, "A Study of the Instructional Personnel in the Public Schools of St. Thomas, Virgin Islands of the United States," mimeographed (St. Thomas Public Library, July, 1954) ; and *A Comprehensive Survey of Education in the Virgin Islands* (New York: Center for School Services, School of Education, New York University, December, 1963) .

activist parent-teacher associations that act as militant lobbies to improve the local public school systems in the States; thus the more affluent parent, both native and continental, turns naturally to the private foundation. A 1966 directory issued by the Department of Education in Charlotte Amalie offers a numerical estimate of the consequences: in that year there were (inclusive of all grades) a total of twenty-two public schools and seventeen private and parochial schools in the three islands.[12] The job that the public school should be doing is obviously being done in large part by the private school, which finds itself characteristically hard pressed, with long lists of waiting entrants. It is not surprising that the private-school authorities begin to press government for financial aid, thereby threatening to jeopardize the funds that are presently set aside for the public-school sector, not to mention the possible unconstitutionality of such a policy, should it be adopted.

But there is more to it than that. The situation introduces, in effect, a dual educational system, with all of the resultant inequities. The public school takes on, quite recognizably, a lower-class image, the private school an affluent middle-class image. At the same time, a color distinction makes itself felt, with the public school becoming overwhelmingly black and Puerto Rican, and the private school in large part light-skinned and white. The result is that the ordinary Virgin Islands child attends what is in effect a segregated school, obtaining an education that is shaped by factors of skin color, language, and parental income. Local educators have themselves compared the situation to that prevailing in the worst of mainland southern states, where an alliance of white parents and lawmakers finds devious ways to avoid the public-school system by sending white children to private schools and then proceeds to request state aid to help finance the operation, thus leaving an impoverished public system to the poor and the black student. And that the public school in the Virgins case is impoverished is beyond doubt. There are too few schools for too many pupils. The overcrowding is notorious. Discipline problems abound, to the extent that the Wayne Aspinall Junior High School in St. Thomas is referred to casually by everyone as "Vietnam." There is a chronic shortage of school materials, and one teacher, indeed, has become something of a folk hero around the islands because, driven to desperation, he finally went out to the town refuse dump and collected paper, pencils, erasers, and a few odd books. One of the more ludicrous consequences of this state of affairs is that nearly two-thirds of the students of the St. Croix Central High

12. Virgin Islands, Department of Education, *Directory 1965–1966 Public, Private and Parochial Schools of the Virgin Islands of the United States* (St. Thomas, 1966).

School cannot swim, due to the absence of any adequate facilities; yet every schoolchild in the islands lives at the most only a few brief miles from the sea. The only child who has suffered worse is, of course, the alien child, barred from the public school system until only very recently, when the courts finally adjudged aliens to be "persons" within the meaning of the Fourteenth Amendment and thus entitled to equal protection under the law. Yet despite that breakthrough the island press is still full of hostile comment about "faceless droves" of alien children flooding the schools, so much so that it looks as if the myth of alien responsibility for crime will now be accompanied by the further myth of alien responsibility for the educational crisis.

The problem of teacher recruitment has equally undesirable results. As native teachers attend mainland colleges and universities to earn a baccalaureate or a higher degree and then remain there, owing to more attractive opportunities than those awaiting them in the islands, the local school system has been driven more and more to the practice of stateside recruitment. In 1960, less than 10 per cent of the teaching staffs were continentals; today, only a decade later, the figure is nearly 50 per cent. Yet the mainland teachers bring many vexatious problems with them. There is a frighteningly high turnover, for they come unprepared for the cultural shock that awaits them. They must pay exorbitant rentals for indifferent housing, when indeed they can find it. "It is most unfortunate," a Department of Education report wryly admits, "that we must tell applicants that their rental on a gross biweekly salary of $207.69 will begin at $165.00 per month." They can find few of the fringe benefits, such as teachers' insurance schemes, which they are accustomed to in the States. There are even fewer opportunities for the continued professional training they naturally seek. More profoundly, they are rarely prepared to meet and absorb the racial-cultural facts of their new employment. A recent analysis of the problem by a Virgin Islands teacher has pointed out that many applicants who are quite willing to work with colored children are reluctant to work with a supervisor or an administrator who is colored, which is the prevalent Virgin Islands situation. Too many of these recruits are attracted by what is misleading, if not downright mendacious, soliciting by the Department. "Lovely natural beaches, cheap silver and china, beautiful nights and friendly people in a setting of old world charm," the teacher's report acidly comments, "are the assets which can be used for tourist appeal. These are not necessarily the attractions which will provide us with a hard-working stable teaching population." The proper and alternative approach, it is urged, can only be one that honestly tells the prospective mainland teacher what he is likely to meet with, warts

(277)

and all. Perhaps the only alternative is a Peace Corps type of approach, in which the emphasis is placed on service and sacrifice.[13] In the meantime, lacking that sort of approach, the presence of such a large percentage of mainland professional strangers in the system gives the local classroom more and more the appearance of black children being taught by white alien teachers, most of whom rarely stay for more than a year, hardly long enough for them to learn and cultivate the habit of cultural empathy. It is a situation fraught with real social danger, in which the native schoolchild is taught more and more by a harassed, culturally perplexed young stateside teacher who is anxious to return as quickly as possible to what he or she regards as "civilization" on the continental mainland.

It is hardly suprising that the last few years have seen the rise of a militant teacher unionism in the islands, culminating in the affiliation of the St. Thomas Teachers Association and the St. Croix Teachers Representative Council with the American Federation of Teachers. A study of the recruitment campaign and the subsequent negotiations with the local government makes it clear that the teachers finally decided that only a general collective bargaining system could give them the tenure protection so long denied them, and that in order to obtain that protection, in view of the intimidatory practices so long utilized against them, they would have to call in the aid of the mainland union movement. It is worth noting that the call for assistance happened to coincide with a growing awareness on the part of the mainland leadership of their responsibilities and obligations to the struggling teachers in the semicolonial situations of the American off-shore dependencies, including Guam, the Canal Zone, and now the Virgin Islands. The extraordinary record of the neighboring Puerto Rican Teachers Association since its foundation in 1911—including struggles to defend the political rights of its members, the organization of a teachers' cooperative, the establishment of one of the most remarkable teachers' hospitals in the Americas, scholarship systems, credit for housing, arrangement of life insurance, radio and TV programs in the area of public relations, a tourist bureau to facilitate teacher travel, and much else—demonstrates what an active association can do for its members and how far, by comparison, the Virgin Islands teachers have yet to go in order to even begin to match such a record.[14]

13. Vitalia L. Wallace, "Recruitment Problems in the United States Virgin Islands," handwritten (St. Thomas, June 16, 1965).

14. For all this, see reports in *Daily News*, Dec. 8, 1967, Jan. 25, Feb. 9, 1968, and in *Home Journal*, Dec. 8, 1967. For a typical example of the plight of teachers under the old colonial regime, see *The Emancipator*, Jan. 30, 1926. For the Teachers Asso-

Yet perhaps the issue that most exercises the minds of the territorial educators and teachers is the relationship between local education and Virgin Islands culture. The debate on the issue came to a head with the local government's decision to request a federal money grant under the terms of the Higher Education Act of 1965 for the purpose of promoting the study of local history, civics, and geography in the instructional program of the local schools. The project was set up by the Department of Education on an ambitious scale, and was federally approved in 1967. The application to the federal Office of Education sharply emphasized the first principles on which Project Introspection was based:

> The steady influx of new residents from the United States, other Caribbean islands, and many foreign countries; the impact of mass media and other means of communication as they become more accessible to the population; improved transportation, and the general rise in the standard of living—all these factors accentuate the need for islanders to become more knowledgeable about their islands in order that they may deal more effectively with problems growing out of the present setting. . . . We believe that the Virgin Islands, committed by choice to the United States of America and all for which she stands [*sic*], must nevertheless have a school system which recognises the important fact that the community differs from other American communities. We are an island territory, until recent years relatively remote from the American mainland. We have a culture of our own that is valuable and well worth preserving.[15]

The writers of the application seem at times not to be sure whether they want to emphasize the thesis of the islands as an American success story which, if taught the native child, will enlarge his positive self-image, or the thesis of the islands as an indigenous culture beleaguered by the larger metropolitan culture. Even so, it is a statement of impressive quality and confronts head on the issue of national selfhood and cultural identity that characterizes the social debate in every ex-colonial society of the modern world.

A number of general observations suggest themselves at this point. In the first place, it should be noted that this debate is in fact not quite as novel as it seems. Every report since the Hampton-Tuskegee report of 1929 has drawn attention to the issue. "Children in these islands," stated that report, "need to have their reading, writing and

---

ciation of Puerto Rico, see full-page advertisement in *San Juan Star,* Oct. 17, 1967; also Teachers Association of Puerto Rico, Pronouncement, "People Must Be Given the Right of Active Participation in the Direction of Their Public Schools," *ibid.,* Mar. 21, 1967.

15. Virgin Islands, Department of Education, "Project Introspection," Application for an Operational Grant, ESEA Title III, mimeographed (St. Thomas, June 8, 1967), pp. 2, 4.

other school activities in connection with ideas and experiences that are genuinely real to them; only in this way will there be any likelihood that what they learn in school passes over into the realities of life around them." Reid, in his book of 1941, noted that the local school curricula had been taken almost verbatim from courses of study established in the school systems of Utah and New Mexico and that, generally, those curricula were insufficiently related to the real life of the community. Bertha Boschulte's report of 1945, which was essentially a spirited defense of the idea of vocational education as against traditional education, reflecting the influence of John Dewey's theories, echoed the same note. "Students," that report stated, "know more about United States history and geography than many Continental students, but they know little about Caribbean history or geography." It added, "Virgin Islands history should be studied as a key to understanding the present social and economic problems. A study of these problems should lead students to see that their solution demands concerted action, that running away when times are bad and returning when there is some artificial boom will not solve the problems." [16] And the lesson was finally emphasized, yet again, in the 1963 NYU report.

The second point to be made, then, is an explanation of why, after an existence in printed reports for forty years or more, the issue has suddenly become so much alive. One answer has already been suggested in the earlier discussion of Virgin Islands culture (see pp. 170–76): it is at once an expression of the gathering insecurity of the native Virgin Islander group as against the culturally invading expatriate, continental, and alien groups and an effort on the part of the professional elite of the native group to enlarge its social power by developing, and controlling, its own equivalent of the new state cultural apparatus that emerges in all of the colonial societies, at any given point, on their way to nationhood. This is not to deny that they feel, with real sincerity, the cultural impasse that their society has arrived at. The principal of one of the schools has put it this way:

> We are dealing here with a population that does not understand and appreciate mainland mores, yet a lot of that orientation inevitably creeps into the instruction process. A few of the kids can adjust to it, many of them want to but can't pay the price, and most of them are just confused by it all. The textbooks and teaching materials we get are middle-class continental, and they usually get

16. See Bertha Boschulte, "Some Weak Areas in Our System of Public Education," reprinted in *Daily News*, June 1, 2, 1950. The study was originally undertaken in 1945, and constitutes a remarkable pioneer effort anticipating much of the present-day debate.

interpreted in those terms. The reading materials are oriented to a different culture, and I don't like that at all.[17]

To talk for any length of time with the educators involved in the remedial program—Mavis Brady, Huldah Joseph, Gwendolyn Kean—is to sense how deeply they feel the fact that West Indian children and parents, even from the most anglicized of the neighboring islands, possess a pronounced sentiment of island identity that the Virgin Islands child and parent seem pathetically to lack.

Yet at the same time—and this is the third point—there is a curious ambivalence, a sensed suspicion of not being quite fully militant, about the program of the Educational and Cultural Center. It has the unconvincing aspect of all folk-culture programs that are arranged by earnest committees. Too many of the plays that have been presented by the St. Croix Center, for example, carry the touch of the old system which uplifts the people to the "nobler" European forms, whereas what is needed is the presentation of West Indian and Puerto Rican plays. If the residual culture of the Virgins themselves is tiny, the picture changes once the islands are seen as an integral part of the wider regional West Indian culture. And if that is so, it follows that the West Indian alien must be seen as an ally in the struggle against the American cultural penetration. Yet so far there is little evidence that that truth—which ought to give rise to a binational front of black native and black alien—is appreciated, or its implications seized. Even more, there is the contradiction contained in the fact that while the Virgin Islands educational commissars talk about the dangers of anachronistic continental values in the school system they continue to recruit continental teachers at an increasing rate, the majority of whom, through no fault of their own, inevitably act as the carriers of those values. There is also the contradiction involved in stressing the need for a more indigenous teaching force and then recommending for candidacies in the Creativity for Education program five consultants who, with the single exception of a Puerto Rican, are stateside professional persons.[18] What is needed is a massive crash educational program which would effectively use the latent talent of the islands' young people, whose vivacity and readiness to help out are rarely appealed to in any creative sense either in the home or in the school.

But to embrace such a program would inevitably involve facing the

17. Principal, Wayne Aspinall Junior High School, quoted in John Egerton, "Education in the Virgin Islands," *Southern Education Report*, reprinted in *Virgin Islands View*, November, 1967.
18. "Project Introspection," pp. 31–34.

(281)

fundamental truth that it is impossible to seek to ameliorate an American disease—the fact that the school in the Virgin Islands is not an indigenous institution created in response to local needs but a stateside system introduced, with only slight modifications, to serve pedagogical-social purposes strictly American in their character—by bringing in yet once more the American prescription of cure. The fact that there is no Virgin Islands ingredient in the school is not to be seen, as so much of the local commentary sees it, as merely a regrettable error of policy or judgment but as an inescapable consequence of fifty years of American cultural imperialism in the island territories. The school is not an end in itself. It is shaped by the social, economic, and cultural forces that weigh on the society as a whole. Virgin Islanders have perhaps failed to see this because every step in their school system, including this latest Project Introspection enterprise, has been taken in conjunction with American pedagogical consultants, the high mandarins of the ultra-Deweyite theory that education not merely reflects social reality but can fundamentally reshape it. It follows, then, if this line of analysis is correct, that the school can only be rid of the American cultural imprint when the society as a whole is rid of it. But for most Virgin Islanders at this stage of their political development, perhaps this reality is so difficult to accept that, like the rich young man in the Scripture story, they will go away sorrowing rather than be prepared to embrace its harsh imperatives.

The fact that the islands have their roots deeply implanted in both cultures, insular and metropolitan, also helps to determine the character of communications. On the one hand, much of the communications pattern is still that of old-fashioned, traditional small-island life, based on gossip and word of mouth. The drinking shops are social centers in a way that the American-type saloon bar is not; they are rather like the English pub. The popular attitudes toward work and time still reflect much of this social gregariousness, the well-known West Indian street life. This, in a way, is an isolationist life, in which people feel cut off from the rest of the world. "Happenings in the Virgin Islands," opined a local newspaper editorial a generation ago, "often in a most peculiar manner correspond to or resemble events in the larger outside world, though humbler and often somewhat debased, owing to the smallness of our conditions which are not favorable to the presentation of the heroic. This, undoubtedly, to some extent works against any comparison of ourselves and our own conditions with the ideals and events of other places, and makes it difficult to draw strength and encouragement from local happenings." [19] Yet on the other hand the rapid boom development, along with the vast improvement of travel and communications with the continental United States, has replaced this older style with a pseudo-modern pace. There is daily service of the *New York Times;* there is a large demand for the *San Juan Star;* there are stateside television programs. It is true that tourism tends to dehumanize social relationships, for it engenders a social atmosphere of hospitality without friendship, public relations without private feeling, commercialized personal relations based on economic acquisitiveness. At the same time, the tourist as a person is not always the cretinous globetrotter he is sometimes pictured as, and at his best he is bound to put new ideas and attitudes into local circulation. Isolationism grows more difficult to sustain, either as a fact or as an ideal. An efficient rapid transit communications system to Miami and New York is a sine qua non of a continuing tourist boom. So, Virgin Islanders are intensely air conscious, just as they were intensely sea conscious in the earlier period of maritime communications.

Of the local mass media, television, of course, is the latest, in the form of two Virgin Islands channels and six Puerto Rican channels whose signals reach all of the three islands. Most of the programs originate either from the States or Puerto Rico, although the local-made programs are there, including the emergence of the local TV personality conducting her own program, like Joyce La Motta with her "Pueblo Show." There is also, since 1968, a public TV system.

The newspapers possess, by contrast, a remarkable ancestry. The *Royal Danish American Gazette* appeared in St. Thomas as early as 1770; it was reported in 1926, as an illustration of the antiquity of that paper, that the merchant Alvarez Julien had at that moment in his possession a copy dated November 5, 1796, printed in Christiansted, that contained the text of President Washington's Farewell Address to Congress.[20] The Danish tradition was autocratic, and right up to 1917 the three public newspapers bore their titles as government property and their editors were required to pass an examination before the police authorities before being licensed. The papers tended to be, then, bulletin boards for official notices, a characteristic still discernible in papers of the present day such as the *St. Croix Avis.* At the same time, that kind of government press law did not prevent the emergence, in the Danish period, of independent editors like Leroy Nolte, John Benners, William Murta, and John Lightbourn, whose liberal tradition was carried on after the transfer by editors like Conrad Corneiro, Abram Smith, and Alton Adams,

19. A. H., "Small West Indian Pen Sketches," *The Emancipator,* Aug. 15, 1931.
20. *Ibid.,* Jan. 13, 1926.

as well as by the creators, like Jackson and Francis, of a more radical type of newspaper. After 1917, these editors fought the new U.S. Navy regime, which was almost as hostile in its own way to an independent press as the Danish regime before it. Jarvis carried on that struggle after 1930 with the establishment of his *Daily News.* The story of these small-island editors against colonial bureaucracy is a heroic one. It constitutes the basis, usually unacknowledged, of the state of the press in contemporary society.

Considering the difficulties all small-island presses face—the absence, noticeably, of a professionally trained reporting staff—the Virgin Islands press has always been astonishingly good. A columnist like Jean Larsen of the *West End News* would do justice to any quality London or New York paper. The weekly magazine *Carib* gives its readers good regional coverage. The *Daily News,* under the editorship of Ariel Melchior, has carried on its fine tradition of independence, Melchior himself being cast in the mold of the maverick small-town editor for whom no topic or person is too sacred to deal with. His publication, for example, of the full list of political posts in the local governmental structure, graphically illustrating the extent of government patronage, was a public service no other paper would have dared provide.[21] The importance of such a paper, granted the obsessive secrecy with which Virgin Islands government is conducted, is incalculable. Only too often, newspaper ventures are simply used as platforms by aspiring politicians on the way to higher things. Certainly, Senator Ottley's editorship of the *Photo News* between 1945 and 1951 can be so described, while the *Home Journal* of today, also under Senator Ottley's guidance, is regarded by many as the defender of official policy and of the Ottley-Paiewonsky political machine that controlled that policy until the changeover of 1969. But nothing perhaps so damningly illustrates the inability of the Virgin Islands political-business mind even to begin to understand the meaning of the idea of freedom of the press as the sorry story of the short-lived and ill-begotten paper *The Virgin Islands Times* after 1963. Conceived by Governor Paiewonsky and his friend Leo Harvey of the alumina big business enterprise in St. Croix as a frankly political weapon with which to fight their Crucian political foes, its successive editors were controlled by a Virgin Islands senator carried on its payroll as a "reporter" at $500 a month. This situation so discredited the paper with the local St. Croix community that it finally died of unpopularity, with its editor being ignominiously dismissed by the paper's Washington lobbyist and then being driven to the local airport by a junior accountant whose assigned

21. *Daily News,* June 12, 1967.

task was to deliver his airline ticket to the editor only when that unfortunate individual was safely astride the boarding stairs of his plane to New York.[22] There is, as the newspaper critics of the local political machines have pointed out, a vast difference between a public relations organ specifically set up, like the *Times,* to give a consistently favorable picture of those who are paying for it, and a newspaper which because of its historic position in the community is under an obligation to speak only the truth.[23]

There are, of course, other forces working for the general cultural elevation of the society. There is a public library service under the able directorship of Enid Baa that only wants more generous financial support from the legislature to improve on the job it is already doing. Every visiting scholar to the islands knows that the von Scholten collection of historical documents in the main St. Thomas library is one of the best in the Caribbean, and the library's photoduplication laboratory is excellent.[24] There are the bookshops—mainly established, let it be noted, by imaginative continentals—that serve a tradition started early on by the poet-bookseller Tram Combs; these include Jeltrups, Palm Passage Bookshop, the Ad Lib Center. There was the *Virgin Islands View,* a magazine run by Allen Grammer until his untimely death, which gave Virgin Islanders the best popular critical journalism since perhaps Jarvis. Not the least service the magazine rendered was its regular reprinting of selected chapters from the older writings on the islands: those of Gurney, Thurlow Reed, Taylor, Wenzell Brown, and Jarvis. That in itself was a boon, considering that the local schoolchild has had to learn about his own society largely from mediocre books such as Anderson's *Up and Down in the Virgin Islands* and Child's *Our Virgin Islands.* There is, finally, the work being done by the Virgin Islands Council on the Arts, in which valiant contributions have been made by native and continental alike, such as the St. Croix pianist and composer Stephen Bostic and the former corporation executive Byron Case. For all of its temptation

22. John Simon, in Sunday Magazine, *San Juan Star,* Jan. 7, 1968.

23. Editorial, *Daily News,* Jan. 19, 1968.

24. St. Thomas Public Library, *Micro-Film Catalogue 1967* (St. Thomas: Bureau of Libraries and Museums, Department of Education, 1967). This sort of work on the part of the Virgin Islands library staff is carrying on the earlier tradition of the federal government agencies. See, for example, *Bibliography of the Virgin Islands of the United States,* ed. Charles F. Reid (New York: H. W. Wilson, 1941). This outstanding bibliography was begun as a Works Project Administration project under the original sponsorship of Mayor LaGuardia and was later transferred to the federal government, with general responsibility being placed in the hands of Dr. Rupert Emerson, then director of the Division of Territories and Island Possessions in the Department of the Interior. For the later work, see Enid M. Baa, "Development of Public Libraries in the Virgin Islands," Focus Magazine, *Home Journal,* Jan. 17, 1971.

at times to preserve the merely archaic in the song and dance traditions, the Council has been a forceful instrument in the forging of a new relationship between the government, the public, and the arts.

The background to all this is characteristically Caribbean. Like all other colonial societies in the region the Virgins were a mimic society, copying the worst features and denied the best of its respective metropolitan cultures, Danish and then American. In Père Labat's sharp phrase, everything was imported into the West Indies except books. The resultant anti-intellectualism is the legacy with which the contemporary society, seeking its own unique identity, must perforce deal. Within the framework of that general condition, even so, each individual island sustained its own peculiar experience. In the case of the Virgins, the peculiarity was especially marked.

Because, to begin with, the Virgins were the entrepôt center of the Antillean mercantile colonial system, they were part of a multilateral rather than simply a bilateral system. One outcome of that was the multilingual virtuosity of the ordinary Virgin Islander, which caught the attention of every traveler to St. Thomas and St. Croix. Up until the early twentieth century, apparently, it was not unusual to meet a hotel clerk or a wharf worker who spoke English, French, and Spanish with equal ease. Yet that gift has obviously declined as the connections of the island populations have become narrower, restricted more and more to the United States and the English-speaking northeastern Antillean area (including even Dutch Saba and Dutch/French St. Maarten). The linguistic isolation that this has led to is not unlike the isolation which after 1700 converted Barbados from an English-French-speaking plantocracy to its present-day cultural anglophilism; and the cultural loss has been equally severe in both cases. The Caribbean is a multilingual region, and to the degree that any one of its island societies loses its multilingual character the capacity to participate meaningfully in a full Caribbean life is thereby impaired.

This is especially ironic in the case of the Virgins since—apart from the multilinguism noted above—the society was markedly successful in the eighteenth and nineteenth centuries in solving the problem of finding a common language, a lingua franca, that could weld all of its disparate elements into a workable communications system. The solution was the rise, after 1750, of the well-known Negro-Dutch-Creole dialect of the slave population. The scholar who made this his special field of study, Pastor Jens Larsen, has told that remarkable story in his book. What is now a dead language constituted, for something like a century and a half or more, a Creole speech giving rise, through the tremendous translation work of both German Moravian and Danish Lutheran cleric-scholars, to its own written literature of church hymnals and Bibles and testifying to a high rate of literacy in the slave population. The Virgin Islander thus discovered very early, as Larsen points out, that his language had some respectability about it and thereby developed, three-quarters of a century before Emancipation, not only the ability to read but also the sense of dignity that came with it.[25] Negro Creole later became the means of awakening a cultural curiosity which only English—with which no Creole dialect could compete—would satisfy. While the Danish Crown was able to encourage the development, through active patronage, of a Creole dialect while resisting the temptation to force Danish on its subject populations, the American republic was unable to do this. Thus the opportunity of doing for the "calypso English" of the modern period what was earlier done for the Negro-Dutch-Creole dialect has been neglected.

The island society still has to build up a flourishing civic life. Too many of its institutions work for their own narrow ends rather than concerning themselves with the wider community. The peevish remark of one local senator, speaking to the St. Thomas Chamber of Commerce, typically expresses the situation: "I've been legislative representative for fourteen years and you've only invited me to speak twice. Yet if I do anything wrong you raise hell." [26] There is reason to believe, however, that the foundation of the College of the Virgin Islands (1963) may make some difference. It is pertinent at this point, then, to discuss the contribution that the college might make in the twin fields of education and communications.

Going back to its origins in the Hollis report of 1958 and the later work of the Virgin Islands College Commission, there can be little doubt that, notwithstanding the attacks of its many local critics, the college has fulfilled a number of needs. Its undergraduate program has helped the school system toward recognition of stricter educational standards. The teacher training program in collaboration with New York University promises a breakthrough—but only a breakthrough—in the vexing problem of recruitment of trained personnel for the schools. The adult education program, in which night classes educate islanders in a large variety of subjects, also strikes a new note, although this scheme was not a part of the original plans for the foundation. The college helps to establish the precedent that it is not always necessary to go abroad in order to

25. Larsen, *Virgin Islands Story*, chaps. 9, 10. See also Henry S. Whitehead, "Negro Dialect of the Virgin Islands," *American Speech*, Vol. VII, no. 3 (February, 1932).
26. Interview, Senator Fritz Lawaetz, March 20, 1968.

receive education. It gives a new status to the teacher as such, in itself a significant thing when it is remembered that, as a recent critical report has pointed out, some 28 per cent of the Department of Education and the school system's staff are administrative personnel, with all of the excessive bureaucratization that that means. The recent innovation of a Caribbean Heritage course indicates a new and welcome reorientation of studies for any student body located within the Caribbean area. At the same time, the presence of the visiting scholar—a political scientist like Roy Macridis or an economic historian like Richard Sheridan—helps the college in its effort to demonstrate exactly what the intellectual life means. Also, as the college holds the conference, the seminar, or the evening public meeting, it becomes a visible symbol of disinterested inquiry into the problems of the society. The resident faculty member likewise begins to compete as an authoritative voice on societal problems with the politician, the newspaper editor, and the bureaucratic head. This is something completely new for the insular, inward-turned society, and it is eminently welcome. Thus the college helps to fulfill one of the many dreams of Jarvis. One day, surely, a Virgin Islander of the stature of Jarvis will be president of the college.

That much having been said, it is hard to withstand much of the criticism of the college, not all of which is by any means the product of spleen on the part of politicians or ex-faculty members. From its very inception the college was conceived by Governor Paiewonsky and his wealthy business friends as a grandiose monument both to his gubernatorial record and to their status as culture-conscious "friends of the Virgin Islands." Because their ambition was so much more political than educative, the college, instead of growing slowly and experimentally as it moved into uncharted seas, was pushed by the governor and his Board of Trustees into overprecipitate growth, and almost on the same principles that Government House pushed tourism or industrialization. Hence the changeover to a four-year college in 1970, which was a gross repudiation of the founding decisions. Hence the planned subsidization of high-school students, many of whom were obviously unfit for collegiate entrance, in order to bring enrollment figures to an appropriately impressive total. Hence the lowering of academic standards in order to attract students—there exists already a small file of bitter statements on this score by one-time faculty members who valiantly refused to give in to that pressure—and the general encouragement on the campus of an atmosphere of tropical euphoria. Criticism yields to a demand for loyalty, best illustrated in the masterly evasive language in which the early interim director tried to explain away the scandalous fact that the college is situated next to the St. Thomas airport, thus creating a terrible noise problem from which no teacher or student can escape: "This will obviously be inconvenient for lecturing professors," he wrote, "but many of them will have come from campuses bisected by major highways, railroads, trolley lines, etc., and I feel sure they will accustom themselves to Caribbean air traffic without great suffering." [27] That spirit of Panglossian optimism, hiding unpleasant facts under the glib rhetoric of the professional educational mind, has played havoc with the ability of Virgin Islanders to recognize the full price they have had to pay for the direction in which the college has been taken.

All this is regrettable, for there is a place in the Virgins, just as in Jamaica or Martinique, for a really indigenous university which will offset the damage done by the imposition of the imperial intellectual tradition on the colonial mind. There are a number of reasons in the Virgins case why the venture has been so disappointing. It has been, to start with, too much a creature of wealthy continental patrons with nothing but their money to commend them. They develop a proprietorial air toward the recipients of their donations, in return for which they get written up in the sycophantic local press as veritable Renaissance Medicis. One such article on the millionaire patron Henry Reichhold, for instance, tries to convert what is patently the self-made businessman into a veritable statesman. Not the least of the damage the patrons wreak is that instead of creating a genuinely Caribbean center of learning they merely re-create the American model, with its premises shaped by yet another wave of continental experts. This situation is summed up in Reichhold's argument that "there is a burgeoning interest in these islands not only among those who live here, but also in numerous departments of the Federal Government, among giant industrial corporations, among major banking interests, among scientists and engineers and among educators." [28] How much the academic side of the college has been sacrificed to these other considerations is illustrated by the bizarre situation in which even its ultimate physical site depends on which group of powerful business interests wins the fiercely conducted battle of the new jetport: the one group, identified with the businessman Isidor Paiewonsky, which wants to expand the present airport lest a new one elsewhere

27. Quoted in Allen Grammer, "C.V.I., Boon or Bust?," *Virgin Islands View*, January, 1967. For the critical reports of the comptroller of the Virgin Islands on the college, see Office of the Comptroller, "Audit Report No. 265–66–98, Accounting Administration, College of the Virgin Islands," mimeographed (St. Thomas, 1966), and "Audit Report No. 266–66–98, Personnel Administration, College of the Virgin Islands," mimeographed (St. Thomas, 1967).

28. Quoted in Roy Gottlieb, Focus Magazine, *Home Journal*, Nov. 5, 1967. For the alleged involvement of Reichhold in charges of graft with relation to city government affairs in New York, see *New York Times*, Jan. 10, 1968.

threaten its business interests in town, or the other group, identified with the former governor and his American hotel syndicate associates, which wants to locate a new super jetport in the lagoon area of eastern St. Thomas, with all the massive despoliation of a remarkable tropical nature preserve that would entail.

There are other forces, too, at work. There is the obsession of the college builders with mere size, what Herman Wouk in his critical memorandum termed both the innate tendency of all bureaucratic structures to expand and the appetite for prestige; these criticisms, it is worth noting, President Wanlass failed to meet in his rejoinder to that memorandum.[29] The hastily arranged conference of scholars on some particular topic, usually presided over by an *eminence grise* from a state-side university, half of whose time during his visit must be consumed in hastily reading up on the nature of his host society, or the appointed faculty member who is there only because he is in search of a viable doctoral topic and, once the topic is exhausted, will disappear to greener pastures—these are not unknown in other Caribbean area universities, but it must be admitted that the College of the Virgin Islands has had more than its fair share of both. Nor is this offset by the official claim that, with some 20 per cent of students being non–Virgin Islanders, the college offers an international cultural flavor of immense significance for the Caribbean. The truth is that most of those "foreign" students come either from the United States or the nearby British West Indian islands, which hardly constitutes a genuinely Caribbean mixture likely to have much fundamental influence on the main body of native students.

Other, more particular difficulties exist. There is a growing dissatisfaction among the student body with the heavy preponderance of continental teaching staff (at least 70 per cent) , some of whom lack empathy with the local scene. Caribbean-oriented courses suffer from meager library resources, for there is nothing in the college library comparable, say, to the Richard Moore collection of Negro history materials at the Centre for the Study of Multi-Racial Societies in Barbados. Granted the short life of the college, it is only natural that a tenure system is just beginning to emerge. There is, too, a fear among the more dedicated faculty members that they are getting the mediocre high-school graduates, while the more talented graduates are going, as before, to stateside institutions. The disgraceful collapse—to use the words of the Wouk memorandum—of the Caribbean Research Institute, set up originally

29. Herman Wouk, memorandum, *Long-Range Future of the College of the Virgin Islands,* reprinted in *Virgin Islands View,* January, 1967; and "The Costs of Higher Education," *President's Newsletter, College of the Virgin Islands,* II, no. 1 (1966) , 1–2.

as a semiautonomous unit of the college, is another example of premature, grandiose schemes ending in near-disaster. The few research publications that the Institute has put out since it really began functioning
in 1965 are mostly action-oriented reports in the areas of geography,
conservation, and oceanography; only one, Norwell Harrigan's analysis
of the social ecology of the British and American Virgin Islands, is in
the social sciences. This output can hardly sustain the bold claim of the
Institute's founders that it would become a vital center for research in
both the natural and social sciences in order to serve the entire Caribbean
area, including both the Antilles and the Caribbean borderlands from
Mexico to the Guianas.

It is only fair to say, however, that in one field the Institute has
been remarkably successful. That is its series of projects, under Dr.
Edward Towle's able directorship, aimed at the conservation of the
natural, historical, and human resources of the Caribbean as a whole.
The Institute takes a frank and bold view of its task here:

> After surviving eons of geologic evolution, hurricanes, floods, drought, tropic
> sun and, in more recent times, five centuries of colonial exploitation, the islands
> of the Caribbean now confront a new kind of hazard, a virtual tidal wave of
> people, spilling out of the continental melting pots, seeking permanent or
> temporary respite from the urban revolution. Drawn by idealized concepts of
> tranquil islands in the sun, this flood-like migration into the Caribbean basin
> is having far-reaching, occasionally promising and potentially disastrous effects
> upon all aspects of island life.[30]

This is no exaggeration. There is, for example, a noticeable absence of
legal protection for historical sites, which are consequently falling prey
to the amateur archaeologist and the souvenir hunter; in similar fashion
marine life succumbs to the scuba diver, sand beaches to dredging and
construction companies, and hilltop silhouettes to housing developments.
The preservation of the environment, natural and historical, has thus
become almost the leading concern of the Institute. The preservation of
the Fort Berg military fortifications at Coral Bay, St. John; the study
of the rare Anegada iguana species; the excavation, in conjunction with
the St. Kitts government, of the submerged seventeenth-century city of
Jamestown off the island of Nevis; a systematic survey of existing legislation in the western hemisphere relating to historic sites, shipwrecks,
and artifact recovery; a master card file on shipwrecks in the Caribbean

30. Quoted in Margaret Zellers Lenci, "A Program to Guard the Treasure that
Gilds the Caribbean," *New York Times*, Nov. 30, 1969, sec. 10. See also Caribbean
Research Institute, College of the Virgin Islands, *Annual Report*, 1969.

area—all these projects illustrate the pioneer work being done. Not the least valuable aspect of the program, perhaps, is its regional frame of reference, helping to emancipate Virgin Islanders from their traditional insularity in at least one field of regional cooperation. To the degree that this aspect of the college develops, it can be a real force for good in the area.

12

~~~

The Machinery
of Government

Like all the Caribbean colonies, the Virgin Islands have been governed by the imported constitutional models of the respective metropolitan centers, first Copenhagen, then Washington. The governmental institutions of the present-day period are thus colonial replicas of those models, with their legal-constitutional framework derived from the major metropolitan enabling acts—the Danish Colonial Law of 1906, the terms of the 1917 transfer, the 1917 Act of the Congress to provide a Temporary Government, the first and second Organic Acts passed by Congress in 1936 and 1954 respectively, and, most recently, the Elective Governor Act of 1968. The highlights of the islands' constitutional development, as shaped by those acts, were essentially four. There was, first, the 1931 transfer of the administration of the islands from the Navy Department to the Department of the Interior; although that transfer was effected by a presidential order and not by statute, it had the important result of facilitating civilian rule in St. Thomas and thereby democratizing, in part, the climate of politics. There was, second, flowing out of that, the 1936 Organic Act, which replaced the old rotten borough system with universal suffrage—the significance of which must be seen in the light of the fact that, remarkably, Congress retained the structure of the Danish colonial system almost intact in its government of the islands for the twenty years between 1917 and 1936. There was, third, the liberalization of the legislative branch by the 1954 Organic Act, which abolished the old separate municipal legislatures of St. Thomas and St. Croix and replaced them with a single legislature, thus facilitating the drive toward unified government. That second Organic Act also defined for the first time the status of the islands as an "unincorporated territory," for it is the astonishing fact that Congress waited some thirty-seven years before making up its mind on that vital matter. Fourth, and finally, the Elective Governor Act replaced the presidentially-appointed chief executive with a locally-elected governor, with all the tremendous implications for the democratization of the executive branch which that change carries.

The institutions—executive, legislative, and judicial—that govern Virgin Islanders today have emerged from these changes. They are the constitutional dress that clothes the spirit in which they function. (The character of that spirit, which really means the character of local politics, requires separate treatment; see Chapter 13.) They are also forms that reflect, in their limitations, the historic status of the islands as a colonial territory, that is, the peculiar creature of federal discretion as that discretion has been mirrored in the policies adopted by the relevant congressional committees and administrative agencies that have had to deal with the islands. That, in essence, constitutes the problem of political status (which also requires separate treatment; see Chapter 14). In a quite special sense, the discussion of Virgin Islands governmental institutions cannot be divorced from the discussion of local politics and of constitutional status. The three areas are inextricably bound up with one another.

There are two general points worth emphasizing by way of prelude. First, changes in the organizational powers and governmental structure of the island territories have traditionally emanated from the federal legislative and executive institutions. But the establishment in 1964 of a local Constitutional Convention, composed of delegates chosen by popular vote in the elections of that year, marked a turning point, and the report of that convention, although by no means a radical document, at least gave notice that initiative, if not final policy, had shifted to the Caribbean end of the federal-territorial axis.[1] The terms of the debate on institutions—the office of the governor, reapportionment of legislative districts, the question of a resident commissioner, and so on—will now increasingly be set by what Virgin Islanders want, not by what Congress thinks they ought to want. What this change means can perhaps be appreciated from the fact that whereas in the 1920s congressional committees could consider, with impunity, a proposal to transfer the islands to the gubernatorial jurisdiction of Puerto Rico (the old colonial game of using the outlying possessions as pawns on the metropolitan political chessboard), in the 1970s such arbitrary treatment is impossible, as was

1. "Proceedings of the Constitutional Convention of the Virgin Islands," December 7, 1964, to February 27, 1965, mimeographed (St. Thomas, 1965). The Convention adopted a draft for a revised Organic Act, pp. 246–67.

shown by the quick dispatch given the suggestion a few years ago that the islands be attached in county status to the state of Florida.

The second general point to underline is that, although still in dependent status to congressional government, the islands over the years have gradually acquired a wide ambit of internal autonomy. Congress has developed a "hands off" policy in an increasing number of areas. In the executive branch, for example, Governor Pearson was effectively removed by means of the Tydings Committee investigation of 1935. But it is doubtful if Governor Paiewonsky could have been similarly removed in the 1960s, even though a comparable congressional investigation in 1967 was in fact made of the irregularities of the 1966 election in the islands. In the legislative branch, likewise, the same investigation, although noting with some acidity those irregularities, as well as the attempt of the local ruling political group to institute grossly political control of the strategic Boards of Elections, at the same time revealed a marked reluctance to intervene, using as its excuse the fact that such practices were inevitable in the traditional American type of patronage politics, where the spoils go to the "ins" and the grievances to the "outs."

This permissive attitude can be interpreted in different ways. It can be seen as a genuine liberalism on the part of Congress and the relevant federal agencies, promoting the art of self-government in the islanders by insisting that they find their own solutions to their own problems. Or it can be seen as the end result of habitual indifference on the part of Congress and agencies alike. Certainly, there were members of the 1967 investigation by the Subcommittee on Territorial and Insular Affairs who saw it the latter way. The Department of the Interior officialdom, those critics felt, had tended to treat the Virgin Islands too indulgently, and this attitude had been encouraged by the failure of the relevant congressional committees to be sufficiently vigilant in their demands upon that officialdom.[2] Congressman Morton's angry questioning of the leading officials of the Department of Labor and the Office of Territories of the Department of the Interior over their signal failure to intervene in any real way on behalf of the defenseless alien worker in the island economy brought out the fact that all the glib rhetoric about self-government for the islanders really amounts to the withdrawal of federal protection from a group of people for whom the local political leadership has shown, at least up to now, very little sympathy.[3] There is, obviously, a real dilemma here. Yet the point to be made at this

2. U.S., Congress, House, Subcommittee on Territorial and Insular Affairs, *Election of Virgin Islands Governor: Hearings,* 90th Cong., 1st sess., 1967, pt. 1, pp. 342–45, 381.

3. *Ibid.,* pt. 2, pp. 680–700.

juncture is that the federal policies, whether construed as liberalism or neglect, have had the effect of placing upon the Virgin Islanders an ever increasing responsibility of coming up with their own answers to the problems that beset their society. The machinery of insular government reflects that development.

The office of the governor as a presidentially-nominated colonial administrator was terminated, of course, with the final passage of the Elective Governor Act. But the basic characteristics of the office have naturally been shaped by the long experience (1917–70) of the appointed executives, and especially by the unique experience of the Paiewonsky administration between 1961 and 1969. The powers, duties, and functions of the office in fact have remained substantially unchanged throughout the years: the executive order of 1931 retained by implication all the statutory powers and duties of the earlier 1917 legislation, as did the 1936 Organic Act, while the Elective Governor Act in the main altered only the mechanism of appointment. The last of the appointed governors—Dr. Melvin Evans (1969–70)—was, looking at the matter from this viewpoint, as much a presidential creature as the first of them, Rear Admiral James Oliver. As the governorship thus enters its new phase it is important to remember that much of its character has been shaped by the earlier experience.

Within the framework of that subjugative character—the fact that all the governors served at the pleasure of the president and were under the supervision of a cabinet officer in Washington—there did occur, of course, substantial changes in the office over the years. The transfer to civilian rule in 1931 meant the replacement of the naval-type governor with the civilian-type governor; that is, a generally autocratic chief executive, bound by naval tradition and discipline, allowed great scope of authority by the Navy Department and serving a relatively short term, was replaced by a generally more liberal civilian chief, usually possessed of a wider social and political background and staying long enough in Government House to cultivate a deeper interest in the colony and its people. The former was limited only by the 1917 congressional statute; the latter was more severely limited by the Organic Acts, which introduced, if only implicitly, the separation of powers doctrine into the situation. Under the naval administration, governors on the whole exercised powers only in the context of a concern for immediate matters such as public health, sanitation, and education; under the civilian administration of the Interior Department, the individual governor, frequently pressed by his Washington bosses, was more and more obliged to concern himself with the broader socioeconomic needs of the islands. With the passage of the 1936 Organic Act the governor was also increasingly subjected to the pressures of local legislative leaders and political groups. In brief, there occurred during this period a structural transformation of the office; it changed from that of a colonial administrator invested with all the necessary military, civil, and judicial powers pertinent to the operation of a newly acquired naval base to that of a second-string civilian executive, operating within the regulatory guidelines of the national constitutional system. Successive governors, although legally still accountable only to the president and the secretary of the interior, felt increasingly obliged to acknowledge an accountability, not yet stated in statutory language, to the local public electorate. So much was this the case that when Mr. Paiewonsky came up for senatorial confirmation as President Kennedy's gubernatorial choice in 1961 he and his friends clearly felt that the best argument in his favor was that, although an eminently successful and wealthy businessman, he commanded overwhelming support from the mass of the low-income groups in the islands.[4] Those hearings also made it clear that any successful candidate for the post would henceforth have to possess the enthusiastic support of most of the leading local politicians—as, of course, Paiewonsky did at that time.

For the decade of his power, then, Governor Paiewonsky left his mark on the office as surely as did Muñoz in the case of the Puerto Rican governorship. Even his bitterest critics conceded that he brought to it zest, energy, and the social idealism for which his family had long been noted. He was his own man, seeing himself as carrying the full power of presidentially-delegated authority, and his peremptory dismissal of the grossly presumptive proposition of a local newspaper editor that both of them should share the power, as terms of a private arrangement, established that fact at the outset.[5] He managed to exact some degree of recognition from the body of state governors, a demonstration of that fact being his treatment at the State Governors' Conference held in St. Thomas in 1967. That, of course, was far short of being accepted as a political or constitutional equal, for he was neither popularly elected nor did he, by virtue of his office, participate in the national elections. He achieved an efficient and cohesive relationship between the executive and legislative branches, something no other governor had been able to do. He brought flair and polish to Government House (Herman Wouk is said to have helped write some of his early speeches). Work processes

4. Senate, Committee on Interior and Insular Affairs, *Nomination for Governor of the Virgin Islands: Hearings,* 87th Cong., 1st sess., 1961, pp. 53–55, 114–16.
5. *Election of Virgin Islands Governor,* pt. 2, pp. 494–95.

were immeasurably speeded up; indeed, the governor made the telephone an instrument of executive generalship long before President Lyndon Johnson did so. In brief, he converted the office from an amateur to a professional entity. That, of course, was due in large part to the fact that he was a professional politician. Having been both a leading member of the old local Council between 1936 and 1946 and a national committee-man for twenty years in the Democratic Party, he was in truth a regular Democratic *politico* in a way that Pearson and Hastie were not, and he put his understanding of the Washington scene and his vast network of personal relationships with stateside politicians into the service of the governorship. By the time that he stepped down in 1969 the governor-ship was in fact a positive executive post, albeit restricted by the fact that it still remained a nominated one. The Elective Governor Act merely constituted legal ratification of the fact.

Paiewonsky's achievement was based on the clever marriage of busi-ness and politics, for he brought at least two characteristics of his business self into the new post. First, it was pretty much a one-man show, almost as if he thought that he might run Government House as he had run the family business on Main Street. He rarely allowed departments to function without his direction; even more rarely was he willing to delegate authority. The exasperated observations of a local reporter illustrated the unfortunate consequences of this excessive centralization in the decision-making process: "Mrs. Blake said I had to see Mr. Berry-man. Mr. Berryman said I had to see the Governor. I haven't seen him for fear he'd say I had to see God." [6] This monarchical character of the office was further reflected in the fact that there were no cabinet meetings as such, but only individual meetings of commissioners with the governor or, occasionally, large conferences on particular issues.[7] In the second place, the governor brought with him the businessman's flair for effective and costly advertising. A Public Relations Office was set up, under the guidance of successive stateside newspapermen or public relations special-ists, to project the image of the government; it operated on the principle, as one of those directors put it, that "thousands of stories mean thousands of tourists" and that "millions of words mean millions of dollars" to the islands. Vast sums, comparatively speaking, were used to finance promotional gimmicks like the Virgin Islands exhibit at the Caribbean Pavilion of the New York World's Fair, despite the fact that only a few businesses from Puerto Rico and the government of the Dominican Republic elected to take a chance with the hazards of such investment,

6. Bill Frank, in *Daily News*, Feb. 1, 1964.
7. Interview, Louis Shulterbrandt, assistant to the governor, March 22, 1968.

hazards which the Virgin Islands government did in fact encounter.[8] It is suggestive that one of the largest items of the 1964 audit of the governor's office included a payment of some $38,000 to a Puerto Rican public relations consultant firm.[9] The paraphernalia of promotional advertising that accompanied the semicentennial celebrations and the Governors' Conference in 1967 portrayed a governmental regime assiduously milking every ounce of publicity value out of its activities. The results of all this were (1) an increasing rate of mobility of personnel between the business sector and government service, and (2) a new degree of professionalism in government as a whole. With reference to the latter point, it would certainly have been difficult by 1969 for Governor Paiewonsky to tell the sort of story that his predecessors could tell about the small-island, amateurish character of the governor's job, such as Governor Merwin's quaint account of being awakened in the middle of the night by a telephone operator to be informed, vaguely, that there was a fire somewhere in town.[10] Yet there are many Virgin Islanders who feel that as Government House has become more sophisticated it has also become more remote.

Be that as it may, the office is certainly one of the busiest under the American flag. A typical day will find the governor making arrangements for setting up a new press bureau in St. Croix, organizing the swearing-in ceremonies for administrators for St. Croix and St. John (appointed by the governor), discussing the federal Headstart program with his educational advisers, deciding whether to receive a delegation of protesting hotel people angry at yet another cutoff in the water supply, looking at reports on population pressure or alien problems, signing a bill to permit taxis the use of bus stops, discussing the next legislative session with his aides, and all the while in constant telephone contact with Washington regarding, say, proposed legislation likely to affect Virgin Islands interests. Added to that sort of daily agenda there are other accumulating duties and obligations. There are speeches to give: to the local Chambers of Commerce, at the graduation ceremonies of the college, at the local churches when any of them celebrates a historic anniversary, and sometimes to the San Juan Press Club. There are receptions for visiting dignitaries, not an insignificant chore considering that the islands have

8. Office of the Comptroller, "Audit Report No. 176-64-70, Department of Commerce, Virgin Islands Exhibit at Caribbean Pavilion of New York World's Fair, 1964," mimeographed (St. Thomas, May 10, 1965).

9. Office of the Comptroller, "Audit Report No. 149-64-99, Professional and Consulting Services, Government of the Virgin Islands, 1958–1964," mimeographed (St. Thomas, August 27, 1964), Schedule A-2, p. 16.

10. *Election of Virgin Islands Governor,* pt. 1, pp. 239–40.

become a favorite vacation spot for stateside politicians seeking a rest after a grueling political campaign. There are special functions at Government House; at one such function Governor Paiewonsky received a gift of the original desk set used by Governor von Scholten in signing the Emancipation Proclamation of 1848. There is, again, always a political public relations image to protect (Governor Paiewonsky once wrote a letter to the *San Juan Star* protesting the alleged inaccuracies of the report of an interview held with him). Governor Evans, in turn, has become adept at the television address, adroitly putting the bed-side manner of the professional medical man to new use. All in all, these two governors have taken a positive view of the office, pushing to the outer limits of active interpretation all of the powers vested in them by both the local statute book and the federal directives.

In one way, it might be argued, all this has produced an American-style chief executive. That, in part, is true. The powers conferred on the office by the various acts of 1936, 1954, and 1968 correspond in large measure to those enjoyed by the typical state governor. They include, among much else, general supervision and control of all executive and administrative departments; the power of pardon and reprieve; the power to commission all officers he is authorized to appoint; the authority to introduce bills in the legislature and to attend or depute another to represent him at legislative meetings; the power to call on naval and military commanders to help in occasions of invasion, insurrection, or rebellion; the general obligation to execute federal laws applicable to the islands; and so on. The office has acquired all of the statutory trappings of a state chief executive. Politically, too, it has become similar to the typical state courthouse in the sense that Governor Paiewonsky replaced the old political neutrality and aloofness of his predecessors with a full-fledged political identity, becoming openly recognized as a leading chieftain in the ruling Unity Party and getting deeply involved with that group in a legislative-executive partnership. Governor Evans has become similarly involved since 1970 with his territorial Republican Party.

Yet it would be palpably erroneous to see the office as this and nothing else. For there were, and still are, markedly emphatic peculiarities and eccentricities about the office that spring from both the colonial relationship with Washington and the special conditions of local island life. The colonial ingredient, to begin with, imposed a peculiar personality on the office. As Adolf Berle told a congressional committee as far back as 1926, the islands hang to the United States by a slender thread and the appointed governor is therefore the only connection, as distinct from a merely local legislature, they have with their ultimate government in the United States. He is cherished, then, as an inestimably valued lifeline to the "mother country." [11] Yet at the same time there resided a fatal contradiction in that status, for the appointed governor was both the delegated representative of federal interests and the custodian of local territorial interests. He was the one by virtue of being appointed by the president and organizationally accountable to the secretary of the interior. He was the other by virtue of the fact that after 1961 the Interior Department policy became one of giving larger scope to internal self-government and more autonomous decision-making to the dependent territories, or in the words of an important speech by the assistant secretary of the Department, the adoption of a self-denying ordinance, a commitment to restraint, a desire to prevent oversolicitous guardianship.[12] It is painfully clear, however, that the appointed governor was never able to establish a happy medium between those two conflicting loyalties. Governor Paiewonsky's own description of the various ways in which his administration sought the guidance of federal expertise makes it clear that St. Thomas was always willing to consult Washington in important matters.[13] When real differences of opinion arose, on the vexatious questions of water pollution and the alien problem, for example, the governor was caught between his dual obligations. The differences dramatized the fact that, as a colonial governor, he was the servant of two masters. He was thus driven into a situation where he had to walk a sort of tightrope. To lean too heavily toward the federal side was to invite the charge by his local enemies of sacrificing local interests. To lean too heavily toward the native side was to be told by his Washington superiors—and there is a wealth of public correspondence to illustrate this—that he was forgetting his obligations as a federal public servant. He was driven to the strategy of delicately pushing the federal officials on each issue as it arose to see how far they were willing to let him go. That, in turn, depended on the degree of liberalism or conservatism on the part of the particular federal administrators involved. Certainly, not every director of territories was as able and liberal as the distinguished scholar Rupert Emerson, who was the first occupant of that post.

There are special conditions of island life that add to the gubernatorial burden. The governor, to begin with, must run a machine in triplicate, since all services must be repeated for each separate island entity, with all the expense which that involves. The governor, in effect,

11. House, Committee on Insular Affairs, Subcommittee, *The Virgin Islands: Hearing*, testimony of A. A. Berle, 69th Cong., 1st sess., 1926, pt. 2, p. 72.

12. *Election of Virgin Islands Governor*, pt. 2, pp. 676–80.

13. *Ibid.*, pp. 497–98.

is running three separate governments, two major and one minor (in St. John), unified under one control. More than that, however, he is running a machine that is astonishingly centralized, even monolithic in character. Ever since 1954, when the Organic Act brought together the islands for the very first time as a unified whole, every level of government has become increasingly concentrated into, as it were, a concentric web with the nerve center in Government House in Charlotte Amalie. Virgin Islanders are, of course, denied the congressional or the presidential vote. But even more unfortunately, they are also denied any real voting power in the structure of local government, since there is, in effect, no local government structure below the executive-legislative level. All board, commission, and authority members are appointed by the governor with legislative consent, with the result (as the members of the visiting congressional committee of 1967 discovered to their astonishment) that the Virgin Islands is the only governmental entity in the entire United States whose citizens do not enjoy a measure of local democracy through their power to regularly elect the members of the various boards— education, planning, tax, public utilities, and so on—that control so much of their daily life. It has been urged, in defense of this situation, that administrative efficiency is thus facilitated. It would be more correct to argue, on the evidence, that it has led to a patronage system in which, contrary to the American idea of local government, most boards are composed of a majority of government employees who owe both their livelihood and their board membership to the administration. Congressman Morton wisely observed:

> I think the gap in the democratic process in the Virgin Islands is not the question of whether the Governor is elected or not. It lies in the question of whether there are elected officials at a low enough level so that the people can do business with them on a day-to-day basis.

He added:

> There has to be a degree of inaccessibility of a high government official, the Governor, for example, and members of his immediate official family. But in the counties and in the States and in the municipal governments, throughout the country, there are elected officials who are very responsive to the constituency. I am speaking of aldermen, city councilmen, county commissioners, registers of wills, people in the courthouse organization who are elected and do have this real sense of responsiveness to these people.[14]

There is much to be said, then, in favor of a reform, already accepted in principle by the local legislature, which would add to the number of

14. *Ibid.*, pp. 566, 584.

popularly elected officers in the government—possibly three island administrators, or three city mayors—who would take over housekeeping duties from the central government. It is worth noting that a new Board of Education, based on the elective principle, is already in operation, as well as Boards of Elections for St. Croix and St. Thomas–St. John, with three seats going to independent candidates on the latter board in the 1968 election: a refreshing sign.

The absence of local democracy clearly calls for a real broadening of the elective base of political life in the islands. This could, of course, lead, as some of the local witnesses told the 1967 committee, to administrative fragmentation and possibly to a return to the parochial island feelings, so inimical to the growth of a unified Virgin Islands national identity, that characterized the period before 1954. There is room for argument here, and a compromise has to be reached between the rival considerations of local accountability and administrative tidiness. But the point to be emphasized here is that, in the absence of a broad elective base, the office of the governor performs all the functions of a state and local character as well as those of a federal character. He is expected to be almost literally everything: governor, mayor, county commissioner, chief of police. Admittedly, he receives support from loyal friends in all those three areas: from local party ward heelers, from his legislative majority, from his many friends in Washington. But, by the same token, he also receives pressures from the same areas: from civic groups and discontented citizens, from the legislative minority group, from independent congressmen, as well as from congressmen whose constituents visit or reside in the islands. It is, on any showing, a massively overworked office.

This, then, was the office of the governor as it was on the eve of the passage of the Elective Governor Act. It is pertinent to ask how that act will affect the future development of the office. To begin with, it will end the dualism of loyalties, at least in its most acute form. The elected governor will be first and foremost the servant of his new electorate, owing his primary allegiance to it. He will be able to speak more confidently to the federal authority from that stance, and to take a firmer stand when there are quarrels with that authority. Congressman Carey put the point graphically in his discussion of the minimum wage dispute. "I suspect," he observed, "on the observation the gentleman has made about the elected Governor, one of the reasons is that if Governor Paiewonsky were to get tough with the Secretary of Labor, he would be told to go take a jump in the bay. But if he were a Governor elected by the people, he would do something or he would not be elected

Governor any more."[15] The submerged discontent, long harbored, over not being able to elect the man in Government House will curb the temptation to blame Washington for everything. At the same time, it will be redirected against the elected head of state, who will then be obliged to reorganize his sense of priorities. In a somewhat different way, the change will also transform his political aspect. Much of the local political discontent over the years has been traceable to a feeling that, constitutionally, an appointed governor should be a nonpartisan and impartial agent, in the mold of the governor in the old British crown colony system, and that Governor Paiewonsky had grossly violated that rule, especially in his unashamedly political activities at the time of the 1966 election. As an elected governor, the successful candidate will no longer be inhibited by those considerations. He will become both chief of state and titular leader of his chosen political party.

The changeover will also mark a pause in activities on the federal level. The elected governor will have less to do with his federal duties, and more to do with his state and municipal duties, hitherto much neglected. The islands will thus finally terminate their historic connection with the Department of the Interior. There will remain, of course, residual federal powers untouched by the elective governorship: the application of federal laws to the islands, the question of the control of federal matching funds, the problem of security, the responsibilities attaching to federal property, the continuing obligations of the relevant federal regulatory agencies, and so on. All of these are matters that relate intimately to the larger question of political status. It suffices to say here, perhaps, that for the sake of clarity they might in the long run necessitate the drafting of a federal relations statute comparable to the statute that seeks in the Puerto Rican case (1952) to draw defining lines between the ambit of federal authority and that of local commonwealth authority. It is certain, for example, that the present system of constant interchange between the federal establishment and the local government on matters such as the management of federally-owned submerged lands in the islands or the regulatory duties of the Civil Aeronautics Board will remain as a permanent feature of the relationship.

There is one final aspect of the governorship worth looking at. Since the man makes the office as much as the office makes the man, it is of some interest to note the occupational background of the men who filled the local gubernatorial post throughout the appointive period. Pearson, Cramer, and Hastie were all college professors, but only Cramer was in the field of government. Harwood was a retired judge; de Castro was a

15. *Ibid.*, p. 698.

seasoned administrator; Alexander was a businessman-engineer; Gordon and Merwin were practicing lawyers; Paiewonsky was a businessman; while the last of the appointed governors, Evans (1969–70), was a professional medical man. Without minimizing the individual gifts of these governors, it is fair to say, generally, that there was nothing special or unique in their training or knowledge which singled them out as public administrators, with the exceptions of de Castro, who had spent a sizable part of his life in that field, and Cramer, who had an academic background in it. Only three of them had been actively engaged in politics at the time of their appointment. Speaking, then, of the majority of the appointees, whatever they came to know about administering the Virgin Islands government they learned after taking office. General knowledge of the area, as distinct from particular knowledge of local government, was of course a different matter. Hastie was perhaps the first appointee (1946) who had a prior knowledge of the area, acquired in his capacity earlier on as assistant solicitor in the Interior Department and as a federal district judge. After him, all of the native appointees, by their very nature, came armed with such knowledge. None of them, it is perhaps safe to say, were great governors in the style of colonial governors elsewhere in the Caribbean, such as Olivier in Jamaica, Lethem in British Guiana, and Tugwell in Puerto Rico. Pearson and Hastie were perhaps the most liberal. But both of them ran aground on the rocks of the general truth that, reacting against the peculiar pressures of a colonial situation, the liberal at home becomes a conservative abroad. Paiewonsky brought to the office all of the genius of the able business-manager type. But his vision of the general good was limited by his assumption, as a businessman, that what was good for business was good for the Virgin Islands. It has taken a governor like Dr. Evans, trained in the public health service tradition, to insist that indiscriminate "development" along business lines can at times run counter to the general good.

There are two other offices peculiar to the old machinery of government—those of the government comptroller and the government secretary —that merit a special note. Although both were modified by the Elective Governor Act, they throw an interesting light on the special peculiarities of that machinery.

The office of the comptroller was established by the Revised Organic Act of 1954; its occupant was appointed for a ten-year term by the secretary of the interior, was organizationally accountable to him, and was invested with the general responsibility of inspecting and auditing the entire financial operations of the territorial government. It was a controversial appointment from the beginning. Along with the governor, the comptroller personified the sovereign power of the federal government; he was immune to local control, yet possessed authority to enter into practically all departmental operations of the local government, granted the fact that there is hardly a single administrative enterprise of any department that does not carry an element of federal matching funds at some point; while the length of his appointed term and the statutory definition of responsibility that covered his appointment conspired to make him in reality a semiautonomous official. It is hardly surprising that from the outset the office was highly unpopular.

There can be little doubt, at the same time, of its enormous value. The various reports put out by the comptroller's office demonstrate how its function as watchdog helped to pinpoint the weaknesses and irregularities of a governmental machine not always too careful in its fiscal-administrative processes. Over a period of time those reports exposed the expensive experiment of the Altona housing project as based on an unwise physical location and poor engineering; noted the vast increase in governmental personnel without any appreciable improvement in the general infrastructure of the public services operated by the relevant departments; unearthed the minor scandal in which the Industrial Incentive Board granted more than a million dollars in tax subsidies to a Milwaukee publisher who did little more than proofread articles for his feature magazine from his St. Croix mansion; criticized the predilection of the government's departments for hiring outside professional consultant firms for costly services which could frequently have been gained by utilizing skills available within the federal government; took the College of the Virgin Islands to task for accepting responsibility for the payment of the moving expenses of a faculty member who was taken over from one of the local departments when the legal obligation belonged to the first employer; noted the deficient standards of the physical facilities offered by the St. Thomas Park Authority in the Magens Bay area; and commented on the widespread habit of paying salaries beyond the statutory schedules of the payrolls of the Department of Education. The examining process itself served an important function. Once the report was forwarded to the appropriate department and to the governor's office—but only after all significant findings of the preliminary investigation had been discussed with the personnel involved in the particular operation—a conference was usually held with the head of the department or agency audited; after this a period of forty-five days was allowed for the government to research the audit findings and make their comments as to agreement or disagreement and as to action which would be taken. The entire process, in brief, was a combination of a bookkeeping-auditing role and a management audit. It kept departmental officials on their toes. The findings were invariably widely publicized in the local press, and the governor was frequently obliged to issue statements.on matters which otherwise, with inevitable detriment to the democratic process, might never have been raised.[16]

Even so, the termination of the office and its replacement with a comptroller who will act only as an external auditor of the transactions of the territorial government, in recognition of the continuing federal interest because of direct and indirect federal financial contributions, is long overdue. The office was born of Senator Butler's effort of 1954 to curb the area of Virgin Islands self-government by means of the limitations that were placed at that time upon both the amounts and the purposes of the territorial share of matching funds, as well as the stipulation that those amounts and purposes be approved by the president or his designated representative. The entire exercise was based on the general argument that the special financial relationships between the federal and local governments justified an extra-special federal supervision of territorial spending. Yet, as Professor Friedrich pointed out in his advisory memorandum of 1957, the argument, in all of its detail, was eminently fallacious. It was argued (1) that the return of the federal income tax to the island justified the position taken by the Butler committee. The answer, briefly, is that if the historic principle of no taxation without representation is invoked, the federal income tax ought not in fact to be locally levied at all; and if it is levied it can only be considered a matter of administrative convenience, certainly in no way as a form of federal support for the islands. It was argued (2) that the return of federal internal revenue to the local treasury, mainly on rum sales, also justified the position. The answer, there, is that just as in the case of Puerto Rico the return of such revenue is justified on the grounds of the unusually low per capita income of both of the offshore territories; indeed, the return of the revenue could be seen in one way as merely comparable to the federal subventions to mainland farmers as another low-income group deserving of special treatment. It was argued (3) that the federal grants-in-aid justified the thesis identified with the figure of Senator Butler. The answer to that argument, of course, is that the grant-in-aid program applies to all the states of the union, and is not peculiar to the Virgin Islands; it is based increasingly on the idea that more and more aspects of American life are national, not local or regional, in character, and that the federal government

16. See, on all this, *ibid.*, testimony of Peter Bove, comptroller, pt. 2, pp. 625–73.

thereby possesses a substantial partnership interest in the multitudinous programs set up to meet the problems. The argument, altogether, fatally misapprehends the special character of the federal state in American life. There is hardly anything uniquely favorable to the Virgin Islands in the fiscal relationship with Washington that justifies the continuation of a comptroller's office such as that conceived in 1954.[17] Whether the successor-office will be best served by an officer to be appointed as before by the secretary of the interior, as recommended by the Interior Department officials in the 1967 hearings, or by the elected governor, as recommended by the 1965 Constitutional Convention, remains to be seen. The first method has in fact subsequently been adopted. But both recommendations, it is worth noting, violate the seminal principle that auditing and related financial controls should be removed from the control of those administrative officials whose activities are being thus supervised.

The office of the government secretary, before its supersession by the office of lieutenant governor in the Elective Governor Act, stood for fifty-odd years (like the mission centers of the old *Camino Real* in southern California) as testimony to the American ability, in odd fits of uncharacteristic eccentricity, to retain and absorb pieces of institutional furniture inherited from colonized political cultures. Taken over from the Danish system, the office of government secretary was incorporated almost unaltered into the American governmental structure, where it stood out as a curious anomaly. Not unlike the office of the colonial secretary in the old British crown colony regime, it carried more independence and prestige than the title suggests. The very fact that its occupant was appointed directly by the president, with the recommendation of the secretary of the interior, made him in effect a second governor; in fact, he was by law acting governor during the absence of the governor. No consultation with the local governor about the appointment was required, and in many cases none took place. Inevitably, then, the secretary was in the majority of cases unpopular with both the governor and the legislature. He made his reports directly to Washington in the early days; in the later period reports were transmitted to the governor. Some of the long-term vendettas between governor and government secretary have become legendary; that between Governor

17. Carl J. Friedrich, "Report to the Organic Act Commission of the Virgin Islands Legislature on Five Proposals for the Amendment of the Organic Act, with Reasons," mimeographed (Cambridge, Mass.: Harvard University, March 1, 1957).

Harwood and Robert Morss Lovett and that between Governor Paiewonsky and Cyril King are perhaps the best known in island political
lore.

In its scope and functions the office was a veritable Dickensian
Circumlocution Office. Both Robert Herrick and Lovett, as they described
it over thirty years ago, were hard put to discover any clear rationale
of the duties imposed on them. Herrick (under Cramer's governorship)
had to deal with, among other things, problems of smuggling, the school
system, the representation of government in the old Council, discussions
of a new bank with Washington officials, and the perusal of budget
proposals. "Mine," summed up Herrick, "is a curious Danish office, a
catch-all, a Secretary of State for Lilliput." Lovett found himself a general
factotum in social welfare matters, dealing, among much else, with
problems of stateless Virgin Islanders left out of the citizenship arrangements of 1917, the need for a new school law, eradication of tick fever,
discussions with Antiguan authorities on problems of illegal entry, cooperation with the Civilian Conservation Corps in the opening up of
subterranean water resources on the islands, and the handling of father-
less children. Later, new functions were added by the 1954 Organic Act
and the Virgin Islands Code, so that in its last years the office was
responsible for some aspects of practically every phase of local business
activity: corporations, licensing, banking, real property assessment and
taxation, insurance, recording of documents, passports, trademarks and
patents, and control of alcohol. In all of his various official personalities—
administrator of the Uniform Commercial Code, commissioner of insurance, registrar of trademarks, chairman of the Banking Board—the
secretary had to assess and collect all filing fees, franchise taxes, and
so on, prescribed by the Virgin Islands Code. It would be difficult to
imagine a governmental office that gathered together under one roof
such a bewildering collection of oddly assorted legislative, administrative,
and judicial duties, and thereby constituting such a gross violation of
the separation of powers doctrine. It was hardly surprising that it drew
upon itself the jealousy of both the executive and legislative branches.
Inescapably, then, it was replaced by the office of lieutenant governor
in the Elective Governor Act. Yet that change, bringing the situation
more into line with standard American practice in the individual states,
may only replace one built-in structural conflict with another—the
political rivalry between governor and lieutenant governor so characteristic of much of state politics. It is at least worth putting on record that
a single dissenting vote in the 1965 Constitutional Convention, that of
its secretary, Warren Brown, was cast against the acceptance of the

(309)

lieutenant governorship on the ground that it would set up, in his phrase, a two-governor situation.[18]

The legislative branch, like legislatures everywhere in the colonial situation, has always played a secondary role in the islands. It can indeed be argued that the legislature under the Danish regime, although placed in that secondary role, at the same time enjoyed a prestige and certainly powers which were later denied to it under the American regime. Thus, although the 1936 Organic Act gave it for the first time a really popular electoral base, the 1954 Organic Act placed a new limitation upon the right of the voter to vote for all of the members at large, a limitation not abolished by Congress until 1966; and an island official as respectable as Attorney James Bough has opined that Senator Butler's main reason for enacting the limitation in 1954 was to insure minority representation, which actually meant a racist-minded consideration for the white continental group.[19] It was equally late in the day that Congress finally granted the legislature the right to fix the salary rates of its own members.

As presently constituted, the legislature is a unicameral body of fifteen members, who are elected to two-year terms. It derives its main powers and duties from the 1954 act; this situation will continue until Congress decides to write the third Organic Act for the territory, which might include some of the reforms recommended by the 1965 Constitutional Convention. As from 1967, the legislature works through eleven standing committees. Following American state practice, vacancies are filled through appointment by the governor, who also possesses the authority to call special sessions. A two-thirds vote of the legislature is necessary to override his objections to legislation. The 1968 Elective Governor Act also grants to the legislature the right to initiate a referendum election for the purpose of removing the governor from office.

Being unicameral, the Senate has no other house to compete with for attention or prestige. Yet few would claim that it has been an impressive body. For far too long, mainly because it was dominated by the overwhelming power of the Unity-Democratic bloc, it has been run autocratically. Under the rules, the president is chairman of the all-

18. Warren Brown, in "Proceedings of the Constitutional Convention," p. 233. For the office of the government secretary see, for example, *Annual Report, Office of the Government Secretary, Fiscal Year 1967* (St. Thomas: Government Printing Office, August 15, 1967).

19. James A. Bough, "General Introduction to the Constitutional Evolution of the Virgin Islands," Remarks prepared for the Conference on the Evolving Status of the Virgin Islands, mimeographed (St. Thomas, March 29–April 1, 1968), p. 11.

powerful Rules Committee, which is comparable in the power it wields to the Ways and Means Committee of the federal House of Representatives. That, coupled with the fact that there is no seniority principle in the appointment of committee chairmanships, so that such appointments pass into the hands of the president or, alternatively, are the result of private trades by the different legislative groups, gives the president almost absolute power over the legislative agenda and even over the outcome of legislation. For years the president was Senator Earle Ottley, who used his power to the full. Not surprisingly, then, debate in the house has tended to be desultory and unexciting; it could hardly avoid being so, considering that the bulk of legislation introduced is approved by voice vote of members on the same day that it is brought up, and that, as minority members have frequently complained, their first knowledge of most bills has to be hastily gained by going over them as they are read aloud to the chamber by members of the staff of the executive secretary. It is small wonder that the visitors' gallery seldom contains more than a handful of listeners at best. Hopefully, the new legislative situation after the 1970 election—in which no one group holds a majority of votes—will improve matters. It is bound to better the lot of the minority groups.

The legislature suffers from other characteristic shortcomings: inadequate office space, shortage of secretarial staff, an almost nonexistent research staff, and the complete absence of a legislative reference library. These familiar complaints have been exacerbated over the years by the feeling of the minority members that they have been discriminated against in the allocation of the services that are available. For years they fought to obtain even a semblance of proper office space. Having a closet to sit down in, in Senator Hamilton's phrase, does not make for creative legislation.[20] There is one legislative counsel, but he obviously cannot prepare drafts or do any kind of meaningful research for fifteen members. Added to all this has been the complaint that members were underpaid. A sixty-day regular session, along with frequent special sessions, placed a real financial burden on members, especially those from St. John and St. Croix who had to try to live on a meager, fixed per diem allowance of twenty dollars in Charlotte Amalie. Senator de Lugo's bitter remarks on this situation in the debates of the 1965 Constitutional Convention were typical.[21] They were met in part by the legislative decisions of 1966 and 1967 to raise members' salaries to an annual figure (as of 1967) of $9,000. But the long years of niggardly payment have

20. *Election of Virgin Islands Governor*, testimony of Senator David Hamilton, pt. 2, p. 591.
21. "Proceedings of the Constitutional Convention," p. 180.

set the pattern of a socioeconomic background of legislators profoundly unrepresentative of the general electorate. The directory of the 1967–68 legislature thus identifies, out of a total of fifteen members, nine business-men (two of them bar proprietors), two real estate agents, two attorneys, one medical doctor, and one editor-publisher.[22] The absence of any sort of academic representative is understandable. Even so, it is to be hoped that the College of the Virgin Islands will sooner or later provide legislative recruits, following the pattern of the neighboring University of Puerto Rico, which has given the San Juan legislature some of its most able minds—Severo Colberg, for example, and José Arsenio Torres. What is more surprising is the almost total failure of the Virgins labor–trade union movement to contribute legislative talent, a failure all the more noticeable when it is compared with the vast success in this area of the labor and union movements in such neighboring Caribbean societies at St. Kitts and Antigua. It is worth noting that the precedent of recruiting political candidates from the ranks of retired civil servants was tried in 1968, when the Democratic Party persuaded Louis Hestres to run (successfully) for senatorial office. Yet it can hardly be said to have been a markedly successful move, if Senator Hestres' inept handling of the controversial Dorothea land transactions of 1969—in which he failed to answer satisfactorily charges that he had personal interests in a land transfer matter involving the legislature—is any indication of his political acumen. It probably takes a seasoned veteran of the territorial political wars to emerge unscathed from that sort of embarrassing situation, so typical of Virgin Islands affairs. The 1970 election, finally, produced a number of new faces on the legislative front, many of them, encouragingly, extremely youthful persons.

It is true that much of the general legislative condition—the deficiency of office space and adequate technical aids, for example—is the sort of weakness endemic in legislative bodies everywhere, including the British House of Commons, and so cannot be laid at the door of colonialism. At the same time, the condition has the general result in St. Thomas of producing a legislative body of, in the main, part-time amateurs, most of them naturally concerned with their own business enterprises outside the Senate. They undertake little, if any, of the sort of intensive fact-finding committee investigation that must be at the heart of the legis-lative process if it is to mean anything. So, investigations on the really crucial issues of island life tend to be done by other, outside bodies—for example, the reports of the Social, Educational Research and Develop-ment body (a private research organization) on the alien question, the

22. "Directory, Legislature of the Virgin Islands, 1967–1968," mimeographed (St. Thomas, 1968).

Department of the Interior report on water resources, or the University of Massachusetts report on natural resources. The report of the Reapportionment Commission set up by the Senate in 1967, based on public hearings in all of the three islands under the able chairmanship of Senator Farrelly, is perhaps an exception to this rule.

Two additional factors aggravate this situation. The first is that the Senate, largely composed of businessmen, is hardly a radical body ideologically. Its debates from time to time on the alien question, for instance, have been invariably unsympathetic. Also, it would be difficult to imagine any one of its committees writing the sort of report, such as that of the University of Massachusetts on natural resources, that recommended a moderate program of public ownership of beaches and recreational areas before they are all alienated into private hands. The second factor is the general subservience of the legislature to executive leadership. The vast majority of legislative measures originate in the governor's office, are drafted by members of the attorney general's staff, and are invariably passed by an easy majority vote. This is a reversal, interestingly, of the earlier situation before the Paiewonsky governorship, when a constant tug of war took place between the two branches, as the 1938 fight with Governor Cramer and the 1955 fight with Governor Alexander dramatically illustrated, with the old legislative bodies playing an aggressive role in the legislative-executive relationship. The changed relationship after 1961 was largely due to the development of organized party politics and to the concurrent disappearance of the independent legislative member, who was always, in the colonial situation, driven to play the role of the people's tribune against the alien executive power. Thus, in the earlier period, certainly up to 1957 or so, most legislators were elected as independents on the strength of their personality appeal, and many of them served for twenty years or more—Earle Ottley, Robert Fleming of St. Croix, and the late Julius Sprauve of St. John. The later period has seen the replacement of that independent type with the party machine candidate; and one of its consequences has been the development of party loyalty at roll-call time, with the majority party organization smoothing the lines of communication between the Senate and Government House.

It is always the exception that proves the rule. The executive and legislative branches became once more separated in their respective ideological positions when Governor Paiewonsky resigned his office in 1969 as a consequence of the Republican Party victory in the United States, with a Republican president anxious to replace a Democratic incumbent in Charlotte Amalie with a man of his own party. That led, successively, to Acting Governor King's "caretaker governorship" for some four months and, after that, the brief incumbency of Republican Governor Evans. During that period, the colonial situation reasserted itself, with the Democratic legislature fiercely taking a stand against Washington appointees in Government House. Both sides excelled in the use of their respective offices for the purpose of building up political good will with an eye on the 1970 gubernatorial campaign. On the one side, the legislative majority used its power to fight Government House on a number of issues; and this was accompanied by the attempt of the Ottley-dominated union movement to embarrass the Republican executives by organizing strike movements within the government service itself. On the other hand, both King and Evans used their veto powers to strike down legislative measures clearly designed to cultivate the voters. The list is instructive: vetoes against a suggested financial appropriation to the local chapter of the Boy Scouts of America, a suggested financial appropriation to the senior class of St. Joseph's High School for the purpose of undertaking a "cultural" tour of the Caribbean islands, and various private bills to issue special pensions to individual civil servants in violation of the governmental retirement system. This renewed aggressiveness of the legislative branch is, of course, welcome, for it keeps government on its toes. But only too often it is, in such circumstances, oriented to partisan maneuver rather than to the public interest.

As a territorial dependency the islands are of course subject to the federal judicial system. The second Organic Act set up the District Court of the Virgin Islands, which possesses, like any U.S. district court, jurisdiction in all cases arising under the Constitution, treaties, and laws of the United States, and also constitutes an appellate court for all inferior courts in the territory. The judge of the District Court, which was placed under the general jurisdiction of the Third Judicial Circuit, was a presidential nominee, as was also the United States Attorney for the Virgin Islands. Apart from a few matters of detail, and some heated argument about the question of judicial appointment for life, the 1965 Constitutional Convention found no reason to change any of this.

What this has meant, essentially, is the export of the American system of law and politics to the islands, along with its consequences. As far as the islands have been concerned, the major consequences have been two. Firstly, there has been the usual American interconnection between the two worlds of politics and law, which overlap as professions. The politico-legal careers of Governor Gordon in one decade and of Judge Farrelly in another sufficiently illustrate that point. Secondly, the American instrument of the judicial review of executive and legislative behavior has been introduced into local politics. The local political forces have not been slow in utilizing that instrument. The series of court battles that followed the passage of the new Election Code of 1963 illustrate that process, involving as they did the effort of the majority group in the legislature to impose a loyalty oath on electoral candidates and, more particularly, the internecine struggle between the two factions of the Unity-Democratic Party for the right to use the party name in the forthcoming elections. The documentation of those battles, as in *Alexander* v. *Todman* and *Williams* v. *Todman,* and the series of open letters written by Judge Maris of the U.S. Court of Appeals for the Third Circuit to Governor Paiewonsky and Senator Ottley show how the American system encouraged a litigious politics in the islands.[23] They also show, incidentally, how the federal principle added to that politics by means of the rivalry it engendered between the federal judicial officers in the territory and the local judicial force. One of the more entertaining episodes in the judicial and legislative investigations that followed the alleged irregularities of the 1966 local elections was that in which the chief investigator of the Department of Public Safety in St. Croix, as a witness before the local Committee on the Judiciary, found himself in an agonizing jurisdictional dilemma, since he was also in the service of the office of the U.S. Attorney and thus owed allegiance to both local and federal jurisdictions. That dilemma was only resolved for Mr. Groneveldt, the officer concerned, by the posthaste arrival of a letter from the U.S. Attorney, in the middle of his testimony, ordering him to desist as a witness. No episode could have better revealed how the dualism of the federal system imposes aggravating conflicts of allegiance in those public servants who occupy the indeterminate territory between the two jurisdictions.[24] The end result of all this is that today there exists in the islands an elaborate and sophisticated legalistic politics, with all factions bringing in their hired legal talent from stateside to further their cause. It is certainly a far cry from 1926, when the young Adolf Berle could tell an earlier congressional investigating committee that he was the only lawyer in the whole United States who had ever made a study of the Virgin Islands situation.

23. *Election of Virgin Islands Governor,* pt. 1, pp. 144–48. The relevant court cases are Civil No. 260—1964, District Court of the Virgin Islands, District of St. Thomas and St. Croix, July 17, 1964: *Alexander* v. *Todman,* 231 F. Supp. 365 (D.V.I. 1964), and *Williams* v. *Todman,* 231 F. Supp. 368 (D.V.I. 1964).

24. *Election of Virgin Islands Governor,* pt. 2, pp. 538–39, 580–87. For an earlier description of the Virgin Islands judicial branch, see Judge Herman E. Moore, "The Virgin Islands and Its Judicial System," *Daily News,* July 7, 9, 10, 1945.

Yet it is the debate on legislative district reapportionment over the last few years that emphasizes most pointedly the intimate connection between the different parts—executive, legislative, and judicial—of the local governmental machinery. The Reapportionment Commission set up by the Seventh Legislature in its 1967 session was prompted by a double mandate: (1) the congressional amendment of 1966 directing the local legislature to reapportion, and (2) the collective decisions of the U.S. Supreme Court after 1964 on equal voting rights, emphasizing as they did the importance of the historic principle of one man, one vote. The first mandate was, of course, expressly addressed to the territory of the Virgin Islands, the second only indirectly so. The public hearings of the Reapportionment Commission, however, made it clear that its members felt the pressure of both mandates.

The reapportionment debate, perhaps more than any other single issue of insular life, graphically underlined the special peculiarities of the Virgin Islands situation. There is, to begin with, the peculiarity of the unicameral legislature, which makes it impossible, through the fictional equality of areas of population in a second chamber, for a smaller island unit like St. John to achieve parity in that fashion with the two larger units. There is also the peculiarity that no elective structure exists beneath the territorial legislative level, which makes it particularly urgent that the representative principle at that single level should operate as perfectly as possible. That situation will continue, of course, until the base of elections in the islands is broadened. There is, speaking more generally, the peculiar fact that, whereas in the continental United States the reapportionment problem has been one of gross overrepresentation of the rural counties as against the city vote, in the Virgin Islands, on the contrary, there is the tendency of the city areas to override the outlying country districts.

The reapportionment situation has found characteristic expression in two problems: (1) the debate between the advocates of the at-large representative principle and the advocates of the subdistrict representative principle; and (2) the celebrated St. John problem. As far as the first problem is concerned, the advocates of the at-large principle urged that any retreat from the principle by way of setting up smaller subdistrict electoral areas would mean a return to the sectionalism of the old days. In the words of a Frederiksted witness before the Reapportionment Commission, "I am totally against any further subdivision of St. Croix. I don't see why we should draw a line between the middle and say two from Frederiksted and five from Christiansted, seven from St. Thomas and one from St. John. Let them be from St. Croix, from St.

Thomas and from St. John. That's the Virgin Islands." [25] The at-large principle is thus seen as a guarantee of the political integrity of the island territory as a whole. The advocates of the subdistrict principle, to the contrary, urged essentially that their proposal would produce representatives more knowledgeable of their local constituencies. In the words of a St. Thomas witness, "I don't see why you should take a senator from Red Hook to represent somebody down at Carrot Bay. I think the whole idea is to have a senator in your district that you can go to immediately. You don't want—if somebody is bothering you, and you think it is a matter in which your senator can help—you don't have to get in a car and go to Red Hook when you can go around the corner and talk to him." [26] There is, clearly, some virtue in both arguments. An outside observer might perhaps only venture the opinion that in a territorial area where only a few miles separate any one point from another it is hardly credible that a legislative representative elected on the at-large system cannot look into everybody's problems in a constituency that typically carries just a thousand or more voters and not do the job efficiently.

The problem of St. John is more complex. With its 400 or so votes the island logically should be denied a legislative seat if the one-man, one-vote formula were rigorously applied; and that fact explains the long-standing proposals that the island should be attached to a larger legislative district in one of the other two islands. Yet the arguments of the St. John residents in support of separate representation are difficult to resist. The island should retain its identity as a separate district, it is argued, for a number of compelling reasons. It is, to begin with, divorced both geographically and sociologically from St. Thomas and St. Croix. Its tourist problem is acute, since its ratio of visitors to resident population is the highest in the three islands, requiring police, garbage disposal, housing, health, and road services out of proportion to tax revenues and normal population. Most important, however, is the unique situation arising out of the fact that some two-thirds of the island's usable land belongs to the National Park, depriving the island of both potential tax revenue and potential population growth; the land available, indeed, for population growth and settlement is uniquely restricted in a manner which does not limit the population growth of St. Thomas or St. Croix. The creation of the National Park, in other words, has effectively circum-

25. "Report of Commission on the Reapportionment of the Legislature of the Virgin Islands and for Other Purposes," testimony of Allen A. Christian, mimeographed (St. Thomas, August, 1967), p. 85.
26. *Ibid.*, testimony of Croxton Williams, p. 131. For criticisms of the district representative scheme from the viewpoint of a proportional representation advocate, see testimony of Allen Grammer, reprinted in *Virgin Islands View*, February, 1968.

scribed economic and population growth while at the same time imposing a peculiar burden of public service on the local inhabitants. For all of these reasons the St. John homesteaders, almost to a man, feel that their problems can only be handled effectively through direct, personal, on-island contact with a local representative. They conclude their claim with the reminder that the U.S. government has in fact already recognized the island as a distinct governmental unit through the establishment of separate immigration, customs, and naturalization offices there. Any political surgery, then, that would attach the island, for representational purposes, to St. Croix or eastern St. Thomas is rejected out of hand.[27]

There is much merit to the argument. The population-suffrage ratio ought not to preclude consideration of other values and factors. Constitutional commandments, as Justice Fortas pointed out in his dissenting opinion in the *Midland County* case of 1968, are not surgical instruments intended to destroy important political and social values on the altar of the one-man, one-vote principle too rigidly applied. Such special values are patently present in the St. John electoral case. But there is more to it than that. Even a short visit to the island will convince the visitor that the St. John populace is confronted with a formidable problem. The people live, literally, on the fringes of a vast park protected by the awesome power of the federal government. They are almost at the point where, in the words of one of their spokesmen, they feel like Indians living on a reservation. A recent episode occurred in which the islanders, suddenly faced with a move in Washington to condemn the rest of their land because they would not sell to the Park, financed the trip of a special representative to the capital in order to voice their objections; this illustrates the kind of special crisis likely at any moment to emerge from that situation.[28] It is perhaps not too much to say that—as at least one St. John witness openly averred in the reapportionment hearings—there is a potential Anguilla-type secessionist situation in the dependent status of St. John in the total Virgin Islands scene. In that sense it constitutes a characteristic problem of the region; for throughout the Caribbean there exists this form of secondary colonialism, as it were —Tobago with reference to Trinidad, for example, or the Grenadines

27. "Report of Commission," testimony of St. John witnesses, pp. 149–203. See also Independent Democratic Club of Saint John, Memorandum presented to Subcommittee on Territorial and Insular Affairs, *Election of Virgin Islands Governor*, pt. 1, pp. 286–88.

28. "Report of Commission," testimony of George R. Simmonds, pp. 173–74. For the leading U.S. Supreme Court cases in the reapportionment matter, see *New York Times*, Feb. 18, 1964, Apr. 2, 1968. For a full discussion of the issues involved, see Royce Hanson, ed., *The Political Thicket: Reapportionment and Constitutional Democracy* (Englewood Cliffs, N.J.: Prentice-Hall, 1969) .

with reference to St. Vincent, or Carriacou with reference to Grenada—in which the minor partner of a relationship initially organized by the former colonial metropolitan power feels aggrieved by the neglect it suffers at the hands of the major partner. This, like the alien problem, is something the Virgin Islands government must face and solve or perhaps be broken by its failure to do so.

13

~~~

Parties and Politics

Virgin Islands politics, as must be clear by now, exhibit all the characteristic features of small-island colonial life. There is the interplay of personalities in preference to the serious debate of social issues. There is the use of politics as a form of social recreation, so that the degree of personal investment in political talk and activity is one of the highest, literally, in the world, certainly higher than in Puerto Rico, where the status debate has long been the national pastime. There is the inflated importance of government, to the degree that survival. in business frequently depends on favorable political contacts with the ruling political group. Added to all this is the peculiar communal psyche that arises out of compressed life on circumscribed islands, whereby everything outside seems remote and unimportant compared with the excitements of the local drama, and the great national and international events come through, as it were, filtered, bereft of their real impact and nature. There is, finally, the additional component, born of colonial status, of the psychological obsession with what Washington says and does, whereby the local politics are made even more complex by the Virgin Islands tendency to look to Washington for help; one of the consequences is that the already fierce political situation in St. Thomas is intensified by the periodic intervention of the major political forces in the national capital. In the words of a Washington correspondent who writes knowledgeably on the Virgins, this is tantamount to taking a smallpox victim and inoculating him with the bubonic plague in the hope of curing him.

The historical evolution of the insular politics falls into certain fairly recognizable stages. During the 1917–31 period it was a struggle of the old Council leaders against the benevolent despotism of the Navy regime. In the period after 1931 until the passage of the Elective Governor Act it was a struggle of the more activist local editors and Council members against the appointed governors, who as presidential creatures were always suspected of being under the control of the Washington power structure. Both of those periods, in turn, were characterized by the administrative tutelage of the federal bureaucracy, and the local political leaderships were drawn into perennial conflict with federal officials, described by one local leader as persons who occupied big positions but who were in fact little men. After 1936, with the advent of popular suffrage, politics took on a new mass base, giving rise to the emergence of real political parties with their rationale in popular support. The current stage is the struggle for the popular governorship unleashed by the passage in 1968 of the Elective Governor Act. There were, of course, subsidiary stages of development, such as the evolution after 1954 of an all-island politics as distinct from a sectional politics; however, that development is as yet incomplete in the sense that the separate factions of the political struggle can still more or less be identified with their respective St. Thomas or St. Croix strongholds.

Each of these stages produced its own unique features. There was, for example, the bitter quarreling of the more forceful Council members with each colonial governor, sometimes degenerating into the old West Indian game of seeking to frighten him into submission. This was, of course, a struggle arising out of the colonial character of the governorship, for the fact that a governor could be a popular liberal, like Governor Hastie, or the son of a Georgia slave, like Governor Alexander, or even a native son, like Governor Merwin, did not save him from ultimate popular obloquy. Few of them were spared the whip of caustic comment in the press; one wit in 1942 observed tartly that no press release had yet been issued from Government House crediting the governor with holding back the hurricane which the weather forecast had predicted for that year.[1] The local leader Roy Gordon quarreled openly with Government House in 1954 on the issue, no less, of the reception ceremonies planned for the new governor, insisting that he, as a Republican national committeeman, and not "half baked Democrats," should be allowed to drive immediately behind the gubernatorial car.[2] Governor Hastie committed a grievous blunder in an otherwise able administration by his open and bitter attack upon the Progressive Guide candidates in the 1948 election, and the electorate's rejection of his advice showed that public opinion was unlikely to follow an appointed executive in a

1. Violet Melchior, "Good Day, My Friend" column, *Daily News,* Sept. 2, 1942.
2. Quoted in *ibid.,* Mar. 1, 1954.

vendetta against popularly elected legislators. Similarly, Governor Gordon provoked a memorable episode in island political history in 1958 when a mass meeting addressed by St. Thomas Labor Union leaders ended in a protest march to Government House, following a series of unpopular decisions by that chief executive.

The politics of the 1931–68 period was, in a typically colonial fashion, a patronage politics, with both governor and legislative chieftains fighting hard to monopolize the fruit that fell from the appointing power. Payroll padding, "jobs for the boys," well-paid appointments to persons often scandalously incompetent, bringing in stateside "experts" frequently no better than local candidates and sometimes worse: all became thriving themes of political intrigue and talk. Local leadership was particularly incensed at the habit of appointing continental persons usually ignorant of the local scene. The long running battle over the top appointments to the Police Department was perhaps the best-known example of all this. The office of director of police became in truth a sinecure for outside friends of Government House, despite the fact that able natives, like Stanley Coulter of Frederiksted, had shown that they could fill the office more than satisfactorily. The old Municipal Council of St. Thomas was driven in 1942 to debate whether it should pay the living and hotel expenses of two police officers sent to attend a course in San Juan since the Council critics saw that as the only means left to them of protesting conditions in the department.[3] This situation, moreover, is of more than historical interest. That the irritant still continues is shown by the attempt of a group of white continentals in 1967–68 (including, however, one prominent native islander) in St. Croix to get rid of the native police commissioner, Otis Felix, and replace him with a stateside person. They proposed this action on the grounds that they considered Felix unfit for the position and could not find a citizen of the islands with sufficient drive and experience to qualify as his successor— an *idée fixe* of a certain kind of continental. The racist assumption behind their attitude was unwittingly revealed by their observation that "The kind of attitude embodied by the chief officer in Frederiksted who walks around in bare feet with a rope around his middle, must go. This is not the Congo."[4] The politicking that went on at much the same time over the appointment of Commissioner Ellison was also symptomatic, for it gave rise to the same sort of angry private intrigue and public debate, with different political figures taking different sides on

3. *Proceedings of the Municipal Council of St. Thomas and St. John,* June 11, 1942, reported in *ibid.,* June 15, 1942. See also *West End News,* Feb. 28, 1944.

4. See series of letters by Charles W. Goit, Lt. Elmer James, and Mrs. Ann Abramson, in *West End News,* Jan. 18, 1968.

the matter, and all of it exacerbated by the fact that Ellison was yet another stateside candidate for local office. Appointments to the strategic post of commissioner of education have unleashed similar political struggles, the latest being the growing struggle between Commissioner Harold Haizlip and the Independent Citizens Movement (ICM) members of the Board of Education. In most of these cases a characteristic situation develops in which a stateside candidate, however able he may be, enters unsuspectingly an island politics much more murderous and acrimonious than anything he might have met on the mainland. The appointing power during the period under discussion also became involved with the issue of island rivalries; the position of the commissioner of commerce, for instance, is vital to the cruise-ship tourist trade, and Crucian business firms have always felt that St. Thomas has been favored in the appointments. Their demand that "we must have someone who is solid on St. Croix" is typical of the attitudes that arise.[5] All in all, appointments under the nominated governor regime were too readily made as rewards to continental friends for political favors. The 1956 episode in which local opinion rallied against the rumor that Connecticut Republicans planned to nominate Stamford Town Chairman Frank Pimpinella as Virgin Islands federal judge when that post was vacated by Judge Moore shows what an important role merely political considerations played in local appointments. And it is perhaps too early to say that that sort of thing does not still continue.[6]

These were the kinds of issues that were debated in campaigns of vitriolic character assassination. Political corruption in the islands is probably not any worse than the sort uncovered, for example, in the 1969 federal investigations of state government malpractices in New Jersey. But it has been accompanied by a peculiar bitterness and jealousy, a temptation to expose the social background of opponents in the most lurid terms possible. Rattling the skeletons that are hidden away in practically every family closet in the racially mixed West Indian societies is an old game, and the Virgin Islands politicians have not been averse to playing it. Even the sanity of opponents could be called into question; there was a hilarious exchange between Roy Gordon and Omar Brown in 1944 in which the latter, having been accused by the former of being "mentally afflicted," published sworn statements of medical doctors that there was no record of mental disorder under his name in the files of

5. Statement, St. Croix Chamber of Commerce, quoted in *St. Croix Avis*, Feb. 18, 1965.

6. Mrs. Audrey Vanderpool Harrison, letter to *Stamford Advocate*, reprinted in *Daily News*, Feb. 17, 1956.

the municipal hospital.[7] It is true, however, that much of this is disappearing as the more sophisticated radio or television address replaces the old-style political meeting and parade. In a political democracy, which the Virgins have been since 1936, it becomes increasingly difficult to invoke the cruder forms of social snobbery. So, candidates rarely now suffer the public examination of their private lives. There is, however, a new, more subtle intercourse between wealth and politics, generated by the intimate connection between government, business, and organized labor. The charges laid against Senator Ottley in 1970, in his capacity as editor of the *Home Journal,* for allegedly accepting advertising fees from the former Paiewonsky government without benefit of competitive bidding, are illustrative of the issues that will more and more arise out of that intercourse. The spoils, to put it another way, are now much larger as both government and business become more corporate in character. The comparatively minor peccadilloes of a generation ago—the effort of 1944, for example, of a group of local French and Puerto Rican businessmen to make a killing on the use of imported slot machines [8]— have been replaced by far more lucrative opportunities.

But perhaps the most striking features of the Virgins political profile in the post-1936 period have been (1) the effective incorporation of the masses into the political process, and (2) the concomitant transformation in the character of the political elite. The one change produced the other. Universal suffrage converted the masses from spectators into actors. They could now make or break politicians and political careers. That in turn helped to destroy the old class system of social recognition as a basis for legislative membership. The 1938 election, followed by that of 1940, handed legislative power over to the Progressive Guide group of younger men recruited mostly from the colored lower-middle class: men like Valdemar Hill, for example, who was a federal officer in the Civilian Conservation Corps; Earle Ottley, who started his long public career as a *Daily News* sports columnist; and, later, Ron de Lugo, who started his career as a radio commentator. That, of course, was, in the main, St. Thomas. The change did not reach St. Croix until the elections of 1946, with the rise of the liberal movement in the Crucian rural areas under the leadership of young men like Walter Hodge and Louis Brown; Darwin Creque has related in his book how their radicalism was born of their unhappy experience of racial discrimination in their wartime U.S. Army service in the New Orleans area.[9] The old groups of the town

7. Exchange of correspondence, *Daily News,* Jan. 19, 21, 24, 1944.
8. For this episode see political advertisement, "Open Letter to a Local G.I. Stationed in Puerto Rico," *ibid.,* Oct. 30, 1944.
9. Darwin D. Creque, *The U.S. Virgin Islands and the Eastern Caribbean* (Philadelphia: Whitmore, 1968), pp. 115–17.

burghers and landed gentry were thus displaced, politically, by the rising colored talent from the lower social levels. It was a bitter and difficult struggle. Island social life had bred both an attitude of reluctance on the part of Virgin Islanders to be identified with anything of a public character and a real fear of associating themselves with innovative organizational work of any kind. In addition, the entrenched group fought its rearguard actions with methods that were not too admirable; a typical example was the effort of what a local newspaper called the "Cliveden set" of a group of continentals, supported by the Crucian oligarchs and certain U.S. southern elements, to destroy Judge Hastie's nomination as governor in 1946 by a campaign in Washington of vicious slander that in its character anticipated the later rise of McCarthyism in American life.[10]

These processes all combined to produce organized political parties as they exist today in the islands. The campaign platforms of the Square Deal ticket in the 1940 and 1944 elections set the pattern of formal political organizations based on general public membership and espousing a coherent program of social and economic betterment. The organizations were statutorily recognized by the Election Code of 1962, which legally acknowledged and controlled them, as well as providing for the election of Territorial Committees by party members and the proper selection of candidates for general elections by means of party primaries. Party loyalty rather than legislative individualism became the order of the day. The concept of party loyalty had become so widely accepted by the 1960s that the Unity–Democratic Party-controlled legislature of 1966 was able to pass the now famous "loyalty oath" bill requiring all party legislators to adhere indefinitely to the policies announced by their respective party organs (a provision later struck down by the courts). The independent candidate ran an increasingly hazardous course. Earle Ottley could win as an independent in 1946, but the continental resident publisher Allen Grammer lost ignobly as an independent in 1966. The 1970 election, in turn, revolved around the three-way struggle between the Democratic Party, the Republican Party, and the newly formed Independent Citizens Movement. The last-named group, despite its name, was not so much a collection of independent candidates as it was a highly organized new "third force" in local politics; and its newly elected members to the Senate act as such in the transformed legislative scene. It is true that Attorney General Francisco Corneiro undertook a valiant struggle to win the Democratic gubernatorial nomination away

10. See account of the nomination hearings for Governor Hastie, *Daily News*, Mar. 29, 30, Apr. 3, 4, 5, 6, 10, 1946. For a similar reactionary note in the later nomination hearings for Governor Alexander, see *ibid.*, Mar. 22, 23, 24, 25, 1954, and esp. supporting statement of Perry W. Howard, *ibid.*, Mar. 25.

from Farrelly. But he acted throughout not as an independent or as a party maverick but as a loyal party member seeking, in the best American fashion, to challenge what he saw as the highhanded behavior of the party "bosses." It is clear, in sum, that as the modernizing process makes Virgins society more highly structured and stratified its characteristic problems become likewise more institutionalized, demanding collective expertise for their solution. That in turn places a heavy premium on political organizations offering some sort of planned program to the electorate. Singlehanded legislative adventurism thus yields to group work.

It is still too early to say whether the Virgins politics will finally mature into a two-party system along American lines or a multiple-party system along French lines. It is certainly true that a discernible move has been made in the direction of the two-party model. Such a model seemed to be shaping up as early as the 1950s. The turning point in that development was probably in 1952, when the local Democratic Party decided to sponsor candidates for election, and in turn the liberal nucleus of the then defunct Progressive Guide and the short-lived Liberal Party combined to form the Virgin Islands Unity Party. It is also true that the small amount of theoretical discussion on politics has tended to assume that the island patterns must as a matter of course follow the continental patterns. It is of interest to note that when Carlos Downing came to write his authoritative articles of 1956 on the two-party system in the islands he assumed unquestioningly the moral and practical virtues of the model. In an almost Burkean encomium he argued that, if fully adopted, it would bring the Virgin Islands people closer together in their political views, establish uniformity of purpose in policies, set up a common ground between the legislative and executive branches of the territorial government, enhance the respect generally due to the people's representatives, and impose proper responsibility and accountability on the legislative membership. All that was needed, the argument concluded, was the steady improvement of the embryonic Virgin Islands party system along the lines laid out by the historical evolution of the party system in the United States.[11]

There is a bizarre quality about the sort of politics and political party life that have grown out of this background in the Virgin Islands. This observation does not refer to the fact—certainly bizarre enough in itself—that, during the Paiewonsky period, the Virgins were the only

11. Carlos Downing, series of articles, *ibid.*, Jan. 17, Mar. 7, 8, 1956, Jan. 18, 21, 1958.

place in the United States where it was possible to witness the spectacle of a Jewish governor ruling in alliance with a black legislature, with a handful of white continentals seeking to penetrate the inner corridors of power. It refers rather to the fact, generally speaking, that there exist side by side a political rhetoric borrowed from the American scene and a set of characteristic features that are wholly and peculiarly local in origin and nature. The very names of the various factions jostling for power—Unicrats, Donkeycrats, Eagles, Victory 66, Mortar and Pestle, mixed up with the use of Democrat and Republican titles—indicate a veritable political zoology which confuses most outside observers, including visiting congressmen. Virgin Islanders themselves will assure the outsider, with almost perverse glee, that it is all too complicated, too much governed by esoteric rules, for him ever fully to comprehend. The proclivity for politics certainly runs deep and fierce; an American reporter in the islands a generation ago felt constrained to report that it was not an unusual experience to stop a small child on the street and have him tie you up in a political discussion that would do credit to the Chicago Roundtable of the Air.

The local practitioners claim, to begin with, that the political system is a two-party one. But this is true only in a special sense. It is certainly not true in the sense of "party government" as extolled by American theorists like Herring, Schattschneider, and Ranney, that is, a system of two separate and definable major parties that alternate, with reasonable frequency, in power. It is, rather, a modified one-party system in which the dominant party—until 1970 the Unity–Democratic Party—has regularly won most of the votes and public offices, but has been faced at the same time by an opposition party regularly nominating candidates, campaigning for them, winning a sizable minority of votes, and occasionally obtaining governmental power for brief periods. This is not unlike the political situation in states like Florida and Vermont, yet it is more complicated. Whereas in those states there exists a straightforward confrontation between the historic two parties, in the Virgin Islands this has never been so, due to the entirely different historical evolution of the local party structure. The party factions as of today grew, in fact, from a single organizational source, the Democratic Club (going back to the 1930s), with the old Unity Party members taking over the organization after 1962 (when their party was dissolved) and subsequently engaging with their chief rival, the erstwhile Democratic Party officialdom, for both the control of the organization and the prestige of its name. That, in essence, was the meaning of the astonishingly complicated series of maneuvers from 1963 through the elections of 1966. Those maneuvers can only be understood if two things are remembered. In the first place, since local political parties began in effect in the New Deal period (with the emergence of the old Progressive Guide), they have always had a stamp of Democratic welfarism about them, and Governor Paiewonsky, with his twenty years of service as a Democratic Party national committeeman, put the finishing touch on that image. Second, and conversely, the Republican tradition in the islands has been weak and negative, and for years has been identified with the unpopular group of white continental reactionary landowners and businessmen, especially in St. Croix. To have any sort of dealing with the Republican Club, then, was to receive, electorally speaking, the kiss of death.

The result is that there existed, certainly until 1970, a viable two-party system within the one dominant party. It is worth looking in some detail at the 1960s struggle for control of the party, since it shows how absolutely necessary it was for the faction seeking victory to effectively seize control of the Democratic machinery. The struggle was set off as early as 1960 when Ron de Lugo defeated Mr. Paiewonsky for the territorial seat on the Democratic National Committee, a defeat which, it is said, Paiewonsky never forgave, despite the fact that de Lugo was one of his most ardent champions in the 1961 congressional hearings on his gubernatorial candidacy. That was followed by the governor's slowly forming alliance with the Unity Party set, and the depth of the political emotions involved can be seen in de Lugo's angry letters to the governor in 1962, accusing him of failing to fulfill his role as leader and titular head of the Democratic Party in the islands and of failing to direct patronage posts to "qualified, deserving and loyal Democrats." [12] By the time of the 1962 elections the rift had become an open break, with Unity Democrats and Independent Democrats drawing the lines for a bitter contest for control of the party organization. The Unity faction proceeded to use its legislative majority to launch what its opponents regarded, probably correctly, as a calculated attempt to destroy them.

The grand strategy of that attempt certainly makes fascinating reading. There was, to begin with, the inventive but relatively harmless name-calling. The original Democrats were dubbed just a "social club" by the Unity latecomers (always a telling point in any West Indian society), while the governor labeled de Lugo a "pet poodle on the leash of the St. Croix Chamber of Commerce" (always a telling point with the St. Thomas electorate, which has traditionally liked to dismiss the sister island as hopelessly conservative). The more serious punitive measures started with the new Election Code after 1962, in which the supervisor of elections was appointed by the governor and the legislature, immedi-

12. Text printed in *St. Croix Avis,* Nov. 27, 28, 1962.

ately raising suspicions that the officer was just one more part of the kingmaking machinery of the majority party and that the situation was leading to an elective process too politically partisan in its operations. The same code included the now famous "loyalty oath," designed in fact to frustrate the coalition of the minority Democrats and the Republicans; it was struck down later by Judge Maris with the acid comment that it would have had the effect of binding legislators to the party leadership without individual freedom of thought or independence of action, tied and delivered like bunches of beets.[13] The provision of the same code that there should be no similarity in the names of political parties "which would tend to confuse or mislead the electors" paved the way for the Unity-Democratic faction to appropriate the valuable property of the Democratic Party label, an appropriation sealed by the success of the victorious faction in getting itself accepted at the 1964 Democratic National Convention held in Atlantic City as the legitimate delegation— a success largely made possible by the fact that the Credentials Committee at that convention had been too wearied by the Mississippi Freedom Delegation fight to concern itself with the complexities of the Virgin Islands quarrel. Later legislation succeeded in making compulsory the device of symbol voting—always a source of confusion to voters—as well as to have all primary candidates run at large, a requirement favorable to the Unity faction since it would have given a well-disciplined majority almost complete victory.

Added to all this was the increasing use of governmental power in the service of the now openly acknowledged Ottley-Paiewonsky machine. This was fully documented in the 1967 congressional hearings: the dismissal of key employees who remained faithful to the original Democratic Party; the transfer of certain positions away from the Civil Service classification so that career employees thus transferred would have no recourse to appeal if dismissed; the creation of numerous new unclassified posts in order to reward party supporters; intimidation of career employees who dared even to socialize with certain members of the

13. *Alvin Canton and M. Juancito Shackleton* v. *Henrita Todman, Supervisor of Elections, Appellant*, F. 3d (CA, October 24, 1966), reprinted in *Daily News*, Oct. 27, 1966. It is possible to argue, of course, that this judgment goes too far in its support of the doctrine of full individual accountability, giving full rein to irresponsible political individualism, insofar as it asserts that the American "democratic heritage can best be preserved if legislators are free to employ in the discharge of their duties their own individual views and judgment in the light of their personal responsibility as representatives of the whole community." That this might be so was recognized by some members of the congressional investigating committee of 1967. See remarks of Congressmen Carey and White, U.S., Congress, House, Subcommittee on Territorial and Insular Affairs, *Election of Virgin Islands Governor: Hearings*, 90th Cong., 1st sess., 1967, pt. 1, pp. 49–53.

opposition group; and intimidation of voters who resided in public housing units (in 1967, for example, there was a large total of 6,703 persons residing in low-cost public housing in the islands). Much of this, in turn, was given the inferential stamp of official approval by the openly partisan participation of the governor in the 1964 elections. All of these methods—the governor's actions, the use of government personnel and resources, the amendments, frequently introduced at the last moment, to the Election Code—made it virtually impossible for any opposition group to meet the governmental party machine on equal terms. Such impossible conditions of electoral procedure were introduced that in the 1966 elections the minority Donkey Democrats were forced to run under a coalition Victory 66 banner with the local Republican Party. It is worth noting that members of the congressional investigating committee looking into the alleged irregularities of those elections took Senator Farrelly severely to task for his failure to continue the investigations of his own local committee into those irregularities.[14]

The myriad consequences of all this in the island political scene were, and still are, frequently odd and even hilarious. Deprived by court decisions of what it regarded as its rightful title, the minority faction was forced to invent odd labels—Donkeycrats, for instance—to avoid the ignominy of accepting the Republican label. The minority candidates had to fight as much in the courts as at the polls; in the words of one of them, it is not getting elected, it is whether you can win in court or not. They also had to resist the persuasive pressure—especially of visiting congressmen to whom only the Republican-Democratic terminology is meaningful—to move over into the Republican fold. This, of course, they have been reluctant to do, a reluctance that is reinforced when a Republican figure like ex-Governor Merwin can shock the community, as he did in 1967, by a recommendation that because the local economy was "overheated" Congress should eliminate the free-port status of the islands by placing them within the U.S. customs boundary. So, for years, there existed the absurd situation in which a group of candidates ran on the Republican ticket but claimed that they were Democrats, while their Democratic opponents wanted them to declare themselves Republican in order to saddle them with an opprobrious title. "They stole my party from me" became the rallying cry of the dissident group. Correspondingly, the local Republican chieftains rallied their own forces by warning that the Donkeycrats were likely to plan a takeover of the Republican machine, in much the same way that the Donkeycrats had

14. For all this, see *Election of Virgin Islands Governor, passim*. See also David B. Kimelman, "Divided Democrats: A Study of the Two-Party System in the Virgin Islands" (Master's thesis, Yale University, 1966).

suffered from the Unicrat takeover of the Democratic machine after 1963.

Yet in many ways this was a factitious civil war. That was evident from the partial reconciliation that took place in 1968. Several vital factors precipitated that move. On the one hand, the narrow margin of the Unity victory in the 1966 election persuaded the majority leadership that it could not risk going into the 1968 election without healing the factional breach; on the other hand, the Donkeycrat alliance with the Republicans was breaking down as the St. Croix–centered Republican group looked forward, correctly as it turned out, to a national Republican victory in the States, with all that would mean in terms of Washington patronage for their cause. The readiness of the Democratic majority to talk was reinforced by (1) the growing infiltration of "black power" ideas into the movement, thus weakening the unity of the party, and (2) the emerging internal struggle for the nomination of a candidate for the first elected governor in 1970, also calculated to upset party unity. The reconciliation was further made possible by the removal of former Governor Paiewonsky from the scene, insofar as one item of the merger agreement was that the first elected governor would have to be a native-born Negro, thereby making it possible for those Donkeycrats who had become mortal Paiewonsky foes to return to the Democratic fold without entirely losing their political dignity. It is even possible, indeed, that the agreement can be interpreted as an effort on the part of the colored political oligarchy to close its ranks in the face of the growing political power of the white transplanted mainlanders, that is, to reaffirm the carefully nurtured thesis that birth in the islands gives the colored native a preferential legacy in politics and government. That, if correct, would be a sort of conservative application of the "black power" ideology.

All this constitutes, in a way, a record of the methodology of Virgin Islands politics. There were, naturally, sideshows to the main circus. One such was the long vendetta that was waged by the Ottley-Paiewonsky machine against Government Secretary Cyril King during the 1960s. "It is part of the political game in the Virgins to drive a wedge between the Governor and the Government Secretary," observed Robert Morss Lovett a generation ago, speaking from his own experience as occupant of the latter post. Lovett's own quarrel with Governor Harwood in the 1940s had shown itself in minor irritants, such as the governor's instructions to his chauffeur that the government secretary not be allowed to use the official gubernatorial car. What Secretary King had to endure, however, was a sustained drive by the legislative majority to whittle down the importance of his office; this was occasioned by his decision to remain loyal, as an Independent Democrat, to the original Democratic

Party. His punishment took the form of successive legislative acts removing one agency after another from his control, even going so far as to move vital employees from his office to other departments. It is impossible to read the record of that process without agreeing with the secretary, in his report of 1967, that it constituted a partisan and unrestrained exercise of legislative power designed to embarrass, humiliate, and harass him.[15]

A further subordinate element of the political picture has been the stubborn persistency of interisland rivalries. The introduction of the unicameral legislature and the at-large constituency system in 1954 was supposed to have had the effect of generating a really unified politics. Yet the temper of island parochialism still manages to survive, and continues to yield its political expressions. That is hardly surprising, granted recognition of the fact that the three islands have quite different problems. The unique problems of St. John have already been noted. So it is not surprising that the leading political entity in that island for years has been known as the St. John Independent Democratic Club. Similarly, St. Thomas and St. Croix remain defiantly separatist in their attitudes. The division, in fact, between the Unity (Mortar and Pestle) faction and the Donkeycrat faction was in large part a division between the St. Thomas Democrats and the Crucian Democrats. That explains why, during the period of factional strife under discussion, it was always a Unity-Democratic tactic to upset the enemy in the St. Croix stronghold. Ron de Lugo put the point succinctly in his evidence before the 1967 congressional committee. "It is," he observed, "a very simple thing. The main strength of the Mortar and Pestle wing is in St. Thomas. Our strength is in St. Croix and St. John. As close as these two political power structures are, all you have to do is to cause confusion in St. Croix, keep the vote down in St. Croix, and get the vote out in St. Thomas, and that is it. Simple as that." [16] That explains, too, why it has been hazardous for a candidate from either island to run on an at-large ticket rather than on a one-island district ticket, as Senator de Lugo himself found out to his cost when he was narrowly defeated in the 1966 election because he made exactly that mistake. It is rare to find the vote-getter who can win handsomely in all three islands. The surprising support, however, that the new Independent Citizens Movement garnered in both St. Thomas and St. Croix in the precedent-shaking 1970 election might indicate that as both islands begin to face more or less similar problems as modernization breaks down their traditional

15. *Annual Report, Office of the Government Secretary, Fiscal Year 1967* (St. Thomas: Government Printing Office, August 15, 1967), pp. 88–89.
16. See *Election of Virgin Islands Governor*, pt. 1, p. 113.

dissimilarities the insular character of voting patterns may likewise disappear.

How much of all this general temper of parochialism will in fact remain now that the elective governorship is beginning to influence the general political party picture is problematical. The 1970 election showed that the influence was already at work. It undoubtedly helped to stimulate the growth of new party alignments. There was the remarkable stimulation given to the Republican Party forces. There was the emergence of the Independent Citizens Movement. There was the decline of the Unity-Democratic dinosaur. Beyond doubt, those were surface phenomena indicative of very real subterranean forces at work. There was something of a burgeoning Virgin Islands nationalism in the appeal of the ICM, as well as an embryonic response to the vague feelings of racial insecurity embodied in the "black power" sentiment. The overthrow of the long Unity-Democratic Party reign suggested that its power to intimidate the electorate has been exaggerated, and that there was present in fact a new independence of voter spirit, especially in the growing middle-class sector of the private housing developments. What larger import these elements presage, of course, only time will tell. It is at least certain that the island political party scene is undergoing a process of serious revision.

Whatever the process of revision may mean it seems safe to say that, definitionally speaking, the Virgin Islands political system still remains highly pragmatic in character. It is no longer the opportunistic pragmatism of the individualistic politician going it alone. It becomes increasingly difficult for politicians like Frank Jacobs and Lloyd Joseph in St. Croix to behave in flagrant violation of party policy. Only the peculiar conditions of life on St. John have made it possible for a politician like Theovald Moorehead to conduct himself as the independent tribune of his constituents. The pragmatism, on the contrary, that is the hallmark of the system is operating in the area of ideology; for apart from the general concept of social welfare it would be difficult to discover any real ideological content in the elements of the system. Both ICM and Democratic Party candidates—Cyril King and Alexander Farrelly—in the 1970 campaign were ideologically liberal, emphasizing essentially the same program of general improvement of the basic infrastructure of island public services. Furthermore, the secret maneuvers that went on after the election among all three party legislative groupings with an eye to the organization of a majority legislative alliance graphically illustrated how the minority group of Progressive Republican senators was willing to come to an agreement with either of the other two senatorial groups; the sole consideration, for all sides, was the search for an alliance that would give them the largest benefit. Within the loose framework of party organization the one factor that seems so often to determine interparty understandings is that of personal rivalries based on accumulated animosities. What stood in the way of a Republican-ICM legislative amalgamation, according to political gossip after the election, was in fact the Republican resentment of the fact that the Crucian Moorehead family had subjected Governor Evans to vicious personal attacks during the campaign period. The minor controversy that accompanied Mr. King's failure to attend the governor's inauguration is another example of the intensely personalist atmosphere of the island politics. Since every political system requires its safety valves, this habit may well play a therapeutic role in compressed island societies.

Political energy is mainly consumed in the endless and apparently meaningless maneuvers of factions and individual politicians. It is true that at one time Governor Paiewonsky attempted to insist that the Donkeycrats were composed of the conservative upper class of the colored people while his own Unicrats were concerned with grass-roots folk seeking to become middle-class.[17] But that thesis is belied by the mass support that both groups were always able to muster, resulting typically in closely run elections with many candidates winning by extremely tiny margins. It is true, too, that for years it has been a fruitful political ploy to hold up the white continental business group as reactionaries and thereby to emphasize, by contrast, the social liberalism of the native groups. But this again will not bear examination. Senator Ken Alexander belonged to the majority Democratic group, and Senator David Hamilton to the minority Democratic group; yet both are domiciled mainlanders, the one in real estate and the other in the automobile franchise business. Senator Hamilton, indeed, successfully filled the role of Donkeycrat leader necessitated by the decline of Ron de Lugo's political career after 1966, and it would have been impossible to do that had he been a conservative in the manner, say, of men like Gordon Skeoch, representative of the old landed Crucian oligarchy and long bereft of any real political influence.[18] Likewise, there are signs that the younger set of educated continental professionals are beginning to take their political civics seriously, so much so that a rejuvenated Republican Party has

17. Quoted in *Daily News*, June 14, 1967.
18. See Roy Gottlieb, "David Hamilton—A Man of Many Names," Focus Magazine, *Home Journal*, Dec. 3, 1967. Senator Ken Alexander, as a businessman-senator, reports that he spends three-quarters of his time during sessions and one-half of his time in out-of-session periods on legislative business (interview, March 19, 1968).

emerged in the last few years, getting away from the old image of negativism and obstructionism, under the leadership of able young lawyers like Ronald Tonkin in collaboration with their native counterparts like the young business executive Evan Francois.

But a viable two-party system, along Democratic-Republican lines, is still only nascent. Meanwhile, since politics, like nature, abhors a vacuum, the political debate continues to concern itself, apart from the struggle for office and power, with the trivia of island life. The Police Department, the planned new jetport, the pollution of the St. Thomas harbor, the kinds of plays put on by the cultural centers (public opinion here is still very Victorian), the scandalous condition of island roads, Caribair service, government contracts for housing projects—all become lively issues both in private gossip and in the newspaper political columns. Heated debate even develops around the proposal that the islands should abandon the left-lane driving rule and change over to the standard American right-lane rule. The scurrilous comment that accompanied the undignified squabble about Secretary King's occupancy of a house situated on the grounds of the College of the Virgin Islands illustrated to what low levels this sort of insular parochialism can descend.[19] Another example of how petty the political struggle can get was the effort on the part of Peter Bove's enemies in 1969 to smear him when he was under congressional consideration as President Nixon's candidate for the governorship; this included the resurrection by the Drew Pearson column of a charge allegedly brought against Bove, in his capacity as comptroller, of making improper advances to girls in his office. The charge, fortunately ignored by the congressional committee, does indicate that the earlier style of character assassination in territorial politics may not be as obsolete as is sometimes assumed. There are times when it seems that Virgin Islanders can only rise above this temper of corrosive divisiveness when they are confronted with a challenge to their collective *amour-propre* from outside, for example by a series of rather exaggerated articles in the *New York Times* in 1969 which annotated the growth of racist attitudes in the islands, whereupon they close ranks in defense. Such reports, it is generally felt, gravely imperil the tourist trade, the continuing development of which is accepted by all politicians as a central article of faith, much as sugar was regarded in the politics of the Caribbean sugar islands until only recently.

Altogether, then, it is a politics of personality rather than of principles. At the same time it is not a cult of personality of the kind endemic in the neighboring Puerto Rican political system. The tradition of

19. See, for example, "The Political Observer" column, *Daily News,* Dec. 8, 1965.

Hispanic authoritarianism has meant that the brooding omnipresence of the *lider maximo* has characterized every generation of Puerto Rican political life. This has not been the case in the Virgins; not even the most powerful of their politicians—Senator Ottley, for example—have played the tremendous charismatic role of the great men of Puerto Rican politics—Barbosa, Santiago Iglesias, Muñoz Rivera, Muñoz Marin. In part, this is because of the relative absence of a powerful pre-American cultural influence. In part, it is because the continuing tenacity of the Spanish language in Puerto Rico against the intense pressures of Americanization has kept Puerto Rican politics a Spanish-language politics, while the different development in the Virgins, where English has remained the dominant linguistic instrument, has facilitated the Americanization of the spirit as well as of the structure of politics. The powerful individualism of American politics, as well as its anti-hero bias, has thus the more easily entered into the dependent colonial politics in St. Thomas.

That temper of individualism has, to go one step further, been reinforced by the aggressive individualism of island life. The Virgins, like Trinidad (and unlike Puerto Rico), have been a raucous, highly individualistic society created, historically, by the emergence of a social-ethnic fabric in which different racial and cultural conglomerates live precariously side by side, tolerating one another according to the unwritten rules of the social truce, but rarely collaborating for common purposes. In such societies, it is difficult for a genuinely national politics to grow up, for that requires (as in Puerto Rico) the base of a culturally homogeneous mass populace ready to yield up its loyalty to national hero-figures. So, just as in Trinidad the East Indian section still remains aloof from the controlling colored Creole political party, with the white Creole groups standing on the sidelines, in the Virgins the ruling political party has been for years that of the Creole native Virgin Islanders, with a handful of Puerto Ricans and white continentals allowed entry with secondary status, while the alien mass was left outside. All groups will agree, as Senator David Puritz told a visiting congressional subcommittee in 1966, that "the American political and governmental system is the finest method of governing the collective lives of a people yet devised by man."[20] But they are hardly yet capable of producing the flesh and blood of a common social purpose, founded on mutual trust, with which to encompass the skeleton of the politico-constitutional framework. The political leaders they come up with, including governors, are

20. Statement to Subcommittee on Territorial and Insular Affairs, U.S., House, 89th Cong., March 6, 1966, in *Proceedings*, Virgin Islands Legislature, March 15, 1966, p. 14.

sectional chieftains rather than national statesmen. Whether the elective governorship can change that is problematical. It is at least disconcerting to note that in the last few years it has been widely believed in the islands that many white continentals were opposed to the Elective Governor bill because it meant the certainty of a colored chief executive in Government House.

The ideological weakness of the local party life in large part flows from this sectionalism. A black nationalism, perhaps, could unite native Virgin Islanders and West Indian aliens into a new political alliance. But such a spirit is as yet poorly developed, and what there is of it retains the old Negro self-help message, summed up years ago in Jarvis' lecture to the Progressive Guide: "Forget Massa in the cold, cold ground. He is where he deserves to be. Allow Marian Anderson and George Washington Carver to enjoy their fame. Work individually and collectively for tomorrow as they did yesterday." [21] Alternatively, there could conceivably develop a politics of anticolonial nationalism, rooted in the idea of national independence. A leading stateside newspaper noted, when the Unity Party was beginning to form in the 1950s, that its members were slightly left of center and a somewhat nationalistic group.[22] But the party has hardly been that in its subsequent period of power. It has, in fact, willingly accepted the dependent status of the islands, seeking only to modify the status along the lines of the Puerto Rican commonwealth system. There is, then, a noticeable absence of the Puerto Rican type of status politics, not to mention anything comparable to the Puerto Rican *independentista* factions. There is a well-established habit in the island political debate of referring enviously to the Puerto Rican constitutional development as a model to be followed. But it has always been a reference to the pro-American elements of the Puerto Rican system, never to its anti-American elements.

In the absence of any grand, unifying principle, the local politics is marked by a temper of small-town bourgeois civics. Any collection of campaign statements by candidates will reveal that the two things most of them will mention with pride are their stable, respectable family life and their periods of service in the U.S. armed forces. The programs they advocate will concentrate on the mundane things of life: better roads, better police and educational services, more recreational areas, home ownership, improved air services, more efficiency in government, and so on.[23] This, of course, is unavoidable and indeed desirable in a repre-

21. Reported in *Daily News,* Feb. 18, 1944.
22. Article in *Cleveland Plain Dealer,* quoted in *ibid.,* Apr. 1, 1958.
23. Campaign statements by majority of electoral candidates in *Virgin Islands View,* October, 1966.

sentative system. At the same time it leads to a veritable dearth of informed discussion on the larger, transcendental issues.

It is not difficult to determine why—apart from the reasons already cited—this is so. In the first place, ever since the transfer the islands have consistently lost their best, most educated talent to the mainland, where the educational and occupational opportunities have lain. It is true that it is difficult to document that loss, since no statistical analysis of the emigration has been undertaken. Nor is there much known, from a statistical viewpoint, of the nature of the island colony in New York. But that the colony, for fifty years or more, has been large, and that it has had a high proportion of professional people in it, is common knowledge. It is of some significance, too, that when native Virgin Islanders write on the problem of leadership they tend to concentrate on the leader figures that have arisen from the mainland colony; an example is the recent series of articles in the local press by Geraldo Guirty, himself a returned exile. There is something about the island life-style that discourages local professional persons. That can be seen in looking at the indigenous second generation of Puerto Rican Virgin Islanders, for example, where the professions remain poorly represented, despite the fact that the group has become fully integrated into the educational system. Thus, there is not a single Puerto Rican lawyer or doctor among the Crucian Puerto Rican community and only one Puerto Rican lawyer in St. Thomas. The Puerto Rican talent is apparently emulating a pattern set earlier by the native Virgin Islanders.

Second, the absence of any center of higher education, until only recently, has aggravated the resultant anti-intellectual tone of life. By comparison, the inestimable influence of the University of Puerto Rico (founded in 1903) on the growth of Puerto Rican ideologies, as well as the way in which the University of the West Indies (founded in 1948) has in recent years helped forge a new relationship between the student body and the masses in both Trinidad and Jamaica, illustrates the heavy cost that the Virgin Islands society has had to pay for the absence of such a university in its own life. Thus, resultantly, the characteristic feature of colonial experience—the dependence of the colony on the mother country for ideas and values so that it becomes difficult for the colonial person to think out his own solutions to his own, fundamentally different, problems—has been grossly aggravated in the Virgins case. The model, always, is the American theory and practice, in politics as in everything else. So, when Representative Shirley Chisholm, campaigning for Cyril King's Independent Citizens Movement in the local gubernatorial race in 1969, compared that movement to the Fusion Party that put Mayor La Guardia in power in New York a generation ago, she was unwittingly providing just one more example of this colonial mentality in the Virgin Islands personality. Until an independent intellectual class develops in the islands, this tendency to encapsulate local experience in North American imagery will continue to hold that personality captive and to frustrate, among much else, the growth of a genuinely independent politics.

It has been argued by one of the veteran practitioners of Virgin Islands politics, Carlos Downing, in a rare attempt to furnish some theoretical foundation for the system, that the provincial type of party, unaffiliated to any of the national stateside political entities, simply serves to aggravate the confusion and ineptitude of the system. This lack of affiliation helps to explain why most islanders are ignorant of the history of the national parties, knowing only that Lincoln was a Republican and Roosevelt a Democrat. It leads to an absence of synchronization between what happens in Washington and what happens in St. Thomas, so that (as in 1952 and 1968) a Republican administration in the national capital is embarrassed by not being able to find appropriate allies in sufficient numbers in the colonial capital. The only way to end this unsatisfactory situation—the argument goes on—is to have local party entities affiliated in a logical fashion with their national counterparts. A local legislature divided more or less equally between Democratic and Republican parties will ensure that there will always be a ready approach to Congress from both sides, equally recognized. Thus a Republican-dominated Congress in Washington would look favorably on the local Republican group, and similarly a Democratic-dominated Congress would enjoy the confidence of the local Democratic group. In this way there would always be friends in Washington, regardless of how the party lines were arranged at any one time in the national capital. The Virgin Islands political groups would never run the risk of being isolated.[24]

The argument proceeds throughout on the assumption of the need for an intimate correlation between the metropolitan and subordinate party structures. It even defends the entry of continentals into local politics as beneficial since many of them will have useful contacts on the mainland. Moreover, it goes on to place the thesis within the terms of colonial loyalty:

> Further, it may be stated that provincial parties give the impression *per se* of having nationalistic tendencies. This, of course, is not the case with respect to

24. Carlos Downing, *Daily News*, Jan. 17, Mar. 7, 8, 1956, Jan. 18, 21, 1958.

the Virgin Islands, but outsiders seem to get this erroneous belief which certainly does the islands no good. Having this wrong opinion as to the patriotic spirit of the people as true Americans, the following question is at times asked by some mainland politicians: "Inasmuch as the people of the Virgin Islands have no use for either the Republican or Democratic parties why do you come to us for help rather than making your own way as you do in your politics?" There is hardly a reasonable answer that can be offered to such a question as things stand.[25]

The inference is clear that a separatist politics is dangerous and undesirable and that the future of local parties rests in a dependent alliance with the mainland forces.

Is this argument valid? Obviously, an answer in part depends on whether the question assumes continuing constitutional integration of the islands with the United States or considers possible independence. Yet, even assuming the continuing integration, there is room for discussion on the argument. It is of course inevitable, granted the appointive and regulatory powers of Washington, that the two political structures should be heavily intermixed. The behind-the-scenes machinations that went on between local political leaders and the secretary of the interior, as well as the chairman of the Democratic National Committee (not to mention the curious story of the mission of two agents from the Interior Department to the islands at the same time), with reference to the Paiewonsky candidacy for the governorship in 1960–61,[26] and Governor Paiewonsky's own account of how he kept in touch during his term of office with the Washington bureaucracy[27] demonstrate the wide scope of possible, and legitimate, interference by Washington in local affairs. With the appointed governorship Washington exercised a kingmaking power, which will naturally decline with the elective governorship. But it will not quite disappear. Personal and political contacts will still make it possible for the national party system to influence local political careers, in much the same sort of way, for example, that Cyril King was able to capitalize on his early period as administrative assistant to Vice-President Humphrey during the Johnson presidency. The continued affiliation of the island parties to the national parties, with the right to send alternate delegates to the respective national party conventions and to elect members to the respective national committees, further increases that possibility. A local figure like Roy Gottlieb, who is a member of both the Territorial Committee of the local Democratic Party and a

25. "Two Party System: The Virgin Islands," *ibid.*, Jan. 17, 1956.
26. Senate, Committee on Interior and Insular Affairs, *Nomination for Governor of the Virgin Islands: Hearings*, 87th Cong., 1st sess., 1961, pp. 81–86.
27. Senate, Subcommittee on Interior and Insular Affairs, *Election of Virgin Islands Governor: Hearings*, 90th Cong., 1st sess., 1967, pt. 2, pp. 496–500.

Democratic Party national committeeman, thus becomes a sort of broker between both ends of the axis.

The trouble is, of course—and this is the danger of the Downing thesis—that the relationship is not one between equals. Washington, with its enormous federal funding programs, has much to offer the islands, while St. Thomas has little to offer in return. It can give a handsome job as federal customs collector to the wife (who is now retired) of its own native son, Councilman Raymond Jones, county leader in the New York Democratic system; or create remunerative private consultantships for friendly ex-congressmen; or offer a tropical holiday during the winter period to visiting congressmen. But beyond that it can hardly go. However, the national interventions in local politics can frequently be disruptive, distort the real issues, and generate passions that do little good and much harm. The islands are ruled, much of the time, by "congressional government" through the medium of the relevant congressional committees. Yet a look at the way in which the Republican and Democratic members of those committees exploit their perennial visits to the islands to further their own partisan views, instead of adopting an objective attitude to what they see and hear, shows that the islands are used as a pawn in the Washington political game. Nor can it plausibly be argued that it is legitimate for mainland forces to interfere in island politics because Virgin Islanders after all interfere in stateside politics. Once again, the power to intervene is unequal. It is doubtful whether there is any truth to the claim, heard from time to time in St. Thomas, that there exists any real local influence on stateside elections—for example, the claim of certain Unity leaders in the 1950s that they controlled sufficient votes in California so that Congressman Clair Engle could not be elected without Unity Party support.

Continental affiliation, patently, has the effect of converting the local parties into satellites, to some degree, of the big stateside political machines. It facilitates the growing Americanization of local politics. Even the pantheon of heroes is mainland American, rather than local, so that whereas Valdemar Hill's books, *A Golden Jubilee* and *Rise to Recognition,* do full justice to the great figures of the local colonial freedom movement—Hamilton Jackson, Rothschild Francis, and the rest —it is significant that their names are rarely heard in the present-day speechmaking ritual of the political process. It is noticeable too that the characteristic properties of the stateside political game repeat themselves in the Virgins. There is the same fund-raising style of expensive testimonial dinners at the lush hotels, the same use of car-stickers and buttons, the same recruitment of public-relations firms to boost candidate images, not to mention the similar structure of electoral procedures,

(341)

party conventions, party primaries, and so on. It is immaterial, then, to suggest, as did many witnesses during the numerous committee hearings that were held on the matter of the elective governorship, that the election of the new-type chief executive ought not to coincide with the national presidential elections since the local issues would then become entwined with the national issues. They are, in fact, already so entwined. A dependent politics arises naturally out of a dependent colonial status. The consequence can only disappear as the original cause disappears.

There is one final point to note. Any political system is all the better if it receives healthy and continuous criticism from genuinely independent sources. A grave weakness of Virgin Islands politics is that little of such criticism exists. The reasons are apparent: a system of governmental employment which makes professional advancement for far too many people dependent on the good will of ruling political figures; a notable absence of independent institutional forces; and the lack, until recently, of a local university helping to form a class of informed citizens. So, what political criticism there is only too often is tainted by political self-interest. The leading "political analyst" of the *Home Journal* is at the same time a powerful figure within the Democratic machine, while the editor of the *Daily News* has his own political ambitions, having run, unsuccessfully, on an independent ticket in the 1968 election. There is a separate strand of criticism that comes from politically-minded continentals, but the fact that as fellow citizens they have a full right to participate is not always willingly conceded by natives. It is regrettable, then, that much of their criticism is often couched in strident and exaggerated tones. Too many of them, undoubtedly, suffer from a messianic conviction that they have been called to purify the local politics. That politics, it is true, is sufficiently corruptive in character. But it is probably not worse than the sort of corruption unearthed recently, for example, by the Knapp Commission in New York City. And it becomes grotesque distortion to compare it, as some of the continentals do in their more excited moments, with Huey Long's Louisiana or even Hitler's Germany.

Those mainland academicians who have concerned themselves with the islands cannot, of course, be so arraigned. They cannot be blamed for the fact that they are frequently identified with their official hosts of the local dominant groups, nor for the fact that those groups sometimes bring in academic advisers merely for the purpose of conferring an aura of academic respectability on decisions that have already been made. Some of them, it is true, manage to see that the islands' future possibly lies more with their Caribbean neighbors than with the United States—Professor Roy Macridis, for instance. But even then it is doubtful if they would go so far as to argue, as do native writers like Valdemar Hill, that the emergence of a truly united Caribbean, with the Virgin Islands as a member, would require that every foreign nation, including the United States, relinquish its Caribbean possessions. The more typical temper of most of the visiting academicians is one of constitutional conservatism. Their contribution—speaking now of most of them, for they constitute only a handful of persons, in any case—to the first volume to be published by the local college in its political science series, *The Virgin Islands, America's Caribbean Outpost: The Evolution of Self-Government,* can hardly be considered exciting, reflecting as it does the more staid elements in contemporary American political science developments.[28] Its very title, "America's Caribbean Outpost," suggests the colonialist viewpoint from which it is written. Some stateside political scientists, furthermore, have not been averse to using unscholarly and unreliable sources like the Evans book of 1935, with its vividly expressed animosity toward Virgin Islanders, to prove that the native populace is "unfit" for further steps in self-government. It is hardly surprising that the most fruitful kind of criticism tends to come from groups like the radical minority of students and faculty at the college who are beginning to realize that the writings of the Trotskyite-nationalist West Indian C. L. R. James are far more appropriate to their colonial condition than the advisory briefs of Ivy League political scientists whose premises are firmly set in orthodox American constitutionalism. Only a Caribbean political science, perhaps, rooted in the experience of the islands, can produce the sort of work that will help terminate the near monopoly that the politicians have had for so long over the Virgins public debate.

28. James A. Bough and Roy C. Macridis, eds., *The Virgin Islands, America's Caribbean Outpost: The Evolution of Self-Government* (St. Thomas: College of the Virgin Islands, 1970) .

14

~~~

The Problem of Status

In many ways the central malaise of life in the Virgin Islands is their continuing status as an "unincorporated territory" of the United States. What that means, essentially, is that in the absence of precise congressional grants of rights, citizenship in the islands does not carry with it the full plenitude of rights which inheres in citizenship in any of the fifty states. That differentiation is a result of the fact that the Constitution of the United States does not extend of its own force to unincorporated territories under American jurisdiction.[1] In the absence of the enactment of a bill of rights by Congress, only some properties of the national Constitution apply to the islands.[2] So, for example, citizens of the islands are not entitled as of right to the guarantee of jury trial in criminal cases.[3] What rights they do enjoy flow from the general fact that there are certain fundamental rights protected by the Constitution which apply to the islands of their own force and therefore are not dependent for their viability on a specific congressional grant.[4]

It can perhaps be best appreciated what denial of rights is involved by noting the major recommendations of the 1965 Constitutional Convention in St. Thomas. These included (1) election of a governor and a lieutenant governor by popular vote, (2) abolition of the limitation (in the 1954 Organic Act) on voting for legislative members at large, (3) representation in the U.S. Congress through a resident commissioner or delegate to the House of Representatives, (4) participation in national

1. *Dorr* v. *United States,* 195 U.S. 138, 24 S. Ct. 808 (1904); *Soto* v. *United States,* 273 F. 628 (3d Cir. 1921).
2. *Granville Smith* v. *Granville Smith,* 349 U.S. 1 (1955).
3. *Balzac* v. *Porto Rico,* 258 U.S. 298 (1922).
4. *Downes* v. *Bidwell,* 182 U.S. 244, 21 S. Ct. 770 (1901).

elections for the U.S. president and vice-president, (5) abolition of the presidential veto of local laws, (6) appointment of a comptroller by the local governor with advice and consent of the local legislature, (7) amendment of the Organic Act of 1954 by the local legislature, or by popular initiative through a referendum, or by a constitutional convention, and (8) authorization of the local legislature to fix the salaries of its own members, effective upon the election of a succeeding legislature.[5]

Today, over five years later, only three of these recommendations have been acted on by Congress. The most important, of course, is the right to elect the governor and the lieutenant governor by popular vote. The two others are minor concessions: the removal of the limitation on the vote for members at large and the right of the local legislature to fix its own salary levels (the latter thereby finally ending the financial embarrassments attending legislative membership). The Organic Act of 1954, imbued with Senator Butler's conservative temper, still remains the chief constitutional instrument. Congress can still annul local legislation (a right that has never been exercised, its mere existence, perhaps, being sufficient to curtail legislative extremism in St. Thomas). The right to the presidential vote, recently a lively issue in Puerto Rican demands on Congress, seems as far away as ever. The Elective Governor Act retained the thoroughly unpopular office of the comptroller, appointed by the secretary of the interior, thereby almost certainly ensuring repeat performances of the kind of acrimonious quarreling between that officer and the local government forces that has always marked the relationship. So far-reaching, indeed, is the comptroller's power, under the external audit concept, that it will certainly remain a thorn in the flesh of any local government in St. Thomas.

Most of these issues have been fought over for years. The long history of the fight for adequate representation in the national capital by means of a resident commissioner is as good an example as any of the forces that have been at work generally in the national-territorial relationship. As far back as 1945 the old Legislative Assembly petitioned for the idea, while in 1948 and again in 1952 popular referenda were overwhelmingly in favor of the reform. The secretary of the interior added his own weight to all this both in 1947 and 1949 in letters to the Speaker of the House of Representatives. The Committee on Public Lands approved the idea in 1949. Persons as eminent as Judge Hastie, former Governor de Castro, and former Congressman Fred Crawford all added their voices

5. "Draft to Provide for the Revised Second Organic Act of the Virgin Islands," in "Proceedings of the Constitutional Convention of the Virgin Islands," December 7, 1964, to February 27, 1965, mimeographed (St. Thomas, 1965), pp. 246–67.

in support of the claim. In the majority of these cases the argument was advanced, naturally enough, on the basis of the principle of self-determination within the American system. That was clearly in the minds of the members of the 1965 Constitutional Convention when they recommended a resident commissioner patterned after the relevant provision in the 1952 Constitution of the Puerto Rican commonwealth.[6] More latterly, Senator Hamilton from St. Croix has added some practical considerations of a new character springing from the acceptance of the elective governorship. He told a congressional committee:

> A territory, while not nearly of the same magnitude as a State, shares many of the same problems in that it is a separate political entity and therefore must at all times be ready to seek out or speak out on legislation that affects its well-being. To saddle an elected Governor with the responsibility of maintaining an alert, effective administration in the territory, at the same time staying abreast of congressional activity, in addition to dealing with all of the Federal departments, is simply too heavy a load for one man to handle successfully. An appointed Governor, by the very nature of his appointment, receives the cooperation and support of the Federal administration. An elected Governor might very well find himself at odds with the Federal administration and in the position of having to spend more time in Washington, protecting and promoting his own program, than in the territory, where he belongs. . . . In my opinion, a bill to elect our Governor is incomplete while it does not provide for a Resident Commissioner.[7]

It is in many ways a summation of colonial rule that all of these considerations, both moral and practical, have for thirty years or more been received by Congress with indifference, inaction, and even outright hostility. Congress, on the whole, has evinced two attitudes. The first is one of cost: a resident commissioner, it is claimed, would be an expensive item for the federal government to maintain. Yet it has been estimated that the cost might in fact be no more than $50,000 a year, or just over a dollar a year for each person in the islands. Virgin Islanders, rightly, have always been particularly incensed by this tendency to put a price tag on an issue that is, overwhelmingly, one of moral and constitutional right. The second congressional attitude has been perhaps even more insulting to local pride. It has taken the form of insisting, in a tone of high indignation, that the islanders have no right to complain about anything that comes within the ambit of congressional authority. "In

6. For all this, see the record on the struggle for the resident commissionership in U.S., Senate, Committee on Interior and Insular Affairs, *Virgin Islands Report,* 83d Cong., 2d. sess., 1954, pp. 73–79. See also the 25-point plan for the Virgin Islands, by Representative Fred Crawford, in *Daily News,* May 4, 1950.

7. House, Subcommittee on Territorial and Insular Affairs, *Election of Virgin Islands Governor: Hearings,* testimony of Senator David Hamilton, 90th Cong., 1st sess., 1967, pt. 2, pp. 589–90.

advancing your plea for self-government," Secretary Seaton wrote to the Unity Party group that organized the protest march of 1958 on Government House, "you should bear in mind that only the Congress of the United States has the authority to determine the political status of our territories." [8] "Members of our Committee," the chairman of the House Interior Committee magisterially informed the St. Thomas reform groups by letter in 1958, "have told the Virgin Islanders on innumerable occasions that additional powers and responsibilities would be granted when Congress in its wisdom deems such extension can be justified and managed in a capable manner." [9] The tone is one of parental righteousness exercising itself against a wayward child. And for years, it must be added, it was only a small minority of congressmen—Wayne Aspinall, Fred Crawford, and Adam Clayton Powell, for example—that championed the islanders' cause.

Confronted with such inflexible attitudes the island forces have been reduced to a strategy of inventing plausible facsimiles in order to gain a voice in the federal capital. The strategy goes back thirty years or more; and because it illustrates so well the helplessness of the colonial politics *vis-à-vis* the metropolitan politics, it is worth noting in some detail. To begin with, after World War Two there was the device of the paid lobbyist in Washington, hired by the local legislature. But the method ran into trouble when Governor Merwin, in some acrimonious correspondence with the local Senate president, charged that the lobbyist, by holding talks with Interior officials, was invading the jurisdiction of the governor's office working through the Office of Territories of the Interior Department.[10] The legislature throughout the same period attempted to meet the problem by the passage of legislation setting up an Office of Delegates in Washington. But such bills were successively vetoed by governors—by Governor Harwood in 1944, for instance, and by Governor Gordon in 1956. Governor Gordon's veto message cited constitutional grounds: specifically, the Organic Act of 1954 recognized the secretary of the interior as the presidential agent in charge of incorporated and unincorporated territories, and for the territorial legislature to nominate a delegate to the national capital with power to deal directly with federal officers was in effect an illegal attempt to administratively bypass the secretary.[11] Governor Harwood's earlier veto message to the old Legislative Assembly used language so sharp that it

8. Cited in Valdemar A. Hill, Sr., *A Golden Jubilee: Virgin Islanders on the Go under the American Flag* (New York: Carlton Press, 1967), p. 162.

9. Quoted in *Daily Gleaner* (Kingston, Jamaica), Mar. 21, 1958.

10. Exchange of correspondence, Governor Merwin and president of the Senate, in *Home Journal*, Jan. 20, 1959.

11. Quoted in *Daily News*, May 16, 1956.

can perhaps only be explained in terms of the excited indignation let loose in the officers of the federal hierarchy by any action on the part of the territorial assemblies to claim independent representation for themselves. "This ill-considered legislative action," Harwood lectured the Assembly members, "does not inspire confidence in the ability of the present legislative authorities of the Virgin Islands to assume a greater share of the privileges and obligations of their government." [12]

Thus balked by executive opposition the legislative forces turned more and more to the device of the occasional delegation appointed to lobby in Washington on particular matters. As early as 1944, indeed, the method had been used to persuade the War Production Board to cease linking the islands with Puerto Rico and thereby ignoring the special problems of the islands. Ten years later the method was used to lobby Congress on the terms of the pending new Organic Act; some of the delegation's recommendations at that time, such as the elimination of the presidential veto over local legislation, are still unmet. A radio address of Senator Lawaetz in 1958, reporting to Virgin Islanders on his trip to Washington (in that case, a mission sponsored by the governor), demonstrated the amount of ground that could be covered by an energetic delegate: testimony before the Senate Subcommittee on Irrigation and Reclamation with particular reference to a desalinization plant for the islands, discussions with Interior officials on the dechartering of the Virgin Islands Corporation, lobbying on behalf of the island cane growers, and an investigation of progress on plans for harbor development in St. Thomas and St. Croix.[13] Yet all this was intermittent rather than continuous representation of island interests; and only recently has it been replaced by the first elected full-time representative of the islands in the federal capital.

Even so, the islands still remain, as it were, colonial beggars knocking at the metropolitan door. The island representative is not even the non-voting delegate that his Puerto Rican counterpart is. He is not entitled to a congressional office; he is denied membership on committees; he has no access to the floor of either chamber; and, of course, he has no voting power. He has to meet, furthermore, a general congressional attitude of skepticism and unhelpfulness, summed up in the recent complaint of the Puerto Rican resident commissioner: "What I have to overcome is the attitude among Congressmen who tell me, 'Of course, you people don't

12. Quoted in *ibid.*, Jan. 10, 1944.
13. Text in *ibid.*, Apr. 10, 1958. For an account of the activities of an earlier delegation to the federal capital in 1922, see letter of Adolph Sixto to Emil Berne, July 27, 1922, in *St. Croix Tribune*, Aug. 11, 1922.

pay any federal taxes, so you really can't expect too much.' " [14] The answer to that innuendo, which Virgin Islanders are not slow to offer, is that since they have no representation in Congress the principle of "no taxation without representation" applies, and although they do not contribute to the federal treasury (for that very reason) their youth do in fact make the ultimate contribution of service in the U.S. armed forces. It is not surprising, then, that attempts to modernize and strengthen the office of the island representative in Washington have come only from Charlotte Amalie: for example, a recent act of the territorial legislature withdrew its old impeachment power against the holder of the office, replacing it with the proviso that he can only be removed by the electorate through a special referendum.

The point to underline is that the islands continue to be governed by the political science of "congressional government"—government, that is, by an instrumentality in which they have no membership and over which they have no control save that of moral suasion. That instrumentality not only exercises a major decision-making power over most aspects of territorial life, but—despite the growth of internal self-government—it also exercises other powers such as, anomalously, the right to determine the electoral basis of the territorial legislature. Congressman Burton's remark in the 1967 hearings, "We are still the governing board, so to speak, of the territories," aptly summarizes the position. It is doubtful if an instrumentality more unfitted for such a role—the governance of dependent areas—could possibly exist. The average congressman must of necessity respond to a priority of obligations: first to his constituency, second to the national interest, and only last of all to the peculiar interests of the dependencies. He must be specially motivated to make himself an authority on the problems of people who, after all, are not constituents but merely colonial clients, as it were. The seniority rule means that the chairmanships of the strategic committees, from the viewpoint of those clients, are filled on the basis of considerations quite removed from those problems. Senator Tydings in one period and Senator Butler in another personified, in their patriarchal attitudes to the Virgin Islands, the sort of irreparable damage that can result. The Virgin Islands, then, like Guam and American Samoa, must always wait at the end of the line. Even in its domestic setting Congress moves at a glacial pace. It moves at a pace even more glacial when it comes to needful legislation for the overseas dependencies. Considering the extensive time periods it has taken Congress to discuss the ideas of the resident com-

14. Quoted in *San Juan Star*, Jan. 14, 1970. For the office of the resident commissioner for the Virgin Islands, see *ibid.*, Jan. 22, 28, 1970.

missionership and the presidential vote, it is safe to assert that it will take it veritable light-years to even begin discussion of statehood for the islands.

The territory, in brief, is altogether at the mercy of Congress. Even when the congressional system provides a friend at court—such as in the person of Congressman Aspinall as chairman of the House Interior Committee—it is the result of accident, not of policy. The same is true of the various federal agencies that control and supervise so much of the territorial activities. Everything that the territory gets is given as a favor, not as a matter of right. It is perhaps the small, odd exemplifications of this generally humiliating condition that hurt the islanders' pride as much as anything: the fact, for example, that the islands, like the other dependent territories, are not regarded as United States territory for the purposes of drug control in international traffic, or the fact that what passes for a territorial flag is nothing more than a copy of the U.S. Navy ensign, made the islands' official emblem by naval order in 1921. Caribbean colonial history has a long record of riots triggered by such apparently minor irritants. The record could still repeat itself in the Virgins.

Congressional rule for the islands means, in essence, at best a government of benevolent paternalism shared by the Interior Department and the appropriate congressional committees. Granted the nature of American executive-legislative relationships, those two agencies have never managed to adopt a common, coherent policy toward the dependency. If Assistant Secretary Carver's speech of 1960 is taken as the ideal statement of Interior policy, Washington sees itself as engaged in a partnership with St. Thomas, making itself responsible only for matters imbued with federal substance. Congress, contrariwise, has oscillated between outright neglect and overweening paternalism. The old attitude of federal officialdom, even as recently as the 1950s, was of course almost completely colonialist, as was demonstrated in statements like that of Harry Taylor (former administrator in St. Croix) in 1953:

> The clamor there [in the Virgin Islands] is for more self-government and not for more efficient self-government. What they have been doing with what they've got is disgraceful, and mere change of form will accomplish little until they grow up, accept the responsibilities of self-government, and evidence mental and moral capacities and qualities adequate to its proper exercise. And that goes for the electors as well as the elected.[15]

15. Letter, *Daily News*, May 22, 1954.

Such disquisitions force the Virgin Islanders into a narrow strait jacket of norms and value judgments that arise, historically, out of the comparatively limited experience of the Anglo-American party system over the last century or so. No effort is made tb ask whether that experience is pertinent to the problems of a Caribbean colonial society emerging from a quite different historical experience. Consequently, Virgin Islanders are endlessly lectured by visiting congressmen and academic mandarins about the general desirability of the Washington model. But it is doubtful, for example, if the separation of powers doctrine is at all practical in such a Lilliputian society, any more than—to speak in comparative Caribbean terms—the doctrine of the anonymity of the civil servant is practical in the tiny societies of the former British West Indian islands, characterized by such high degrees of social intimacy, to which the Westminster model has likewise been so uncritically exported. In both cases the metropolitan model has been transferred by the imperial officialdom to the dependent colonial society as a sacred article of faith; and if the colonials have failed to learn the lesson they have been denied their final graduation ceremonies.

The second observation to be made on the thesis of "evolving status" is that the phrase itself presupposes a gradualist development of constitutional status in which each step, one improving on the other, has presumably taken place in response to some prearranged grand policy shaped by Washington. Yet it would be difficult to think of a thesis more fictional in character when compared with the real story. In actual fact, there has been no progressive movement, in a style of social Darwinism, from lower to higher levels. Civil government in 1931 was, admittedly, an improvement on naval government in 1917. But the Organic Act of 1954 was in many ways retrogressive, adding new federal controls over the local governing entities rather than enlarging the promise of self-government contained in the earlier act of 1936. Nor was advance, when it came, the fruit of a forward-looking statecraft on the part of a beneficent federal government. It was, on the contrary, as Assistant Attorney General James Bough pointed out in 1968, the result of continuous agitation in the islands and persistent pressure on Washington by means of innumerable petitions, resolutions, and delegations to the federal capital.[22] The island forces have had to fight, frequently at the cost of much anguish and bitterness, every inch of the way against the lethargy and obstructionism of the Washington governmental labyrinth. To call this in any way an "evolutionary" process is to place an interpretation upon the record not warranted by the facts.

22. See "General Introduction to the Constitutional Evolution of the Virgin Islands," in *ibid.*

Reading the history of that struggle brings out the astonishingly heavy-handed attitude of Congress to island aspirations. The general tone has been schoolmasterish: Virgin Islanders must learn to "behave," to have "respect" for Congress, in return for which good behavior they will receive their prize when the head office so decides. But what is equally astonishing is that Virgin Islanders themselves, despite their readiness to fight hard for what they want, have been generally compliant in the face of that attitude. The lengths to which the islanders will go in order to please or placate Congress must be seen to be believed; it constitutes a veritable Uriah Heep-like posture of fawning appeasement. Any show of militancy on the part of the more daring spirits in their midst is immediately met by pained admonitions to "behave" on the part of the more cautious elements. The angry reactions, to take only a single instance, of Senators de Lugo and Lawaetz to the Unity Party protest march of 1958 are symptomatic: that action, they urged in shrill tones, was one of power-mad and small-minded politicians calculated to alienate even the most friendly of congressmen.[23] The contrast, indeed, between congressional arrogance and Virgin Islands deference is so marked that it requires an effort at explanation.

In part, what is at work here is the obsession with what Washington says and does. Everyone looks to Washington for aid, guidance, inspiration. Everything local is thus seen not in terms of local values and experience but through the distorted prism of the metropolitan values and experience. This produces both a profound self-distrust, almost self-contempt, in the colonial person and a readiness at the slightest provocation to raise a hymn of praise to all things American. In 1931, at the height of the American economic crisis, a local radical newspaper did quote approvingly from Erich Remarque's attack on patriotism in *The Road Back*.[24] But that was a rare exception; more generally, Virgin Islanders of all viewpoints have been the loudest carriers of American chauvinistic patriotism. It was perhaps permissible that a local conservative like George Audain should have talked of the 1917 transfer as "but the beginning of that immutable decree of Providence through which other territories will eventually come under the Stars and Stripes. This is particularly true of the European possessions." [25] But even a Virgin Islander as trenchantly critical of American colonial policies as Ashley Totten could, in almost similar vein, speak of the American democracy "that spreads its mighty hand of sympathy to the four corners

23. For all this, see Senator Ron de Lugo, text of radio speech, in *Daily News*, Apr. 17, 1958; and Senator Fritz Lawaetz, text of radio speech, in *ibid.*, Apr. 10, 1958.
24. *The Emancipator*, Supplement, July 11, 1931.
25. "Transfer Day Address," *Daily News*, Apr. 1, 1942.

of the world," a view not altogether excused by the fact that it was uttered in the midst of the war against the Fascist powers.[26] From time to time the more perceptive of island spokesmen will recognize what is going on, and the damage it does to Virgin Islands life and personality. Lionel Roberts saw it in 1933. He told his colleagues of the Colonial Council at that time:

> A very unfortunate place is our little island. At the will of Tom, Dick or Harry it is swayed to compare sometimes with the United States, sometimes with England, sometimes with Puerto Rico, and every other place under God's sun; but never with itself and the things consistent with and necessary to its own government.[27]

The general consequence of that habit was, as a local editor saw it at much the same time, the growth of a fatal and directionless ambiguity in island attitudes. He wrote:

> Our characteristics are purely imitative. We have no history. Whatever the racial traits and characteristics of our ancestors, they were fairly well consumed in the melting pot of slavery. . . . Although slavery was abolished in these islands in 1848 it is still but of yesterday. Two generations ago we were nearer portraying our true characteristics than we are today. We are still characterless, not to say without native or racial ambition.[28]

It cannot plausibly be argued that these sentiments express the peculiar conditions of Virgin Islands life before American ownership finally brought with it, after the termination of World War Two, some tangible measure of American prosperity and affluence, for it is easy to match them with comparable utterances today. It would almost be possible to argue that prosperity and affluence have given the sentiments a new edge, a new sense of profound loss, that they did not possess in their earlier embodiment. The series of congressional hearings throughout 1966, 1967, and 1968 on the matter of the elective governorship, for example, gave Virgin Islanders one more opportunity to prove their patriotism to visiting congressmen, and the more independent of them an opportunity, likewise, to note the abject character of the attitude. One of the witnesses put it as follows:

> The long struggle, the anxiety, the disappointments, the setbacks, have had its effects on our fortitude and morale. It has caused chronic frustration and multi-complexes to affect segments of the people of the Virgin Islands. Because we do not have self-government, some of us have developed paternal complexes,

26. Letter to Representative John Dingell, House Ways and Means Committee, April 22, 1942, in *ibid.*, May 14, 1942.
27. Reported in *ibid.*, May 19, 1933.
28. Editorial, *The Emancipator*, Aug. 9, 1937.

running to members of Congress, with all their troubles, real and imaginary, as political fathers and protectors. Others advocate that since over the years Congress has not seen it fit to yield to our repeated requests for a greater measure of self-government, that self-government is not good for the people of the Virgin Islands, it is bad and dangerous and we should have none of it.[29]

The passage dramatically illustrates what happens under colonialism to the communal psychology of a dependent people. It leads to drastic self-abasement. It corrodes self-respect. It blunts the edge of any sentiment for freedom. Some of the ultra-patriotic declarations of loyalty to flag and constitution by native witnesses during the same hearings give the impression that on occasion some Virgin Islanders, political leaders as well as private citizens, live on their knees.[30] In part, the phenomenon here under discussion is the outcome of the atmosphere of profound uncertainty in which the islanders live. What Congress gives, Congress can take away. Where so much of insular livelihood depends on special privileges enacted by congressional legislation there is always the fear that the privileges may be whittled down or even abandoned for reasons extraneous to Virgin Islands considerations.

All this helps to explain why there has never been a Virgin Islands *risorgimento* of anticolonial nationalism, with independence as its aim. For years even the slightest mention of self-government or autonomy provoked a negative reaction from the islanders, because they felt that it was an indirect affront to their pride as U.S. citizens. The same sentiment now accompanies any mention of independence. The 1965 Constitutional Convention thus adopted a resolution on status in which it declared itself "unalterably opposed" to independence and in favor of the closest association with the United States as an "autonomous territory," although that term was in no way fully defined. There can be little doubt that the resolution reflects the feelings of the effective majority of the islanders.[31]

Any keen observer of the Caribbean scene is driven to reflect that there are other peoples in the area that have suffered from the blight of the colonial psyche and have nevertheless moved on to independence. Why have the Virgin Islands not followed suit? The answer, apart from those already offered, lies perhaps in a comparative analysis between the Danish and the American colonial legacies. Whereas the Spanish in Puerto Rico left behind them a powerful Hispanic imprint on people and

29. *Election of Virgin Islands Governor,* statement of Henry E. Rohlsen, pt. 1, p. 171.
30. *Ibid.,* pp. 165, 357, 362, 375.
31. "Proceedings of the Constitutional Convention," Resolution on Status, pp. 269–70.

culture, in the Virgins the Danish heritage was weak and impermanent. The persistency of that legacy in Puerto Rico, especially in language, gave Puerto Rican nationalism a linguistic base that has been absent in the Virgins. The cultural-ethnic homogeneity of Puerto Rican life, at the same time, as contrasted with the heterogeneity in the composition of the Virgin Islands society, as already noted, conferred upon Puerto Ricans a common sense of cultural nationality, of *puertorriquenidad*, which Virgin Islanders have lacked; it is suggestive that the term "native Virgin Islander" still signifies only that section of the polyglot society that is native-born in the islands.

At the same time the element in Puerto Rican nationalism that feeds upon a romantic image of the Spanish past can do so because the Spanish era ended at a time (1898) which no generation of contemporary Puerto Ricans can really remember. In the case of the Virgins, on the contrary, there is a sizable element of older people who can still remember the reality, as distinct from the myth, of the Danish past. The sense of grate-fulness for the benefits of American rule is thus reinforced by the compari-son those people can make with the comparatively poor record of the Danish kingdom. The gratefulness, in turn, is reinforced by the fact that Virgin Islanders can see no alternative, in the short run, at least, to retaining the American connection. It is in this sense that, savoring the fruits that flow from the connection, they want what they get rather than get what they want. And if any of them complain they are likely to be reminded—by the chairman, for example, of the Senate Interior and Insular Affairs Committee at one time—that they are better off than their Caribbean neighbors living under other metropolitan powers.[32] Most of them, however, appear contented with what they have, and will readily agree with the Virgin Islands exiles living in Puerto Rico who, contrasting the turbulence of Puerto Rican status politics with the comparative lack of interest in status matters by Virgin Islanders, utter prayerful thanks that in St. Thomas at least people realize that their political status will somehow be eventually resolved and leave it at that.[33]

What, in any case, are the status alternatives? There is, to begin with, statehood, with the islands possibly gaining that goal as a unit joined to Puerto Rico. There is the possibility of union with the British Virgin Islands, where cultural similarities and economic interdependency lend credence to the "single group" theory. There is the idea of remaining

32. Quoted in *Daily Gleaner,* Mar. 27, 1958.
33. D. R. Primoshic, letter, *San Juan Star,* Apr. 16, 1967.

annexed to the United States but at the same time seeking a relationship of "closer association" with the immediately neighboring West Indian territories, so much alike ethnically. Should any of these alternatives prove impossible, mainly because of opposition within the United States or, in the case of union with the British Virgins group, from the United Kingdom, there is the final possibility of independence, which would leave the islands free to choose whatever type of larger Caribbean alliance they might want. It is worth discussing all of these alternatives in some detail.

Statehood, to begin with, would probably not be financially feasible. While the present grants-in-aid and matching funds payments would continue, the new burden of federal income tax would almost certainly be an impossible one for the territorial treasury to take on. Apart from the consideration that Congress is not even beginning to consider the possibility, it is doubtful if many islanders have seriously thought out the wider implications. In constitutional terms, it would mean absorption into the centralized federal governmental structure in which, to employ the phrase of Justice Roberts, the individual states are not so much coequal partners as they are administrative districts of the federal government. It is no longer the case, as it was fifty years ago, that federalism permits the state to become a laboratory of social and economic experimentation. As a state capital, then, Charlotte Amalie would have no more power of maneuver in such experimentation than, say, Bismarck, North Dakota, or Raleigh, North Carolina. Even more portentous is the consideration that statehood would accelerate the processes of cultural absorption, for the advent of statehood would mean—as happened in the cases of Alaska and Hawaii—an immediate influx of Americans seeking opportunities in new places. Most of them would be white, and this would help to tip the racial balance in the islands even more against the native group. Recent estimates suggest that in the seven years after 1960 the percentage of natives in the total population declined by more than 10 per cent. Statehood would engender an even more precipitate decline. It is obvious that sooner or later the territorial leadership must begin to think seriously about some sort of population control, perhaps by a policy of restrictive entry. Statehood, of course, would make that impossible.

Statehood, then, is at the moment illusory. It does not seem possible even for Puerto Rico, where since 1968 a local pro-statehood Republican administration has been committed to the ideal. For Charlotte Amalie, union with the British Virgins group, to create a "greater Virgin Islands," seems more plausible. Norwell Harrigan's pioneer work, "A Study of the Inter-Relationships between the British and United States Virgin Islands," has discussed the matter for the first time in detail. The lengthy brief (to speak of some earlier documentation) presented by the governor of the British Virgin Islands in 1954 to a visiting congressional committee at Roadtown spelled out the essential facts of the case.[34] About one-third of the St. Thomian population at that time were of British Virgin Islands stock. Economically, St. Thomas was the "town" and the British Virgins were the "country" of a single economic community. Some two centuries of continued intercourse, at every level, between the peoples of the twin entities had produced a single ecological system which was then threatened by the arbitrary application of U.S. naturalization and immigration legislation. The brief, of course, simply argued for a humane application of that legislation to meet a peculiar situation. It did not draw the logical conclusion that the economic and cultural intermixture could only end in some form of amalgamation.

Yet amalgamation, as the Harrigan study (1969) makes abundantly clear, could create as many problems as it would solve. If, from the point of view of Roadtown, it were amalgamation with an independent U.S. Virgin Islands, the connection would make sense. But in practice it would mean amalgamation with a sister group that is increasingly Americanized in its public policies. It would mean, for a sizable element of local opinion, the loss of an English identity still cherished. It would mean the importation of all the social problems, including racism, which they see in the American Virgins. There would be the problem, too, of integrating two politico-constitutional systems entirely different in character. Most important of all, however, is the fact that in recent years the British entity has begun its own economic recovery, based on a new influx of private capital in the tourist and construction sectors and on enlarged government spending financed from the United Kingdom treasury.

Yet the irony of the situation is that British Virgin Islanders, aware of what is happening in the neighboring American territories, seem bent on repeating the same pattern of bringing in outside venture capital, with all that it ensures: the alienation of land and property to external shareholders, in this case real estate and financial operators from London; the development of Bahamian-type tourist resorts, priced for the wealthy after the fashion of the Rockefeller operations in St. John and Virgin Gorda, and of which the now scandalous deal with the Bates-Hill consortium group regarding the small island of Anegada is the best-known example; and not least of all the threat of a reversion to the racist social patterns of the nineteenth century as white residents begin to settle and stake their claim in the boom. This, in effect, still following the U.S. Virgins pattern, becomes an alliance of vested interests between the financial intruders anxious to "make a killing" and the local mercantile-

34. *Relationships between the British and American Virgin Islands,* text in *Daily News,* Dec. 24, 28, 29, 1954.

trading families (the Penns, O'Neals, Pickerings, and Dawsons), with the outside "developers" receiving the lion's share of the profits. The position is made all the more hazardous by the fact that, as Harrigan points out, the small British Virgins do not have much of an experienced leadership class or a sophisticated administrative machinery to withstand the tremendous pressures brought on them by these outside forces.[35] The British islands, in brief, are caught between the devil and the deep blue sea. On the one hand there are the private interests seeking to capitalize on the natural resources of the islands, resources which, paradoxically, are in effect destroyed as they are "developed," a process well under way in the American Virgins. On the other hand, they cannot expect much help from Great Britain since British governments since 1945 have been steadily dismantling their colonial properties in the Caribbean, undertaking in fact a clearance sale for any buyers.

The idea of "closer association" with at least the Eastern Caribbean area is logical in the sense that historically and culturally the Virgins belong to that area. The very title of Darwin Creque's book—*The U.S. Virgins and the Eastern Caribbean*—testifies to that link. The annual report of the governor in 1940 insisted that "the language, the *mores,* the political organization, the planter system of agriculture, all owe more to the British West Indies than to the Danish State." The American influence, of course, has balanced that, while the later immigrant influx from the Leewards has in turn counterbalanced the American impact. The historical past of the Virgins is indelibly Caribbean. But so is the present. Thus, the intra-Caribbean movement of the populations of the Leewards and British Virgins to the American islands is only one of the latest in a series that go back for centuries; the movement can be seen as corresponding, in the immigrants' condition of voluntary servitude, to the entry of Chinese and Indian indentured labor into the area in the nineteenth century; while even the movement of white continentals to the islands reproduces, in modern guise, the old Caribbean distinction between the "Creole" (native Virgin Islander) and the "homelander" (continental) . The enforced bilateralism of the American connection, in which practically everything—trade, education, movement of persons— has concentrated in the direction of the United States, means that this Caribbean aspect has been neglected, even turned away from. There is

35. For all this, see Norwell Harrigan, "A Study of the Inter-Relationships between the British and United States Virgin Islands," mimeographed (St. Thomas: Caribbean Research Institute, College of the Virgin Islands, June, 1969); *The Island Sun* (Roadtown, Tortola), Oct. 26, 1968, May 10, 1969; and "Inside the British Virgin Islands," Focus Magazine, *Home Journal,* Sept. 3, 10, 1967. See also John P. Augelli, "The British Virgin Islands: A West Indian Anomaly," *Geographical Review* (New York) , Vol. XLVI, no. 1 (January, 1956) .

much evidence to suggest that in 1870 St. Thomas was an international, multidimensional community, while in 1972 it is a hermetic, one-dimensional community. There is at least room for exploring the possibilities of regaining that Caribbean role, of replacing the present bilateral relationship with the States with a series of multilateral relationships with other Caribbean societies. How far that could go—whether, for instance, it could mean membership in the Caribbean Free Trade Association (which is the first step in the region toward creating a unity based on West Indian interests and objectives)—would depend, of course, on the willingness of Congress and the administration in Washington to permit experimentation within the framework of the national trade and customs barriers.

If it turns out that the American connection makes such experimentation impossible, then Virgin Islanders who care for their Caribbean identity may be driven to the point where they find it necessary to examine the concept of independence within the Caribbean framework. Even to begin to do that would constitute a traumatic experience, since there is probably no dependency complex anywhere in the region so deeply entrenched in the collective mentality of a Caribbean people as is the case with Virgin Islanders. For many of them independence would seem not a step toward freedom but simply abandonment by the United States. Yet it is not entirely unimaginable that some day the concept will become part of the serious political debate in the islands. If and when it does, certain basic considerations will by their very nature present themselves. There is the consideration that independent Caribbean neighbors like Jamaica and Barbados have shown that it is possible to undertake a prosperous tourist industry without benefit of metropolitan privileges. There is the consideration that it would not be inconceivable to work out, when the time comes, economic terms to a treaty of separation that would ensure stability during the period of transition from territory to independent nation. There is the consideration, not the least important, that an independent Virgin Islands would become a natural candidate for membership in those embryonic forms of regional cooperation which, in the long run, must come to constitute a Caribbean Economic Community.

There is, above and beyond all else, the consideration that, despite their top layer of Americanization, the Virgin Islands exhibit many of the leading properties that characterize Caribbean life in general throughout the region. They share with Curaçao a polyglot racial-social structure in which, in the Virgins case, a combination of Jewish mercantile families and Protestant American entrepreneurs, and, in the Curaçaon case, a combination of Sephardic Jewish business houses and Protestant Dutch

(363)

entrepreneurs run and control economies based on black labor. They share with Trinidad a dangerously schizoid situation in which political power rests in the hands of the black majority and economic power in the hands of the local and expatriate white minorities. They share with the Bahamas a type of tourist economy in which an unskilled or at best semiskilled black labor force is made restless by the near presence of white tourist affluence. And they share with all of those other Caribbean sister societies, for the very reasons here cited, the danger that the growing popularity of the "black power" ideology will erupt into the sort of mass riots that swept Curaçao in 1969 and Trinidad in 1970. Not least of all, the islands all possess in common, in one way or another, the problems that have been emphasized in the recent scholarly literature analyzing the relationship in the modern world between territorial size and political independence: the inordinately high costs of public administration in relation to population size; the overreaching and pervasive impact of government on everyday life; the difficulty, almost the utter impossibility, of separating civil service administration from politics; the excessive rigidity of social structure; and, generally, a small-island life-style that makes anonymity almost impossible, with the concomitant threat to civil liberties.[36]

It is frequently argued that independence can only be suicidal for groups like the Virgins, with their absence of resources, tiny size, and prolonged dependence on outside patronage sources. There are a number of weak points in the argument. To begin with, the theory of "resources" is inelastic; it fails to appreciate that an apparent liability can in effect become a resource. Thus, in the 1940s a surplus labor force in Puerto Rico was regarded as a crippling liability, yet was transformed into an asset for the expatriate capital-sponsored industrialization program of the *Populares*. In similar fashion, an independent Virgin Islands republic would not lose the tropical basis of its tourist industry, nor indeed is there anything in such an industry that is incompatible even with a socialist economy. The land area of St. Croix can be dismissed, from the viewpoint of an industrialization-oriented economics, as a dead loss; from the viewpoint of a planned agriculture-oriented economics it can be seen, more positively, as the basis of a production program offsetting the excessive reliance on American imported foodstuffs. It could be argued that

36. For the recent literature on these problems of size and independence, see Burton Benedict, ed., *Problems of Smaller Territories* (London: University of London, Athlone Press, for the Institute of Commonwealth Studies, 1967); Rupert Emerson, *Self-Determination in the Era of Decolonization* (Cambridge, Mass.: Harvard University Center for International Affairs, 1964); and Stanley A. De Smith, *Microstates and Micronesia: Problems of America's Pacific Islands and Other Minute Territories* (New York: Center for International Studies, New York University Press, 1970).

the islands would be better off with less rather than more stateside capital investment. Industrial complexes like the oil and alumina operations in St. Croix, being capital-incentive, bring few positive advantages to the local economy. They generate few new jobs; they alienate resources that could be used more rationally; and in their social aspects they create an artificial wage-salary imbalance in the local economy and tend to give rise to company industrial settlements (like the well-known case of Mackenzie in Guyana) characterized by racial ghetto arrangements dividing white expatriate staff and colored work force.

There already exists a great deal of self-confessing public comment on the part of the Puerto Rican planners on these matters, especially on the fact that their program, vastly indiscriminate, has failed to concentrate on those labor-oriented, quality industries that could most benefit the local economy. The Puerto Rican program of expatriate capital-sponsored development has solved few of the Puerto Rican social problems: massive unemployment, social inequity, cultural disorientation, and the rest. There is no reason to assume that the consequences of the Virgins variant of the program will be any more pleasing. The policy of permanent reliance on foreign investment, indeed, is based on the Rostow theory of economic growth, which presupposes a transition from a "take-off" economy to a "mature" economy, leading, as the final stage, to a self-sustained economy. It is evident that, in the Puerto Rican case, the theory has collapsed, for what marks the present state of the economy is a seemingly permanent need for foreign investment, leading to a spiraling growth of both public and private debt. The alternative—far short, after all, of being the Cuban alternative of socialist development—could conceivably be that of controlled quality craft industries, after the Swiss fashion, catering to a multilateral international market. But only an independent economy, with full freedom of trade and customs policy, could undertake aggressive economic planning of that character, as, indeed, small Caribbean neighboring economies such as Barbados are already undertaking.

There is, further, the question of size. Historically speaking, there has been little necessary relationship between size, national independence, and civilization; more particularly, it is a fact that societies no larger than the Virgins have opted for independence. What is often overlooked is the contemporary environmental climate, as it were, of that choice. Much pessimistic comment assumes that independence, in the 1970s, means a nineteenth-century option; that is, a country's being thrown utterly on its own resources, in the manner of Haiti or the Dominican Republic. That, it goes without saying, is not so. Independence takes place within the framework of interdependence. International public opinion makes it difficult for a metropolitan power to abandon a former colonial possession without accepting some responsibility for its continuing economic health; with the former British colonies in the Caribbean that has taken the form of continuing protective guarantees for the sale of basic cash crops—sugar, bananas, and citrus fruits—in the United Kingdom market. This becomes a fresh application in international relations of the doctrine of reparations. It has been well stated by the United Nations representative of the Trinidad government:

> An administering power is not entitled to extract for centuries all that can be got out of a colony and when that has been done to relieve itself of its obligations by the conferment of a formal but meaningless—meaningless because it cannot possibly be supported—political independence. Justice requires that reparation be made to the country that has suffered the ravages of colonialism before that country is expected to face up to the problems and difficulties that will inevitably beset it upon independence.[37]

A Virgin Islands independence would require the itemized expression of that principle in the clauses of a treaty of separation. For the American side, that would mean at the least provisions for a graduated scale of economic aid to the island group for a period sufficiently prolonged to enable the local economy to absorb the loss of the federal largesse. It would mean a readiness to give such aid without attaching onerous conditions. Virgin Islanders have not been slow to point out that the purchase monies of the 1917 sale went unilaterally to Denmark, with none going to the islanders, just as in the earlier case of slavery emancipation in the British West Indies the compensation awarded by the British Parliament went only to the planter class, with none going to the freed slave population. For the Virgin Islands side, a move toward separatism would require a serious stocktaking of its implications. It would mean exploring the possibilities of new multilateral relationships with other societies in the area, new associational groupings, and membership in the relevant international organizations. Domestically, it would mean frank acknowledgment of the truth that every new problem as it arises cannot be solved by yet another federal grant; that, in fact, the gross inequities of the class system will require not only the ultimate reshaping, perhaps even the abolition, of that system but also a readiness for sacrifice, both personal and collective, which so far few Virgin Islanders demonstrate. Independence, or autonomy, does not solve the social question. It merely clears the decks of the irrelevant colonial question, so that undivided attention can be given to that more profound issue.

37. Sir Ellis Clarke, quoted in *The Federal Negotiations 1962–1965 and Constitutional Proposals for Barbados* (Bridgetown, Barbados: Government Printing Office, 1965), par. 26.

Much of all this, obviously, belongs to the future. Virgin Islanders are a cautious, prudent people, unlikely to rush into anything novel or unsettling. Few of them, as yet, seem ready to consider seriously any of the status alternatives here discussed. They have been shaped, after all, by the traditional Protestant ethic, first Danish, then American, with its stolid, bourgeois reluctance to change the status quo. That being admitted, however, the very pace of the changes that are taking place in the islands must sooner or later break down that conservatism of temper. There are already signs that the more sensitive of island leaders are becoming uneasy about some aspects of the "progress": the growth of middle-class housing ghettos, the new crime rates that reflect poverty and class envy, the sprouting, in large hotels and condominiums, of the faceless buildings of the international architectural style, and not least of all the cultural pollution of island life by the materialist values of the American acquisitive society. What those critics have yet to learn, perhaps, is the hard lesson that they cannot remain part of that society and still hope to insulate themselves against the intrusion of its characteristic features.

To the degree that the islands persist in their schizoid role—trying to be North American and Caribbean at one and the same time—the ambivalence will create increasingly acute problems. Their comparative economic prosperity will be envied by other Caribbean economies. But their subordinate constitutional status will continue to be lowly regarded as the price they must pay, apparently, for that privileged condition. To the extent that they are satisfied with that status, profoundly humiliating as it is, the progressive forces within the Caribbean area will come to see them as the Judas-traitor of the cause. An excellent example of this general truth is the difference between the Virgin Islands attitude toward the Anguilla issue and toward the later Culebra issue; in the first case Virgin Islanders, including the press, were willing to support the Anguillan cause because it merely meant embarrassing the British government, whereas in the second case there was little enthusiastic support because to defend the Culebran cause involved a direct challenge to Washington and to American naval interests. Nor can the fact that the U.S. Navy and its personnel spend heavily in the Virgins ports be discounted in all of this. Nothing, that is, must be done to kill the goose that lays the golden eggs.

This all adds up to a politics of opportunism. It means cooperation with the American presence and an effort to make the best of both worlds. This kind of opportunism, it is true, can be defended as a necessary policy arising out of self-interest and preservation. Thus, Valdemar Hill, in his later book, *Rise to Recognition: An Account of U.S. Virgin Islanders from Slavery to Self-Government,* advances the thesis that the status issue might be solved if only the islanders would recognize and nourish a triangular loyalty: as natives of the Virgin Islands, as West Indians, and as citizens of the United States. The only difficulty, of course, with that line of argument is that it assumes that the three loyalties are coeval and not inconsistent with one another. It assumes, furthermore, that the American power would be willing to accept the other loyalties as complementary to, rather than competitive with, loyalty to itself. It remains to be seen whether American policy-makers in the Caribbean area are capable of admitting those other loyalties in a dependent people. For the truth is that in the Caribbean area, to employ a distinction recently used by Senator Mansfield when speaking of the Pacific area (where American military imperialism holds a myriad of small tropical islands for its use), there is not merely an American presence in the area, there is an American preponderance.[38] The use of that preponderance—in the Cuban invasion, the Santo Domingo intervention, the underground intervention in Guyanese politics, even the minor scandal of the Culebra affair—indicates that the American power has reverted to the "big stick" policy in defense of its regional interests. Such a policy can have the end result of nullifying the substance of independence for the small nations of the areas, leaving behind simply the fiction of sovereignty. It is palpably self-evident that the only way to reduce the danger thus posed is for the Caribbean forces to band together to form a united Caribbean power that can to some extent withstand the American pressure. There is certainly evidence that a new sense of common Caribbean awareness is growing up in the hitherto disparate and separate elements of the more radical Caribbean forces.

Where the tiny Virgin Islands will elect to stand on this transcendental issue of Caribbean life, now or in any of the future Caribbean crises, still remains to be seen. It might be premature to assert dogmatically that the Virgin Islands habit of appeasing Washington has by now gone so far that the answer to that question is already determined. Politics is not always, in a vulgar pragmatic sense, the art of the possible. It is sometimes the art of the seemingly impossible. No Caribbean scholar in the 1950s would have dared predict the emergence of socialist Cuba, any more than British scholars would have forecast in the 1960s the rise of the separatist-nationalist Celtic movements in a British political system traditionally regarded as the classic prototype of the unitary state. The whole Caribbean area is in ferment, from Cuba to the Guianas. It is inconceivable that the so-called American Caribbean (Puerto Rico and the Virgin Islands) should remain permanently insulated from that

38. Quoted in *New York Times,* Oct. 1, 1967.

process. There is still time for both Puerto Ricans and Virgin Islanders to begin to honor the message of Sir Grantley Adams' admonition to the leaders of the old Anglo-American Caribbean Commission in the West Indian St. Thomas conference of a generation ago:

> We wish to say to you, Sir, that the age of the plantation system is gone, and equally we wish to say that the age of having us as military or naval outposts of empire is also gone. We West Indians are determined to take you at your word and to say, as you have said in the joint statements of your two governments, that the object of this Commission is that the West Indies should be run by West Indians of whatever race or nationality.[39]

That objective still constitutes the West Indian destiny. By historical legacy and geographical location Virgin Islanders, as much as any other Caribbean people, have a moral obligation to seek its fulfillment.

39. Quoted in *Daily News*, Mar. 1, 1946.

INDEX

Index

Columbus, Christopher, discovers Virgins, 4
Combs, Tram, 182, 192, 285
Commerce, commissioner of, 323
Communications, 282–87
Community consciousness, 256–58, 262–63
Comptroller. *See* Government comptroller
Constitutional Convention (1965), 19, 308–11, 314, 344, 346, 358
Constitutional framework and metropolitan law, 293–96
Constitutional model: of Copenhagen, 293; of Washington, 293
Construction industry, 125
Continentals, 12–13, 42–67, 179–98; and arts, 183–84; and class, 179–98; in community life, 193–98; in the culture, 190; and the economy, 182–84, 192–98, 334; family life of, 184; in government, 193, 322–23; as a marginal group, 181; as "natives," 156; occupations of, 181–85, 193–97; and politics, 334–35; population of, 179; and racial prejudice, 186–87, 189–91, 250; and religion, 267–68; and social prejudice, 185–93; as a socio-racial group, 154
CORE, 255
Corneiro, Conrad, 283
Corneiro, Francisco, 48, 325
Cornell report (1967), 129, 133, 136
Cost of Living Survey (1944), 94
Coulter, Stanley, 139, 322
Cramer (governor, 1935–41), 69, 72, 79, 83, 99, 304, 305, 309, 313
Crawford, Fred, 105; on representative in Washington, 345; on self-government, 347
Creolization process, 260–62
Creque, Cyril, 172
Creque, Darwin, *The U.S. Virgins and the Eastern Caribbean*, 21, 324, 362
Culture: American influence on, 183–84, 190; Council on the Arts, 170–72, 194, 280–82, 285–86; cultural shame, 167; Danish influence on, 171; deculturation, 175–78; Eurocentric, Blyden critique of, 260; folklore, 101, 172; Jarvis on, 159, 161, 165, 167, 168, 173; Jewish influence on, 171; and nationalism, 20, 359; Negro influence on, 171; Protestant-Puritan ethic influence on, 163; Taino-Arawak influence on, 171; West Indian influence on, 172–74, 288

Daily News, 79, 102, 165, 244, 284, 324, 342
Dalton, Robert, *Mothers and Children*, 246
Danet, Theodore, 205

Daniel, V. F., 115
Daniels, Josephus, *Cabinet Diaries*, 58, 71, 160
Danish Colonial Law of 1906, 45, 48, 221, 293
Danish National Museum, 173
Danish Organic Act (1852), 74
Danish plebiscite of 1916, 39
Danish regime (1815–1917), 4–11, 25–41; architecture, 25, 143, 173; community, 4–6, 26, 154, 167; culture, 171; economic policies, 6–7; education, 38; heritage, 20–21, 359; language, 33, 38; medical service, 38; nostalgia for, 72; religion, 31–32, 265; slavery, 29–32; Transfer, 14, 26, 39–40, 157, 351
Danish Royal Commission of 1903, 39
Danish royal edict of 1831, 29
Danish West India Company, 4, 5–7, 9, 11, 12, 26, 27
Davis, Morris, 79, 259
Dawson, William, 110
Deane, Philip, *Caribbean Vacations*, 130
Dean Stark, Charlotte, *Souvenir of St. John*, 187
Delegate in Washington, office of, 99, 347–48
Democratic Club, 327
Democratic National Committee, 110, 244, 328
Democratic National Convention: of 1944, 244; of 1964, 329
Democratic Party, 158, 325–29, 330, 332, 334
Desalinization plant, 141
Diaz, Luis, 208
Diaz Morales, Aureo, 213
Dickinson, Thomas H., 59
Dietrich, Robert, *Steve Bentley's Calypso Caper*, 181
Dingell, John, 98
District Court of Virgin Islands, and federal judiciary, 313–15
Dober, Leonard, 265
Dorr v. *United States*, 43
Dorsch, Frederick, 179
Dougherty, Romeo L., and racism of Navy, 113
Douglass, Frederick, 56
Downes v. *Bidwell*, 43
Downing, Carlos, thesis of, 106–7, 112; and cooperation of metropolitan and island parties, 339–42; and the two-party system, 326
Dudley, George, 158
Duffy, Hugh, 183
Dutch presence, 4, 5, 8
Dutch Reformed Church. *See* Religion

Economy, of Virgin Islands, 121–53; alien and, 217–38; and budget de-

DEMCO